A torturingly competitive facade thriving on the likes of the weak, Rabbit's hat-trick ability is second to none. Any young, brash Aussie willing to time and time again butt heads with Dane Kealoha in the late '70s and early '80s had to have confidence to spare and a game plan to outsmart the devil himself.

It's a wonder he ever let Mark Richards reach his four World Titles and didn't grab them for himself. This competitive nature is one which novices cannot comprehend and world champions can only dream of mastering. Articulate, personable, calculating and stylish. Rabbit defines an era of innovation and individuality.

KELLY SLATER

bustin' down the **DOOR**

The original 'Bustin' Down The Door' (from an article published in US *Surfer* magazine in 1976) described the arduous task of breaking down the barriers that stood between us, the *Free Ride* generation, and our dream, professional surfing.

As the sport's pioneers, it has been our job to lay the foundations, to chart the waters.

Every step became a precedent, from touring to getting our administrative house in order. Even in retirement there have been new doors to bust down, new frontiers to map. This is the story of that journey.

RABBIT

new edition of the cult classic

bustin'
down the
door

wayne
Rabbit
BARTHOLOMEW

with tim baker

HarperSports
An imprint of HarperCollinsPublishers

TO BETTY

For all the years of struggle and sacrifice, and your belief in my dream.

Harper*Sports*

An imprint of HarperCollins*Publishers*

First published in Australia in 1996
This edition published in 2002
by HarperCollins*Publishers* Pty Limited
ABN 36 009 913 517
A member of the HarperCollins*Publishers* (Australia) Pty Limited Group
www.harpercollins.com.au

HarperCollins*Publishers*
25 Ryde Road, Pymble, Sydney NSW 2073, Australia
31 View Road, Glenfield, Auckland 10, New Zealand
77–85 Fulham Palace Road, London W6 8JB, United Kingdom
2 Bloor Street East, 20th Floor, Toronto, Ontario M4W 1A8, Canada
10 East 53rd Street, New York NY 10022, USA

National Library of Australia Cataloguing-in-Publication data:

Bartholomew, Wayne, 1954– .
Bustin' down the door
2nd ed.
Includes index.
ISBN 0 7322 7479 6.
1. Bartholomew, Wayne, 1954– . 2. Surfers – Australia –
Biography. I. Baker, Tim. II. Title: Busting down the door.
797.32092.

Cover design by Luke Causby, HarperCollins Design Studio
Printed and bound in Australia by Griffin Press on 79gsm Bulky Paperback

8 7 6 5 4   06 07 08 09 10

contents

author biographies

WAYNE 'RABBIT' BARTHOLOMEW, 47, is the 1978 World Professional Surfing Champion, 1999 World Masters Champion, and current CEO/President of the Association of Surfing Professionals. Rabbit and his peers pioneered the professional surfing circuit, travelling the world on the proverbial shoestring to a handful of scattered events until a unified World Tour was formed in 1977. Rabbit was rated in the top 5 in the world for eight consecutive seasons and distinguished himself with his cavalier approach to the big waves of Hawaii and his fierce competitive nature. Today, Rabbit lives in an apartment overlooking his beloved Kirra Point, with his partner Shelley and baby boy Jaggar, and can be found getting his share of set waves on any good day.

TIM BAKER, 37, is a former editor of *Tracks* and *Surfing Life* magazines, and is currently a contributor to *Surfing World*, *Surfing Life*, *Deep*, US *Surfing* and numerous other surfing magazines around the world. His work has also appeared in *Rolling Stone*, *Playboy*, *Inside Sport*, *GQ* and *The Sydney Morning Herald*, and he has been shortlisted for the CUB Australian sports writing awards. Tim lives in Currumbin, Queensland, with his wife, Kirsten, and is still working on his great unfinished surfing screenplay and novel.

Bartholomew and Baker in earnest conference, near Bells Beach, Easter '96.
Steve Sherman.

acknowledgments

I would like to express my deep appreciation to all Rabbit's friends and family who helped in the research for this book. They opened up precious and private chapters of their lives and entrusted me to represent these priceless memories faithfully. I hope I've repaid that trust. To all the friends of Rab's I never got to — I'm sorry, but I console myself with the hope that this book may prompt more vivid storytelling of the as yet untold chapters in Rab's life, and the surfing folklore generally. To Rab's immediate family, especially, thanks for your support and faith.

I would also like to thank chiropractor Matthew Butel for fixing my neck when I'd spent too long hunched over the computer. Also Brian Ford from F & J Computer Services for saving my arse when my laptop spat the dummy. I'm indebted to my family and dear friends Picko, Jigger, Sharon, Mandy, Denis, Heidi, Al, Helen and Helen for never letting on if they got fed up with me prattling on about this book. Thanks also to Geoff Armstrong at Harper*Sports* for the faith, editor Ali Orman for her happy faxes and phonecalls and enchantment with Rab's story, Louise McGeachie for an inspired design job and Liam Hillier for his creative illos and crafty maps. Thanks to photographers: Lee Pegus, John Bilderback, Jeff Divine, Larry Moore, Peter Crawford, Steve Sherman, Peter and Jan Wilson, Jeff Hornbaker, Dan Merkel, Bob Barbour, Johnny Charlton, Dick Hoole, Jack McCoy, Richard Harvey, Sylvain Cazenave, Chris Van Lennep, Ted Grambeau and Peter Morrison.

And mainly, I want to thank Rab for showing me how fully life can be lived.

TIM BAKER

acknowledgments

I'd like to thank all my surfing buddies for their contributions to this book. We shared some fun times and I only hope there are good sets on their way for you.

I'd like to pay a tribute to Mark Richards, Shaun Tomson, Cheyne Horan and Michael Ho. Their enduring friendship means a great deal to me, the sport of surfing is enriched by their contribution.

My friends on the Gold Coast, especially Mont, Denis, and Andy Mac — thanks for always being there. To Bill Callinan, thanks for backing me and believing in surfing. The Snapper Rocks Surfrider Club, especially Bruce, Mont and Lorraine, Deaney, Reg and the kids, I look forward to our next club round and barbie at KH Park.

To Paul Hallas, Gill Glover and Al Byrne, thanks for 20 years of great surfboards. Hot Stuff, for life.

I can only hope that a healing will result from this outpouring. I especially hope my mother Betty can accept that there are some things an only son must do to find peace of mind. I'd like to thank all my sisters for their love and support. I love youse all.

I could hardly contain my excitement when I found out that Harper*Sports* wanted to publish my life story. I was right in the middle of another Bali grommet campaign, with my old mate Mark Warren, when the fax arrived.

I am so grateful for Tim's unfaltering dedication to this project. To leave a highly-paid editorial position at Morrison Media, to sacrifice a year of his life to bring the Rabbit story to fruition, I am eternally grateful. It has been a fun project. Baker's stamina has astounded me, his patience has blown me away and his ability to come home with the goods would do the Canadian Mounties proud. Thanks mate.

To all the surfers in all the lands, thank you for allowing me the freedom to ride the waves that head your way.

Well, I guess the only thing left is to get on a plane and leave the country till this thing blows over. Nah, just kidding.

RABBIT

Bustin' down the door

introduction

A lot has happened in Rabbit's life since the first edition of *Bustin' Down The Door* came out in October '96. He's landed pro surfing's top job as CEO/President of the Association of Surfing Professionals, guiding the world tour he once dreamed of as a teenager. He's won another world title, in the newly formed Masters Championships for pro surfing's founding fathers. He's seen his father and his eldest sister fighting for their lives in hospital and, with that resilient Bartholomew spirit, come through against daunting odds. And he's finally fulfilled his life's dearest wish: producing, with his lovely partner Shelley, a beautiful baby boy.

I had some trepidation embarking on a new final chapter for this revised edition of Rabbit's life story. Pulling the first edition together nearly killed me and I knew hooking up with Rabbit always meant a hair-raising ride. The word came from publishers HarperCollins in August 2001 that the book's fifth print run had sold out and they wanted to update it for a reprint. At the time, Rabbit was juggling the new experience of fatherhood, steering the treacherous path of international pro surfing, and preparing for another world title campaign at the Masters in Ireland and the crucial European leg of his revamped ASP world tour. Amid all this, I had to burrow my way into Rabbit's den and extract his account of the last five fateful years.

We covered all the intrigue and turmoil of his rise to become pro surfing's Juan Antonio Samaranch (he hates that!), and the tumultuous passage of his agenda of sweeping reforms to the ASP world tour, with its threatened rebel tours, surfer unrest, heated board meetings and multimillion-dollar deals. Rabbit recalled it all with typically vivid verve and drama. What we didn't get around to was the personal stuff — love, family, life — the stuff that matters most. I was forced to sweat on the arrival of a promised fax of Rabbit's handwritten version of his equally compelling personal life over the same period, scrawled in that frantic angular freehand with which

Rab's written missives spill forth and laced with the same electricity his passionate hand gestures generate when he's talking. As promised, it eventually got to me. Rab will string you out and confound you, go underground and be unreachable at the most inopportune times, duck and weave and avoid difficult issues when it suits him, but he always comes through with the goods in the end.

I'm immensely proud of the collaboration that produced the first *Bustin' Down The Door*. Serious newspapers said nice things about it, but the best review it ever received was a hand-carved quote in the back of a toilet door at Duranbah, where someone had seen fit to record Rab's theory that surfing was the perfect barometer for your life: 'When you're surfing well and often, life seems to unfold smoothly easily. If you're surfing badly or not often enough, you've obviously strayed from your path as a surfer.' That the book had been so honoured by an unknown surfer at his local beach gave me a great kick when I discovered it during one early-morning surf session.

My other favourite bit of feedback, which I've been waiting for a chance to re-tell, was on the south coast of NSW, where a mate and I picked up a young hitchhiker toting a Tommy Peterson fireball fish surfboard. 'Where'd you get the board?' I asked, curious how a kid from the south coast bush was riding a classic board shaped by the brother of the great MP, up in Tweed Heads, over 1000 k's to the north. 'I read Rabbit's book,' the kid told me, oblivious of the part I'd played in it. 'I just had to see it all for myself, so I hitched up there.' He'd surfed Kirra, Snapper, Duranbah, met Tommy Peterson and bought one of his old boards, and returned home to put the savage little dart of a surfboard through its paces on that coast's exquisite reefs and beaches. The chance encounter warmed my heart.

So thank you to everyone who read the first edition, or picked up this one, for believing that storytelling — reflecting on our past in this mad fast-forward world — is still worth something. Books are a bit like surfboards: handmade, time-consuming, barely profitable. The countless hours hunched over your tools shaping and finishing the things, trying to iron out every last bump, can be hard on the body and mind. But when they deliver their buzz, there's nothing else you'd want to be doing. Enjoy the ride.

TIM BAKER

carving out bushtracks

I was conceived during the Great Floods of '54. I put it down to the weather — mum and dad were shacked up, they couldn't get outdoors. With the rain came the biggest cyclone on record round here. The press dubbed it 'the Great Cyclone' with a central pressure of 970 hpa. The eye of the cyclone passed directly over Coolangatta, and 40 inches of rain fell in just one day. The whole of the Tweed Valley was under water, and at Kirra Point six foot walls of water broke over the shed and washed cars down the road, piling them up outside the Kirra Pub like toys. The surf probably pumped for weeks on end with barely a soul to ride it. Nine months later, on November 30, 1954, I was born.

My father, Don, or 'Bart' as he was commonly known, was a school teacher and a respected deep-sea fisherman. On the one hand, he was a stern disciplinarian at school but on the other, he used to run with a pretty wild crowd of characters and disappear for weeks on fishing trips. My mother, Betty, was an accomplished dance teacher, and they were both popular and strong-willed characters in their own right. Dad was president of the local Lions Club and mum was president of the Lady Lions and they used to clash just in the strength and presence of their personalities.

I am the second eldest of five children, and the only boy. My earliest recollection of home life is manipulating my sisters Wendy,

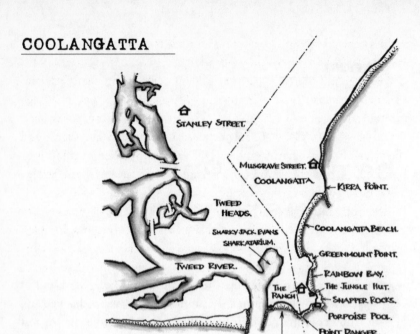

Cindy, Heidi and Louise to do the washing up, the chores and cook me food. I became pretty good at that.

In my mind's eye, I picture my early childhood like an Australian bush version of *Huckleberry Finn*. We lived at Razorback, an area of dense bush and farms behind Tweed Heads, on the Queensland and NSW border, at the southern end of what is now known as the Gold Coast. Down the back of our place was the Tweed River and McGuinness's farm. This was our playground — the bush, the river, the farm. My best mate at school was an Aboriginal kid, David Garrett, who ended up becoming a representative rugby league player; he and I were inseparable. I used to hang out at the Garrett's house after school and all weekend and I became a bit of a bush kid, running with the Tweed Aboriginal kids. We used to build treehouses, skin snakes to make belts, and we never went anywhere without our bowie knives.

Early mornings were devoted to fishing trips down to the Boyds Bay shed. I'd hop along the moored beach boats out to the middle of the river and fish for bream by myself in the dawn half-light. This legendary gang of fishermen, the Boyds Bay brothers, would all be in their ramshackle old shed, still finishing up an all-night poker and drinking session. Their colourful language would drift out across the river but I couldn't decipher it. They never seemed to mind me bounding across their row of boats and I'd invariably haul home half a dozen bream for breakfast, then head to school.

As I got a bit older, I discovered the beach. I carved out my own bushtracks from the back of our place down to Coolangatta. I could just duck out into the backyard to play after school, take the bushtrack into town and play the pinball machines and still get back in time for dinner. I began to lose interest in the bush once I had a taste of the town and beach life and became streetwise to all the opportunities they held.

The centre of my early aquatic activities was Jack Evans' porpoise pool at Snapper Rocks. There were three pools — a baby pool, a middle pool where swimming classes were held, and a long, almost Olympic-size pool. This is where local character 'Sharky' Jack Evans, 'the Man of the Sea', kept his dolphins. Then Jack moved to larger, more elaborate premises at Duranbah and opened 'Jack Evans' Porpoise Pool and Sharkatarium'. Then the swimming club took over the pools.

I was a member of Jack Woodward's Snapper Rocks Swimming Club. Apart from learning the basics of swimming, we used to muck around in inner tubes and perform all kinds of raucous dives off the diving board, and just hang out in the pool, going off all day long. The boldest of us kids used to make our way outside the swimming pool and go over to this spot in the rocks called the 'suicide hole' where the waves would go right over the top of you. I've seen generations of kids doing this and they still do it today. The suicide hole at Snapper is one of those places where you have to carry out your first dare. You go up to this gap in the rocks and face the incoming swells and bob down behind this ledge just in time to let the waves crash over you.

Carving out bushtracks

So even though I wasn't straight into surfing at an early age, I was still a bit of a water baby. Whenever it was hot, there'd always be someone in the neighbourhood driving down the beach and we'd all clamber in and go down for a big, mass bodysurf in the Coolangatta or Rainbow shorebreak.

The only disruption to this early love affair with the sea came the day I nearly drowned at Greenmount Beach. I was seven years old, frolicking just beyond the shorebreak, when a sandbank collapsed and I was sucked under the waves and out the back. I was gone for all money and my uncle Michel from Moruya, up on holidays, came in and hauled me out. I distinctly remember the view from under water, looking up at this watery image of my uncle Michel reaching down to pull me out. Strangely, this little section of Greenmount Beach, this very same sandbank, became the setting for some of my most defining moments in surfing in later years — where I first paddled a surfboard out into the waves at age 10, and where I first really hit my straps in the speed stakes at age 16.

BETTY: 'He was the happiest little boy, he had a lovely nature ... I believe little children can actually see things, little spirits. They're around everywhere, they really are. He had this little friend, this imaginary friend called Jimmy. I'd be sitting watching and they'd have great conversations together.'

My introduction to surfboard riding wasn't a happy one. During the Christmas holidays of '65 I helped Kerry Gill carry his surfboard down to the beach, one of us at each end of this huge board, every day for the entire holidays. He was the best little surfer in town. Nine years old, red hot, and he had everyone's respect. His parents owned this amusement hall at Tweed Heads, Gill's Cafe, where we played on the trampolines, the pinnies, pool, and basically hung out. I'd help him carry his surfboard from the amusement hall

Bustin' down the door

to Greenmount Beach. When he finished surfing and came in, we went through a well-rehearsed ritual.

I'd go, 'Are you going to give me a go today?'

And he'd go, 'Nah.'

'Righteo, let's go back to the pool hall then,' I'd mutter forlornly.

This went on every day for the whole of the holidays. Finally, it was the last day of the Christmas holidays and we were down at the beach. We'd gone through the whole rigmarole, the whole ritual, and he'd come in and I just didn't want to know about it any more. The surf was perfect, offshore, really pretty, inside Greenmount.

I said, 'Are you going to give me a go?'

And he's gone, 'Yep.'

I did the full double take. 'Really?'

'Yep. Here's the deal. You swim out the back, you swim all the way out the back.' He thought I was pretty hopeless and I'd chicken out. 'I'll paddle the board out and when you get out behind the breakers I'll give you the board.'

It sounded like a hell of a deal. Save me all that trouble of paddling the board out. I thought, I'll swim out, no worries — I'd bodysurfed and surf-o-planed and had a bit of water sense about me. Next thing I knew, I was out the back at Greenmount, he'd got off the board and bodysurfed in, and suddenly it was just me, sitting on a surfboard out the back of Greenmount. It was a sparkling, crystal, perfect day, and I thought, this is unbelievable. I'm surfing. I'm part of this whole deal. I feel so fantastic. Next second this wave was peeling down Greenmount Point towards me. I couldn't quite judge where it was heading but it was a big one. This bodysurfer took off about 50 metres further out, and he was good, real good, this guy. He was headed towards me and I was sitting on this board, and it suddenly dawned on me that I didn't know how to manoeuvre it. I could see the guy coming but I hadn't mastered the technique of sitting on the back of the board and swinging it around, like I'd seen others do. In the end I was yelling at the guy but I couldn't budge the board. He came cruising along this wave, 'Dum de dum de dum' … straight into the nose of my board. The wave exploded, the board went shooting up into the air, I went under and came up trying to figure out what had happened. This guy came up next to me with this hole in his head. His whole forehead was opened up, and he roared at me, 'You great galoot.' And that was all he had to say. My adrenalin was pumping so hard and I was so scared I just swam straight to the beach. I didn't stop, I didn't look back, I didn't even look to see where the board was. I hit the beach at a full run and I ran all the way home. And that was the end of surfing. I'd had my go. I'd nearly killed a guy and I hadn't even caught a wave yet. I was so freaked out I didn't touch a surfboard for a year.

I remember my dad going away on long fishing trips and I can see in hindsight the gradual breakdown of the family unit. It was one of those things that I was a bit oblivious to until it actually happened, because those sort of things just didn't go on then. People didn't just up and leave — you stuck it out. But we were different, and when things came to a head it all happened very quickly. My dad went away for a holiday to the Great Barrier Reef with well-known fisherman and diver Ben Crop — these are the sorts of guys my dad used to run with, fishing and drinking and having a fine old time. He came back three weeks later than he was supposed to and we were gone. This was unprecedented. Before we left, mum had laid the cards on the table — she called a meeting with me and my older sister Wendy and explained the situation, and I said, 'Let's go.' I remember clearly giving the vote to go. 'Let's do it, let's move it down to Rainbow Bay.' So, we just up and left. We moved out of the family house and moved to Rainbow Bay right in front of the surf and I became the man of the house, at 11 years of age.

And that began our period of hardship. I don't know what the poverty line is but no money in the coffers and no food in the fridge is pretty poor in my books.

Bustin' down the door

WENDY: 'Our house at Razorback was once a block of units, the Bahama Flats, opposite the Patch at Coolangatta. Dad bought it and had it cut in half and moved on a big truck right up to Razorback. We moved in when I was four, so Rab was two. There was upstairs and downstairs and it was just all little flats. I thought it was great. Dad split it in half and we lived in one half and they rented out the other half for a few years. Then child number three came along which was Cindy and so Dad knocked a hole in the wall and made the whole top of the house the family house, and then Heidi and Louise came along, and we took up the whole lot. It looked very big and lonely stuck on a block of land all on its own, because there was nothing around it. We lived in the boondocks ... I remember our last night there, Rab and I kissed all the walls of the house goodbye before we left.'

RAINBOW BAY

Once the decision was made, a friend of the family's came by and in several trips just moved us down to a classic little beach house right across from Rainbow Bay, called the Ranch. We got everything into the house and I announced, 'Okay girls, fix things up. I'm off to the beach now.' And I just went out cruising, getting the lay of the land, as if this was my first duty as man of the house. I went over Rainbow Bay with a fine tooth comb, seeing what opportunities for fun and profit it presented. It was a feeling of absolute freedom.

I'd already spent a lot of time on the beach and knew a few of the local characters. I had a part-time thing going hiring the surf-o-planes at Greenmount Beach, just round the corner. I worked for Billy Rachinger (or Billy Rak as everyone knew him), a beach boy who ran a beach hire business with his partner John Cunningham, a legendary lifeguard. John had once saved Brian Henderson from Bandstand, who's now a national news presenter — John was a super hero. And Billy, he was just the smoothest operator, as he is to this day. He had the surfboard hire and the showers and I used to hang there with him, because the other end of the beach was just too cool. That's where all the older guys, all the classic surfers, used to hang. We were at one end with the beach hire, the surfboard hire, the showers; in the middle was a kiosk with snow cones, ice creams and dagwood dogs; and at the other end there was a little park where Ron Rico used do his magic act and the Bee Gees used to play, before they were anybody.

> BILLY RAK: 'They'd all start out helping and then you'd leave them to it and when you come back there'd be no-one there. They'd all be out on the boards.'

The Greenmount crew were the original soul surfers, among the first humans in Australia to embrace surfing as a way of life. They created a rich legacy, with nicknames like Snake, Bonus, Jingles, Little Scunge, Thumb, Big Scunge. The hottest local, Greg Selladoni, held place of honour, his deeds in the surf and the pool hall revered by the faithful. On his 18th birthday 'Sella' was killed on the Burleigh 'S' bends, going hard on his shiny, new Bultaco motorbike.

Greenmount, Rainbow and Coolangatta — the whole strip — became my turf. There was the beach and parallel to the beach was the main street with all the pool parlours and pinny machines. Once I moved to the beach I never went further inland than the main street. It might not sound like a big deal today, moving from Tweed Heads to Rainbow Bay, but back then it was two different worlds. Tweed Heads was the bush and I was a bush kid, and Rainbow Bay was the beach and that's where you became a beach bum. But it didn't take me long to adjust to the beach culture.

Beachcombing was one source of income, helped greatly by the big cyclones of '67, the year we moved to Rainbow Bay. These were the biggest cyclones since '54 and they just destroyed the beach. I used to sift through the erosion for hours on end. It was like an archaeological dig — there were 50 years of lost coins on that beach and I found most of them.

Society didn't cater for divorce or single-parent families in the mid–'60s. There were no family courts, no mandatory maintenance, no

Bustin' down the door

single mother's benefit — we did it really tough. Dad was dirty about us moving out and wasn't prepared to support the family, so we were out on our own. We had no money coming in, except for mum's dance school. Mum was always popular and her dance classes were famous. Even before the separation, she'd drag me down every Saturday morning to ballet class, she tried and tried and tried to get me to do it.

WENDY: 'Mum always tried to get Rabbit to be a part of her dancing but he'd always somehow do the Rabbit disappearing act. Once, it seemed like she finally cornered him into appearing in this concert at the old RSL. There were all these different acts — I did a cha cha with a girlfriend, and there was this little black and white minstrel act that mum was going to put on and somehow she'd got Rab in as one of the minstrels. There were three young boys in it and they did their faces in the full Al Jolson thing, black face, big white eyes, the striped vests on, and they had this little routine to do. They were just about to go on and Rab fainted. Completely fainted on the floor from absolute fear. We were all leaning over him and looking at him and he was so pale, he was so white and freaked out, you couldn't even see the black on his face, the white came through the black. And he never made it onto the stage.'

Eventually mum realised I wasn't going to have a bar of it and she said, 'If you're not going to do it, you have to join the nippers,' the junior section of the surf lifesaving club. I thought, oh God, I can't think of anything worse. Two disgusting options. This is when there was a full-scale war on between the surf lifesaving clubs and the surfboard riders — you either belonged to one or the other. The regimented club rules, the march pasts, the togs, the caps — they just didn't fit my street agenda, so I'd take the money for nippers every Saturday morning and make a detour to the amusement arcades.

Mum had ballet classes in the CWA hall right across the street from Greenmount Beach, where the McDonald's is now, and I'd walk out of there on my way to nippers but I'd take this left-hand turn because three doors down was this insane slot car racing place called the Lazy Jay, and I'd invest my nipper money in the slot cars for hours and hours. Then I'd duck down to Funland where they had 60 pinball machines (I'd mastered about 30 of them), and I'd scout around until I found a machine with a free game on it or a few stray coins. I was on to anything that moved in there. I'd get eight free games up and then sell them to some sucker for 20 cents. It was a business.

I'd just started to get all these little rackets going when we left Razorback, so when we moved down to Rainbow Bay suddenly I became master of my own world. I was free. Nothing could keep me away from those pinnies. On the way to the bus they were there, on the way home they were there, and on the weekend they were there. Coolangatta was like Disneyland — three pool parlours, big ones — the Lazy Jay with the giant slot car races and there was Funland with two levels of pinball machines. But it was absolutely forbidden to gamble in Queensland, so over the Tweed side they had the little gambling places, where I mastered the pinball-style, on-line machines that they played for money. My favourite haunt on the Tweed side was Gill's Cafe, where the older guys would actually give me money to get the machines going and clock a few credits up for them. This is where I earnt the nickname 'Rabbit'. I was in at Gill's Cafe one Saturday morning just completely dominating the on-line machines. I was actually running from machine to machine — I had them all going. And Goober Barnes, a well-known surfer from Tweed Heads, just looked at me and went, 'You're a Rabbit.' And it stuck.

KERRY GILL: 'The shop was a real good hang in those days. All the surfers from both Kirra and Snapper used to come. We had a snooker table out the back, mum and dad used to make hamburgers and fish and chips and milkshakes and things. We had on-line machines, sort of like an early model poker machine that you could win money on ... Rabbit was a genius at it. He had

Bustin' down the door

the gift of being a master at playing them, and he never used to lose, so a few of the blokes after work, like Terry Baker, would come in on a Friday afternoon and grab Rabbit and go, "Hey son, get over here and win us some money." Then I remember mum sort of cottoning on to what they were doing and she tried to sort of outlaw that, much to the disgust of Terry, and Rabbit too because he used to make a few bob out of it.'

THE ROBIN HOOD DAYS

That's why it took me a little while to get into surfing, because there was a lot going on. I could make money on a Saturday morning, just roaming around the town. We all became insanely good pool players, playing for money, hustling and, with one thing and another, I used to provide a fair bit of money for the family. I had legitimate jobs as well. I had a paper run, and I used to go down to the Dolphin Hotel and the Tweed Pub selling the afternoon *Tele*. The real money was down there with the drunks getting the tips. I had it down to a fine art. I'd stand outside and put on the full bung arm just to get a bit more money. And I'd pick up all the empty bottles around the place.

I'd come home and just lay money on the table. I remember one Friday afternoon we'd hit rock bottom. Mum was devastated. There was no money and no food in the fridge, it was the weekend and we'd all come home wanting some food and it was down to war rations. I'll never forget it. Mum said, 'Well, it was good enough for your grandmother,' and she put a block of lard on the table and it was lard on toast for dinner. And I just said, 'Nuh, we're not eating that,' and whipped out a $20 note and laid it on the table. Twenty dollars was a lot of money then. Mum didn't even ask where it had come from. She just started crying. And it was chiko rolls and chips for dinner. I'll never forget it — the chant went up. 'We want chiko rolls, we want chiko rolls.' That set a precedent, when things were real low mum would always be hoping I'd come home with a twenty.

So I had quite a little empire going. I had my normal paper run, I had my tips from the drunks, I had my bottle collecting industry, the hire boards and the trampolines. The pool and the pinnies were just for my own entertainment. I was making a bit of money ... but nothing like the sort of money I could make stealing off the tourists.

It all started this day I was going round searching the beach for coins. This took a lot of work — you'd walk all the way from Coolangatta to Greenmount and come home with less than five cents some times. For two hours' work. But I remember one day looking down and there was a towel and a shirt and a bloody fat wallet sticking out of it. Without really thinking about it, I whipped down and emptied that wallet. It was a quick 18 bucks. I went, wow, too easy. I kept it quiet, but I knew I had a new industry here. I knew it was bad but, honestly, every Friday night I tried to put a $20 note down on the kitchen table. The rent was $22 and mum could cover that with her dance classes, but it would always get to a crisis point by the end of the week, and the crisis was always averted when I put the money on the table.

There was a spectacular finish to my life of crime however. It all blew up this day that I was doing my paper run. I seemed to have developed this survival instinct and I was constantly thinking of how I could pull something off. I couldn't even afford a pushbike, I'd hocked my pushbike and had to walk my paper round. I was walking down Tweed Street and we were absolutely destitute. I got two bucks a week for that paper round but that wasn't going to get us through. I walked past this car and it had a wallet on the dashboard, and it was the biggest temptation I'd ever seen in my life. It was big and thick, and it looked like it had juices running out of it — I'd never seen anything more tempting in my life. I ended up doing the block, walking around in a quandary. Will I? Won't I? I shouldn't. I couldn't. But I am walking around the block. And I doubled back around, and came past again, whistling to myself. It took less than a second. The window was open and it was gone. I continued my paper round, the wallet in my bag, and I went to the Tweed Bridge, scrambled underneath where no-one could find

Bustin' down the door

me, like a troll, and I started going through my takings. There was $32 cash, which I pocketed, and all these cards and stuff that I thought were worthless. I got a paint tin, stuffed the wallet in the bottom of it and filled it with rocks and threw it in the river. Perfect crime. I walked out from underneath the bridge and saw two priests walking towards me. I thought, I'm gone, I'm busted. The priests walked right up to me and one of them said, 'You have done a very bad thing, son.'

I just looked at him and said, 'Yes, I have,' and I returned the money. I don't even know how they found me, but that finished my life of crime. I never stole another thing in my life because I felt like God was watching. Of course, the police were involved and I was taken home and presented to my mother, and she was crying. It was a bad scene, but served its purpose. I was definitely heading a bit delinquent. The head policeman from Coolangatta had lived opposite us at Tweed and always had a caring attitude towards our family. He knew that we were doing it really tough and he already had me pegged. Once I got caught he started calling by and counselling me. He went and fronted dad, and that's when dad started providing some support.

By then, I was 12 years of age, and that had all happened — my juvenile delinquent days were behind me …

> WENDY: 'My very first job was in a real estate and my first wage, I got 16 pounds and I gave mum half of it. It's just the way it was. And anything Rab earnt he helped out too. We all just helped out when we could … I don't know how she did it. I don't know how she fed us all.'

SAVED BY THE SURF

It wouldn't be the first time a kid's been saved from a wayward life by sport, but surfing came along at a really good time for me. I'd been on the perimeter of the sport for a couple of years, looking in from the outside.

When we moved down to Rainbow Bay, every morning I would wake up and see the surf. Every single morning, these perfect waves breaking through Rainbow Bay and no-one surfing, except Peter Bryant and Billy Grant. They were a bit older than me, but we all used to hang out at school together. They surfed every morning before school and every afternoon after school. For a whole year I watched them surf. I'd watch them from this swing — which was like a long plank of wood that swung back and forth like a pendulum on metal poles — in the park nearby. (There's a scene of me riding the same swing in the '70s surf movie *Free Ride*.) In the mornings I'd get up and do the dawn patrol and while they went surfing, I'd ride the swing. I still wasn't game to go back in the surf after my first experience, even though the swing was probably more dangerous. There was metal all around me, and I'd practise walking the board and nose riding and all the moves while I watched them surf. One fall and I could have killed myself.

I used to push it pretty hard on that swing. Sometimes I'd get it going as high as I could without touching the bars, and experience that moment of weightlessness at the very extremes of its swing. But it got to a point where you couldn't hope to ride out the drop back down without steadying yourself by momentarily holding on to the bars. That really helped me with my late drops in surfing. I came to deploy that technique at Pipeline, in Hawaii, many years later, when I'd have my arms outstretched on take off, just steadying myself by hanging on to the lip on the way down. It was exactly the same technique. They've taken all those swings away now because they were so dangerous.

I used to ride the water's edge on my skimboard, and I'd play cricket on the beach with my sisters — but I just wasn't ready to go back out into the surf and, besides, we could never afford a surfboard.

Then one afternoon, Peter Bryant (or 'Mont' as I came to know him) came running down the beach to where I was playing cricket with my sisters — I'd just belted another six. He said to me, 'Stop being a sissy. Why don't you come surfing?' And I've gone, 'Alright then. When?' And he goes, 'There's a friend of ours coming down from Brisbane this Saturday. He's going to bring a board.'

Bustin' down the door

That Saturday, the guy arrived at 10.30 am and I went down to officially begin surfing at Snapper Rocks. Timmy Bryant, Peter's younger brother, started first, and Peter Grant, Billy's younger brother, started second. And then it was my turn, and I went out at Snapper Rocks on this board, about nine feet long, this red board, and I paddled into a wave, took off, got to my feet, turned the board ... and I was good. I was already good. A year of simulated surfing had paid off — big time.

> MONT: 'I remember coming in with my board and there's Rab surfing on the swing, and I remember seeing him on the beach and thinking, the poor guy, he's got four sisters and there he is on the beach playing cricket with his sisters, and here am I, I've got three brothers and I'm surfing.'

The feeling of confidence I suddenly had out in the surf was overwhelming. I had barely entered the ocean in the year since my first, ill-fated attempt, and now this giant barrier had been broken down. I could join in with my buddies before and after school and on weekends, and suddenly I became the keenest surfer on the beach. You couldn't get me out of the water. Even though we still couldn't afford a surfboard, I made an art form of borrowing whoever's board I could lay my hands on.

I soon felt comfortable surfing at Rainbow and exploring its various nooks and crannies. When no-one was watching, I'd actually surf this little wave inside Rainbow Bay called Little Mali — my own private little break that no-one else would have even considered a surf spot. There was this outcrop of rocks that divided the point and was generally considered an irritant that broke the flow of a nice, peeling point wave. For some reason, I found it intriguing to surf near the rocks. Waves break differently when they break over rock or reef. You get a bit of a power surge off them and weird boils and bubbles. Sometimes I'd surf clean over the rocks at high tide, and other times I'd be dodging rocks at the lower tide and I became quite good at it. I think that helped me in later years because we didn't have any reef breaks around here, but I found my own reefbreak at Inside Rainbow. Of course the waves were only six to eight inches high, but it still prepared me for some of the more challenging waves I'd tackle later in life.

Entering the surf altered my whole universe. The street scene and its various attractions suddenly didn't have quite the same lustre and everything revolved around the beach. Right where the seafood restaurant is now at Rainbow Bay there used to be a classic place called the 'Jungle Hut' and this was our new hang-out. It was done up in the style of a Hawaiian beach hut with palm fronds around the ceiling and a sand floor. We knew the family that ran it and all us kids, the Grants, the Bryants and the Bartholomews, used to hang there. We made friends with the younger son, 'Boorai' Curtis. He surfed too and most importantly, his family had this amazing old surfboard that dated back to the '40s or '30s. It was huge. I couldn't even lift it but he let me borrow it. All I had to do was get the board from outside the Jungle Hut, round the back, get the nose of it under my arm (because I couldn't get my arm around the middle of it), and he said that it was okay to drag the thing along by the nose. So I'd drag the board across the road — it was such a tough old beast of a board it actually made a mark in the road, as I went back and forward. I had my own groove in the road, and I'd drag it over there and just flop down the hill, drag it along the sand and just surf and surf the thing all day long. You couldn't turn it, but once it got going everyone got out of your way. The rocks didn't matter either — nothing could stop this board. When it finally got worn down by all the abuse we used to fix it with mosquito netting and grass clippings and industrial resin in some of the crudest ding fixing exercises in history.

Being mates with Boorai had other advantages too. He'd let us in the Jungle Hut after hours because they had a couple of pinball machines in there. I had everything I could possibly want right there at Rainbow. We'd sneak in after hours, and we'd have milkshakes and chocolate sundaes and play pinball, all while the parents were sleeping upstairs.

One thing about surfing is, as soon as you feel like you've mastered one spot, you realise there's a new threshold to tackle

Bustin' down the door

somewhere else. I'd become confident at Rainbow, but the more abrupt waves just up the point at Snapper were still out of my league. I remember one day surfing through Rainbow and the swell was up. Snapper was a good solid six feet and Rainbow had some good lines coming through. It was the biggest swell I'd surfed, and I took off on this wave and it was easily triple the biggest wave I'd ever caught in my life. I was completely out of control, but somehow I was going the right way. I was going across the wall of the wave, but travelling so fast it blew my young mind. Surfers were scattering and diving off and a lot of guys' boards went in to the beach on the same wave as me. As I paddled back out buzzing on the biggest hit of adrenalin of my life, this giant guy, an older guy, paddled up to me, steam coming out his ears, and said, 'Right Rabbit — you pick waves your own size.' He gave me a full dressing down. It was my first lecture from an elder on how to conduct myself in the surf and made quite an impression.

In 1968 and '69 they held the Queensland Titles at Snapper Rocks. I just thought I was nowhere near good enough to be in the cadets (under–15s) and didn't have any interest in competing. But both years I sat and watched every single heat. It wasn't the idea of competition but just the surfing itself that I was entranced by. There were some incredible surfers in it — Peter Drouyn, Graeme Black, Robbie and Wayne Deane, Keith Paull, and in the juniors there was Andrew McKinnon, Michael Peterson and Peter Townend. Absolutely incredible surfers and perfect surf. I sat there on a hill that is no longer there now. I called it Pat Riley Hill, after the father of a good surfing mate of mine, Sean 'Reg' Riley. Pat started surfing late in his life — he bought a board for his eldest son but he didn't like it so Pat started taking it out. Pat and I sat on this bench on the hill and we'd meet there every day and watch the contest. The next year we met there again and did the same thing — just sat there and watched this incredible display of surfing together. Pat must have been about 30 at that time, and he was really the first older guy to sit me down and give me advice. That had a huge influence on me, watching those State Titles accompanied by Pat's commentary on the various styles of surfing. Peter Drouyn was unbelievably good, and he won in '68, and this local guy Graeme Black won in '69. I found I had the ability to really study their surfing and subconsciously I would kind of replay their surfing over and over in my mind. I'd lie in bed and conjure up an image of the Robbie Deane roundhouse cutback or the Peter Drouyn vertical re-entry or the Graeme Black figure eight cutback into the whitewater. I really wanted to do those things in *my* surfing, but it was hard on the old Jungle Hut board, or jumping from one borrowed board to another.

I'd always ridden a variety of boards. I used to look forward to the guys coming down from Brisbane, the 'Brisoes' — who generally got a hard time from the local surfers. There was this one guy, Rod Frawley, who had a 7'11" Woosley surfboard, which itself was a super small board for the times. It was just the coolest board. It had a paisley design on the deck and he'd let me ride it on Saturdays in between his surfs. I used to sit there like a faithful lapdog waiting for a turn.

I guess a few people must have noticed we were doing it tough and had seen how keen I was, because one day in 1968 there was a knock on the door. I went out and there was Wayne and Robbie Deane, and Robbie had this tiny little surfboard under his arm. It was 6'8" which in those days was incredibly tiny, verging on ridiculous. 'This is for Rabbit,' they said. They didn't give it to me, they sold it to me for this incredible deal. It was like $40 for a brand new surfboard they'd made themselves. The deal was I could pay it off at a dollar a week, and I could handle that. They wanted to do it that way, they wanted me to actually have to work for it. Instantly, I had the most amazing surfboard on the beach. I'd walk around and everyone would be ogling it, I was so proud of that board. It really picked up the pace of my surfing because it was so different from Boorai's board, which I couldn't even lift.

Suddenly, with my own board, I really felt I belonged. I felt a part of this exclusive club. I didn't know it, but that board really put me at the cutting edge of the shortboard revolution. It was probably one of the original cutdown surfboards. Pretty soon, surfers were all chopping a foot at a time off their surfboards to make them more manoeuvrable — but I'd been a given a head start.

I started surfing Snapper a lot more, and my universe started to expand on land as well. My older sister Wendy was going out with a fairly well known local surfer and he would come by and take the little brother to the movies on a Sunday night. I started hanging around in the shadows of the Greenmount scene, where the hip, older crew hung out. I was watching the beginnings of the whole youth revolution in Australia. The Beatles and the Rolling Stones had captured the imaginations of an entire generation. There was a certain look — the Levi Strauss blue jeans, the white sneakers and some groovy Hawaiian shirt or even some hole-riddled T-shirt, and you were just the coolest dude on earth as far as I was concerned.

The authorities were unnerved by the evolution of a strong youth culture — it questioned the whole status quo of getting a job, working hard, getting married, getting a mortgage, raising a family. Teenagers were living for today and rebelling against the system. The police started cracking down on the Greenmount Beach scene, using the draconian vagrancy laws of the time. They'd come down and do a raid on the beach and if you were caught without a dollar in your pocket you'd get arrested for vagrancy and thrown in the lockup. Most of the crew didn't have a dollar in their pockets, particularly after a Friday or Saturday night — Sunday they definitely didn't have a dollar in their pockets. The police would come down in this mad rush and the guys in the cool, blue jeans would dive off the rocks at Greenmount Point and swim to Kirra. It was the most amazing thing I'd ever seen.

Australia had also just been hit by the spirit of the Summer of Love. Coolangatta wasn't quite San Francisco, but flower power was making an impact. People were starting to wear the beads and the paisley, only two years before it was all crew cuts, Elvis and James Dean.

Not everyone was possessed with the new spirit of communal love, however. Around that time I saw my first real act of localism. There was this young, local guy named Robbie Pearce who was the ultimate punk. He used to wear the bomber jackets and the boots. He was a full-on rocker, with the grade 1 haircut, but he was also an incredible surfer. He was completely ambidextrous, he could surf goofy or natural, and he had the most amazing surfboards I'd ever seen. He was sponsored by Merrin surfboards, and he had this design of his own called the bat fin, which had a scalloped trailing edge like a bat wing. This guy was so innovative and so far ahead of his time, and he was also incredibly good on the trampoline. When I was working on the trampoline he'd come over — he always had his henchmen with him — and I'd see him coming and yell out, 'Robbie, Robbie, please come on,' and he'd come straight up to me and give me a wailing backhander straight across the face. He'd come in and just take over. But he taught me how to do the backflips and all the tricks.

I once saw him punch out this guy, Benny Jaw. Robbie just snapped for no apparent reason, probably some minor hassle over a wave, and punched him out in the surf. I'd never seen anything like that before. I didn't know that happened in the surf. It seemed like street life had somehow encroached into the surf, and the whole dog-eat-dog, pecking order attitude in surfing was being formulated.

Then, one day, mum came in and said, 'We're behind on the rent and they've had a gutful of us, we're out of here.' We were evicted. Mum announced, 'We're moving to Kirra.' We moved to Musgrave Street, the front street at Kirra — right across from the surf.

Bustin' down the door

Chapter 2

kirra

irra seemed light-years away from Rainbow Bay, even though it was just the other end of Coolangatta beach. It was like moving to another country, I was that excited. Kirra was a legendary place where the waves broke in freight train cylinders, spinning down the point, and a particularly hard-core breed of surfers rode them. I hadn't been round there since the early days — before the family broke up — when my dad used to take me there to watch the great Billy Stafford Junior surfing. I didn't even know what I was watching then.

I gingerly went down to Kirra Beach after school and had a few beachbreak surfs during the week. I didn't consider myself ready to tackle the more challenging point.

This is fun, I thought, nice punchy beachbreaks at Kirra. But I was really looking forward to my first weekend at Kirra, when I could surf all day long.

That first Saturday morning, I got up super early. I could tell it was a hard offshore wind, and I looked out the window and there were these lines of swell stacked up out to sea.

The surf was six to eight feet and not a drop of water out of place. I thought I was watching one of the wonders of the world that morning. My little board looked hopelessly inadequate for the conditions. And the surf was packed. During the week Kirra had been deserted and suddenly there were 150 guys out. The lineup

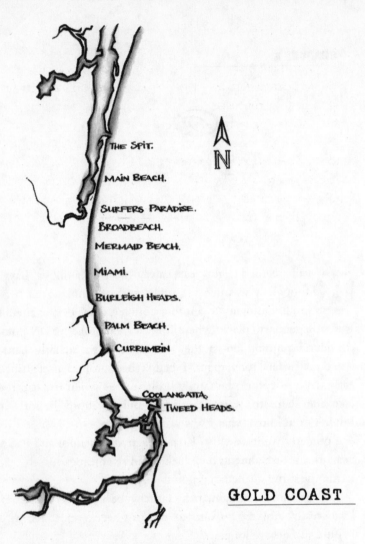

THE SPIT.

MAIN BEACH.

SURFERS PARADISE.

BROADBEACH.

MERMAID BEACH.

MIAMI.

BURLEIGH HEADS.

PALM BEACH.

CURRUMBIN

COOLANGATTA.
TWEED HEADS.

GOLD COAST

was a mass of action and colour. There were red boards, red and white striped barber pole boards, blue boards, yellow boards — every colour imaginable.

The longboards had a lot of trouble at Kirra, because the wave was so fast and hollow. This was before legropes, guys would kick their boards out before the wave shutdown and the boards would get caught by the offshore wind and spiral through the air. You'd see a wave rifling down the point and boards flying everywhere.

Bustin' down the door

Still, they were all out there, all the Kirra locals, and I watched from the Kirra shed — just mesmerised. One thing I knew, I wasn't going out there. I was happy to be king of the shorebreak that day. It looked so dangerous, and it actually was, because guys were always getting run over and boards were always coming in on the rocks and getting wrecked.

That was my first impression of Kirra, this six to eight foot day, and I realised that there was this whole other plateau of surfing that I had to get to. I'd progressed to surfing out the back at Rainbow, and even ventured up to Snapper, but suddenly I was back in the shorebreak at Kirra. Out there was another world.

TRYING TO MAKE IT TO THE SCHOOL BUS

I continued going to school at Tweed Heads after we moved to Kirra, but now I had to walk around Kirra Point to Coolangatta to get the school bus every morning. Everyone else at Kirra went to Miami High, further north. I was living in Queensland but I was still going to a NSW school. I had to get past the temptations of Kirra Point to even make it onto the bus.

It was the start of a new school year, an event that had the misfortune of coinciding with the start of the cyclone season. The surf was just incredible that year and I'd walk around the point at Kirra every day and some days it would be just unbelievably flawless, like the perfect waves I'd draw on my school books. I'd be looking at the waves, empty on a Monday morning, after battling the crowds all weekend — it was too much for me. That's when I started having a bit of trouble getting to school. There were some Monday mornings when I just could not go past that point at Kirra. I'd go down to the shed on Kirra Point and underneath this shed became my little hang-out. I had a mate called Dave MacDonald, 'Macca', who lived at Kirra and his parents were much more lenient than my mum, he was allowed to take a few days off here and there. I used to leave my board at his place, and Macca and I would plan the whole thing when we knew it was going to be perfect.

One particular school day we were out surfing Kirra all by ourselves and I looked up at the top of Kirra hill to the Coolangatta State School and I saw these figures over the fence, looking down at us. I instantly recognised them as the Peterson brothers — Tom and Michael — two hot, young, local surfers. Me and Macca were out at perfect Kirra by ourselves, this is when there was 100% employment and there was no dole. There was no-one around — only a couple of stray school kids, and we were surfing these beautiful waves by ourselves. It must have been too much for the Petersons to bear, because the next moment I saw them making a trail down the hill to the surf. That began a beautiful relationship, because they started stashing their boards under the shed as well. We weren't close friends, we went to different schools and hung out with different crowds, but it was a bit of a bonding — the shared defiance of truancy.

The Peterson boys were also in the idyllic situation of having a teacher, Dr Edwards, who shared their fascination with the surf. I was so jealous, so green with envy, because I'd see them going by in a big old Holden with their boards on the top. I'd be thinking, I can't believe this, what sort of life have these guys got? Teachers don't take you surfing, they try to stop you from surfing. Dr Edwards would actually go and pick up the Peterson brothers and take them surfing before school. Queensland schools seemed to be a paradise compared to NSW schools.

Sure enough, I got caught wagging school from time to time — the cane would come out and I'd get the cuts, but I figured a perfect day at Kirra was definitely worth four of the best. They were great times, being a young truant when the surf was perfect. Each spot had its designated hang-out and at both Kirra and Greenmount there were sheds conveniently located on the points where we could hide out. The only time it wasn't worth it was when me and my mate from Rainbow Bay, Mont, got caught wagging in the shed at Greenmount Point by my mum. Mont's dad found out and promptly packed him off to boarding school for three years. It was really heavy. Mont was the best surfer out of all of us and he was robbed of some good years there. I was devastated.

MONT: 'My old man was so heavy on wagging days off school ...
He's even said to me in later times, he now thinks that he did
the wrong thing. At first he didn't mind us surfing, he bought
us our first boards, but after that, that was it, because all this
crew just converged on our house. It was pretty heavy, it was
like a cancer then, because they just couldn't get us out of the
water.'

THE WORLD OF KIRRA

When the surf was really good I still occasionally made it round the
Point to the school bus. But I'd be on the bus thinking to myself, gee,
I wonder what it's like around the next point. I wonder what it's like
down the coast. I wonder what it's like up the coast. And I wonder
what it's like around the rest of Australia. I wonder if there's 100 of
these Kirras around the place. It used to really baffle me: Is this what
the surf was like everywhere? Of course, years later I found out that
Kirra is a one in a million, but I didn't know that then.

It was perfect timing for my surfing to move from Rainbow to
Kirra — where I could learn to ride the more challenging waves.
And I had a board that could ride in the tube. I was so lucky
to have that little 6'8" the Deane brothers made me, because the
bigger boards of the day just couldn't fit into the extreme curves of
the Kirra barrel. It was a daunting task edging my way out the back
at Kirra, but little by little, and by scrutinising the surfing of my
heroes, I moved on from the shorebreak.

My progress was only set back by a bout of double pneumonia
that kept me out of the surf for three months. I made the mistake of
going surfing with a severe case of the flu and my condition quickly
worsened. I lost weight and my surfing fitness vanished and I was
reduced to a skinny waif. In a way, that really spurred me on because

I figured, okay I'm behind now, and when I finally recovered, I attacked the surf with a new vigour — to make up the lost time.

Kirra virtually became my world. If I wasn't surfing, there was enough going on around the beach scene to keep me amused in daylight hours. Doug Rowton had the local kiosk, and in there he had pool tables, a couple of pinball machines and the juke box, and that was the hang at Kirra. Just down the road from there old Johnny Charlton had the hire boards and he started taking me under his wing. I was just this little rat that would be hanging there all the time, looking for hand-outs and bumming off the older guys. Johnny Charlton gave me a job during school holidays and on weekends, hiring out the surf-o-planes and surfboards. This was quite a prestigious position for me because Michael and Tommy Peterson and I, we all used to think this number 19 hire board was the bee's knees. It was the best one Johnny had and we'd all fight over who got to ride it. As soon as one guy fell off, the others would just run down, grab the board and take off and surf it. We had our own boards but we used to love riding that number 19.

It was round this time that I got my second board — a Hohensee cutdown. My Deane Brothers cutdown was a very sought-after board, and I had to take bids for it. I finally sold it to my best mate Macca for $21 and I threw in my paper run as well — my board and my paper run for $21. It was a great deal. Then with that $21 I went to Hohensee and bought a $45 dollar board and put a $21 deposit on it. I paid it off at a dollar a week again, so it was a beautiful deal … until I fell behind in the payments. At one stage, I owed about five week's instalments, the grand sum of $5, which seemed like the greatest financial burden imaginable. But Lawrie Hohensee could see I was a keen, young surfer and allowed me a bit of leeway. It ended up taking me about nine months to pay it off.

That board went unreal and I thought my surfing was progressing in leaps and bounds. I remember coming in after having a really good surf on my new board, and I thought I was surfing really well. And Johnny Charlton said to me, 'Rabbit, you're surfing too much like a tin soldier. You've got to loosen up.' This kind of devastated me for a while because I thought I was ripping. It really made me start thinking about the mechanics of connecting all the turns and movements. I'm glad he said that to me. He knew I was super keen and he'd give me these little tidbits every now again that always made a huge impression on me. Old Johnny Charlton still lives just round the corner from me — he can be found on any day there at Kirra. He's a gem.

JOHNNY CHARLTON: 'I was very lucky to have the beach hire rights here in Kirra in the years of hire. Now it's different. Everyone's got money, the kids have got their surfboards ... I started with surf-o-planes, 80 old surf-o-planes, rubber, and then to the boards. So all the kids, after school, they'd get a free hour to cart all the surf-o-planes, all the beach umbrellas, the wigwams, and then the surfboards, up to the pavilion. They'd do 360s on the surf-o-planes and the Brisbane people had never seen this, kids doing 360s on rubber surf-o-planes, and they wanted one, so it boosted my business. Actually, I used them up in a sense. Slave labour with children (laughter) ... that's why they're all champions. They learnt on my heavy boards, paddling big boards out there. Tough as nails. By the time they were 14 or 15 there were a lot of champions around. Kerry and Robbie Gill, Wayne and Robbie Deane, Peter Drouyn, Rabbit, Graeme Black. And Rabbit ... I used to watch him. He was very small, a small build in those days ... but he'd get out there. He had a heart. He'd get out there and have a go at the big stuff ... He'd get thrown upside down but he'd fight back and they learnt on those heavy bloody boards that I had and it made them tough.'

Macca and I had identical fibreglass skateboards. We would find a corner pavement at Kirra and practise our bottom-turns and cutbacks endlessly. The skateboard boom of the '60s had died out in Australia but an older guy made us up fibreglass decks shaped like our cutdowns and we attached the wheels ourselves. Unlike the skateboarders of the coming '70s re-birth, we were doing surfing turns on our crude skateboards — they were purely on-land, surfing simulators as far as we were concerned. They no doubt helped our development and we were soon turning harder and doing snaps in the Kirra shorebreak.

My local hero at the time was a guy called 'Hacka' Allen, he kind of took me under his wing and taught me how to shoot pool. Hacka Allen was an incredibly talented surfer, I could sit there for hours watching him. He hardly ever had his own equipment and he could ride anything. If he wrecked a board on the rocks he'd just borrow another one, and he started borrowing mine and Macca's boards. Macca had this beautiful Joe Larkin board. We loved it when Hacka borrowed our boards, even though he'd wreck them — just run them into the rocks. He opened our minds to what our boards could do. Even on our little boards, he was still walking the board, he could hang heels on a 6'8" and walk back up the board like a moon walk and he'd do all that stuff out the back, do the classic cutback, bring it into the shorebreak and then come through the shorebreak and get down on his knees and hang one knee over the nose. Just unbelievable stuff — very theatrical. And then he'd just let the board go up onto the rocks and we'd go scrambling down the rocks to try to save it.

It was a great form of entertainment, watching boards get washed up onto the rocks at Kirra. When a set would come through and wipe everyone out or catch them inside, the boards would come straight in and just get annihilated on the rocks. There was a little eddy in the corner of the Point where the boards would congregate and there'd be about 15 boards floating in there getting worked on the rocks and all the Kirra locals would be sitting there cheering. Boards were just cracking in half, being destroyed beyond repair, and no-one would move to save them.

When we'd get a classic day at Kirra I used to just hope and pray that the great surfers from the northern end of the Gold Coast, Peter Drouyn and Paul and Rick Neilsen would come down and surf it. If Peter Drouyn came down I would get out of the water and just stand in the shed and watch him, because no-one surfed

Bustin' down the door

Kirra like him. He was just majestic. The most perfect style, incredible speed, and he'd attack it with absolute gusto. He was doing arches and carves that I'd never seen anyone do at Kirra.

I'll never forget the day that Peter Drouyn returned home in 1970 having just won the Makaha International in Hawaii. The day of his victorious home-coming, Kirra was flawless, and he went out there and put on the best display of surfing I've ever seen in my life. To this day, I've never been more impressed by any single surfing session. He was on this little mini-gun, the Hawaiian spear, which was the latest design from the Hawaiian Islands. He surfed Kirra with this speed and style that was supreme. I'd never seen surfing like it and I think it was the first time I became really conscious of the importance of style in surfing. Paul Neilsen also had this silky smooth style. When the Neilsen brothers came down they'd often bring David 'Baddy' Treloar from Angourie, Baddy was another guy who had a great influence on me. Those guys attacked the place on big days — eight foot days on low tide, before the big groyne, when Kirra could handle a bigger swell than it can today — and the waves would just be dredging out. To me the waves looked impossible to ride, and to most people they were. But these guys would come out and just master the place — doing incredible stalls at the base of the wave. Tube-riding was really only in its infancy, so they were mainly just hotdog surfing — carving up big waves as if they were a little, playful beachbreak.

I consider myself really blessed to have been surrounded by such great surfers. Apart from the older guys, Michael Peterson (known as MP) and Peter Townend (PT) were two of the hottest juniors in town, and they used to have a running duel going just down the beach at Greenmount. I'd walk around Kirra Point after school, look down and see a set of waves at Greenmount Point, and nearly every day I'd see PT with this white mop of hair and a pink board going along on a wave. You could see his beautiful, weaving style even from a distance. And the very next wave, always, you'd see these big roostertails of spray, and it was MP, doing these really aggressive carving turns and throwing up bucket loads of water. Even though Kirra would be perfect they'd be busy going at each other at Greenmount. I'd be happy to go to Kirra and surf with my mates, kids my own age like Steve Harge, Wayne Noakes and Macca. We weren't yet super-competitive, but we had a good energy going and we were riding out the back and really having a go at it, egging each other on.

Although I was now going straight, I was still always working out ways where I could get a fiver in my pocket. As I was walking home from school one day, I looked down on the rocks along the Point and lo and behold ... there was a penguin. A fairy penguin. And my first thought was, there's money to be made out of this. I climbed down and grabbed this penguin around its belly and stood by the side of the road, in my school uniform, hitchhiking south to get to Jack Evans' Sharkatarium. I got picked up by a local guy who was notorious for dropping acid, and I'm absolutely certain he was tripping at the time. I jumped in his VW, sat in the front with this penguin flapping away on my lap, and he just looked over at me and went, 'Where are you guys going?' I said, 'Jack Evans' Sharkatarium,' and he didn't bat an eyelid. There were no explanations to make — this seemed the most normal thing in the world to this guy.

So he dropped us around there and I went up to the legendary Sharky Jack and tried to sell him the penguin. When he didn't go for that, I suggested a reward might be in order for rescuing the penguin. 'Yes, Rabbit,' he said, taking possession of the bird, 'come back tomorrow and we'll get the newspaper here to take a photo and we'll have a reward for you.' But I didn't get a chance to go back because in the *Daily News* the next morning there was a photo of Sharky Jack with the penguin handing it over to one of the officials at Seaworld. The penguin had escaped from Seaworld, at Southport, and somehow made its way down to Kirra. Sharky Jack took full credit for rescuing the bird and returning it.

I got no reward and no picture in the paper. Sharky had snaked me.

THE SHORTBOARD REVOLUTION

There's always been a bit of conjecture in surfing on the subject of the shortboard revolution. Boards went from 11 foot to nine foot overnight after Nat Young won the World Title in San Diego in 1966 on a board cut down and refined by his design buddies, Bob MacTavish and George Greenough. But that's only part of the story. In 1968 and '69 most surfers were still riding 9' and 8'6" surfboards. There was a second stage to the revolution that happened in about 1969 when people like the Deane brothers and Drouyn just started chopping a foot off a week. Of course, it went to the other extreme and we tried to ride some pretty ludicrous boards. At one stage I was riding a board 5'4" long by 21" wide at Kirra. It was like a big disc and was actually a kneeboard, but anything went amid the spirit of design experimentation.

Nowhere was that spirit more evident than at the Hohensee factory. Lawrie Hohensee (the guy who had extended my loan period on my last board) ran a board business where Drouyn and the Neilsen brothers all got their start, and that was the cutting edge of the cutdown era. What helped the spread of the cutdowns was the fact that they were very accessibly priced. They were the old 10'6"s, stripped of their fibreglass and re-shaped and re-glassed with a modern fin. Recycled boards, so to speak.

Of course, performance surfing changed in parallel with these design changes. One year it was really cool to do the big fade on the longboard, do the s-turn and then walk the board. If you could walk the board and walk back and do it with real style or hang 10, you were incredible. Then, almost overnight, high speed, aggressive direction changes became the real focus.

Drouyn developed this amazing cutback and the Deane brothers were tearing it up. As boards started to come down in length and became more manoeuvrable, the classic Queensland cutback started to evolve. MP took it on and made it the cornerstone of his new aggressive approach that was to revolutionise surfing. Even though I was younger than the guys who were setting the pace, my little 6'8" had placed me at the cutting edge of this performance revolution. In 1969, MP was still riding an eight foot board, but his boards were ahead of their time in their own way too. I remember the day his brother Tommy said to me, 'I've got Mick's board, the magic board,' and we took it for a surf. We weren't game to surf Kirra, so we snuck over to my little spot at Inside Rainbow and surfed it there until MP tracked us down. Of course Tommy hadn't got his permission at all, he got smacked around the head and MP took the board back, but I loved that thing. It was a magic board and it was a thrill just to ride it to try to figure out what MP's secret was.

So I was riding a variety of equipment from an early age — longboards and shortboards and most of the weird variations that popped up along the way. And then suddenly, it all went shortboard — the longboard was dead — and the guys who didn't make the transition just disappeared. There was some sort of juncture in surfing there, when suddenly everything that had come before was considered old school. It was like the dinosaur. The longboard and the longboard faithful, they just faded out — faded out to the pub, or faded out to the hills. The era of flower power and the prevalence of magic mushrooms out at Pigabeen Valley, inland from the Gold Coast, might have had a bit to do with it too. A lot of people did get on that trip — literally. At the same time there was a new crew of very aggressive young surfers entering the water on the new equipment and surfing in the new style. Just in Coolangatta you had me, MP and PT, and we were already pretty aggressive. It was a radical change. We were super-competitive and we were on small boards doing the new manoeuvres; in a lot of ways the longboarders must have suddenly felt like strangers in their own sport.

This was also the golden age of the old 8 and 16 mm surf movies, but all we were seeing were longboard movies. There was a surf show on TV every Saturday afternoon hosted by Stan Richards, and it was all this Californian footage — all longboards and tandem surfing. We never, ever saw any footage of shortboards. It was happening live in front of our eyes but there was no reference to it in the surf media of the day. Even the magazines remained predominantly longboard oriented, until *Surfing World* magazine came up and did a feature on Queensland. I had my first shot in a magazine and we were all riding small boards at big Kirra. After that, we began seeing photos of the big Queensland cutties and MP started getting a little bit of exposure.

There was another giant influence in surfing which came rumbling up the Pacific Highway from down south every Summer. North Narrabeen was a super power then and in 1969 and 1970 they came up and spent the whole of those summers at Coolangatta and showed us what it was all about. They partied hard and they surfed hard — Col Smith, Tony 'Wicka' Hardwick, Steve Cooney, Mark Warren, Grant 'Dappa' Oliver, Simon Anderson and Terry Fitzgerald. They did some great surfing and turned us on to new ways of approaching our waves and new surfboard designs. But they didn't have it all their own way in the water. This was when the McCoy twin fin was starting to take off and I remember sitting back with MP one day at Kirra and Dappa and the North Narrabeen guys were trying to ride Kirra with 4'9" twin fins. That's when we got to the ridiculous point in the shrinking of surfboards. They'd go, zip, zip, zip, along the wave but they couldn't get to the bottom of the wave to do a bottom turn. We already knew we needed to have these longer, mini-guns for Kirra to handle the speed and cover the distance of the Point. But they were going, zip, zip, zip, until they just spun out, and they'd go flying through the air. We'd sit there on the beach, howling. Kirra was such a demanding wave that it was actually dictating design. Surfboards were evolving so fast, but Kirra would sort them out.

Around the same time, an almost Jesus-like figure from the distant southern depths of Victoria materialised on the Gold Coast and blew all our minds. I remember me and this mate of mine Bruce 'Bucky' Perriot, we walked round to Greenmount and there was this guy riding this green board, and I'd never seen anything like it in my life. He was doing these figure eight cutbacks off the foam, it just seemed like he could go anywhere on the wave. He had the most perfect, loose style. Of course, it was Wayne Lynch. We sat there and watched this guy surfing and just went, well, that's got to be the best in the world. And he was, at that time, he was definitely the best in the world.

That same night, he was sleeping on the beach at Greenmount. He'd just come up from Victoria and it must have seemed like a tropical paradise to him, he just plonked himself down and slept on the beach. During the night the police came and dragged him off the beach, took him to the border, and kicked him out of Queensland. When we found out, we were absolutely mortified that this revered figure could be thrown out of the state.

Wayne had a huge influence on surfboard design. At the time I was influenced by MP's boards, and Gordon Merchant (who would eventually become the driving force behind the hugely successful Billabong company) had just developed the tucked under rail with the big raked fin at Joe Larkin's surfboard factory. Gordon was singing the praises of his design and saying that it was the reason why Wayne Lynch was able to do what he did. He had these forgiving rails at the front and this hard edge at the back. Such things had never been thought of before. As the boards were coming down in size no-one actually thought to change the rails. All the design subtleties were just starting to happen and the Joe Larkin factory became the new hot spot. Terry Fitzgerald came up from Narrabeen and spent a year on the Gold Coast and worked out of Joe Larkin's factory. Of course 'the Sultan of Speed,' as Terry was known, was incredible at Kirra. I don't think he was as good in the tube as the locals but he was faster and better on the face and he had that incredible style. It seemed like design breakthroughs were being made every week at Joe Larkin's factory during this time and the principles of good surfboard design that came out of that place in 1969 and '70 are still applied today.

One other great surfer whose development I was lucky enough to witness at close quarters was Mark Richards — MR. His late father Ray and mum Val owned a unit at Rainbow Bay and I watched him every school holidays since he was 10. He had a gawky style, kind of knock-kneed with arms flapping and board squiggling all over the place, all the while decked out in iridescent pink Midget Farrelly trunks.

Mont and I couldn't believe this kid. He was perpetual motion from take off at Little Mali to step off at Greenmount Point. On

Bustin' down the door

the run-around his parents, and surprisingly his mother more so, would remonstrate with him about a particular subject and send him back out again for another round. Having been raised on the classic Queensland pointbreaks, we were into style and found it highly amusing to watch this spectacle.

About two years later, I think it was early '71, I went to the top of Duranbah Hill and saw some guy sending giant roostertails off the back of this wedge breaking off the northern wall, a good 500 metres away. He caught three more as I gave hot pursuit. The guy was whipping this little green board past 90 degrees every cuttie. As I paddled out, to my horror, I saw that it was the kid in the fluoro trunks. MR had gone from the ugly duckling to the graceful swan. I knew right then I was watching the surfing of the future.

THE ANIMAL ERA

This era of surfing has gone down in history as the animal era — partly because of the aggressive new style of surfing popularised by Nat Young, and partly because of the notorious animal acts of the surfers of the day. Surfers could never hold a function at the same venue twice — ever — and my first taste of a surfing social event was a beauty.

I'd been spotted as a prospective talent by some of the older guys at the beach. Paul Daley, who was a very respected surfer, was the president of the Kirra club and Darryl Eastlake (now a TV sports presenter) was also involved as a surfing promoter, and they organised for me to come to my first presentation night. I hadn't been to any competitions, but I was invited to come along to this night at the Kirra Beach Hotel as my introduction to the club. They came and picked me up and took me to this function where the guests of honour were Ma and Pa Bendall, a classic old surfing couple from the Sunshine Coast who were our closest thing to royalty. Pa Bendall was an amazing character. The first time I laid eyes on him I was paddling out at Rainbow Bay and as a wave came through, this head popped up in front of me. It had this grizzled face and long, grey hair and an eyepatch and a big, bushy beard. I thought it was either King Neptune or the spirit of some lost pirate arisen from the deep, but it was Pa Bendall bobbing up after a wipeout. He and his wife had both been surfing as long as anyone could remember and they were esteemed guests of honour at any surfing social occasion of note.

Ma and Pa Bendall sat up at the top of the room and the booze flowed and things slowly degenerated. When someone threw a sandwich and it hit Pa Bendall in the eyepatch, things quickly degenerated. Someone else threw a custard pie or some big dessert thing and it landed right square on the picture of Queen Elizabeth and the room just blew up. This evening caused a giant split in the local surfing scene — people walked away from surfing and never came back because they were so appalled by the behaviour this night. And this was my introduction to a boardriding club. You had the Windansea crew from up the coast, the Kirra crew and the Snapper crew all having food fights and brawling and it spilled out on to the streets. Chairs were thrown, the place just got destroyed, and I was kind of impressed. Wow, this is insane, I thought to myself. The president of the club came round to mum's house with his tail between his legs a few days later and apologised profusely, as I'm sure he was doing all over town throughout the next few weeks. He said to my mum, 'I hope this doesn't put Rabbit off. We're not like that.' But he needn't have worried about me — far from being put off, I was fascinated by this collection of wild characters and their raucous ways.

So I joined Kirra. My first club contest victory was at about six foot Kirra in the cadets, or under–15s. There was Macca and myself and several other young guys and I won, surfing out the back at good-sized Kirra. I was totally stoked and I went home and told mum (she was very proud of me), had lunch and hurried back down the beach to watch the open final. It had already started when I got there and the organisers kept asking, 'Where's Blacky? Where's Graeme Black?' The final was under way and he was in it. He was the best surfer at Kirra at the time and he'd already won the Queensland Title off Peter Drouyn and he'd won the 1969 Queensland Title at Snapper Rocks. He was the best goofyfooter in the land of right-handers, which meant he nearly always surfed on his backhand. Wayne Lynch was the only backsider I'd seen who was better. They were still calling for Blacky when I saw him come out of the Kirra pub, and he had a bit of a swagger on. He'd been in the pub for a couple of hours, which was not unusual. As he crossed the road I went running up to him and said, 'Blacky, your final's on.' He didn't run, he just kept walking up the Point, got his contest singlet, paddled out and just blitzed them and won the final. That was kind of mind-blowing to see and it was probably the beginnings of a proud Australian surfing tradition for ripping in the surf no matter what sort of abuse you'd inflicted on yourself. That was the era.

Soon I was also being wooed by Windansea, who were based up at Surfers Paradise. Windansea was like a super club. The original Windansea club was formed in California and then some of their surfers came out to Australia and started chapters at Manly, in Sydney, and Surfers Paradise, recruiting all the big name surfers of the day. There was no money involved — just the prestige of belonging to this famous club. In my eyes, the surfers in the Windansea club at Surfers Paradise were all superstars. The rivalry between clubs was intense. Darryl Eastlake had become involved in Windansea and he had the gift of the gab even then, and finally convinced me to go in one of their contests. So up I went to Surfers Paradise, where the beachbreaks were thumping at about six feet. I went in the juniors and won. I went in the new members section and won that, and because I won both those divisions, I got put in the opens and I made the final. Here I was, this skinny, young kid from down the coast and I was in the final with Peter Drouyn, Paul and Rick Neilsen, Richard Harvey and some other huge names of the times and I got second to Drouyn. People were just stunned. I went to the presentation and collected three huge trophies. No-one at Kirra knew anything about this and I imagined Surfers Paradise was so far away they'd never even hear about it. But of course they did find out, so I instantly had to get all my trophies and head back to Kirra and explain myself. I went to the next meeting at Kirra and I had to stand there and swear black and blue that I'd never join that club. But I had all their trophies and after much deliberation it was decided that I'd performed a brilliant ruse against our bitter rivals. I was a sensation for doing that. Even MP thought that was really something, so I got some heavy respect for that one.

THE AUSSIE TITLES

The 1970 Australian Titles were held on the Gold Coast at the peak of my grommethood. Me and Macca got the week off school and things were so cool back then that we left our boards on top of Greenmount Hill for the whole week. We didn't even take them home, we just left them there under a rock for a whole week and we'd just come back the next morning and there they'd be.

Those Aussie Titles really blew my mind. Wayne Lynch was like the Messiah, he had this incredible presence, and was untouchable. It was his fourth Australian Junior Title in a row, and he was already a legend at 18. He had the long hair, he really did look like Jesus. I was a reserve for the Queensland team and I didn't get a start. I didn't even want a start. In the juniors there was Lynchy, MP, PT, Mark Warren, Grant Oliver, Andy Mac — a super hot crew. But the real action was in the open final — Drouyn, Keith Paull, Ted Spencer, Midget, Nat Young, and Baddy Treloar — and each one of them had incredible style. I felt like I actually saw my lineage right there before my eyes. I saw where I fitted into the big picture. Drouyn was my super hero, but Nat was like a god — a distant figure of awe and reverence. Midget was just this incredible mythological figure arisen from the past. Keith Paull was the guy who I thought had the most beautiful style and Ted Spencer was unbelievable too. Drouyn won, Ted Spencer got second, Keith Paull third and Nat and Midget were relegated to a little bit up the back.

It was perfect Greenmount every single day and Nat, perhaps frustrated by the stiff competition, finally blew up. He came along this wave, did this giant snap and hit a rock and snapped his fin clean out; he just stood there and bellowed and roared like an animal. We were sitting up the Point, just stunned, and he started swearing and spitting the dummy. It was the first major tantrum I'd seen in a surfing contest. Stan Couper, the president of the Australian Surfriders Association, came marching down the hill, this elderly, very straight kind of Victorian administrator. He marched Nat up the hill, virtually by the ear, and he just gave him this incredible dressing down and threatened to throw him out of the Australian Titles. And Nat pulled his head in.

But they were all superb, they were all super heroes, larger than life, and I witnessed it all. Drouyn was the victor. He showed me what show business was all about. He had a guy who carried his boards, a caddy, and the caddy wore this cowboy hat and he would carry his board around everywhere and Drouyn would walk around just supreme, like Marlon Brando, and so on top of it all. Nat couldn't touch him, no-one could touch him.

And then MP and the other juniors put on quite a show. They were just raw, they hadn't quite got their act together and Lynch was so far ahead of every one at that time, but I could tell MP was going to be a great then. I could see Nat and then MP following in his footsteps, and somewhere between Drouyn and Nat was my path. It was like a meeting of the gods and it all happened right on my home beach. I think those Australian Titles had a lot to do with the formation of my dream as it started to unfold a bit later.

SATURDAY NIGHT'S ALL RIGHT FOR FIGHTING

Coolangatta was a pretty wild town in the late '60s and early '70s. It had evolved from this quaint country town, ideal for peaceful family holidays, to a kind of wild western frontier town where almost anything went. With its pool halls, pinball parlours, the thriving beach culture and the famous Danceland dance hall, it was the perfect hotbed for the fermenting youth revolution.

My friend Bucky Perriot and I would look on in awe at all the action that went down on a Saturday night. I was allowed to go and stay at his place on the weekend. His older sister was friends with my older sister Wendy, and we all used to go into Coolangatta on a

Saturday night. Me and Bucky, we'd be out there playing the pinballs, and the older crew headed to this incredible place called Danceland. Right next to it there was a cafe called Gerry and Ivo's and this was where the surfers hung out. Just down from that was the Capitol Theatre and just up from that there was a rockers cafe called Butsy's. It was taboo for the surfers to go there and the rockers would never go into Gerry and Ivo's, but they'd all go into Danceland. We'd see all the surfers coming in and they'd all been getting pissed, and the rockers would be hanging out at Butsy's and then they'd all file into Danceland too. You could hear this incredible music going on inside, the Beatles and the Stones and Manfred Mann and I remember when that song by Russell Morris, 'The Real Thing,' came out, that was just the most awesome song of the times. We never got to go inside Danceland — it was the most intriguing thing to us, just imagining what actually went on in there. But just hanging around there was an incredible experience because it was Saturday night and sure enough, sooner or later, you'd hear the cry go up — 'Fight!' We'd be playing the pinnies, and someone would go, 'There's a fight outside Butsy's,' and we'd drop everything and go running up the road. The surfie–rocker wars were unbelievable. You'd hear all week that the rockers from Brisbane or Murwillumbah were coming down to beat the crap out of the surfies, and this is where the Kirra, Snapper and Greenmount guys would forget their rivalries and all link together and stand as a big front. There were actually three factions, because usually the Aborigines would come in from Chinderah and then it was on. Everyone would be pretty pissed and it would just be this giant, rolling fight up and down the main street of Coolangatta.

And so weekends consisted of surfing Kirra four or five times a day, going over the pool halls or the pinball parlours afterwards, then watching the fights on Saturday night. I'd come out of the surf and say to Hacka Allen, 'Oh Hacka, can I come over the pool hall with you?' And he'd take me over, and we'd play doubles — we were nearly unbeatable. He was so good, and he taught me to play pretty good pool. We were a bit like Paul Newman and Tom Cruise in *The Color of Money*. He was the all-time hustler.

Bustin' down the door

It was a pretty incredible time. And when you throw in the era of psychedelic drugs it became really interesting. You'd see all these people coming in to Coolangatta tripping out of their minds on mushrooms. The gold top mushrooms were growing everywhere out in the valleys. There were some unbelievable stories about people who'd never taken drugs in their lives, who'd just gone out and picked some mushrooms, to make a mushroom omelette, and they had no idea they'd just picked 30 gold tops. There were people running naked through the middle of Coolangatta, just going crazy, and ending up in padded cells. There were always incredible stories. Sundays you'd be over at Kirra, just sitting and listening to the post mortems of what happened the night before — who got pissed, who got arrested, who'd gone crazy. The police had this enormous black paddywagon we called the 'Black Mariah' and they would come cruising through town on a Saturday night, you'd always see people in the back that you knew. You were famous if you got chucked in the Black Mariah and then in to Coolangatta jail for the night.

Despite all this mayhem, by day Coolangatta looked like a peaceful country town, with some classic old hotels — the Grand Hotel, the Coolangatta Hotel — they're all gone. They were beautiful pubs. It still amazes me sometimes how much the place has changed and the pace with which development has transformed the Gold Coast. I remember the big drive to Brisbane — you'd have to go up north through Southport and there was one big building, Lennon's Hotel at Broadbeach, it was about six storeys high and we used to think that was just unbelievable.

The big storms of '67 and the erosion of the beaches probably had a lot to do with Coolangatta changing from a family holiday town to a young people's hang-out. Families stopped coming because there was no sand left on the beaches. With the absence of the families, the youth of the day took over the town. It was a wild place. Nothing too serious ever happened, no-one was getting killed or anything, it was just young people getting pissed and having a good time.

Round this time, smoking marijuana became popular among the youth too and the police were waging war. This is when the jackboots came out and the famous 5 am gestapo raids went on. You'd hear the news that 40 people had got busted in one morning and people were going to court for having three seeds. Pot smoking became synonymous with the beach culture in the eyes of the general public. The surfers were really getting the blame for that — surfing had a bad image. The surfers were considered a menace and the full weight of Queensland's severe laws were used to crack down on them. The police would literally run people out of town. They'd bust them and drive them over to the Tweed click gates and send them on their way. But once you got thrown out of Coolangatta, it was common for people to double back around again — and then get thrown out again. A lot of young people were getting criminal records over fairly minor stuff.

I was aware all this was going on but I kept my distance. I knew guys two or three years older than me who were getting into a fair bit of trouble, getting busted for possession and selling. Half the time people were buying a matchbox full of bay leaves or parsley or mixed herbs and thinking they were getting high.

We were happy just to scull a bit of cheap plonk on a Saturday night. A group of us would head down the beach and pass round a bottle and then run amok in town, playing the pinnies and getting thrown out of all the places, and that's about as much as we were into. We still managed to attract the attention of the police though, and finally one of our gang got busted. Bucky Perriot got taken home drunk by the police one night and that kind of pulled us up a bit because the parents cracked down.

The more the public image of surfing fell, the more strongly we wanted to identify ourselves as surfers. The coolest fashion on a Saturday night was if your parents allowed you to go out in jeans and thongs. I was never allowed to do that. If I was going out Saturday night I had to get dressed up, so I'd stash my thongs down the bottom of the stairs, wave goodbye and get my shoes off and my thongs on in the front yard. And everyone was trying to grow their hair long. The big challenge was at school. Schools cracked down heavily on long hair but MP was probably one of the first to let his hair grow long. Bucky Perriot's parents were really cool and he was allowed to grow his hair long. I was never allowed to grow my hair, but I was just stoked that my hair went blonde from all the surfing, so I was going okay.

While the Danceland crew were going dancing, our romantic arena was the roller-skating rink or the Capitol Theatre. We'd go roller-skating on Saturday arvo and mingle with the girls and we'd all plan to meet later and go to the movies. They had the big canvas seats in the old Capitol and the big deal was to sit there with your girl and have a bit of a feel, and you'd all talk about it the next day. And if you turned up at the beach or school on Monday morning with a love bite you were a hero. Bucky Perriot had a bit of a touch with the women and I used to hang in his slipstream. His girlfriend was beautiful and I started going out with her best friend, Rhonda Cross. She was my first girlfriend and I think it was one night after seeing a movie, I walked her home and we both lost our virginity on the soccer field at Goodwin Park. It wasn't very romantic, but it was done. It was accomplished. Then we really got going because Bucky's father was a fisherman and he had a trawler. We started having secret Saturday night parties on the trawler. We'd meet the girls on the trawler and we'd have some drinks; Bucky would be over in one bunk with his girl, and I'd be over in another bunk with my girl. It was heaven … until Bucky's dad busted us one night.

But the girls were really secondary to surfing. Saturday night was a date with Rhonda but we wouldn't ever mingle with them at school or the beach, it would just be like a bit of a wink.

My results at school were suffering because of my infatuation with surfing. I'd gone from being dux of the class at Tweed Primary to the class clown and habitual truant at Tweed River High. I was still in the top 10% in the state for maths, I can remember flying through maths tests but my other marks were plummeting. One teacher failed me outright before I even sat the end of year exam. For some reason, I've always felt like I could straddle opposite ends of the social spectrum, and this may have been developed at school, because I was hanging with the brains in class and the ratbags in the playground.

My sporting prowess didn't extend to all things, but I always had this unshakeable self-belief. This teacher came round one day at school and said, 'We're having this big inter-school carnival and we're short of people. We are desperately in need of some really top-class high jumpers. We need you to be able to jump a minimum of four foot one to qualify for this.' I put my hand up, and declared confidently, 'I can do that,' and he said, 'Are you sure?' And I must have seemed sure, because they didn't even put me through any trials or anything. The day of the carnival arrived and all the different schools were there; it was a big deal. I turned out for the high jump, and they set the bar at four foot to start. So I strode purposefully at the thing, hurled myself at it, and discovered that I could jump about three foot seven. I got nowhere near getting over the first hurdle. I was in disgrace, but for some reason I wasn't the least bit embarrassed. I wasn't good at athletics, but I had an unfaltering belief in my ability to do anything.

PT was different from the rest of us slovenly surfers. He was impeccable. Not only would he have these clean-as-a-whistle surfboards, immaculate clothes and carefully groomed hair, but he would record every contest result, and every newspaper clipping about himself. At school he never wagged a day. He was a very conscientious student. I, on the other hand, was in the running for the premiership for who got the most cuts of the cane. The winner would get something like 60 cuts a year, and I was going alright. I was up there. I really was squandering my potential as a student, but I was getting a bit of respect in the schoolyard.

Towards the end of 1970, my mother's divorce settlement came through and she announced that we were moving to Sydney. I left Tweed River High in disgrace. I owed three years of textbook fees and I was definitely not an honour student.

Mum wanted to get a ballet class going in Sydney and she had some quite high-profile contacts in the dance scene down there. So we moved to Sydney, into a place on the beach at Curl Curl, just north of Manly. We had more money than we'd ever had before, and every day my mum and my sisters would go and enjoy the sights of the city. Sydney Harbour boat cruises, Taronga Park Zoo, shopping trips into the city, sightseeing. Mum became pretty good at spending money. I was just happy to get a couple of bucks and walk along Curl Curl beach and go and hang out at Dee Why where I met all the local surfers. They took me in and I surfed Dee Why and Curl Curl and saw it as an opportunity to get a bit of a Sydney influence to my surfing.

During the course of my stay there the locals would terrify me with stories about their legendary surf break, Dee Why Point, and when it did come on at eight foot I could see exactly what they meant. It was a reef point break with a really radical take-off section and an even more radical bowl section and I was quite in awe of that wave. I'm sure my sessions out there, and the guidance of the locals like Peter Crawford, Big Ox, the Harris brothers and Jimmy Sasse really helped my surfing at the time. I knew it was doing me the world of good, because the waves were totally different from home, and I knew how many good surfers were coming out of Sydney. So I applied myself to surfing all those seaweedy shorebreaks, and then a couple of times Dee Why Point went off and I made a bit of an impression there.

About three weeks after we arrived in Sydney, mum walked into the house and announced, 'Well, we're broke, we're moving back to the Gold Coast. We've got just enough to see us through to the end of the holidays.' We had a bit of a family meeting and decided we'd go for a holiday to Surfers Paradise, at the northern end of the Gold Coast. So we packed up and moved again, this time into the main street of Surfers Paradise. And, somehow, after the school holidays finished, we didn't leave.

WENDY: 'There was one man who came into mum's life after dad. But he wanted to put us into boarding school while he took mum overseas and that was when she made a big decision. She probably would have been really well cared for and had money, but he wanted to put these kids in boarding school and mum's just gone, no way.'

the  hitchhiker

My world expanded again with the move to Surfers Paradise, and the whole of the Gold Coast became my domain. I became a hitchhiker and I fell into a natural, wandering rhythm; catching rides up and down the coast, as if in preparation for the global travels that lay ahead.

I changed to Miami High, where Andrew McKinnon (Andy Mac), the Petersons and my other friends from Kirra, Steve Harge, Macca and Wayne Noakes, went to school. The headmaster Bill Callinan was very sports-minded, he had represented Queensland in Rugby League, and he'd already heard of me. He interviewed me when I enrolled and asked me what I wanted to do with my life.

'I want to be a champion surfer,' I told him, point blank.

Incredibly, he didn't bat an eyelid. 'I'll back you all the way. As long as you give me respect I'll back you,' he said.

I found it unbelievable for an authority figure to give surfing such recognition at the time. When I was at Tweed River High, I remember reading the back page of the *Courier Mail* and there was a photo of this kid called Mick Murphy riding to school at Miami High with his school uniform on and a surfboard under his arm, with a big story about him going to school to go in a surfing competition. I remember thinking, that's me, I want to be at that school. But it wasn't by design that I ended up there. If we hadn't moved to Sydney, if we hadn't run out of money and moved up to Surfers, it might never have happened.

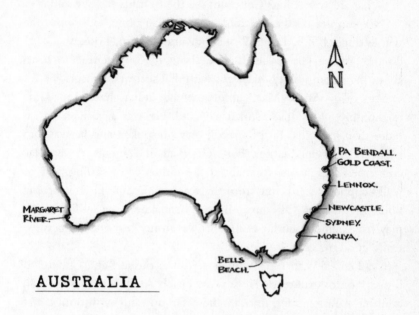

PA BENDALL.
GOLD COAST.
LENNOX.
NEWCASTLE.
SYDNEY.
MORUYA.
MARGARET RIVER.
BELLS BEACH.

AUSTRALIA

But I wasn't about to break my ties with Coolangatta, and so began my nomadic wanderings up and down the Gold Coast. I made a personal resolve never to ride public transport, so I walked from Surfers Paradise to Miami High School and back every day for three years. I can't even recall the moral grounds of my objection to public transport. The fact was that we didn't have any money, but typically I had to turn it into a noble crusade. I made this stand that I couldn't go back on. I started going to school with Andy Mac, who lived with his mum at Mermaid. I'd walk to his place, we'd have a surf and come in at 9 am and he'd get in his car and drive to school but I'd still insist on walking, get to school late and get in trouble.

Bill Callinan had basically given me an open-ended pass which meant, if I did my work I could do what I wanted. It was like a sports excellence program before there was such a thing. It was all quite unofficial and, of course, I absolutely abused it to the max. I'd be walking out of school and hitchhiking right in front of Miami High School, hitchhiking down to Kirra.

A teacher came out one day to challenge me.

'What are you doing? Get up to see the headmaster,' she said.

'No, you get up there,' I told her. I was so obnoxious about the whole thing. Bill had to pull me aside and explain, 'Look, you can't do this. You've got to be discrete about it.' So I started to learn about the responsibility that went with that sort of privilege.

My mate Andy Mac, unfortunately, didn't have the same relationship with Bill Callinan as I did. He was a year and a bit older than me and a bit of a rebel, very outspoken and he was into transcendental meditation. For conservative elements, Andy Mac confirmed their worst fears about the influence of surfing, and he really copped a hard time from the teachers. I came in at a turning point in attitudes. Of course, Bill Callinan knew my father, which may have helped, and his son Denis was in my year and we became really good mates.

I had a deal with Bill Callinan — he let me surf and I played in the school football team. He was my coach. Andy Mac was the full, counter-culture surfer, into all these far out and new things, and the establishment related that to drugs. There were even a couple of instances where drugs suddenly came on to campus and some surfers got busted which, of course, didn't help matters. But I played in the school firsts football team with Steve Harge and some great footballers, and Bill could see that I was a bit of an all-rounder — I did my football training, I did my school work, and he let me go surfing.

Andy Mac was with the Windansea club, he'd already been to Hawaii, and he seemed incredibly worldly to me. He became a big influence. I regarded the walk to school as good training, and a surf and breakfast at Andy Mac's place at Mermaid became a part of the routine. He was right into health food and his mother would squeeze fresh orange juice and they had muesli and stuff that all seemed terribly exotic to me. Andy Mac would still drive to school and I'd still walk, but now he'd get to school five minutes late and get blown up by the teacher and I'd walk in like 15 or 20 minutes later without getting into any trouble — he could never understand that.

It was during the walks to and from school that I first developed my dream of pro surfing. I would daydream the whole way, and

I never noticed the distance, four or five miles back and forth every day. I'd dream about travelling around the world, going to surfing tournaments and going to Hawaii.

Across the road from Miami High was the Hohensee Surf factory so I'd hang over there at lunch times. That had become the hot spot and that was where Paul Neilsen, Peter Drouyn and MP were making boards. Hohensee had taken over the mantle from the Larkin factory. This was where it was all happening, the cutdowns and the innovations. Then the news came through that Kenny Guddenswagger up at Adler surf centre had offered Paul Neilsen a $20-a-week retainer, and I just went, 'Unbelievable.' It was the first I'd ever heard about someone getting paid to go surfing. Twenty bucks a week. Soon Andy Mac was on a retainer too and this was just a gigantic development. I already had the dream but that just made me go, 'Well, there's something.' Something happened there to support my dream, and it happened right across the road.

Around the same time, the first contests with prize-money were popping up — the Kirra Pro-am, and a thing called the Queensland Open. MP was winning everything but I started coming second or third. I was starting to win things like 50 dollar vouchers at shops, then MP won a stereo and I won a surfboard. Things were starting to happen. I became aware of Hawaii through the magazines, there was already professional surfing on a very small scale in Hawaii then. Nat won the first Smirnoff competition and I read that he won $1000 — that was insane. I was reading or picking up any information I could to support the dream.

But my dream was quite specific. It centred around actually going around the world to all these countries and competing in grand prix events as part of a circuit and actually having a ranking. There was nothing like that happening. There wasn't anything like that happening until six or seven years later. I didn't have any model for this — I wasn't the least bit interested in tennis, golf, car racing or any sports that ran on that sort of system, but somehow the vision was clear to me. I don't know what planted the seed. This is where PT had a bit of an influence, because he had the dream of professional surfing too and he was right into promotion — something that I didn't know anything about. He'd lecture me on promoting yourself, keeping all your news clippings, having a scrap book, so I got a scrap book going. He was very professional about his whole act, documenting everything, and he certainly wasn't scared about selling himself.

Walking to and from school, I continued to spend my time dreaming about professional surfing, picturing in my mind manoeuvres I wanted to do and linking them all together. I still dreamt about going to Hawaii and the circuit and things that just weren't there. I believe I had a vision into the future, because as I remember it, when everything actually happened it was all exactly like the dream, exactly like my vision.

All this time, I was virtually living life on the road. I'd walk to Miami High on a Monday morning, check in at school, do a bit of this and that and then check out. I'd hitchhike straight down the coast, go surfing, and hitchhike back to Surfers in the evening. Then I started not coming home for days on end. My older sister Wendy lived in Coolangatta with her boyfriend and I started spending a lot of time there.

On a Monday night I'd go to the Kirra Boardriders Club meeting and the furthest north anyone else lived was Palm Beach. This was when I realised I had to have a bit of a base in Coolangatta. I'd get dropped off in Palm Beach at 9 pm on a Monday, and there wasn't much traffic going to Surfers in those days so I would find myself at 11 pm standing out there with not a cent in my pocket, in my school uniform with my school bag, still trying to hitch a ride to Surfers Paradise. But it didn't phase me. That's why I became such a good traveller later, when I was travelling the world with next to no money.

I'd leave home on a Monday morning, and wouldn't return until Sunday night. During the week I had to get the bus up to school from Coolangatta and for some reason this trip escaped my public transport boycott. Probably because it was such a riotous bus trip, with Steve Harge, the Peterson brothers, Wayne Noakes — the complete muck-up crew.

I always had to return home on Sunday afternoon because I made a promise that I'd bake an apple pie for the Sunday night baked dinner. I'd go home and eat and eat and eat. My deal was: I had half the pie and the whole family could share the other half. That was quite a tradition. I'd have three surfs at Duranbah (a punchy beachbreak on the Queensland–NSW border) before lunch-time on Sunday then hitch up to Surfers. I'd go down to the park with my sisters and play cricket or soccer, make the pie, and then have the big family dinner. After dinner we'd walk into Surfers and go ten pin bowling and play a few pinnies.

One particular time, during the '74 floods, Surfers was entirely under water. They were rowing the clubbie boats down the main street. Come Sunday afternoon, the girls were convinced I wouldn't be able to make it home this time, but sure enough, I came wading down the street, up to my chest in water. They saw me coming up the street through the floodwaters to get to that family dinner.

I started doing my own circuit training around the house to improve my fitness. I was just making it up, copying a bit of what my heroes did, like Muhammad Ali. But my specific surfing exercise involved jumping up to my feet and reaching up above my head and touching my toes and jumping back down into a crouch. Later on I saw it in yoga classes and they call it 'Salute to the sun'. I just came up with it through the need to exercise those muscles. I knew if I was going to beat MP I had to be completely dedicated to being the best I could possibly be. I saw myself as a dancer on the waves, and I worked constantly on improving my routine, fitness and flexibility. It was ironic that my mum had tried to get me to go to dance classes all those years and I'd steadfastly refused. Now, I was training like a dancer.

HEIDI: 'He used to jog around the house, in and out of every room, in and out, for hours. I remember going to sleep to that, the sound of him jogging around the house.'

PETER DROUYN: 'I don't believe Bugs in those early years was a very forward fellow. I think he was quite shy and I think he might have even lacked a lot of confidence when he was very

The hitchhiker

young. That's the impression I got and I've got pretty good intuition for that because, to a certain degree, I was like that at one stage. And to get out of that shyness, to get out of that not being able to take that big step forward, I used surfing as a means to grow confidence, lift my self-esteem and in doing so get up with the rest of the pack and even go beyond. And I think it was the same for Bugs. And he had a hunger for experiencing the world. I think Bugs wanted to experience the world, not just the local scene.'

In 1971 there was an inter-club contest between Windansea and Kirra at Burleigh Heads. MP and I had never surfed Burleigh before; we went up there in the same car and pulled up and the surf was just outrageous. The Burleigh locals were all there waiting to see us in action, it was six to eight foot and the outside cove was just unbelievable. We were all just standing there, gawking, waiting for someone to make a move. Then someone said, 'Where's MP?' He'd disappeared, and the next minute, there he was sitting out at the Cove. He took off on this wave, just this bottomless sucking pit out the back of the Cove, and he pulled into the thickest, meanest barrel you could ever imagine, disappeared for 12 seconds right across Burleigh Point and just got spat out the end. It just dropped everyone's jaws. It was one of the best tube rides ever at Burleigh at that time and it was his first wave. That was such a boost for us — MP had led the charge and we all took to it with a vengeance. We lost the contest, Windansea won it because they had the depth, but MP, myself and PT, we all did well out there. That was our introduction to Burleigh, and we all started going back there a lot from that day on.

We thrived on competition, us young guys, at a time when most of the established guard in Australian surfing had turned their backs on contests to go in search of their various gurus. After the 1970 World Titles at Johanna, in Victoria, Ted Spencer, Nat, Midget, Baddy Treloar, Keith Paull, they all went off on different tangents. Some of them went to India looking for the Maharaja, and some of them built treehouses at Angourie. Midget went into self-imposed exile. And that's why we came along at an accelerated pace — MP, PT and I,

Mark Warren, Ian Cairns, MR and our whole generation came into a bit of a vacuum. There was nothing there for us. Our elders had vanished. We were these super-competitive rats coming along at a time when transcendental meditation was all the rage. The Beatles were off looking for their guru, everyone was looking for their guru, and yet we were down at the beach training and surfing and into competition and club surfing. We didn't meet our predecessors, we passed in the night. Combine that with the whole shortboard and performance revolution and suddenly, the face of Australian surfing had changed overnight. There was a new crew and a new focus. The surfing media of the day was kind of divided on which aspect of the sport to focus on — the whole 'sport or artform' debate had begun. *Tracks* was interested in what Nat and the others were doing in their treehouses and the whole country soul, lifestyle thing, but *Surfing World* was interested in what we were doing at Kirra and what the super-competitive North Narrabeen crew were up to.

In fact, I can only remember one instance of seeing all our elders together up close after 1970. People all over the world have asked me in the years since, 'Do you remember '71 at Lennox?' It was like a gathering of the elders and I just happened to be there. Nat, Baddy Treloar, Ted Spencer, Keith Paull, and the young crew, MP, and I, and Andy Mac, we were all out there together at Lennox Head, the classic right-hand point on the north coast of NSW. It was six to eight feet, and I remember paddling on to a wave, and I looked on the inside and Nat Young was doing this incredible bottom turn and he just growled at me. I'll never forget that growl, you've never seen someone pull back harder than I did that day. I made the mistake of dropping in on Baddy Treloar and he had the all-time classic kick stall, he came up behind me and kick stalled and whacked me fair in the bum with the nose of his board, kick stalled me right off the back of the wave. I didn't forget that for a while either. It was really intimidating surfing alongside all these massive legends.

That afternoon Nat came in and held court on the Point. Andy Mac knew him, and I was desperate for an introduction to the great man. I kept moving a foot closer as the afternoon wore on, until I'd shimmied up next to him on my bum. I listened to him for hours, and finally Andy Mac said, 'This is Rabbit from up the Gold Coast,' and Nat shook my hand. He was talking about Angourie and the new age of surfing, the keeled boards they were riding and stories about when he and Wayne Lynch went down to Victoria, I was listening in awe. It was an amazing conversation — he really was holding court, nothing less than that. It was like noble royalty on the point at Lennox. That's how I saw it. It was a day of gathering. Surfers from all over the world gathered at Lennox that day. There were some great South African surfers there that day who I ran into at Jeffreys Bay 20 years later, and they still talk about it.

It was a very good season at Lennox in '71, good sandbanks, and plenty of swell. I'd actually gone down to Angourie with Andrew the day before and the talk was that the swell was coming up and it was getting a bit too much for Angourie. The guys from the Gold Coast and Angourie converged on Lennox. It was amazing. Nat was really checking out MP because he knew that MP was the natural heir to his throne. It was great watching Nat watching MP. It was a pretty special day, kind of a turning point, because I had a feeling that day that none of them were ever coming back, that they were gone from the competitive scene. It was like AD and BC, and some kind of torch had been passed on to us young guys.

MP made a great impression that day. He was surfing really fast, really amped, like a natural extension of Nat, whereas Nat and his crew were on longer boards just doing these deep, carving turns. MP was all perpetual motion and energy. It was an awesome session, a watershed session in my eyes — a landmark.

COMPETITION

The Queensland Titles was always a ferociously fought event and with me, Andy Mac, PT and MP fighting out the juniors in the early '70s, I received a great competitive blooding right from the start. Andy Mac was unbeatable in the juniors in '70 and '71 — we were the new guys coming up, but he had the experience to hold us back. This was Andy Mac's time — he even won a contest called the

Bobby Brown Memorial (in memory of the great Cronulla surfer who was tragically killed in a pub brawl) in Sydney and beat Nat and all the heavies. It was the biggest open event in Australia at the time and he brought home the biggest contest trophy I'd ever seen.

I got third in the Queensland Junior Titles in '71 behind Andy and PT, and I started to make a few open finals around the place even though I was still a junior. '71 was also the year of my first big trip to Bells, which is always a memorable part of the Australian surfing calendar. This first one was so epic — with Joe Larkin (who was driving the van), MP, PT and me and Terry Baker. My first-ever trip away, my first-ever big trip to an Australian Titles.

Joe told us, 'Right, you can all bring one cassette to listen to.' Terry Baker picked the Beatles, MP picked Santana, I picked Creme, and PT picked Crosby, Stills, Nash and Young and that was our soundtrack. Whenever I hear any of those bands I always think of that first trip to Bells.

I had no idea how cold it was down south, I went to Bells Beach with only a shortjohn wetsuit (short legs and no arms, when most surfers wore full length wetsuits). We had this incredible trip down there and my eyes were opened to the bigger picture of Australian surfing. We ran into filmmaker Alby Falzon who was putting together *Morning of the Earth* (destined to become a surf movie classic) and we met John Witzig and Phil Jarratt, from *Tracks* magazine, in Sydney.

On the trip south of Sydney, we stopped at a place called Moruya where my dad grew up, and surfed at Moruya Breakwater. We pulled up and it was the best looking left-hander I'd ever seen in my life, not one soul out, and absolutely perfect. We were checking it out, Joe lit up a roll your own, I was waxing my board up and PT was going through his meticulous preparation. He got his pink board out of its cover, put the cover underneath it, applied a perfect coat of wax to it, laboring over every little part. Then MP came around the back of the van and he'd melted a pound of butter and he just went, WHOOSH, and threw it all over PT's board. Then it was on. They were on the beach duking it out, Terry Baker was trying to break it up, Joe just sat back having a cigarette, and I surfed perfect Moruya Breakwater by myself.

We all had to sleep in the one tent and we finally got that organised. It was a three-man tent with four of us in it. Joe was in the van, and Terry Baker had to sleep at our feet, sideways, and I had to be in the middle because I had to separate PT and MP. PT was a very good mate of mine and we were talking away during the night. MP was quietly nudging me, 'Psst, psst, Chine.' He used to call me China, or Chine — short for 'China plate,' rhyming slang for 'mate.' He'd go, 'Come this way, don't talk to that wanker, I'll tune you in to what's going on.' MP was such a mentor for me, I didn't know which way to turn. PT was giving me all this advice about being professional and presenting a good image and promoting yourself. And MP was on the other side going, 'Don't go down that road, you'll end up nowhere,' whispering so that PT couldn't hear him. In the dead of night in pitch black, in a tent at Moruya Breakwater, I had the two extremes of Australian surfing trying to guide me.

The surfing at Bells was incredible. I remember standing on the cliff and I had a flashback to being on the hill with Pat Riley back at Greenmount in '68 and '69. Even though I was a competitor now, I still felt like a spectator just drinking all this in. Ted Spencer blew my mind — he'd become a Hare Krishna and had the most serene, focused presence. Drouyn and Paul Neilsen fought it out for the Australian Title. MR, that gawky kid at Rainbow Bay during school holidays, and I made our debut in the juniors and we both made the top 10, along with Steve Cooney, Bruce Raymond and Simon Anderson. We were a completely new crew. Wayne Lynch was gone — he'd won four Australian Junior Titles in a row and retired at the grand old age of 18.

Bells was notorious for the almost complete absence of women but that year this absolute venice, a goddess, turned up. She was 15 years of age, her name was Patty. I don't know how or why, but Patty and I connected straightaway. I'd come in from Bells in my shortjohn, and I was just shaking from the cold, on the verge of hypothermia, and she came up and put her arms around me and warmed me. It was unbelievable, and I was the envy of all the other young guys. I was only 15 myself and I realised she was too good for me. We were all staying in this house together and one night Patty jumped into bed with me. It was all quite innocent, but I just could not believe my luck. I got up to go to the bathroom and when I came back — Patty wasn't in the bed any more. I looked over and, sure enough, Patty was in Michael Peterson's bed. She came back with us to Queensland and we all became really good friends. She and MP moved in together, I'd go round and hang out at their place all the time, and me and MP would go surfing together.

I was almost like a little brother to MP for a couple of years. One little known fact about the great MP, that goes right against the grain of his rebellious image, is that he was a clubbie. MP was the Australian cadet surf lifesaving champion. But he could never have lasted long in that regimented environment. The MP I knew was super quiet but super intense. I was the same age as his brother Tommy, and MP kind of took me under his wing. We'd hang out at their mum's house at Bellbird Flats and there wasn't one spare bit of wall in the house. MP had wallpapered the whole place with surfing posters, even the doors. We worked it out one day — 80% Nat Young, 15% Wayne Lynch, and then a smattering of Ted Spencer and some Hawaiian shots, but just Nat everywhere. We used to sit there all day just ogling these photos, or we'd hang out underneath the house where they'd set up a makeshift surfboard factory. That's when the cutdown era really kicked in for us. MP would shape them and me and Tommy would try to glass them.

MP shaped me this thing once and then Tommy glassed it purple and glassed about half a dozen cockroaches into it. This board became known as the 'purple people eater'. Some bizarre things came out of that place, but some of the creations were really revolutionary, way ahead of their time, and MP became an accomplished shaper. I was kind of like a guinea pig for his most off-beat creations. MP made me this board for Kirra that was 20 ½" wide by about 5'8" and he drew this weird looking bat on it. He called it 'The Demon'. I walked down the beach with it and PT and his cool crew were sitting there, they started laughing and writing me off. 'You are kidding man, the guy's just made you a monstrosity, he's going to ruin your surfing.' I took the board out and everyone stopped to see me ride it. It wasn't yet cyclone season but there was this perfect little rock break and I went out there and just shut them up so heavily. This board, with its round nose, did the perfect roundhouse cutback. The thing went insane from my first surf. It even blew MP out.

I started surfing Greenmount a bit more because I didn't want to miss out on the MP–PT rivalry. After a mysterious absence, the dreaded Robbie Pearce, the punk that used to slap me round at the trampolines, returned to town. MP and I saw our opportunity to get our revenge. MP had suffered at Robbie Pearce's hands too — he'd once mugged MP and I outside the Coolangatta Pie Shop in broad daylight. He stopped his car, got out, came over and actually stood us up, made MP and I empty our pockets and give him all our money. We never forgot that, it was so humiliating. We didn't actually talk about the incident much, but the day Robbie Pearce returned to town and paddled out at Greenmount MP and I both saw him and had the same reaction. I was in the shed at Greenmount and MP was up the top and without one word spoken between us, we paddled out and just worked him. Just completely demoralised him with our surfing. We snapped over his head, dropped in on him, sprayed his face — without touching him we beat up on him so bad in our surfing that he retreated. We'd waited and we'd gotten good while he was away. We had our sweet revenge.

THE NARRABEEN CREW

With the mass exodus of surfing's elders, and the country soul surfing trip continuing, there were really only two competitive strongholds in the whole of Australia — the Gold Coast and North Narrabeen. Coolangatta and North Narrabeen almost became like sister cities. The Narrabeen guys used to come up every summer and stay at Greenmount Beach for a couple of months. Instead of going to Hawaii they'd come to Coolangatta and just go on the rampage. My sister Wendy and her boyfriend lived in Victory Flats at Greenmount, and the Narrabeen guys would settle in every summer — Fatty Al Hunt, Greg Hodges, Col Smith, a really bad old crew. Fatty Al got me pissed for the first time. He came upstairs to my sister's place one day and announced, 'Right Rabbit, we're going to play cards.' I'd never played cards in my life, and we played a version of strip poker, which would have been an ugly sight (Al's nickname was Sea Cow in those days) except instead of taking clothes off, he'd make you scull a shot of Bundaberg Rum every time you lost a hand. Of course, I lost three hands in a row. This was the beginning of the infamous Narrabeen drinking games, they loved to get young innocents senseless. Of course, I was mindlessly drunk in half an hour.

They were a formidable crew out in the water too. Col Smith's surfing at Greenmount used to hold me absolutely spellbound. To this day, on modern equipment, I've never seen a backhand attack like it. He used to come square off the bottom at Greenmount, go up the face, and because of his long legs and his weird back, he used to be able to go up and go beyond vertical, slam it around and drive down the face beyond vertical again. In the same motion he would bring it around off the bottom and do it again, seven or eight times in a row. We would sit there spellbound.

The Narrabeen crew loved coming up here and we used to look forward to their arrival. I'll never forget the New Year's Eve Greg Hodges fell out of the window at Victory Flats — he went through the roof of Sid Aspinall's surf shop, on the stroke of midnight. They were great days. Tony 'Wicka' Hardwick taught me his famous hangover cure — two cans of ice cold coke at dawn and maybe a cigarette and that was it, that's how those guys were. Even though they used to play pretty hard, it was still innocent days — before hard drugs came into Coolangatta.

AL HUNT (ASP TOUR MANAGER): 'Under Queensland's vagrancy laws, you had to have a dollar in your pocket, or they'd kick you out of the state. This one sergeant was a real prick, he hated surfers. Everyone got kicked out of town by him. He couldn't do anything other than kick you out but he just wanted to get rid of you, but we kept sneaking back in. A couple of times we ended up in the clink there ... One time the police were in my room and they were escorting me out of the state, so they went with me to my room while I got my stuff to kick me out. It was late in the afternoon just after school had finished and Rab could have only been 15, 16, something like that, and there was a set of stairs coming up the side. I'd packed all my stuff, Rab came flying up the stairs, bounces into the room, bounces onto the bed, bounces onto the floor to get his board to go for a surf after school, and he just looks around and goes, "Oops," turns around, bounces on the bed, bounces out of the room and took back off. It was like, boing, boing, out of here, see you later.'

1972 -- THE WATERSHED YEAR

Andy Mac, PT and MP moved up to the Opens in '72 and I finally became Queensland junior champ — the start of a big year for me. I won the Australian Schoolboy Titles at Maroubra, on Sydney's southside, and I got my first board sponsorship. This surfboard shaper named Gill Glover befriended me and started taking a real interest in my surfing at Kirra. MP was the man as far as everyone else was concerned, but Gill really believed in me. He really thought that I was as good as MP and so he became my shaper. He got a job at Hohensee and got me a sponsorship, that was a really big break for me. Pretty soon, I had boards all over the place. I became quite famous for having a board at Andy Mac's at Mermaid, a board at Burleigh, and a board at Kirra.

But the biggest thing that happened in '72 was that I became a world class tube-rider. We didn't know it at the time, but it was the last season of Kirra before the big groyne went in and Kirra fired. That last year of pre-groyne Kirra was the most epic year in the wave's history. It was almost as if Kirra knew something was about to happen and was determined to go out with a bang. MP, PT and I were getting 20 feet back inside the barrel and making it. No-one gets deeper now. It was six to eight foot and 10 to 12 feet round. You could drive buses through it day after day after day after day. It was just cyclone after cyclone.

There was one particular swell that I think was the best I've ever seen Kirra. These American filmmakers came through town and they'd just shot this footage of Drouyn, the Neilsens and the rest of the crew at big Burleigh and the Neilsens brought them down to Kirra. They were mainly focusing on MP but it just so happened that they shot this wave of me. They made a movie called *Dogs Run Free*. I'd love to get this footage, it was just a home super–8 movie but it went through Europe and America and became a minor cult hit. When we got to America, people had heard about me and MP through this movie. There was this sequence where I paddled for this wave and I freefall into it, this big double up at Kirra, and just scraped into the barrel, but it looked like I just got dusted. He just kept filming this wave and the wave went and went and went. The wave had actually shut down ahead of me but instead of bailing out I stuck my hand in the wall and dropped down another level into this next section. The wave opened up again and I was about 20 feet back in the barrel, and the wave just kept going and he kept filming it — and I came out the end. It was probably one of the best barrels ever recorded and it was just me, this kid, I stole the show. They started showing this footage up and down the coast and people started raving about it. 'You've got to see this shot of Rabbit.' And suddenly I made this quantum leap in respect. When I saw it, it was pretty mind-blowing. That's when I realised I was going to rival MP in tube-riding and I'd sort of come of age at big Kirra.

That season, MP, PT and I went to a new level of tube-riding. 1972 was when they were making movies of Gerry Lopez and the crew at Pipeline in Hawaii. It only occurred to me much later that while we were going right at Kirra, Gerry and the boys were doing their thing at Pipe going left. Unbeknown to each other we were both pushing the limits of tube-riding on totally different fronts. It wasn't until three or four years later that deep tube-riding was really documented for the first time, with the movie *Free Ride* and Shaun Tomson's surfing at Off The Wall. But

MP, PT and I were getting insane barrels in '72. There hadn't been a lot of deep tube-riding going on before that. The boards didn't allow it, for starters. I've always considered that the first real, fair dinkum season of barrel riding, anywhere in the world. I used to watch the movies of the Californians and me and MP would say to each other, 'They're not barrel riding. We're barrel riding.'

The '72 season at Kirra was like the last farewell, and then it was gone. Something died, something actually died in the town, some spirit left the town when the groyne went in and Kirra stopped breaking. And of course that set the scene up for all the bad shit, when the hard drug dealers moved in a few years later. We'd heard talk of the construction of a groyne to try to stop beach erosion, but we didn't know what form it would take, how it would affect the surf, or even how to organise ourselves into some sort of effective protest. When the constructions began it was a pretty sad time. In society's eyes, we were just the bums, and no-one would have listened or cared about how important this Point was to us. It was the focus of our lives — our sport, our socialising, our club — they were all based around the incredible waves of Kirra. In my mind, great surf spots are legitimate natural wonders of the world, almost like sacred sites to the Aborigines. But surfers and Aborigines were on about an equal social footing in those days. So there was no chance of stopping it and in fact it was only by absolute luck that the developers stopped where they did. The original Dutch engineers who were commissioned to tackle the erosion problem planned to build an L-shaped groyne that would have blocked the entire Point off. It was only luck that they literally ran out of money. It's a miracle that the Gold Coast's incredible surf survived all those '70s developments and groynes and beach works. The administration responsible ran out of money, and that's the only thing that saved the Gold Coast's surf. Kirra didn't break for a couple of years — there was just a big, deep hole north of the groyne and those amazing barrels were gone. The only consolation was that the swells that used to rifle down the Point started hitting this big offshore reef and on huge swells we'd surf these massive lefts out in the middle of the ocean.

But a real sadness took hold when that Kirra groyne was going up. The council was desperate to stop the beach erosion caused by the big storms of '67, because the beach was the lifeblood of Coolangatta. But this quick fix for Coolangatta Beach and Greenmount Beach only alienated the surfers who were the core of the beach culture, and the people never came back. This signalled the absolute demise of Coolangatta.

The whole exercise seemed to me a glaring illustration of the folly of man trying to tamper with the forces of nature. Kirra used to have a giant caravan park on the foreshore. There used to be three roads running down toward Kirra from the main beach road, heading east. You'd turn off the main road and there were roads that led to the beach. Over 100 metres of actual land got taken by cyclones just after they built the groyne. It just started ripping into the caravan park. This wasn't just beach sand, this was actual land. Nothing man could build was going to stop forces like that.

So I moved my focus to Burleigh, I became a Burleigh boy. Kirra was gone and we shed a tear, but we probably didn't quite realise what we'd lost. We didn't know if it was coming back — we were resigned to the fact that it probably wasn't at that point. But it just so happened that '73, '74 and '75 were epic years at Burleigh so it became a natural migration. I'd surf D-bah and Snapper and then when the swell came up I'd go and surf Burleigh.

I was starting to travel a lot further afield now too. There was the Queensland Titles and Bells, and the Newcastle Contest and the Australian Titles. At the Newcastle Contest in '72 I developed a great rivalry with the McCabe brothers, Peter and Geoff, and at the Australian Titles at Narrabeen that year, I encountered my new sparring partners. Local surfer Simon Anderson was untouchable on his backhand at his homebreak and MR really came on. Simon won, Mark got second and I got third. They were more advanced in their backhand surfing at that time than I was for sure, because I didn't get to go left that much on the Gold Coast.

The trip to Bells at Easter was another great adventure in '72. Andy Mac's mother had just bought him this brand new Kingswood station wagon — the only problem was he didn't know how to drive. He was hoping it would be an automatic, but no, it was a manual. So basically we kangaroo-hopped from the Gold Coast to Torquay, a small town near Bells Beach. We went to overtake this truck in the Burringbar Ranges and it was nearly the very end of us all. I think Andrew had just finished off a bit of the herbal and we tried to overtake this truck and he could not get it from third to fourth. He could not get it in gear. He got it out and he was revving and revving and the headlights were coming and me and PT were just panic-struck. Somehow we survived, but this was typical of the whole trip. We kangaroo-hopped across Sydney, every single traffic light from one end of the city to the other. Terry Fitzgerald won Bells in '72 and Simon Anderson won the juniors ahead of Dave Byrnes and me. On the way back from Bells we stopped in at Angourie and had all-time Angourie with Nat Young and Baddy Treloar. That was a really rich trip.

THE '72 WORLD TITLES

The World Titles were coming up in San Diego and I trained with PT at the Coolangatta beachbreaks in the build-up to them. Vietnam was at the height of hostilities and it looked like Mark Warren and Ian Cairns were going to go to war, so the Australian Surfriders Association got in touch with me — I was probably going to surf for Australia. I trained and trained and trained and in those few months PT and I both made a really huge progression — when we went to California we were ready for anything. I didn't have the money for the airfare but I got sponsored by Miami High School, and the local Apex Club — all sorts of people donated money for me to go. They had this come-as-you-like day at school: everyone had to put in 20 cents to wear free dress for the day and I got all the money. I was the first international representative for Miami High School at that time, so Bill Callinan must have felt like his backing of me had been vindicated. Bill was sufficiently moved by the occasion to pen a poem in my honour and recite it at a school assembly.

Bustin' down the door

A BURST IN VERSE IN HONOUR OF OUR FIRST AUSTRALIAN REPRESENTATIVE

A black shadow knifing through the swell

I am bemused but my friend starts to yell

A shark with jagged teeth and flashing tail?

A whale about to surface under spouting spray?

A swordfish spearing with upright sail?

A dolphin or porpoise speeding on its way?

I assure my friend he is still alive ...

The shadow is Wayne Bartholomew hanging five!

It was an awesome Australian team for those World Titles. With our elders still in retreat we were the full new crew. There was Simon Anderson, MR, Col Smith from Narrabeen, PT, and Australia pulled out of Vietnam so Ian Cairns and Mark Warren made the team and I was relegated to reserve.

That was the last World Titles, because it was this big lurching dinosaur that eventually had to go. Everyone sensed this would be the last World Titles and it turned into a mega-party. It was such an enormous, unwieldy contest format, with round after round after round, I think it just outgrew itself. Politics were becoming increasingly involved, and surfers around the world were rejecting the idea of competition, but we still went at it hell for leather.

I was in a room with Mark Warren and Terry Baker, the judge, it was a fairly conservative room. Down the corridor there was MP, Andy Mac and PT in a room together, this was the *happening* room. The locals were on to MP — he was the Australian champion who'd already recorded a couple of minor drug convictions at home. He just seemed to attract every weirdo and hippy in town. Strange things started to happen. People were leaving offerings on MP's doorstep — ounces of pot, bits and pieces, notes and gifts. MP didn't quite know what to make of the full-on Californian adulation. It was like all of these people wanted him to be some kind of leader for their counter-culture movement. MP was happy for the gifts, but didn't want to know about the rest of it.

PT was really serious about the contest and it wasn't long before he came to me in a state of panic and asked, 'Hey Rab, do you think we could swap rooms?' And I went, 'Yep, not a problem, I'll move up into that room,' and that was the beginning. MP, Andy Mac and I were a dangerous combination.

The hotel was an amazing scene. We stayed at the Sheraton on this island off San Diego, this man-made island in the harbour where all the surfing nations of the world were gathered. The Hawaiians' rooms were a constant party — the bath was always full of Primo beer. And there were these Peruvians, full-on radical guys with a hot-blooded taste for excitement. All the different countries were going off in their own particular style. The Australians took over the pool area. There were no older, sobering influences because we were all new, young guys and the elder of the team, Col Smith, was the biggest maniac out of all of us. Col became the ring leader. He started diving off the diving board onto his surfboard in the pool, boards were getting flung out of the pool onto people's laps. We were all screaming and hooting and hotel staff kept trying to kick us out but to no avail.

We ended up doing the infamous run down to Mexico. We were all lined up to go through the border checkpoint, but they wouldn't let MR and I through because we were under 18 and we didn't have guardian papers. So the rest of the team went into Mexico for the day and we had to stay outside. They left us with one of the cars and we spent the day at the San Ysidro McDonald's, the infamous scene of the McDonald's massacre some years later, right on the Mexican border. We hung out there for a while but we soon became bored, so I said to MR, 'Let's go for a little burn around the car park.' I drove and MR sat there not looking too sure about the whole deal. I started getting real cocky, doing these wheelies, and MR started to hang on to the dashboard. The more worried he looked the more it egged me on. I was doing burnouts and donuts in the car park — completely illegal, no licence. We were burning around the car park, I'm screaming and tooting the horn, dust going everywhere, and the next moment, CRASH! I've run straight into a light pole and the front of the car's just wrapped around it. MR was in shock. His mouth was moving but the words couldn't come out. He was just opening and closing his mouth like a fish. Eventually, all the boys came back and stories started flowing. They all had bottles of tequila with the worms inside, Col Smith had some great stories about the women, and they'd apparently made quite an impression on Tijuana. No-one seemed to be concerned about a damaged rent-a-car.

MP found plenty of adventure in California and met this local girl who would come and pick him up in a red convertible. On a lay day she came to get him and they took me along. Cruising the Californian coast in a red convertible was quite a thrill for a young Gold Coast lad. We went and surfed Oceanside and just blew these local surfers out of the water. They didn't know who we were or where we came from. They were gawking as if we were from another planet. Then we went to Trestles, one of Southern California's best surf spots, and did the all-time Camp Pendleton raid — we didn't know it was a military base and a presidential retreat. MP's girl pulled in at Churches, a pretty weak beachbreak just south of Trestles and MP and I have gone, this is a hoax, let's go to that wave up there. So up we went, marching along the beach, with no idea that it was a restricted military zone. Next minute, down came the military police, which freaked MP right out. Tricky Dicky Nixon was actually in the presidential holiday house at the time, hiding out from the Watergate scandal, and the military police were on full alert. We were walking along the beach and they charged down and escorted us off the beach.

Just the Californian freeways were a spin out for us Coolangatta boys. We were going along the freeway one day and had a blow out and the team van went out of control. I just remember looking back at an eight lane freeway, watching all the traffic weaving backwards and forwards. It was terrifying.

San Diego gave me the opportunity to see the surfing of the hot new Hawaiians, Larry Bertleman and Michael Ho. I said to myself, these guys are going to be my rivals, they'll be the guys I'll be up against in Hawaii. They already had big names and I was really still waiting in the wings but I didn't mind that at all. I was laying my plans, sizing up my future opponents.

But there was a bit of an air of hopelessness about those World Titles because everyone was wondering, well, what is there for us? These are the last World Titles. Where are we going to go from here? Where's our chance for a World Title? The world professional surfing circuit was still a dream and wouldn't become a reality for another four years. They were really lost years as far as establishing yourself on the world stage went.

There were guys who peaked in that era, that was their time and they didn't get to fulfil their potential. I reckon MP was one of them. There was no World Title for him to win. Terry Fitzgerald, another fantastic Australian surfer, fell right into that void, and so did guys like Jeff Hakman and Gerry Lopez. It was the era of their golden years and there was nothing for them to win except Hawaii.

There was this kind of unspoken understanding that there would be an unofficial rating based on peer respect and magazine exposure. It was going to come down to who was the hottest in the water, and who was seen to be the hottest. We started to become aware of the importance of the photographers to document our surfing, and the Hawaiian winter was still where the most photographers gathered in one place. Pipeline and Sunset were already established as surfing's greatest arenas and somehow we all knew that Hawaii was where we were going to have to prove ourselves in the years to come.

Perhaps it was with that in mind that MP and I snuck away from the rest of the Australian team and jumped on a flight to Honolulu at the end of the San Diego World Titles.

A HAWAIIAN BAPTISM OF FIRE

We didn't even know where Hawaii was on a map of the world. A travelling Victorian surfer who happened to be in town, Stricko, had filled our minds with glorious visions of the Islands. 'Yeah

Michael, Hawaii is where you guys should be. It's awesome, the best waves in the world, easy. That's where the future of this sport lies,' Stricko said. MP looked over at me and without so much as a word we were packing our bags. Our impulse even took Stricko by surprise, we giggled our way past the Australian team manager's suite and down the elevator. We took great pride in the knowledge that nobody else knew our plan. We even snuck past the Hawaiian entourage with our secret.

It was October, 1972. The world was under siege by hijackers and terrorists. As I walked up the stairs to board our flight to Honolulu, I heard all the bells go off. I turned to see MP being frogmarched off by airport security. He'd purchased a switchblade, a big one, in Mexico and walked through the metal detector with the knife under his ever-present leather jacket. What a sight. MP with semi-dreads hanging halfway down the leather jacket, being marched off absolutely expressionless, just like a terrorist. Stricko motioned for me to go on and at the grand old age of 16, I went to Hawaii alone.

At Honolulu I figured out the information scoreboard in the arrival terminal and I coolly met every flight from San Diego. At 9 pm the next evening I hit the panic button. The never-ending school of Hawaiian print shirts that swam by me had fully tweaked my brain. But then, just as a fuse threatened to blow, they showed up. 'What the fuck went down back there?' I dribbled.

'I told them nothing man, just nothing, didn't talk. That really fucked them,' reasoned MP. Stricko gave me a wink and herded us out of the airport. 'I'm heading to Kauai, see you guys on the North Shore next week,' Stricko called out as we bundled into a taxi.

'Where you go, brah?' scowled the driver.

Mick and I looked at each other dumbstruck. 'Rocky Point,' said MP with great authority. The cabbie leered over the back with his scary half-smile, and proceeded out to the country.

'Here you are, brah. Rocky Point,' the driver announced an hour later, laughing ominously. Well, we thought Rocky Point was like Kirra Point with street lights and all the rest, but we were in the jungle. I covered the $56 taxi fare, leaving me with $40 to my name.

The hitchhiker

A wave cracked on the reef. We lugged our stuff down a bush track past some tall A-frame houses and nestled in under a bush canopy right on the beach. I'll never forget that first dawn in Hawaii.

I woke up and MP was squatting by the edge of our tropical pad, staring at perfect three to four foot lefts peeling off. Within minutes we were surfing Rocky Point alone. We were astonished. This little kid, Jackie Dunn, paddled out and we surfed by ourselves all morning.

We couldn't believe our good fortune. Nobody was on to our beachside retreat and we snuck in and out of our lair looking for food and waves all day. But strays always become curious and that night we dragged our boardbags up onto the nearest porch and fell asleep.

I awoke to much clamour. 'Who the fuck are you man? What the fuck are you doing on our land?' demanded this angry local guy. I was packing it and MP had already entered into his silent persona. After an uneasy few minutes this afro-haired guy with hippy glasses appeared and, offering the local a chillum, calmly okayed our temporary presence.

We'd had the good fortune of landing on the verandah of local legends Owl Chapman and Sammy Hawk's A-frame, and they kind of took us in. MP and I were in hog heaven, living on muesli, porridge and bananas, pawpaws and coconuts acquired from the local neighbourhood. We surfed Velzyland (V-land) and Rocky Point day after day and walked around like Alice in Wonderland.

For ten days the swell ranged between four and six feet. Owl and Sammy were spewing. They were calling it flat. We were calling it insanity, like perfect big D-bah day after glorious day.

Then the swell came up one afternoon. We'd surfed perfect V-land in the morning and Sunset was six to eight in the afternoon. MP and I were surfing from deep inside, continuing our tube-riding duel. We didn't have a clue they called this particular section of the reef Boneyards. It offered the perfect backdoor entry into Sunset Point. Even the locals were hooting that day. Their semi-guns were too long to ride the tube at that size whereas our 6'6"s were slotting in pretty deep.

We returned to the A-frame in a triumphant mood. Yeah, we sure had given old Sunset the one-two punch. We openly wondered why Owl and Sammy hadn't joined us in the hideous barrels. Surely they had heard about our tube-riding display? Surely the whole world had heard how MP and I had stitched up Sunset on our first attempt? Where were the dancing girls and why weren't movie offers pouring in?

The next morning we found out. The A-frame began shaking every 20 minutes just after midnight, and a frenzied atmosphere betook the house at dawn. Owl and Sammy were hooting. MP and I gingerly strolled down to the clearing and nearly died on the spot. It was huge. No. Bigger than that. Mountainous peaks were pitching thunderously way out the back of Sunset, gigantic plumes of spray being blown off the back of these magnificent beasts.

Back at the A-frame, Owl was pulling big-wave boards down from the rafters. A fleet of red Brewers was lined up on the wooden floor — a majestic sight. We were scared enough already — then came the bombshell.

'Here Rabbit, this 7'8" finely-tuned RB is for you today. Michael can ride the red 7'10" and I'll stroke out on this here 8'2".' Owl was in full flight. His super confident aura commanded much respect this day.

I gulped and stared at MP, who was deadpan again, only his tapping foot showing a hint of nerves. Even the paddle out was different from anything I'd experienced. The water seemed denser over the deep channel, and I could still only imagine what was waiting for us outside.

Our first pit-stop was in the channel adjacent to where the inside bowl unloads. Surely we didn't have to go through with this! But Owl waved us on and reluctantly I stroked to the outer reef.

I was a good hundred yards further out than anyone else and I still thought I was going to get caught inside. MP entered the fray off his own bat, but Owl had to come and fetch me. When I finally settled into the main lineup, I realised I was out in very special company. The Aikau brothers, Clyde and Eddie, were out, as was Barry Kanaiapuni, Reno Abellira, Tiger Espere and of course Owl and Sammy. The waves were enormous peaks, the strong trade winds standing them up until they heaved over the reef — tons of pure Hawaiian juice detonating in a hideous impact.

I must have stroked for my life a dozen different times before Owl paddled me right into the eye of the pit. Inevitably, a big set rolled in. Owl commanded me to hold my position, every fibre of my being wanted to get the hell out of there, but I stayed put. The fourth wave was a special one, equal to the biggest I'd seen. Owl summonsed me to turn and paddle for everything I was worth, he was coming with me. I stroked furiously, never looking behind, completely trusting Owl's call. With heart in throat, I dropped out of the heavens into the biggest wave of my young life. I'll never forget the sight from the bottom of that beast. I looked up to see Owl snapping under the lip directly overhead, a long way up. I just gunned for the shoulder as he came from beyond vertical into a racing cutback into the very pit of the wave, passing me as I headed for the channel.

A few hours later, a half dozen waves notched on the belt, and 10 years wiser in one fell swoop, I was ready to head back to land. MP and I were pretty stoked, that feeling of personal accomplishment burning deeply within us both. But just as we thought the threshold had been crossed, Owl informed us we were going down to Pipeline after lunch.

It was all a bit much, but looking back I sure was fortunate to have a surfer of Owl's stature — a bona fide big-wave legend — to push us both far beyond our existing limits.

Late in the afternoon of that Sunday Bloody Sunday, MP and I were resting under a tree, totally inconspicuous and totally stoked. To our astonishment a six pack of green and gold trunked Aussies marched down the beach, one board between them. The Aussie team had arrived. The sight of the green and gold Ockers trundling down Ehukai Beach Park kind of shook us a little. The aura around them seemed kind of alien here in the land of kick-back, but there was no doubt a major mission was underway.

Col Smith, the wild man of North Narrabeen, paddled out into classic 12 foot Pipeline. Dappa, Wicka, Mark Warren and Simon Anderson cheered and hooted every time Col paddled for

Bustin' down the door

a set. The North Shore had never seen anything like it. He wisely pulled back on one that Lopez pulled into, then paddled for a real McCoy. Col manoeuvred under the windblown lip like a veteran but then he attempted the classic Smithy, halfway-down-the-face bottom turn. Next second, to the moans and groans from the Aussie team, his board spun high into the air and Col clawed the wave face until he disappeared behind the meanest curtain in the world. Col injured his back and headed home to Sydney. Not long after, MP and I were flying back into a broiling controversy over our conduct and disappearing act. We both knew Hawaii was a place for us to take on a serious mission, and we descended into silently plotting our next mission.

MP never paid me back his half of the taxi fare. We had a falling out soon after arriving home. Three months later I entered the open men's division at the Queensland Titles and we both knew that the friendship and camaraderie between us would never be the same again. We became mortal enemies for 10 years.

Yeah, that first trip was something else.

THE LIFE AND TIMES
OF A SURF NAZI

(An extract from an essay* by Wayne Bartholomew, age 17.)

It's about time we stood up and fought against the ignorance of the straightees. For a long time we've hung back and let people tear what we stand for down and down. First, was our hair colour and length (how they judged us by that I don't know), but then came our free-and-easy approach to life and our style of dress. And then, last but not least, they tore down our lifestyle, i.e. surfing.

We do the most natural thing around and I'm not just saying that to be COOL, even though a few people do it to be COOL. What other thing can one completely tune into nature yet at the same time can hold so much mystery, adventure and versatility?

Most surfers of the past couldn't fathom further than the physical surface of surfing, but now a breed is developing that has unlimited potential. These surfers have hardly any social links apart from their family, and those that they have, have been moulded to suit their flexible lifestyle.

If you can see through the surface of surfing and allow yourself to accept what you see and continue to dive deeper you will find that you can relate what you've learnt to everyday things around you, because you've unlimited yourself and unleashed your mind and imagination upon the thing you're into.

What will begin to happen, even if you are unaware of it at the time, is that your scope of things will expand so that what was once far off will now become positively within reach. It's comparable to advancements in cameras and photography. Your limit is your camera, because it's the link between you and your subject. But with an unlimited lens, your scope increases, and things start taking new proportions.

What was once intangible or indefinable now becomes visibly logic, because your mind has realistically touched it. Your mind is like a very basic telescope and it remains out of focus, until you unleash your imagination and when you are finally one with your mind, which involves controlling external ego and reviewing your freedom, etc, you open yourself up to yourself.

You can discover that this telescope, your mind, has no end. In fact, there is a myriad of different lens channels through which can be seen so much more than you actually see. If you are true to yourself, what you see takes a rationally logic form, simplified to the level of your intelligence, so that is why no-one can judge somebody by their public presentation, both mental and physical.

* This essay was written for a school assignment, but was never submitted. Rab's sister, Heidi, has preserved it for all these years.

the
opens

I t seemed like everything changed when I came back from that first overseas trip. It was 1973 and I entered the open division for the first time, up against my old sparring partners Andy Mac, PT and, of course, MP.

MP was undoubtedly the best surfer in Australia at the time, maybe the world, but over five rounds of the Queensland Titles I beat him straight up. This did not go down well with MP. He became convinced I was stalking him, following him round, watching him, pouncing on any opportunity to surf alongside him and learn his tricks. His girlfriend Patty told me as much, on the quiet.

It was obvious there was no longer room for PT, MP and I in the same club. Kirra Boardriders held its club meetings in the women's toilets of the Kirra Surf Club (because the men's toilets smelt too bad) and one night the club literally self-destructed. You had PT and his entourage kind of running the show because they were the most organised, then you had MP and his henchmen just hanging round looking menacing, and I had my own little crew kind of hanging in the background. MP would do things like sit in a corner all night and drink out of a bottle in a brown paper bag. He wouldn't say a word but, in effect, he'd totally dominate the meeting because we all wanted to know what was in that brown paper bag. He could be incredibly subtle. He wanted people to write him off, but there was never any alcohol in those bottles.

Finally, one night MP's crew attacked PT's crew — all hell broke loose. One of MP's henchmen, Big Eddie, was chasing a guy called Alan Campbell around the women's toilets. Alan tried to hide in a cubicle, but Big Eddie got a hold of him and beat the shit out of him. PT and his entourage walked straight out, marched over to the Jungle Hut at Rainbow Bay and resurrected the Snapper Rocks Surfriders Club that night. Me and my crew kind of tip-toed out and joined PT. The Kirra club was left to MP and his disciples who wanted him to be president; the last thing I heard as I walked out through the smoke was someone putting forward the motion that they had to smoke joints at every meeting.

Snapper Rocks Surfriders Club had originally formed in 1964 and became so popular that the Tweed Shire Council built the Air Sea Rescue building at Duranbah for the club. But there was a catch: the club members had to perform patrols and even wear the surf lifesaving caps. But the patrols weren't well-attended and there was outright revolt over the wearing of caps. Eventually, the council took the building off them and the Snapper Club fell into limbo. When PT kick-started Snapper in '73 Terry Baker began a 10-year reign as president and it soon became one of the strongest boardriding clubs in Australia — as it is to this day.

Whether it was the overseas experience, MP's fierce competitiveness or just my own coming of age, I really started to hit my straps in '73. In those days, a win in the Queensland Titles earnt me an automatic seeding in the Bells Easter Classic, which was a big deal, particularly because Rip Curl wetsuits had just made Bells a professional event. So already I could see my dream starting to take shape.

But at the same time, I had undertaken to finish my HSC. When I went off to San Diego and Hawaii in '72 I barely gave a second thought to the fact that I would miss sitting my leaving exams. When I returned, Bill Callinan talked me into repeating. He argued convincingly that it would be silly to throw away 12 years of schooling and that there was no shame in repeating. Bill knew my father and got in touch with him, to get him to add his weight to the back-to-school campaign. We hadn't seen each other for years, and I was open to the idea of making peace with my father. I undertook to finish my studies. There was some kind of unspoken trade-off at work: respect me and my surfing and I'll fulfil your formal education trip.

But there were only about three of us doing Year 13 at Miami High in 1973, such was the lure of the surf and the beaches for every kid of school-leaving age on the Gold Coast. My leave pass from Bill Callinan was easier to abuse than ever, and with the carrot of pro surfing dangling seductively, this pact was going to prove harder to live up to than I knew.

There was still a sense of a vacuum in Australian surfing. The mass exodus of the tribal elders left surfing in uncertain territory. I wanted to know where my heroes went — it was a bit disturbing that they'd disappeared off the face of the earth. In California, competitive surfing was officially dead and buried. I think it was the aftermath of the Summer of Love. People did not want to know about the system, they didn't want any part of it. US *Surfer* magazine stopped their annual Surfer Poll in which their readers used to vote for the most popular surfers of the year. In the new spirit of enlightenment this was considered uncool and crass. There were no Amateur World Titles. There was no way of ranking anyone in the world.

In Australia, the competitive drive endured at North Narrabeen and the Gold Coast; Newcastle had a bit of an enclave as well — with the McCabe brothers, MR, and Newcastle Col Smith (as opposed to Narrabeen Col Smith). They were basically good, working-class beaches where the locals liked their beer and their competition and you couldn't afford to be a hippy because you wouldn't get any waves.

But really, there was nothing concrete to aim at beyond the Australian Titles. All we knew after that first trip overseas was that we needed to aim our careers at Hawaii. That's all there was —

Hawaii was the international stage of surfing, with the photographers, the filmmakers and more pro contests and prize-money than the rest of the world put together. We knew we all had to go back there at the end of the year and fight it out in the pecking order for those couple of contest invitations. There were only 24 invitees for the Duke Kahanamoku Classic and 22 of them were Hawaiians, and that was the most prestigious event in the world. They'd do odd things too, like only invite the national champions from Australia and Britain. At least 20 Australians would be desperate for a start and there'd be this reluctant, unknown British champion summonsed to surf in a big-wave event that he didn't want to know about. I remember one British surfer, a guy called Tigger Newling, coming down the beach to surf 15 foot Sunset. He was a solid surfer and a lovely bloke, but he did not want to go out in that water. He was in *way* over his head. He didn't want to be out there and we would have given anything to be in his position.

Out of the Australians, Terry Fitzgerald and Paul Neilsen had the inside running — Paul had won the '72 Smirnoff and Fitz was the 'Sultan of Speed' at Sunset. There was no way into the loop except to start this campaign of getting yourself to Hawaii and drawing attention to your surfing. The appearance of the first, modest pro events in Australia then, was like a Godsend to those of us scrimping and saving to get ourselves over to Hawaii at year's end.

In early 1973 the Pa Bendall Contest at Caloundra, on Queensland's Sunshine Coast, advertised a $1500 first prize. We were stunned. Here was a contest just a couple of hours' drive away offering this massive amount of money. We all went up there with dollar signs in our eyes, and I took up a young, local surfer called Guy Ormerod, just to give him a bit of contest experience. I was going for that $1500, as was MP and several others, and the Narrabeen crew came up after it too. The competition was full-on, but I was on a mission. I won every single heat I went in, I won my semi-final, and I went into the final against Col Smith, Richard Harvey, Ron Ford and my little mate Guy, who caused a sensation by getting so far. In a huge upset, MP didn't even make the final.

Bustin' down the door

I went out in the final super confident. The tide turned and started coming in, the surf was small and shifting. I'd sussed out my own little part of the reef that had served me well all through the event and I went straight back out to it for the final. Col, Dick, Guy and Ronny went to this other peak, and I was thinking, these guys have lost it, I'm over here by myself, I've just blitzed them. I came in and the first thing someone said to me was, 'Shit, Bugs, you should have seen these lefts over on that other bank.' Dick Harvey won the 1500 bucks, Guy Ormerod got second, and I got third, which scored me 90 bucks.

Bells was already a fond tradition, but the annual trek down south was undertaken that little bit more eagerly with the news of Rip Curl wetsuits posting $1000 first prize. The National Titles were on in Margaret River, in WA, just after Easter so we set out on a two-month road trip stopping in at Bells on the way. MP won the first Rip Curl Bells Easter Pro and he seemed like the richest surfer in Australia. 'Jesus, I've won a thousand bucks,' was his breathless quote on the winner's dais. The surf was eight to 12 foot for most of the event and some of the Hawaiian big-wave surfers came out for it and really shone in the size. I didn't do much good in the contest, I realised I still wasn't quite in the big league when the surf was up. I put in a respectable performance but I wasn't capable of getting into the top five of that event. MP was just superb — he'd gotten his revenge on me, but there was still another bit of revenge he had waiting for me.

From there it was the long haul across the Nullarbor to the Australian Titles. At least we were doing it in luxury. Richard Harvey had picked us up for the big trip in a brand new car, and there was me, PT and Richard's wife Jan. On the way over, we stopped at Cactus in South Australia, and surfed the cold, perfect, desert waves by ourselves. It was about five feet and we surfed Caves and Castles on the edge of the surreal landscape of the southern desert.

The drive across the Nullarbor was awe-inspiring and I remember being continually stunned by the amount of space all around us. I'd been battling away with my old rivals for the title of best surfer in Coolangatta, and now here I was driving all the way across the country to see who was the best surfer in Australia.

Just before we'd left for the Australian Titles, MP had extended a totally unexpected olive branch.

'Who's doing your boards now?' he asked one day, out of the blue.

'Gill Glover's doing them,' I told him.

'Ay, I'll do you up a board for the Australian Titles, Chine,' he said cheerily, just like old times.

I was stoked. One of MP's magic boards for me to tackle big Margarets for the first time! Even when he produced this thing 6'5" long by about an inch thick I didn't suspect a thing. This was the board I was going to ride 15 foot Margaret River on, and of course I paddled out there — thinking this was the board that would win me the contest — and just got smashed to smithereens.

That set the tone for the Australian Titles, because it was big Margaret River for the duration of the event. I couldn't even get down the wave face on that 6'5", I got absolutely obliterated. MP had completely done me up. Richard Harvey won it, PT got second and MP got third. I was pretty stoked that at least Richard had beaten MP.

Big Margaret River was a real eye-opener for me. I'd been to Hawaii once, got a few waves at big Sunset, and that was the sum total of my big wave experience. It's a wild and woolly ocean in the south-west — big waves and cold water. I came home pretty humbled after that. I thought, gee, there's a lot of work to do here. Richard Harvey won the Australian Title on an 8'1" gun. He had the best equipment, the most experience and he won. That's what I learnt from that trip.

The highlight of the trip back was another stopover at Cactus. We pulled in off the highway and it was a solid eight to 10 feet and just perfect. There was only one person out at Caves, and it was Reno Abellira, the great Hawaiian surfer, and filmmaker Paul Witzig was filming him for the movie, *Rolling Home*. We raced out and joined him, it was an epic session. Reno's surfing was insane that day. He was a major hero of mine, he'd made the finals of the World Titles in '68 and '70. He had that beautiful Hawaiian style and grace in the water and a Zen-like approach to riding waves and life in general that made a big impression on me. To me he was the epitome of the true soul surfer.

WENDY: 'I remember when he left for that trip to WA, it was the biggest trip he'd embarked on at that time. They pulled up to get him at my flat and all I could afford to give him was 10 dollars, and a cake, a fruit cake, and that's all I gave him. He might have had five dollars to his name and that's all he left with. That's what he went to WA with. 15 dollars and a big cake. He went with that and he survived.'

BETTY: 'It used to break my heart when he'd go away and there'd be no money for him to take. That really upset me a lot, but it seemed to make him hungrier.'

For the rest of '73 I was back at school. I'd taken a big break to do Bells and the Aussie Titles — I had a lot of catching up to do. As luck would have it, we got some beautiful big winter swells that year, so I still had a hard time staying out of the surf. It was some of the best big Burleigh of all-time that year. Sydney got hit by two massive swells that produced 20 to 30 foot waves and wreaked havoc along the city's beaches. By the time it got up the coast to us, it had transformed into perfect 10 foot Burleigh. That was a big factor in our development and preparation for Hawaii. These were genuine big waves, something we didn't see a lot of in Queensland. It was almost as if Burleigh was turning it on to help us get ready for the challenge waiting for us in Hawaii at year's end.

But I had another challenge to worry about before Hawaii and big Burleigh wasn't helping that cause one bit. I knew I had to see through my repeat attempt at the HSC and time was running out. It was starting to eat at me. I'd tell myself, my father thinks I'm a loser and I've got to prove him wrong. I also wanted to justify the faith Bill Callinan had shown in me, because I really respected him.

In my darker moments too, I'd start to think, maybe there really is no future in this sport and I'd better get something behind me.

Finally, Bill Callinan pulled me up and said, 'Look, you've come back and repeated. You've either really wasted your time or you've really wasted our time. You don't want to be a non-achiever.' That really hit home.

Soon after, my father tracked me down and said, 'Look, Bill Callinan's been in touch. You're supposed to be repeating Year 13 and you haven't been to school for three months. It's getting a bit much isn't it?' I hadn't had much to do with my father for years but somehow it seemed we'd both decided it was time to get to know each other and make our peace. He offered me a deal: move back in with him in the old family home at Razorback, put the surfboard away for the rest of the year, and just put my head down and study. And that's exactly what I did. I secretly moved out from my mum's, because she had never forgiven my father. Even his name was taboo in front of mum — it would have broken her heart. It was an easy enough secret to keep. She thought I was still doing the circuit up to Wendy's and back again. I'd still go to mum's for Sunday dinner to keep the tradition alive, so she was none the wiser. But I was actually living with dad in our original family house. I was re-living my childhood and in my study breaks I'd go for walks down the back of the house around my old bushtracks.

I really bonded with my dad during this period. He began to respect me for my surfing and for being a good waterman. We had something in common because he was a devoted fisherman who knew all the offshore reefs and had a healthy respect for the ocean. We started doing things together — we went fishing, we'd go and have a beer together — I was 18 and the only son, so it felt like the right time to square things up.

I got a job working part-time at a surf shop in Coolangatta, Clearlight Surfboards, that my shaper Gill Glover and his partner Paul Hallas started up. I was their first sponsored surfer and part of the deal was I also had to work behind the counter. There were a couple of good things about this — on one side of us there was a pie shop and on the other there was a record shop. When business was slow, which was often the case, I'd hang out in the other shops. I struck up a bit of a deal with the pie shop where they'd let me have the stale pies that hadn't sold. I once got busted with 17 meat pies behind the counter, and that's where the stories about my prodigious eating habits really got started.

People would come into the shop all day and tell me how good the surf was, so I developed this theory — if I put up a sign saying 'back in 10 minutes' no-one would know which 10 minutes I was talking about. If I wasn't in the record shop, or eating the meat pies from the cake shop, I was at Duranbah, Greenmount or Kirra surfing. Before long, the shop went broke.

BART: 'Wayne was living at home and he said, "Hey dad, you haven't been to have a look at my shop yet, my surfing shop." So I went down to the surfing shop and I'll tell you what was in it — one bloody, scratched, dingy surfboard, with a dingy pair of shorts hanging off the fin. So, he said, "What do you think of it?" and I said, "Plenty of potential mate." That was the total contents of the shop, a surfboard and a pair of shorts ... When he came home he said, "Gee, there's a nice lady who has got a shop next to mine," and as soon as he said anyone was nice it immediately meant that they'd fed him. So I said, "Right, what did she give you?" And he said, "At closing down time she had 15 pies left." And this is when it went through my mind that there was no fridge in there. I said, "What did you do with them?" And he said, "I ate them," like, what else would you do with 15 pies? And then he said, "What time's tea?"'

In the weeks leading up to my final exams, I wholeheartedly devoted myself to study. I remember walking down my old bushtrack to Greenmount one day during a break and the surf looked alright. Everyone was going, 'Look, there's Rabbit. You coming surfing Rab?'

'Nah. I've got to get back and study,' I told them.

They just went, 'Man, you have lost it.'

I really had to see this through. I was almost like an alcoholic coming off the drink, I was scared that I wouldn't be able to stop after just a couple of waves, that all my discipline and resolve would be washed away and I'd end up bingeing on the surf all day long.

I studied my guts out, sat my exams and passed. I didn't get enough points to get into the university courses that interested me but I was eligible for teachers' college. While my dad had me out of the surf, he took me down to Armidale, which was a bit of an education centre for northern NSW, to check out the various educational institutions in town. I was the Queensland Open surfing champion, and I was staying on a farm, hundreds of miles from the coast. It seemed surreal, but I found I quite enjoyed it and I put on a few pounds, eating big country breakfasts. Each day my dad would take me around the different faculties checking out courses, and he very nearly had me enrolled in teachers' college. He'd actually brought me round and suddenly I was staring at another few years of academic life. But one morning, he made a fatal mistake.

We went downtown this Saturday morning and happened to wander into a newsagent. I was scanning the racks of magazines when I spotted a new issue of *Surfing World* magazine. On the cover were the words, 'pull-out poster'. This was a new innovation in surfing magazines at the time and I could barely open the thing quickly enough to behold this miracle of modern technology. I got to the centrespread and fumbled with the staples to try to get the thing out without tearing it, or drawing too much attention to myself. I managed to get the poster out, unfolded it and was rendered absolutely speechless. There, in larger proportions than I'd ever seen a surfing photo before, was a shot of me in the barrel at Duranbah. And it was a watershot, one of the first watershots I'd seen inside the tube, taken by Steve Core during those winter swells. I looked at this image of myself crouched in a perfect tube and made an instant life decision right there on the spot. All I could say was, 'Dad, drive me to the coast.'

Bustin' down the door

It was a very frosty drive back. Neither of us said a word the whole way. But somehow, my father accepted my surfing from that day on. He could see how staunch I was, and maybe he realised that he'd underestimated the strength of my convictions about surfing. I continued to stay at his place and used it as a base in between my increasingly frequent travels. We still talk about that Saturday morning in the Armidale newsagent. Dad still rues the day. He thought he had me — he'd got me off the beach, I'd had a haircut, I'd put away my surfboard and poured over the books. But once I was back in the surf, I was back with a vengeance.

> BART: 'I was really interested to see him follow on in teaching, but we never nagged or anything like that. In late January, when it was time to book in there at University, we got him in the car. I've always been interested in punting, and we always used to buy the Saturday *Australian*. On the way to the uni we pulled in to Pigeon's paper shop, in the main street of Armidale. It's indelibly printed on my mind, and I bought the *Australian* and he said, "Can I have two dollars fifty? There's a *Surfing World*. Can I buy that?" So I gave him the money to buy that and a full centre page fell out, of him ... And he said, "Do you mind if I go full-time surfing instead of university?" and I said, "Well, you could have bloody told me 300 miles back." We got within a mile.'

There was a brief trip to Hawaii at the end of the year but I still had a long way to go in the big stuff. Terry Fitzgerald and Paul Neilsen were already accomplished in Hawaii and that year Ian 'Kanga' Cairns, PT, Mark Warren and to a certain extent MP, established themselves, and I started to follow big Kanga's lead, in particular.

When 1974 began there was no doubt in my mind that I was going to make surfing my career, I wanted to make my presence felt again, after my study leave. It was like, okay MP, I'm after you now.

A lot happened in 1974 to strengthen my resolve. The Australian Professional Surfing Association (APSA) was formed to administer the growing professional contest scene, and the first Coke Surfabout was on. I won the Queensland Open Title for the second year in a row, and PT started recording the year's major contest results in a little exercise book, formulating Australia's first pro surfing ratings.

Kanga Cairns and Mark Warren came and stayed at my father's house during the Australian Titles, which were held on the Gold Coast in 1974, and I remember us all sitting around the kitchen table, discussing the contest scene. Bart was aware that MP was winning the major events and he started asking us, 'So, how are you lot going to beat MP?' His idea was to form a group and use the buddy system and strength in numbers to beat him. It was less than two years later that Kanga and Mark, together with my old mate PT, formed the Bronzed Aussies — surfing's first professional team — and I've always wondered whether it was my father who first planted the seed in their minds. I think I was too much of an individual to be a part of something like that. Bart also arranged for Kanga, Mark and I to give a talk at the local Lions Club meeting on the subject of 'closing the generation gap'. We caused quite a stir — three young, well-dressed, articulate surfers. Kanga Cairns brilliantly espoused his vision of professional surfing and the image of surfers was turned around in the minds of those present in one evening.

1974 was also memorable for some massive swells that broke on the reefs outside Kirra. Although the mighty Point still lay dormant, something about the shift in the sand flow meant these banks formed around the offshore reefs and we had a couple of incredible 15 foot swells that broke like Sunset way out to sea. MP and I were surfing it at every opportunity, with all our energies directed towards making a big impact in Hawaii next season.

Me and my surfing mates were all super fit and we saw the opportunity to shame our old rivals, the clubbies. The clubbies always seemed to put their patrol flags on the one bit of beach where the waves were breaking best, and then harangue us for surfing too close to the flags. They had the power to confiscate your board and make you pay a fine before you got it back. But we had our revenge.

Anyway, they'd organised this paddle race from North Kirra to Snapper Rocks, and a few of us surfers decided to enter. There was MP, Mont and myself and young Guy Ormerod, all lined up on the beach with our normal surfboards and long baggies. And there were all the clubbies with their big paddle boards and bum togs, just smirking behind their hands at us and our puny equipment.

We all set out on the race, and the clubbies were all knee paddling up from North Kirra to Kirra, round Kirra Point, up Coolangatta Beach, round Greenmount Point, up Rainbow Bay and into Snapper Rocks. Meanwhile, the four of us took off on a straight bee-line, out to sea, out past the shark nets and directly towards Snapper Rocks. Mont had actually paddled into the beach, collected the winner's cheque and left the beach by the time the rest of us finished. MP was looking really good for second, but Guy Ormerod somehow caught a wave and got ahead of him to take second place, MP got third and I got fourth. We scooped all the prizes and had left the beach before the clubbies paddled into Rainbow and up to Snapper Rocks. They ran up the beach thinking they were going to break the winner's tape and it was all over. It was brilliant.

Around this time, I also had another base at Eden Avenue, Rainbow Bay. PT's dad owned a block of flats and it was full of surfers — my shaper Gill Glover and his girlfriend, Paul Hallas, Mike Perry, Geoff Darby and Rusty Priesendorfer. Every time PT's father came around he'd find me in a different flat. He was always sus about me, I wasn't officially living there but for about two years I regularly stayed in that building in between travels. Every time one of the Townend family came down, I'd be in that building but I'd be in a different flat and I'd assure them, 'No, no, I'm not living here. Just visiting.' But I was constantly there. Of course, I always had the good sense and instincts to move on to the next unit just as the fridge got empty or the rent was due. This was my rice custard phase. I virtually ate nothing else. I could surf all day on a bowl of rice custard.

PT, meanwhile, moved down to Cronulla, in Sydney's southern suburbs, he reckoned you had to be in the big smoke to crack the big time. He signed up with one of the top Sydney surfboard labels of the day, Gordon & Smith, and was right on hand for the birth of the APSA. Cronulla was also the home of Sydney sports journalist Graham Cassidy. Cassidy was really the prime mover behind the formation of the APSA and PT was a founding member. He kept waving his exercise book at them, showing off his rating system until they finally accepted it — with a few modifications. Cassidy was the force behind the first Coke Surfabout, and suddenly surfing had a major, mainstream commercial sponsor.

We had the beginnings of a circuit — with State Titles, National Titles, Bells, and the Coke. They were exciting times. When I won the Queensland Title all I wanted to do was get to Bells. In these days we'd head down five or six weeks before the event to acclimatise to the cold southern waters, test new boards and just gather with the rest of the crew. Torquay was just starting to develop as the centre of the Australian surfing industry. Quiksilver and Rip Curl, two of the world's biggest surf companies today, were just in their infancy. All the best surfers in Australia, and a growing number from overseas, headed to Torquay in the weeks before Easter. It was a fantastic gathering. There'd be big days at Bells, and trips down to Johanna along the spectacular Great Ocean Road.

We always looked forward to catching up with the classic Torquay characters. It was a real pleasure to go surfing with Wayne Lynch and Maurice Cole, two of Victoria's best surfers. Even the captains of the industry were a really wild crew. Rip Curl owners

Bustin' down the door

Doug 'Claw' Warbrick and Brian 'Sinding' Singer blew my mind with their ability to combine lifestyle and commerce. There were some wild parties in Torquay at Easter. I used to think Brian Singer was actually in the Rolling Stones and, when I first met Claw, I thought he was like Gyro Gearloose. I thought Claw was batty, this classic guy who'd turn up at Bells Beach in his thongs and socks — he still does — twirling his hair, jumping up and down and rubbing his hands. He was all time, just all time. Those early days at Rip Curl were pretty amazing. The original Rip Curl surf shop was this tiny little hole in the wall, and they started making these wetties. It didn't seem like they were making much money at the time, but those guys definitely had a futuristic vision of the surfing empire. The Torquay surf mafia were the ones who really put it together. You put MP in a long-armed black vest and get a photo of it in the magazines and then make more of them the next year. They were on to that. Rip Curl were the first ones to *really* sponsor anyone. I think they might have paid Nat and Wayne but most guys only got free product. But to get a Rip Curl sponsorship was pretty cool.

All the fine traditions of Torquay social mayhem which survive to this day were established back then. The Torquay pub was an institution. It was the only place open after 6 pm and all roads seemed to lead there. The Narrabeen crew would dominate the pool table — it was deadset near impossible to get on. You had to be willing to shout the pub if you lost and to this day I've never seen Fatty Al lose a card game, a pool game or an argument.

This year, MP's arrival was the talk of Bells. On the eve of the event MP trundled down the muddy goat track at Bells and shredded the place beyond belief. It was like watching Bruce Lee, the kung fu king, on water — so quick and devastating were his moves. MP streeted the field, his frenetic energy making a mockery of the points-for-manoeuvres system.

In comparison, the '74 Coke Surfabout was the birth of slick surfing professionalism. It was all glitz and glamour compared to the earthy Bells event. The surf just pumped for that first Surfabout and we felt that pro surfing's birth into the mainstream had been blessed by the ocean. There were seven or eight rounds of competition all over Sydney's northern beaches with a constantly changing leaders' board. The event got heaps of publicity and when the competition was moved to Fairy Bower, the notorious rock ledge at the southern end of Manly, it seemed the whole of Sydney was lining the clifftop. That day I made a bit of a name for myself amongst the Hawaiians and some of the older guys by charging big Fairy Bower. I'd never surfed the place before and had no idea where the lineup was. I paddled out and saw this wave breaking in front of a really shallow rock ledge and sheer cliff face further up the point — I figured that was the spot. In fact, this area is rarely surfed because it's considered too dangerous. No Man's Land, they call it. I just took off on this thing, with a large number of my heroes like Nat Young, Baddy Treloar and the Hawaiian big-wave legends watching from the cliff. This wave must have been about 10 feet and there was no option but to pull into the barrel or get spread all over the rocks. They were all watching, going, 'Wow, look at Bugs charging.' I was standing in the throat of this thing just totally terrified out of my mind, thinking, let me out of here! I came in after that wave and Baddy gave me a bit of a wrap which meant a lot to me. MP won that round at big Fairy Bower, I got second, and Nat got third; that was a huge boost to my confidence in solid waves against top-level competition.

There was a real buzz about the whole event. It was on the hourly radio news bulletins, all over the newspapers and TV, and the surf just kept pumping. The next day we went to Narrabeen and the results were decided in really good waves. MP won it, PT got his customary second place, and Nat made a spectacular comeback to take third place. In a grand gesture, Nat stood alongside Gough Whitlam at an election rally at the Sydney Opera House and donated his third prize cheque for $750 to the ALP. Terry Fitzgerald got fourth, Simon Anderson got fifth, and I got sixth.

Every contest had a different scoring system and MP was an absolute master at totally exploiting the system. He was convinced that the contest directors were changing the systems to try to stop

Bustin' down the door

his success. PT had been leading for most of the Coke Surfabout and MP just came out in the final round with the scoring system totally mastered — poor old PT saw him catching up and just about had a nervous breakdown.

At the end of Australia's first professional surfing season it worked out that MP was on top of the rankings, PT was number two, and I was number three. The Coolangatta trio had moved into prime position in Australian surfing and a bit of a pattern had formed between us. PT always seemed to finish second, while MP and I would finish first or third.

Graham Cassidy became the head administrator of pro surfing in Australia and I could see that we shared a common vision. We had an instant rapport. Graham was a straight shooter and I always really admired him. He really put Australian surfing on the road to professionalism.

> MARK RICHARDS: 'I can remember at the first Coke at Fairy Bower we caddied for each other. We were the two youngest guys in it and I don't think anyone else would talk to us. Bugs and I were the two little groms.'

> JOHN 'REGGAE' ELLISS: 'Every grommet in Manly was on that hill that day. It was the first time I'd wagged school in my life. The Bower was such a special place in Manly and in '74, I would have been 14 and all your heroes are surfing the Bower at 10 feet. It was the first year of the Surfabout and it was spectacular. If you were a surfer in Manly you couldn't miss it.'

INDONESIA

1974 was also the year of my first trip to Indonesia — the new surf Mecca to the north. My most enduring image from that first trip is sitting in a solitary chair in the middle of a small Balinese warung, semi-conscious and bleeding freely from a gaping head wound.

Children and elders are sitting on their haunches around the room, completely surrounding me. They're smiling, some are giggling, the old betel-nut warriors giving me that unforgettable toothless grin. I've just had my first taste of Uluwatu Reef. The locals seem stoked. Maybe I'm dying and this is some Hindu death ritual. After an hour of incessant eyeballing, the old witch doctor appears, chanting and dancing around me. He fills his right hand with a thick, off-white substance and — 'thwack!' — he presses a mound of it on to my wound, then periodically piles more on until I feel like one of the original mud men of Borneo. But it feels good. My head feels sealed again and I'm caught up in the powerful vibe in the warung. I'm enjoying this and each slap is now heralded by the locals with shrieks of delight. Soon it's over and I'm left to my solitude for several hours, wondering how I'd gotten here.

After a few years of muted whispers, '74 loomed as the first large-scale Indo season. A Sydney travel agent bunged on a quiet package, something like $400 plus a couple of revalidation stickers. Totally bogus air tickets, but we'd already used them successfully to get to Hawaii and Mexico and no-one had been busted yet. It worked something like this: we'd get the bottom of the barrel seven-day excursion ticket, stay six weeks, then whack a reval sticker on and bullshit our way on to the plane. It got critical at times, like when a nosy airline official began poking under the bogus sticker at the original date, but it's virtually impossible to outwit a desperate surfer.

This was the era of the 16 mm surf movie, and no less than three major productions were in progress. Steve Core paid for me to go — he was shooting *Ocean Rhythms*, Dick Hoole and Jack McCoy were doing *Tubular Swells* and Bill Delaney was making *Free Ride*. It was evident that the first major Indo season was going to be documented in its entirety, but when Dicky Hoole started filming

Richard Harvey and I checking in at Coolangatta airport, I had a feeling that things could get pretty strange in the ensuing weeks.

The first unmistakable wafts of Bali overwhelmed us as we got off the plane, and the sensory assault didn't stop there. It was such a trippy place, a real gathering of the world's hip to get their rocks off. Kind of an *Adventure Island* for the chosen ones — survivors and casualties alike from the drug-inspired late '60s and early '70s. Surfers' ears had pricked up with stories of Gerry Lopez at Uluwatu and this insane left that Mike Boyum had discovered in Java.

Everything seemed larger than life. Accentuated. Fresh fragrances were sweeter, bad odours were even more pungent. Everyone seemed to walk slower, talk slower. Bali very nearly seemed like another planet.

That first night, over a few Bintangs, a friend named Don weaved a web of fear with stories of black magic on the full moon at Legian, of guys found dead at Uluwatu with their eyes missing from their sockets, or with sea snakes wrapped around their ankles. Kind of a laugh, but a growing sense of the hidden agenda of the place began rising from deep within.

The pre-dawn activity at bemo corner wasn't too intense back then. A bemo would fire into the alley out of the dawn haze, pick up a few market-bound locals, plus the odd domestic animal, then the whole act would rage off, the intermittent, grinding gear changes breaking the dawn. But our guy sat waiting. We were loaded aboard, not too comfy, but ready to go, and we just weren't going anywhere. Another bemo pulled up, and an exchange took place between the driver and ours. Our driver, Wayan, promptly dropped to the ground and placed a small, patterned flower arrangement on the corner — the traditional Balinese offering. We were off to Uluwatu.

The country was awesome. Rich greens and an insane tropical canopy. Further into our ride, Wayan pulled over and again placed a flower offering, this time by the side of the road, explaining that this offering was for the flat lands. Judging by the offerings lined up on the dashboard, we had several more stops ahead. We pulled up adjacent to some intricately terraced farmland and placed another offering for the mountains. Wayan finally unloaded us at the Ulu track, where two locals were hanging out. Wayan made the introductions. 'Kutut carry Gerry Lopez board. He want to carry Rabbit board.'

Uluwatu before the warungs and busy holiday trade was just a sleepy valley. A few women were carting buckets full of warm soft drinks around, the board carriers were laid back, and the exchange of small monetary offerings seemed to bring pleasure to both parties.

We surfed our brains out. It wasn't perfect, kind of disjointed, tricky on your backhand, but Tony 'Doris' Eltherington, Dick Harvey and Terry Richardson were getting outrageous barrels. Peter McCabe paddled out and systematically plucked the best waves of the afternoon. For nearly a week we surfed four to six foot Ulus and Kuta Reef and didn't put a foot wrong. Then some strange shit happened.

A few days later, we set off to Ulu, Wayan was nervous as hell. Only he knew that he'd missed the 'offering' connection from Denpasar. We didn't even notice going straight by the designated offering sites and we laughed it off when Wayan apologised for leaving no offerings for Uluwatu.

A second staff car pulled up and out trundled the press corps — a band of filmmakers who were by now blatantly poaching on Steve Core's movie cast, namely Richo and me. Extra board carriers were called in and this strange convoy of surfboard and tripod carrying natives and caucasians snaked its way along the primitive path. The first omen appeared not half a mile down the track. Carmel Hoole, wife of filmmaker Dick Hoole, misjudged a step and tumbled onto an outcrop of jagged rocks. A couple of gnarly gashes, and Carmel had to turn back. Strangely, Wayan was still back at the top of the track waiting with the bemo.

The surf was pretty big, a solid eight feet, some bigger sets, but the wind wasn't true offshore, creating ribs on the face. It looked pretty pleasant — big walls neatly terraced, like the countryside, but not every wave was makeable. Pinpoint accuracy was required on take-off, and on his second wave Brian 'Furry' Austen ate it, cut himself pretty badly and was also on his way back to Kuta.

Soon after, I swung around for a solid 10 footer and stroked into the meatiest wedge of my fledgling Indonesian career. Some ugly ribs appeared up the face of the wave, my board went a little squirrelly and I executed a flailing freefall to the base of the wave. As with most impacts, details are a little sketchy, but I distinctly remember the thud of my cranium as it connected with reef. I surfaced semi-conscious and could see Doris Eltherington putting in the big ones to reach me. My leash had snapped and I was groggily checking out the water turning red around me. I managed to throw a leg over Tony's board and he skilfully steered his semi-limp cargo over the inside reef, reassuring me about my board and injury as we took aim for the cave.

The legacy of missing the offering connection was on the scoreboard: Uluwatu 3, Visitors 0. I was clearly knocked up, one of those situations where you can only guess the damage. That's where the locals took charge, led me to the hut and the witch doctor weaved his magic. They even arranged a bemo after the treatment and I clambered in. On the way back to Kuta we picked up a few passengers: a few chickens and a giant pig. As we meandered through Denpasar I struggled to maintain equilibrium. The combination of bemo fumes, pig fumes, cigarette fumes and those rare exotic Balinese smells overcame me. I lunged for the back of the bemo but didn't make it — spewing my heart out between pig's trotters in the aisle.

When I finally got back to Kuta, delirious and barely conscious, they put me in a darkened hotel room where I stayed for three days. Every time the door opened there were purple and black spots all over the place. A doctor visited me and explained, 'You've got major concussion, hang in there.' I don't know what the surf was like for those three days but I was down for the count. Every couple of hours one of the cameramen would come in to see if I was okay. Steve Core had paid for my ticket over there, three major surf movies were in production, and I don't think they really accepted the fact that I was out of action. I got the vibe that they were thinking: What's Bugs doing? We've got movies to make. But every time they opened the door things started spinning. I had to be in complete darkness just to get through this thing.

Finally, one day Dick Hoole popped his head in and politely asked my condition. Shit — no spins, no chunders. I was right.

'Hey Bugs, there's no wind, the tide's high. It looks perfect for Sanur,' Dick said.

I remember saying, 'How big?' And he went, 'Six to eight.' By then it was already a done deal. Before I knew it we were in a bemo, my trusty 7'3" Dick Van Stralen again by my side. I'd lost three days and three nights but I felt good. Ah, a bit of fresh air on the way over to Sanur did me the world of good. We pulled up at the beach just as they were pulling a shark out of the water. It was about six feet long, no big deal, but I remember looking at the shark and going, wow, where am I? Terry Richardson was with me and neither of us had ever surfed the place before. I looked out to sea at the break, still feeling pretty vague. The wave was just going, GRRRRRRR, like a steam train, grinding down the reef. I remember it so clearly. Dick had got me going but he didn't quite grasp how gone I was. Bill Delaney had followed us over there, because I was making *Free Ride* with him. The whole thing had been a bit of a nudge, nudge, wink, wink, routine between the whole lot of us.

So I'm standing there looking at six to eight foot Sanur, a six foot shark on the beach, still a bit unsteady on my feet, wondering where to paddle through the reef. Dick's already traipsing off down the beach with his camera and tripod, setting up. Bill's there going, 'Get out there Rabbit.' In *Free Ride* and *Tubular Swells* you can see my first wave out there, you can see how slow that first part of the wave was. I'm actually riding a wave again, much to my own amazement. I'm coming off the bottom, and I'm coming up and I'm doing a cutback and going, wwhhhooaa! I remember this, this is all nice. And then it went all glassy and I went out and tried a bit of a roundhouse cutback and went, wwhhhooooooo, I'm coming back round and I'm going to hit it off the white water. Alright! And then I just went, WWHHHOOOOOAAAA! Suddenly I was dropping down another level, going, right, here we go. I was already deep when this envelope of lip just threw out in front of me. While I was in there I was acutely aware that there was this barbed coral right

Bustin' down the door

below me. It was like Kirra over reef, and that's the only thing that saved me. It was scary, but somehow I knew I'd come out.

I was back in the saddle, but there was still another challenge awaiting me, back at Ulu. It happened a week or so later. A huge swell hit Bali and Kuta was maxed out. We headed for Ulu — the placing of offerings at the top of our priorities.

Ulu was a churning cauldron of white froth. The only rideable section was way out in the bay off the inside part of the cliff — huge 15 to 18 foot walls of water tapering off into the deeper waters of the next bay. We scrambled over the inside reef and somehow got out. We were on a beautiful roll and definitely weren't looking back.

Doris got the first one, outrunning a gigantic ball of whitewater. We surfed for a couple of hours, the cliffs shrouded in a salty mist way off in the distance, then pondered how to get back in. The only way back up the cliff was through a small cave at its base, but it required pinpoint accuracy and timing, otherwise you were looking at being washed down the coast into the unknown. Dick talked me into paddling to outside Temples and catching a mother of a set into the cave. A huge set built up outside. I paddled over a 12 footer and saw a wave erupt on an unknown outside reef. It was like a huge Pipeline nightmare, minus the channel. I turned and paddled for all my worth on to the next one. My last sighting of Dick was him knee-paddling his 8'1" gun towards the shoulder.

Ulu was like a washing machine, so I proned out and rode the wash through, lining up for an assault on the cave. I could hear this rushing, gurgling sound and I looked over my shoulder to see a tidal surge of epic proportions. It seemed the whole ocean was bearing down on me. Each set wave had gobbled the wave in front as the water rushed off the reef. My 7'6" was hurtling towards the cave so fast I could barely steer it. I drew a bee-line towards the cave entrance. The middle rock loomed dangerously and I bailed. My board went one side and I went the other, hoping for the best. The wave filled the cave and I dug my claws into the sand and held on as the cave emptied back out. My board carrier had a look of absolute horror on his face as I dragged my board and body up the rough bamboo ladder, out of the cave.

I couldn't see Dick from the cliff. A couple of young Balos were shrieking, pointing down the coast. After an hour I started getting worried. We decided to head back to the bemo, thinking Dick might be there already. It was a weird feeling heading back without Dick. Was this yet another cruel twist of Uluwatu fate? You can't imagine my relief at seeing Dick by the roadside near the Padang village. En route to Kuta he regurgitated the whole episode, starting with an estimated 18 to 20 foot wave that deposited him far past the Uluwatu cave. Dick had paddled down the coast and found sanctuary in this amazing nook where a perfectly tapered reef copped about half the size of Ulu with twice the perfection.

Who discovered and first surfed Padang Padang is open to debate, but nobody can lay claim to stumbling upon it in such dramatic life and death circumstances as Dick Harvey. Lopez and company had probably surfed it, but when news of this discovery spread among the movie men, the word was out and the next day Richo, McCabe and Eltherington were documented surfing perfect six foot Padang.

Little could we imagine the scale of the Indonesian assault Australian surfers would mount in the years to come.

The rest of 1974 revolved around trying to get the funds together to get to Hawaii. I'd won about $1200 between Bells and the Coke, but you had to make it last because it was slim pickings after that for the rest of the year. I was feeling the pressure to really establish myself — at the grand old age of 19 I was already feeling like time was running out.

MP's mum didn't help matters. I remember going into the Commonwealth Bank to ask for a bank loan to get myself to Hawaii. Mrs Peterson came up behind me and started telling me, 'If you don't do it this year Rabbit, you never will. You're getting old. Your style's getting old, you're old hat.' She was a scary lady. The thought kind of took root and I remember thinking, that's so heavy, I am kind of getting old, I'm nearly 20. But that was the era. You went in the Amateur Titles, collected your trophies and then you were gone. Guys were retiring from competition at 21. It was a real test of my self-belief; I had to say to myself, no, I'm not ancient, I'm still getting better. Getting to Hawaii at year's end seemed like a matter of life or death.

Bustin' down the door

I got knocked back for the loan, so I got a job at the Grand Hotel, Coolangatta, cleaning out the pub. I'd go in there at 5.30 am and clean out all the swill from the night before, including the toilets.

I decided I was never going to work in the pub again after a rugby team came to stay and had a shit fight in the toilets. I walked out. I was prepared to do almost anything to get to Hawaii but that was too much for me. Still, I'd put enough away for a good solid stint in Hawaii and I felt good about the fact that I'd worked to pay my way. The whole time I was cleaning that pub all I had in my mind was getting back to Hawaii and riding those big waves.

Shortly before I left for Hawaii a good friend of mine, Johnny C, from Burleigh, handed me a book and said, 'You should read this.' I ended up reading *Jonathon Livingston Seagull* over 30 times. I saw the movie 17 times. Watching it was akin to a religious experience. Richard Bach's work inspired me like nothing before — the story of one seagull's desire to break from the flock and follow its dreams mirrored my own desire to break through in Hawaii.

HAWAII 1974-75

Professional surfing was already well-established in Hawaii — it was just a matter of figuring out how to break into the elite club. The protocol then was to write letters of introduction to the contest directors, explaining what a magnificent surfer you were and why you should be invited to their contest. It seems a terribly quaint custom in hindsight but it didn't seem at all odd to us then. We'd all dutifully apply our literary skills to penning the most impressive letters to Hawaiian contest directors Fred Hemmings and George Downing, and wait anxiously for the invitations to arrive in the mail. My mailbox wasn't exactly inundated so the only option then was to fly over, charge like a maniac and draw attention to yourself that way. So off we all flew with stars in our eyes on October 1.

Ian 'Kanga' Cairns had taken me under his wing and virtually tutored me on surfing the North Shore in the lead up to the '74 Hawaiian season. We'd got hold of these US *Surfer* magazines

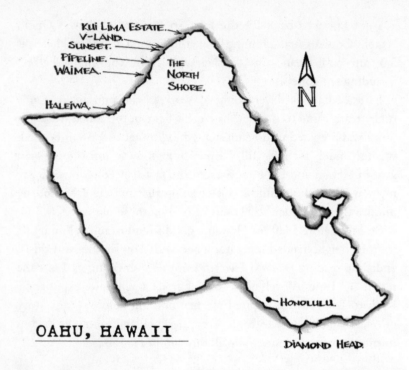

KUI LIMA ESTATE.
V-LAND.
SUNSET.
PIPELINE.
WAIMEA.

THE
NORTH
SHORE.

HALEIWA.

N

HONOLULU.

OAHU, HAWAII

DIAMOND HEAD.

with maps of Sunset, Pipeline and Waimea. The maps showed the reef, the depths and the rips and I used to study them closely. I sat up at night and studied Pipe, Sunset and Waimea — where you sit and how the west peak swings in at Sunset. I had Kanga pointing things out to me all the time and mentally preparing me to have a real dig. I felt a lot more at ease, I felt ready to give it a bit of charge. I was 19, about to turn 20, and there was a feeling that our generation could be the next crew to make an impact if we went on with the job in Hawaii.

The determination to do well in Hawaii among the Australians was intense and a lot of guys overcame some deep-seated fears of big waves. There was even a tradition called Aussie Day — the big, stormy, wild days at Sunset that the Hawaiians wouldn't even bother surfing — they could afford to wait for the perfect days. But us Aussies would go out and try to surf anything, even when the wind was from the north and the ocean was a mass of white caps. The locals would sit out on their porches and laugh at the crazy Australians, but these were the days when we could catch up to them, learn the reef and the character

Bustin' down the door

of the surf spots and get some waves under our belts without crowds — even if the waves were pretty wild and woolly. We'd surf for six hours at a time — Kanga, Mark Warren, PT, MR, me and Bruce Raymond, just going hell for leather. Then they started noticing that we were getting better, and they'd come down to watch us. Pretty soon a few of the younger Hawaiians would come out and surf with us and see that we were getting some pretty decent barrels, despite the conditions. There was a great vibe between us all in the water on those days. We'd all hang out on photographer Bernie Baker's front porch on those windy sunset days. Bernie was the first local to understand our warped sense of humour.

There was a fantastic camaraderie between all the Australians in Hawaii. Geoff McCoy was the gun Australian shaper of the day and his team riders all stayed together in a house at Rocky Point. This became the Australian embassy and we'd go down there, hang out and surf a little break called Monster Mush. This became our spot, mainly because no-one else wanted it — it was such a dreg of a wave. But we loved it. There were some heavy sessions out there with all the top Australians going off.

One of the most important ways to make an impact in Hawaii was to get your photo in the American surfing magazines, so naturally it was important to become tight with the surf photographers. On one memorable morning, American photographer Dan Merkel came by to get Kanga Cairns and I, which was like a major career opportunity. 'It's the best day I've ever seen at Off The Wall,' he said. We'd never surfed Off The Wall and, in fact, few people bothered with it because most of the time it was a bit of a close out, but Jeff Hakman had told us at dinner one night how good it could get. The sand had built up from Ehukai Beach Park to the east, through Pipeline, and through Off The Wall in one grinding, Kirra-like express train barrel. I've never seen it as good — before or since. We charged it and got some unbelievable barrels. I felt like I was surfing perfect, big Kirra and I loved it. It felt like my kind of wave and for the first time I began to sense how comfortable I could become in Hawaiian surf. I really made a lot of ground that day.

Shaun Tomson was arriving from South Africa that afternoon and Kanga and I went to pick him up from the airport — we took him straight back to Off The Wall. It was his first time there too, and we had the most epic session. We were pushing each other further and further inside, seeing who could make the deepest barrel. It was kind of ironic really — we were to become such rivals and Shaun became Mr Off The Wall for his tube-riding in that very location — and we took him there for the first time.

I was excited about Shaun arriving in Hawaii because somehow I knew that he was going to be one of my great rivals. I'd seen him at Bells and the Coke and I just knew, this was my guy. He loved tube-riding, we were the same age, and already you could see that he was a future superstar. I barely knew him but I liked him instantly. He was intelligent, articulate and I could sense that he was going to contribute to the fulfilment of my dream — that here was a surf star ready to win the hearts of the general public. He already had this aura about him, he was a bit aloof, he had the Hollywood looks — he was always going to be a sports star. I figured he was a guy I could run with and bounce off, we could be a foil for each other.

It's weird thinking back on it — I barely knew Shaun at the time, or MR for that matter, we'd never discussed the dream of pro surfing as far as I can recall at that stage, but it was as if we all knew we had the same dream and we were going to help make it happen together.

This intense one-upmanship developed between Shaun and I immediately and we became pretty close that season. Between us I think we really pushed the backside attack at Pipe through our rivalry, just trying to do something more radical, bigger, deeper, more blasé, cooler in the tube. It was just crazy shit at times. I really started surfing Pipe a lot that year, and Shaun and I made a pact. We made a few pacts together, even though we were rivals neither of us wanted to see the other get hurt. We made this pact, and shook hands on it, that no matter what, we'd make the drop at Pipe. No matter how radical the situation, *don't fall off on the take-off at Pipe*, because we knew that was the danger zone. And we

Bustin' down the door

kept that alive successfully for many, many seasons. It was well into the '80s before either of us blew a take-off at Pipe. I got nailed in the tube or out the front of the lip many times but I always made the drop. We both knew, if you didn't make the drop you could get maimed.

Making the drop only really guaranteed a few more seconds of life. I recall pulling into huge barrels, soul-arching or casually looking back as the lip curtained out in front. Once inside, however, it was life or death. Often huge slabs of water would slam down and block the exit. At those moments there was absolutely no chance of a miracle exit. In fact, it always reminded me of the Roadrunner cartoon, when the coyote stops mid-air, gulps and then gets obliterated. Ten minutes later, after thanking God and regaining composure, I'd find myself in exactly the same predicament, facing a nuclear detonation or being squirted along the coral reef on my backside. There was definitely a next-to-be-dead club and I was getting close to being the number one contender.

Letter to Bart, November 19, 1974.

'There will be two major contests while I am here, the Smirnoff and the Duke Classic and last week Ian and I visited the organiser of the Duke and I explained my situation, being that I was stuck right in the middle of amateur and pro division in Hawaii. He told me to write a letter suggesting alternative methods of selecting emerging pro surfers. I thought about it and wrote a letter of suggestion and he was so impressed by my ideas that he compiled a questionnaire based on my ideas and he also gave me a vote in selecting competitors. He told me that it was impossible for me to gain entry to this year's Duke but suggested that I write to the Smirnoff organiser. I did this and included a few more ideas and this organiser was so impressed he included me on the alternate list of competitors which is how Ian got in last year. The Smirnoff began today but I have no idea if I'm in it yet.'

I realised how far I'd come in Hawaii the day of the Smirnoff Pro. MR, Shaun Tomson and I were all alternates, and MR ended up getting into the event. Even though I didn't get a start, a few of us paddled out at Waimea after the final. Bruce Raymond, Simon Anderson and I egged each other on to go out and we surfed big Waimea until dark. I got a couple of beauties — one was easily the biggest wave I'd ever caught. That was a real achievement for me and taught me a valuable lesson: if you go straight to Waimea and get it over with, the rest is a bit easier. It's a strategy Kanga taught me, and we made it a tradition every season to go out for the heaviest surf we could find as soon as we arrived and get the nerves out of our system.

Reno Abellira won the '74 Smirnoff Pro, he was absolutely magnificent that day. He rode the biggest wave I'd ever seen in my life and he became my new super hero. Even though I was pretty pleased with myself, I could see there was still a long way to go.

MARK RICHARDS: 'I'd written Fred Hemmings a letter and said I was shit hot and he should put me in the contest and they (Shaun and Rabbit) were trying to get in as well. That morning we knew this Californian guy, Tiger Makin, who was first alternate, wasn't there. I think Fred Hemmings announced it in the morning, "Mark Richards, Shaun Tomson, Wayne Bartholomew are alternates." So the three of us kind of hung, but we didn't know who was first alternate out of us. Three or four heats into it they started calling this guy for his heat and then with 10 or 15 minutes to go, Fred Hemmings goes, "Mark Richards, first alternate, pay your entry fee and pick up your singlet," and I went, "Fuck, I haven't got any money." I said to Fred, "I haven't got any money," and he said, "You're fucking out. Second alternate!" And Bugs said, "I've got money, I'll pay for you." In hindsight it was a heavy thing for him to do.

Bustin' down the door

My whole career might have been different except for that moment. I got through the first couple of rounds at Sunset, and the next day they moved it to Waimea and it was just huge, and Reno won it. It was kind of like a day when I was forced to go out. I didn't really want to go out, but I knew if I didn't go out I wouldn't get in any Hawaiian contests ever again, and Rabbit would have killed me. That was so big and so scary that after that nothing else was too bad. If that hadn't happened things may have been completely different. I don't think I would have done the same for him. I doubt there were many people who would have done that for another competitor.'

After that Thanksgiving Day swell, we went to Reno Abellira's party and I remember sitting alongside him like I was sitting with Nat back at Lennox in '71, and I was just in awe.

The next day it was still 20 foot Waimea and there were a lot of people on to it, and Kanga went, 'Nah, come and check this out,' and we went and looked at Pipeline.

'See that out there?' he said, indicating huge, Second Reef Pipe, 'that's what Greg Noll rode. We're out there.'

There was no-one out, not one soul out, and I've gone, 'You've got to be kidding, don't ya'?'

But Kanga was on a mission. 'Nah, we're out there,' he said, and so we paddled out. No legropes. I was on a hollow surfboard, playing guinea pig for Kanga's amusement. He'd borrowed this thing and wanted to see how it went in big waves so he sent me out there on it. Just getting out through the rip at Pipe was horrific. Once we'd got into deeper water this gigantic set erupted way out to sea and I've looked at Kanga and he's gone, 'This way,' and I've thought, nah, my instinct says that way, and we separated. He got done like a dinner. This thing broke on his head, and luckily for me it didn't break where I was. I snuck over the shoulder of the set.

I could hear him cussing, he was swearing his head off. You'd expect anyone else to be scared, but no, he was angry. That always stuck with me, he had a good attitude.

So there I was, Bugsy Malone, half a mile out to sea, in uncharted waters, dodging sets, just finding my way round for about an hour or so. Suddenly this set came through and I somehow knew that this was the one to catch. It looked right, and I came to learn that's all you can go on out there — just that it looks right. Like one of those shifting beachbreak peaks but on a massive scale. I went over the first wave, the second wave and the third wave, waiting for the wave in the set that looked perfect. They've got to peak at a certain point and you've got to be right under that point. I remember realising I was in perfect position for this one, putting my head down and just going for it. I took off on this thing and dropped and dropped and dropped and dropped — when I finally did my bottom turn I'd travelled all the way to the inside section just while I was taking the drop. There were a lot of people on the beach by now, but it was so big that it was all misty, and I could only just see the beach. I was coming off the bottom, and this wave lurched, I saw this giant curtain go between me and the beach. This thing was so big and so round that all I was trying to do was stop my progress up the face of the wave. I put all my weight on my front foot and this thing just went over me. I was completely in the barrel of at least a 15 foot wave. The thing spat me out, and I turned and went back to the bottom again and pulled into the barrel a second time and it just shut down on me. I came up and swam to the beach — I knew I'd done something special. As I came up the beach PT ran down and jumped in mid-air, wrapped his legs around me and hugged me, 'Bugs, you've made it, you've made it.' I was elated, but only briefly. Kanga had re-gathered himself and out we went again. That really was the beginnings of the new backside attack at Pipe. Without knowing it, I'd laid down a bit of a gauntlet that day for the rest of my generation of guys. Without ever really sitting down and talking about it, it was understood from that day on that we were all going to go out in anything, take off on anything, pull into anything, to make our names in Hawaii.

Bustin' down the door

MARK RICHARDS: 'I used to get up early and go for a drive and one day Sunset was out of control. It was a huge west and I was going to Haleiwa because that used to be my favourite place and I thought, "I'll have a look at Pipeline." I pulled up and walked across the grass there at Ehukai Beach Park and it had to be 15 feet if it was an inch. Guys here would call it 20 or 25 feet. I think he was out there on his own or with one other guy. But there was just this speck, and it was Rabbit, and I saw him take off on this thing, completely fall out of the sky, he freefell into the pit and just got destroyed. And I just thought, I don't want to be out there, and I bet he doesn't either after that. But he ran up the beach, grabbed another board and was straight back out there. He really embodied that Australian spirit in those years. We virtually were ready to kill ourselves to get in the contests over there, but probably no-one more so than Rabbit, because he was, I think, trying to kill himself. There was no way it couldn't be taken off on — no take-off too late, no situation too radical, no wave too big. He took some pretty severe beatings but he also did some phenomenal surfing. Everyone talks about the backside attack at Pipeline in '75 and '76 with Shaun and Michael Tomson and all those guys ... I think from memory Rab was doing it before those guys at Pipeline. The first guy I saw getting deep at Pipeline on his backhand was Rabbit. This was pre-pigdog. He just did the old, Rabbit, touch your toes and grab your rail and pull in.'

I caddied for Kanga that season too and I learnt a lot in the caddying department. In big waves, each competitor would have a board caddy out in the water with a spare board, in case they lost or snapped theirs. The Duke Contest was also giant that year. It started at Sunset and Kanga had me swimming all over Sunset retrieving his boards. He was a dangerous man to caddy for because he was always taking the most horrendous wipeouts. The cry would go up,

'Bugs, Bugs,' and I'd have to paddle to him with a replacement board and go swimming after the pieces of his other one and then try to paddle in with two pieces of board. The contest was moved to 20 to 25 foot Waimea and Kanga took this unbelievable wipeout. I actually said to myself, 'Well, it might have killed him outright and all my worries will be over.' But no. Up he came and up went the familiar cry. 'Bugs!' In I went. He made me paddle into the impact zone and as soon as he got the board, he yelled at me, 'Go and get my other board and get back out here quick!' He was a hard task-master. His board would be on the rocks or out in the middle of the Bay or in the shorebreak, and I'd be swimming around, going, this is lovely, what a great situation.

My pay for doing this would be a smorgasbord at the Kui Lima Estate, a flash hotel at the eastern end of the North Shore. I'd be so tired I could barely lift my fork. I'd really earnt my money, or at least my 10-buck dinner. Dinners at the Kui Lima smorgasbord became a fond ritual for the Australians in Hawaii. Whoever did well in the contests would shout and we'd all go out to dinner at the Kui Lima smorgasbord. It was a real tradition among us, because no-one had much money. We all stuck together — even though we were all rivals.

MARK RICHARDS: 'Him and Ian were kind of inseparable. They lived together in a place at Sunset Point. They surfed all day every day. He was just in the water all day every day just going for it ... Ian and him used to hit that smorgasbord at the Kui Lima and just clean it out. Due to them the price doubled. You couldn't buy that much food for that price and cook it at home. It used to be five dollars and they put it up to 10 because of Rab and Kanga. That's fact, that's no exaggeration. After a month of those guys going in there and cleaning the place out, the price doubled.'

SHAUN TOMSON: 'In those days the only way to become recognised, to get invitations to the surfing contests, was by making a name for yourself on the North Shore. So that meant

Bustin' down the door

surfing at every break, every day, no matter what the size was. Just really surfing hard and ripping and being really aggressive, creative and radical ... And it was just through our contest surfing, our constant passion, our constant desire to surf great every day at every break. We were intensely competitive and not just in the competition environment. We were so competitive with one another — even though we were really good buddies. Kanga Cairns, PT, Rabbit, MR, my cousin Michael, Bruce Raymond, Mark Warren, we were very good mates. We used to surf a real lot, for hours and hours and hours. It was a really special, passionate era. Everything's changed considerably. That was a really wonderful era. I'm really glad I was involved in the inception of pro surfing. Our whole lives didn't just revolve around competition. They revolved around just surfing radically and surfing great.'

BRUCE RAYMOND: 'If one of the guys won any money, you had to buy everyone dinner. Ian Cairns bought a lot of dinners that season. How could you enjoy your win if your buddies hadn't eaten for two days? I had a budget of $50 a month and lived on rice and oats. That season Rabbit teamed up with Kanga and the first thing they did when they came round was raid our fridge. I remember Mark Warren saying, "Don't feed them or they'll keep coming round," like they were stray dogs.'

After an intense two months in Hawaii most of us returned home for Christmas. I didn't get a start in any of the events. About as close as I got was paying MR's entry fee into the Smirnoff Pro and caddying for Kanga. But it had been an epic trip just the same and I'd made some ground.

I came home and found that news of my Hawaii exploits had filtered back to Australia. I was seen as the new, young turk and

Tracks editor Phil Jarratt rang up and said he wanted to do a major interview. I was stoked. They came up from Sydney and ended up staying at Bart's place — Jarratt, his young mate Steve Cooney (who had an unspecified role) and photographer Frank Pithers. We developed a great rapport and we'd have these dinners and talk about the dream of professional surfing and being a waterman and Hawaii. Then we went down to Byron Bay, and one afternoon we decided to have a few beers. I wasn't much of a drinker, but I went and had a few beers and loosened right up. They started talking about what it was like going to school. I gave this colourful assessment of the Queensland education system, and just swore my head off. It was just beer talk, but unbeknown to me the tape recorder was going the whole time, concealed under a little cushion.

I raced down to the newsagent the day the magazine went on sale and eagerly devoured my first major interview. I looked at all the photos and went, unreal, and then I started reading it and got to this section that was recorded at the pub and it was all f-ing this and f-ing that. I thought, uh-oh, this is too heavy. I was so stoked, but horrified at the same time. In the end, I just thought, oh well, there's nothing to hide any more. I've paddled straight out at

TRACKS INTERVIEW, 1975: 'They had a day where you could fucking wear whatever clothes you want to school and you had to pay money to fucking do it and I just got all the bread from it ... Unreal. Everyone in school pays 20 cents to wear fucking whatever they want to school, fucking really weird gear you know, whatever they liked and it was just a full on unreal day. The teachers were fucking unreal. Everyone came round and just talked so much fucking more naturally. And I got all the bread.'

Waimea on this one. That interview really established me as the wild child. They portrayed me as this rough diamond, this absolute go-for-it guy, a real rebel. I kind of liked the way they portrayed me, but at the same time I was cringing, and I definitely wasn't looking forward to the fall-out.

There was an uproar in the Queensland Department of Education over the interview, but fortunately I was already back on a plane to Hawaii. It was just good fortune that I happened to be returning to Hawaii as the magazine went on sale, and it's a strategy I've adopted many times over the years. When you know there's that kind of storm coming, jump on a plane and be out of the country until it blows over.

HEIDI: 'Mum had sent Louise and I down the shop to buy the magazine, and I remember looking at it and all I saw was F, F, F, F, everywhere, and having it under my arm and not wanting to show mum. Rab had gone the day before as usual. I didn't want to show her, but eventually we couldn't keep it from her any longer so I gave it to her, and Louise and I went and hid for a couple of hours.'

NICK CARROLL: 'Jarratt did an incredible interview with him in *Tracks* where "fuck" was like, every second word. It was famous for that but to me it was a really good interview anyway. He said a lot of really good stuff. He seemed to be really aware of the idea of image, that you would be projecting something that would go beyond you as a person and that that counted for something, so he was already thinking about that. The big quote I think was, "I strive to be unique with as little bullshit attached to it as possible," and I thought, Fuck, he's already thinking about how other people perceive him and he sees that as important, not from any kind of, like, co-dependency problem, but that's kind of part of life, and affects how he would compete, affect the people he was competing against.'

Kanga had said I should go back for the remainder of the Hawaiian season, but I was almost out of money. So for the second time I strode purposefully into the Commonwealth Bank and asked for $500, this time I got it. I felt like I was really throwing the dice this time. I hadn't got a start in any of the contests and funds were low. I wrote a letter off to George Downing, the contest director, saying I was a reserve in the Smirnoff, I'm knocking on the door, I've got next to no money, but I'm coming back. Please put me in the Hang 10 American Pro. And through Kanga Cairns I found out I was the second alternate, and I thought, oh god, it's got to be worth a punt.

That second trip I went back with only 200 bucks to my name. Me and Kanga got our house broken into again and they stole all my money. But that didn't even phase me. I was used to surviving on nothing. What I didn't realise was that there was already a growing groundswell of animosity towards us — the new, brash Australians catching any wave that moved. I thought it was just a random crime, but we'd already put a few of the wrong people offside.

Somehow, I don't know how, I got into the Hang 10 and it was held at awesome Sunset. It was two rounds of competition, with six heats and six surfers in each heat — 36 competitors in all. After the first round I was coming about 19th, and I thought, that's okay, I'm pretty stoked. I ended up coming about 13th in the tournament. But more importantly I got this one classic wave, I backdoored this section and got a really deep barrel. I just went and went and went and I was getting higher and higher up the face of the wave. As the last section came over I came flying through out of control and as I came out I actually hit the lip. No-one could believe it. I thought I was going to die, I didn't mean to do it, but it put me in contention for the best tube-ride. MP ended up winning the best tube-ride though and he won a motorbike, which was dangerous.

That performance was enough to get me a start in the Lightning Bolt Pro at Velzyland. I loved Velzyland — Michael Ho had already taken me there and it was just my kind of wave. These days it's one of the heaviest locals' spots on the North Shore, but back then it had a really friendly vibe, with a lot of great, young Hawaiian surfers doing some amazing surfing —

Larry Bertleman, Buttons Kaluhiokalani, Vince Klyne, Mark Liddel, Lance Hookana, Buzzy Kerbox, Timmy Carvalho and Louie Ferraria. They just accepted me — we were all kids and kids tend to accept kids. I looked young for my age, they all thought I was probably about 16, and I was kind of taken in. They were the ultimate fun gang and I radiated towards them like they were MP and Tommy, totally loose and in sync. I'd look forward to those in between swells, to escape the spartan Kanga regime and hotdog surf with the V-land crew.

In the Lightning Bolt I was coming 12th after the first round, and in the second round I just completely went off. I won the second round and ended up coming third overall. The first round I was still freaked out to be out there with all these incredible surfers, but by the second round I'd realised, hey, there aren't many guys that can surf V-land better than me. My surfing absolutely suits that wave, even better than Kirra, just the way the wave breaks — with tubes and plenty of opportunity for manoeuvres. That was a great moment for me. Third in a major North Shore event. I knew I was going to get invites next year for all the events.

When I came back to Coolangatta I was a hero. I'd got third in a major Hawaiian tournament, I'd done photos with the top photographers, the American magazines had already said they were doing spreads on us. The magazine editors had told us they considered us the new crew and all through '75 they just built us up to go back to Hawaii.

I got a major write-up in the local newspaper as the hometown boy who'd surfed to glory in the killer waves of Hawaii and MP hated that. He had the article up on his shaping bay wall and written across it in giant letters in black texta was the word, 'bullshit.'

the big time

P and I moved to full-scale combat after that Hawaii trip. We'd actually clear the water sometimes, we'd be going after each other so hard. There'd be 20 waves coming through but we'd have to be on the same one. It was unbelievable. We'd drop in on each other, just trying to burn and fade the other one. But all this just served to sharpen my own reflexes. Little did I realise it at the time, but I was getting a grounding in sports psychology and surfing strategy that would serve me well later in my career. No opponent could intimidate me after MP.

Inevitably, things reached boiling-point during an afternoon session at little groyne. I took off on this wave, MP tried to fade me, and then he came off the bottom and went into this searing cutback straight at my legs. I'd seen it coming though, and I got within his turning circle up high on the wave and he passed under me as I came off the top. He just lunged at me, jumped off his board, grabbed me and we went over the falls going at each other's throats, and came up swinging punches. We ended up ripping fence palings off this fence and came to a Mexican stand off, lumps of wood at the ready. People used to congregate just to see us going at each other. He was a scary bugger and he had so much energy: there was no stopping him once he got worked up. But I just felt I couldn't take a backward step to him by that stage.

The Queensland Titles that year was a platform for the hostilities between MP and myself. It was one of the most epic events I've ever been in in my life. The Saturday was absolutely perfect Burleigh and MP was surfing in the heat after mine. In those days they only had the one blast of the hooter to finish a heat and start the next one. As fate would have it, this perfect wave was coming in as they were counting down to the finish of my heat, and MP was already out in the water for the next heat. We both started paddling for this wave as the final seconds of my heat ticked away. I'd made up my mind I was going, and so had MP. The hooter sounded at the very instant we both paddled into the wave, so, technically, it was a scoring ride for both of us in different heats. I was on the inside and I pulled into a deep barrel, and watched as MP slotted into the tube in front of me. We travelled through a couple of sections and I could see a backdoor section throwing out in front of MP. He gunned into the next section and I just squeaked out in front of the curtain as he got spat out the end. We both got incredible scores for that one wave and just stood there riding the wave in, shaking our fists at each other.

The next day Burleigh was out of control and they moved the event to Kirra Point. This was the first time Kirra had broken well since the big groyne went in, and thousands of people from all over the Gold Coast flocked to see it. They tried to run the junior final but only two contestants, my old mate Macca and Peter Harris, could even get out the back. The open final was Peter Drouyn, MP, me, PT, the late Brian 'Furry' Austen, and a guy called Ian Dimond from the Sunshine coast, who was a real solid surfer. There was about 20 minutes left before the start of the final and we were walking round the Point when someone yelled out, 'Who's that out there in the red singlet?'

'Bullshit, it's MP!' someone else exclaimed. There was MP sitting out at eight to 10 foot Kirra Point, the first time it had broken in three years, by himself, just looking at us, already psyching us out. We had to go all the way round to Rainbow Bay to make it out and duckdived huge mountains of whitewater all the way outside Coolangatta Beach — this is still pre-legropes. We got caught by about a 12 foot set out in the middle of nowhere. I had my full Hawaiian big-wave board, a red Barry Kanaiapuni gun, and I was wrapping my arms and legs around the thing trying to hang on to it underwater. I nearly got washed up on the groyne but just managed to pull in behind it and take shelter until there was a break in the sets. PT got sucked around the groyne and got smashed all the way down the Point, he didn't even get out. Brian Austen got washed up on the groyne and got all cut up. The final had been going for nine minutes before I even got out the back, and MP had had it to himself all that time. We were scored on our best five rides and MP got five insane waves and some long barrels. I ended up riding four but I didn't make it out of my best barrel. I got this big drain pipe that got bigger the further it went, but finally this thing got so mean and so round that my board lifted up at the tail and became a missile. For one freaky instant I was travelling along in the barrel not touching the wave or my board, just getting carried along. When my board passed me, that's when it clicked: Ah, I don't think I'm going to make it out of this one. But it must have looked spectacular and, of course, I got thumped and had to swim in and run back around and do it again. It was a real guts and glory final. People were absolutely flabbergasted by how hard we went out there. But no-one could touch MP. He'd won the Queensland Title in '71 and '72 and I'd won it in '73 and '74, so it must have been especially sweet for MP to take that one out. It was serious surfing on big boards and anyone who hadn't been to Hawaii would have had a hard time dealing with it.

The trip up north to the Sunshine Coast for the Pa Bendall Memorial that year was most memorable for the antics of Keith Paull — a great surfer who started behaving a little strangely around this time. I was sponsored by Keith at the time and he offered me a lift up but I'd already arranged to go with my shaper Gill Glover, so I told Keith I'd see him up there. All the competitors gathered at the Pearl Hotel, Caloundra, for the contest meeting that evening and I spotted Keith outside the pub driving his panel van. Next moment, he drove up on to the footpath and I thought, classic Keith, what a way to make your entrance and intimidate your

Bustin' down the door

opponents before a contest. But then he drove up the stairs of the hotel, and lodged the panel van halfway in the front entrance. I was impressed. I thought, all time, he's surpassed MP here. This is the greatest stunt I've ever seen. The showmanship! This is what you do before a contest to psych everyone out, you drive up the stairs into the pub. I was walking over to congratulate him when he opened the door, he got out and his head was shaved bald, and painted with blue, concentric circles. I just stopped in my tracks. This wasn't the Keith Paull I'd seen that morning.

Keith's antics became increasingly weird as the event progressed, culminating in him rolling around in the shorebreak before his heat and telling a bemused TV camera crew that he was an oyster. They are funny stories in the re-telling but the sad truth is not everyone survived this period of surfing too well. For my generation of guys coming through, we were enthralled by all these bizarre and colourful characters, but I could sense the beginnings of a dilemma here for us. We loved the characters in surfing at the time, but we kind of knew we couldn't carry on the same way. If we wanted to fulfil our dream of mainstream respectability and credibility as athletes, we were either going to have to play it super straight or be super discreet. We developed an unspoken understanding: what we did behind closed doors was our own business, but in the public eye we wanted to present ourselves as serious and dedicated sportsmen. It was a bit of a tightrope walk, because at the same time, it was important to me to be respected by the hard-core surfers and I liked being seen as a bit of a rebel and a subversive. We were trying to get the general public to take pro surfing seriously and believe we were serious athletes, and at the same time convince the hard-core that pro surfing wasn't a sell-out, and we were still rebellious surfers in the finest tradition.

Guys like MP became such cult heroes because they put up not the slightest pretence of wooing the mainstream. There was no point MP trying to act straight because he had hair down to his arse, and spoke in low, guttural grunts and mutters, so there was no chance of public acceptability. But he was revered as the uncompromising, animal surfer. Then you had people like Geoff

McCoy, who were super straight to the point of obsession. Geoff would punch you out on the beach if he even suspected you smoked pot. I was trying to strategically pick my line through all this and I think I wound up somewhere halfway between PT's flawless professionalism and MP's anti-social individuality.

A lot has been said and written about surfing's efforts to clean up its image and live down its renegade roots, but that was part of the richness of the times. Surfing has always attracted extreme characters and the success of the whole surfing industry was born out of this culture of wild, live-for-today abandon. But I knew somewhere down the line we were going to have to straighten up a bit if the rest of society was to even begin to relate to us.

BELLS

The '75 Bells event meant another epic trek south, this time with Keith Paull, Andy Mac, myself and Guy Ormerod. MP was on a roll and was virtually unbeatable with his perfect mastery of the points-for-manoeuvres system. My only consolation was succeeding in convincing these two beautiful girls from Manly, in Sydney, that we should give them a ride home.

The night before we left, we were in the Torquay pub with the girls and they still weren't too sure about accepting a lift to Sydney with these young surfers. They were asking us, 'So where is this guy that's going to drive us back? Where's this guy Keith Paull, the legend surfer?' I looked around the pub, and pointed, 'Ah, there he is over there.' Keith was stark naked, except for a pair of ugg boots and a Russian Cossack's hat, and he was doing the big streak through the pub. He was running around, acknowledging the crowd's cheers, and then he did a great jump over the bar, and gave every one a last flip off and went to get out the escape route he'd mapped out — through this door behind the bar. Unfortunately for Keith, the door was locked, and he was nabbed by the bouncers and dragged out. I went, 'Yeah, that's him there. That's my sponsor.'

For some unknown reason, the girls still came with us and I don't know how we did it, but it took us a week to get from

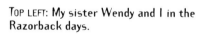

TOP LEFT: My sister Wendy and I in the Razorback days.

TOP RIGHT: The Kirra surf-o-planes, complete with one of surfing's first forms of sponsorship. Courtesy Johnny Charlton.

ABOVE: My mum Betty and a very styling FJ Holden at Currumbin beach front.

LEFT: Kanga and I preparing for a mission at Waimea. I'm about to earn another 10-buck dinner for a near-drowning. Jeff Divine, *Surfer* magazine.

ABOVE: Johnny Charlton's Kirra beach hire. Johnny earned extra income by selling advertising on the surf-o-planes to local businesses. Robert Anthony.

BELOW: The Kirra hire boards. My beloved number 19 must have been out in the surf when this shot was taken. Courtesy Johnny Charlton.

ABOVE LEFT: NSW Premier, Neville Wran, presents me with the big cheque. Dick Hoole.

ABOVE: Michael Ho pips me for the '85 World Cup. Aaron Chang, *Surfing* magazine.

LEFT: Toni and I over the moon after my '78 Stubbies win. Peter Crawford.

BELOW: My first winnings in Hawaii. The Kui Lima smorgasbord took a pounding that night. Jeff Divine, *Surfer* magazine.

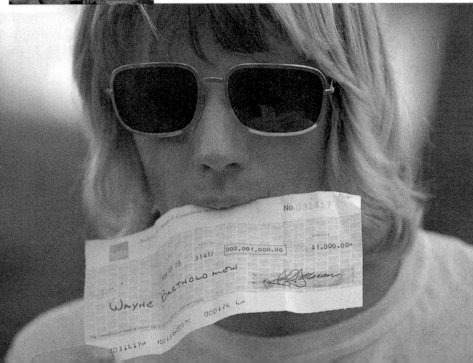

ABOVE LEFT: Mr Smirnoff. In hindsight, maybe 20 grand wasn't enough to have to wear the white suit all around the world.

ABOVE RIGHT: My patented serving style. During my banishment from the North Shore in '76, my tennis game benefited enormously. Peter Crawford.

BELOW LEFT: My late '70s, aspiring rock star phase. Richard Harvey.

BELOW RIGHT: Getting into the vibe on my first trip to Bali. Dick Hoole.

ABOVE: Basking in the glory of my World Title win. I wasn't exactly camera shy. Dick Hoole.
BELOW: In Surfers Paradise for the Julie Anthony Christmas Special, '78. Peter Crawford.

TOP LEFT: Preparing to pounce on a Mexican food cart in a post-surf, feeding frenzy. I came down with food poisoning soon after. Richard Harvey.

TOP RIGHT: Shaun Tomson and I flanked by media and spectators at the '78 Coke Surfabout. Peter Crawford.

ABOVE: Preparing to pull in at the '81 Offshore Pipeline Masters in the controversial pink-and-white Offshore boardshorts. Peter Crawford.

TOP LEFT: Bells '84, my Russian Cossack phase. Here I playfully engage rising young Turk, Martin Potter, in a little pre-heat shadow boxing. Peter Crawford.

TOP RIGHT: Mont and I checking the surf at early morning Kirra *circa* '78. Peter Crawford.

ABOVE: I became obsessed with attempting the carving 360 after the Coke Surfabout posted a $5000 cash prize for anyone who could pull one off in a heat. The prize was never claimed *circa* '76. Peter Crawford.

TOP LEFT: A heavy little snap during an idyllic Tahiti trip in '80. Jeff Divine, *Surfer* magazine.

TOP RIGHT: Toni and I trying to stay warm in the Bells car park, '80. Peter Crawford.

ABOVE LEFT: Checking the perfect geometry of a cyclone swell from the top of Kirra Hill. Peter Crawford.

ABOVE: Chappy and I display our prowess in the kitchen with buckwheat pancakes for breakfast, Hawaii '83. Jeff Divine, *Surfer* magazine.

LEFT: Runner-up Michael Ho congratulates me on my '78 Stubbies win — a classic final against a classic friend. Peter Crawford.

Torquay to Sydney — and we didn't even go surfing. It was the most vicious week in the history of weeks. I spent most of the time trying to find Keith. We'd stop at a roadhouse in the middle of the night and Keith would just throw the keys at me and bolt into the night. Everyone would be panicking, and I'd try to calm them, 'Nah, nah, let him go, he'll be back.' Three hours later, when he hadn't returned, I'd say, 'Righto, let's go look for him,' and we'd just have to drive round in the middle of the night until we'd finally find him cowering under some tree.

By the time we got in to Sydney we were just totally bedraggled. Guy and I had run out of money a week ago, and didn't have a penny to our names. Keith pulled off the highway at Botany Bay and we all asked, 'Where are you going Keith?' and he said, 'I'm taking you all out to dinner — my shout.' He pulled up outside the finest French restaurant in Sydney, and out we got in our hippy gear and ugg boots. By this stage, the girls were just totally disoriented, they didn't know what was going on any more. We must have been quite a sight as we filed in, sat down and started ordering oysters by the dozen and the finest French champagne. Keith was swanning like an aristocrat, bellowing out to the waiter, 'Garcon, more Dom Perignon.' We ate the finest four course meal, all clinking glasses, having a grand old time. Even the girls were starting to smile. At the end of a truly magnificent meal, Keith summonsed the waiter again and very coolly announced, 'Ah ... I've got no money.' Guy and I just looked at each other and went, 'We're out of here.' The bill was something like $800, which was a lot of money in 1975. The others weren't far behind us and we roared away screaming and cackling like lunatics.

We dropped the girls off in Manly, where they made a very hurried, very relieved exit. We went and stayed with *Tracks* editor Phil Jarratt at Whale Beach, on Sydney's northern beaches, before facing the drive back to the Gold Coast. It was a relief to wake up at beautiful Whale Beach to an absolutely perfect day. We were up at the crack of dawn, hoping for an early surf to wash away the highway and the past week's traumas. It was 6.30 am and Keith just reached up and grabbed a bottle of Arak, Balinese rice wine, off the shelf and started guzzling it. Guy and I looked at each other — we'd had enough. We were out of there. All we wanted to do was get away from this possessed maniac. We bolted out of the house and started walking down Whale Beach Road. The next minute, Keith was in the panel van, reversing up the road at 80 miles an hour, door open, hanging out of the car, and he just flew straight past us and disappeared up the road. I remember watching him whiz past and just going, 'See ya' Keith,' as if it was the most normal thing in the world.

It took us two weeks to get from Bells back to the Gold Coast and it was like waking from a bad dream. But we walked straight into a 28-day swell — so all our hardship was pretty quickly forgotten.

There was a powerful momentum building for us to return to Hawaii. The American photographers came out to Australia during the year with explicit instructions from the magazines to focus on me, Kanga, MR and Shaun in the lead up to Hawaii. We'd already had a lot of coverage from the previous Hawaiian season and the magazines were saying, go and get more shots of these guys because we are completely running with them. I guess they could see that we were quite versatile, we weren't just one-trick ponies. We'd surf big waves, small waves, Sunset, Pipe, Waimea; we'd hotdog surf, or tube-ride or take big drops. We'd do well in contests, and charge like madmen in free surfs. We were also building our own momentum, both collectively and individually, and this was all adding to the frosty welcome awaiting us in Hawaii. All the media attention created the impression that there was a jumbo jet full of brash, hungry young Australians ready to run riot all over the North Shore. Really, it was only four or five of us, but it seemed like we were everywhere in '75 — in the magazines, in the surf movies, in the contests — and the Hawaiians were readying themselves for an invasion.

Indonesia became an unofficial part of our circuit, even though there were no contests. The filmmakers and photographers all wanted to document us partaking of the exotic Indo surf experience and we were only too happy to oblige. That added another dimension and a bit of spice to our act, and we saw it as a part of our preparation for Hawaii. We'd go over there with our Hawaiian boards and seek out the biggest waves we could find. We'd also take the soul trips down the NSW north coast to Lennox and Angourie. It felt like we were on a long, glorious roll from one classic surf spot to another with an eager band of cameramen ready to document our every move.

But this heady taste of surf stardom had to be tempered by the reality of returning to Hawaii at year's end and justifying all the hype. And, really, preparing for Hawaii was my main focus all year long. It seemed to me like the whole world was waiting for us to go back. I felt like my surfing had changed gear. I felt I'd gone past a lot of people. I felt like I'd gone past MP at that point in Hawaii. I felt like I'd gone past everyone out of the Australians except Kanga Cairns and MR. I had a lot of confidence. I even felt I was ready to step out of Kanga's shadow. He'd really prepared me. He'd turned me into quite a good Sunset surfer — I certainly wasn't a master of the place by any means at that point — but I already felt I was more comfortable than him at big Pipe.

HAWAII 1975-76

Going into Hawaii in '75 there was no feeling of any barrier being there. I've never anticipated anything more clearly than going back to the North Shore and doing what we did. It was something that MR, Shaun and I never really sat down and discussed — how we were all going to charge in Hawaii — it was an unspoken oath. I just knew Shaun Tomson was going to go absolutely ballistic at big Pipe that year, because I'd sort of laid down the gauntlet in the real nutso stuff the year before. I knew Kanga and MR were going to be insane at Sunset and Waimea. I knew all of us were going to be incredible, and it felt like everyone knew it. We got invited to all the contests, all of us, every single one of us, which in itself was unprecedented. All of a sudden there was about seven Australians in the Duke contest.

Shaun beat me to the punch and got to Hawaii on October 1, me and Kanga didn't get there until the 10th. I rang up a friend in

Hawaii when we were still in Australia and they said, 'Yeah, there's already been a swell at Off The Wall and we've got cover shots of Shaun Tomson,' — that really pissed me off. We went there on a real mission. It was me and Kanga against Shaun. I lived with Kanga all through that Hawaiian season, from October 10 to February 25, and it was the most incredible surf trip of my life.

The whole Australian contingent was on the same flight to Hawaii, Kanga and I teamed up and were first out of the gates. We drove straight to where we were staying, dropped off our stuff, and went down to 8 to 10 foot Pipeline.

'You're not allowed to go left,' Kanga instructed me sternly.

'Yeah, but it's closing out on the rights, there's no rights,' I pointed out.

But Kanga was adamant. 'We're going right on every wave.' People thought we were nuts. Our first surf for the season and we were taking off on close-outs, seeing who could pull in the most casually. I'd go in with my hands behind my back and he'd go in doing a soul arch, trying to outdo each other. I ended up getting a chunk out of my arse and he got chunks out of his legs, we were wiping out every single wave and swimming in laughing. Really laughing. Bellowing. Screaming. It was outrageous — like some kind of adrenalin-induced dementia, I'm sure. We were in the zone — we were right where we wanted to be, doing exactly what we'd anticipated doing all year. It was the Kanga and Bugs show. Everyone had been waiting for us to get there and we did not disappoint. And we let Shaun know that we were catching up real quick.

It was just the best season for surf that year — Sunset and Pipe broke all the time, and we had our own 12 days of Christmas, the surf just getting better and better each day. We were at Pipe every day, surfing with the local crew — Gerry Lopez, Rory Russell, Jackie Dunne — and Shaun and Michael Tomson. We were the only ones out, taking off on each other's waves, dropping in and having fun — all pushing each other.

On one of the meanest Pipe days, there were two guys out who shouldn't have been out there. They were way out of their depth, and the swell was still building. Eventually, it was only me and them out there, and I was only on a 6'8". One of the guys took off on a wave, just to try to get the hell out of there, went down, ate it, came in holding his skull together and died on the beach. I got a wave on second reef, came off the bottom on my little 6'8", saw how it was just lining up for one massive close-out and went for the older skidder out the top. I just squeaked out. I really reckon that one would have hurt me if I hadn't got out. Eventually I got a wave in just before it got totally out of control and was glad to be back on dry land. The next day we were down there again all day.

The 10th day of the swell was Christmas Day and it was one of the best days I'd ever seen at Pipe in my life. I was seeing Michael Ho's sister Debbie at the time, and Michael and I were due at the Ho family's house at Waimanalo, on the other side of the island, for Christmas dinner. I'd surfed Pipe all morning and had the most incredible session, the best one yet, and at about 2 pm I got all dressed up and walked down to Pipe to meet Michael. He said, 'Have you seen how it looks out there now?' We looked out at Pipe and then both looked at each other. 'One more surf,' we both said. We ripped off all our good Christmas dinner clothes and out we went and surfed till dark. We high-tailed it to Waimanalo when we got out but we'd missed dinner, everything. Debbie was just furious, but it was the most epic day I'd ever surfed at Pipe.

It was around that time I started to really abuse my liberties. Michael Ho used to come and pick me up from where Kanga and I were staying and take me to Velzyland. We'd go and park at Michael's friend, Brian Surratt's, house and Michael, Timmy Carvalho and I would go and surf V-land. Michael would say, basically, 'You're here with us, you're a local, you can do whatever you want. You can have whatever wave you want. If someone hassles you, send them in.' Stupidly, I took all this Hawaiian hospitality quite literally and turned into a real little arsehole. As long as I was with them, no-one hassled me and I really abused the system — dropping in and calling guys off waves. One time I got a guy punched out, and it still didn't worry me. I was in a bubble where everything was going my way. The case was building against me beach by beach, but I was oblivious to the whole thing.

We absolutely cleaned up in the contests, like no group of foreigners has ever cleaned up in the Hawaiian contests before or since. We finished one, two, three in the final of every major event — the Duke, the Smirnoff and the Pipe Masters — taking about US$20,000 of a total of $30,000 in prize-money on offer. That was bad enough, but what really started pissing people off was the way the photographers and filmmakers followed us around. The centre stage light was on us the whole time, we were revelling in it, and spouting off at the mouth at the same time. Kanga would be standing there going, 'We're number one now,' and I'd be standing beside him, like the junior partner in crime, going, 'Yeah, that's it Kanga, you tell 'em.' I kind of cringe a little at the memory. We got pretty arrogant with some of our statements, like, basically, the rest of you are just going straight and we're showing you how to ride these waves. We were saying these sorts of things on Hawaiian television. And the same sorts of things were coming out in all the magazines. I earnt two nicknames around this time — one was, the 'Surf Guerilla', because I caught so many waves and dropped in on a fair few people, and the other one was 'Muhammad Bugs'. Talk about fuelling the fire.

It seems incredible in hindsight that I couldn't see the ill will we were generating. I had made some really good friends among the local people and was so caught up in my own glorious world that I couldn't see the writing on the wall. We'd had a couple of little clues, but I still didn't twig. Our house had been broken into and a few things stolen, but I thought it was just random crime. Ian and I were hitchhiking down the Kam Highway after a surf when local heavy 'Fast Eddie' Rothman pulled over and told us to jump in the back of his big pick-up truck. As I jumped in to the back, I saw two snarling pit-bulls in there. But it was too late to back out, we rode all the way to Haleiwa with these two dogs crawling all over us and snarling, and Eddie and his mates laughing their guts out.

I was having such a fantastic time — surfing perfect waves and rubbing shoulders with so many of my heroes. There were great dinners with Jeff Hakman, who seemed to really tune in to the Aussie sense of humour. He was a giant figure and we'd all go out

Bustin' down the door

to dinner with him and pay out on each other, then all go surfing together the next day. All the great Hawaiian surfers were such heroes of mine, it never occurred to me that any of them could be concerned by our presence. I was just stoked to have a rapport and be mixing with guys like Reno Abellira, Eddie and Clyde Aikau and Barry Kanaiapuni.

By late January we were so tuned in, we'd had the 12-day Christmas swell at Pipe, Off The Wall had pumped right through January. We'd been there nearly four months when this beautiful, big, 12 foot, west Pipe swell came through, and Shaun and I had our finest moment at Pipe thus far. I think that day we really dominated the sets and it was clear that Shaun and I were the leaders of the pack. We stamped our presence and justified all the hype that day in two, long sessions. That surfing forms the climax to the movie *Free Ride* and it was classic timing because Bill Delaney needed one clinching moment to make the film, and there it was. Between Bill's land footage and Dan Merkel's incredible water footage, they captured the whole essence of that Hawaiian season for Shaun and I — the backside attack at Pipe.

So I left Hawaii at the end of the '75–76 season with no sense of any animosity towards us. We'd done so much: cleaned up in the contests, monopolised the attention of the world surf media, and charged such a variety of really challenging surf. It was the beginnings of a performance revolution in surfing, and I just expected to return the following year and do it all again.

MARK RICHARDS: 'It was never actually discussed. There was a feeling and a commitment. It was an unspoken thing that we were there to go hard, we wanted to blow people away and we wanted to walk out with big-wave reputations. We didn't care if we walked out or we were carried out. In fact, it was almost better if you were carried out. It was an unspoken pact. We were going to ride big waves like they'd never been ridden before. But I don't think we were trying to outdo each other, we were cheering each other on. That morning that I watched Rabbit out there at Pipe it wasn't like I thought, oh no, now

I've got to go out there. I was watching him, cheering him on ...
It was an unspoken mission, to do shit on big waves that had
never been done before.'

SHAUN TOMSON: 'Twenty years ago I stood on the grass verge
of Ehukai Beach Park with Rabbit Bartholomew, and together
we watched Second Reef Banzai Pipeline in all its glory. I was
19 years old, Rabbit was 20, and with the winter season coming
to a close it was time to think of the future ...

'"So Bugs, what are you going to do with your life?" I asked
him as empty second reef monsters pitched onto coral reef.

'"I'm gonna be a pro surfer mate." It was a revolutionary
thought. To make a living from going surfing. To do what you
really love and get paid for it. Rabbit had total confidence in
his dream. I wasn't totally convinced and was on my way back
to South Africa to complete a law degree. But he got me
thinking. Just maybe it was possible.

'During 1975 I'd won three events and picked up around
$10,000 — a healthy sum 20 years ago. Rabbit and I walked
back to the car, picked up our boards and paddled out
together. Rabbit was my mate and my rival, and he'd just given
me the gift of his fantastic dream. It was a special, defining
moment, a wonderful time gone by when our lives were simple
and our passion pure. Bugs had opened my mind to an option I
hadn't previously considered — Pro Surfer. It had an
interesting, noble sound to it. Maybe it can happen, I thought.
Maybe the dream can come true.'

Bustin' down the door

BETTY: 'I had to represent him for the Caltex Sportsman of the Year. He was up there with Greg Norman and all the top ones. He was nominated twice and each time he was overseas, so I had to go ... But afterwards I was fraternising, it was mostly men, journalists, some fat, old, horrible, unhealthy looking blokes. And I said to them, "Why is it that you people neglect to give the young surfers a good write-up?" And this fellow said, "Oh, you can't compare them with the lifesavers. They're a clean living lot of young fellows." This guy was going on about everything, and he said, "Of course, they've got to be full of drugs to be surfing," and that really got to me. But I thought, I mustn't do any blasting here, I must be really cool and calm. And I said, "Well, I'll tell you something. To me, looking around here, this would be the greatest drug scene I've ever seen." I said, "You've got your hands full of booze and your cigarettes hanging out of your face." ... Needless to say, I was never invited back again and Wayne was never nominated again.'

Rabbit's speech at the Gold Coast Training Association Apprentice of the Year Awards, Jupiters Casino, Gold Coast, Friday, November 10, 1995.

'In 1972 I was a student at Miami High School in Year 12, and I had a bit of a dream. My dream was a thing called professional surfing, and I really believed in it. I was lucky because there were two other people in two other areas of the world — one in South Africa, a young guy at that time called Shaun Tomson, and a young guy from Newcastle, Australia, the great Mark Richards — who also had the same dream ...

'At the end of Year 12 the inevitable question is: What are you going to do with your life? And I'd answer them quite proudly: "I'm going to be a professional surfer." And they'd go, "Yeah, but how are you going to make a crust?" And I'd say, "Well, I'm going to win the World Title." And they'd walk off shaking their heads and go, "Gee, that Rabbit, he's a bit of a worry. I don't know where he's going to head with his life." It was a very unknown field, mainly because it didn't exist. But I believed in it, and me and Shaun and Mark, I guess we set off on a bit of a crusade, in that we believed in our sport, we wanted to lift it up in the public eye, we wanted it to have some respectability and credibility ...

'I remember in early '73 I decided to do something about it, so I put on my best pair of board shorts, and my only clean shirt and I strode confidently into the Commonwealth Bank at Coolangatta to see the manager, to have my five minutes with the manager of the bank. And basically, I said, "Sir, I'm a professional surfer and I need $500 because I've got to be in Hawaii because that's where my future lies." Well, he looked down the end of his glasses at me and said, "You've got to be joking, mate," ... and I walked out of the bank and I didn't get a brass razoo. But at least I knew exactly where I was beginning, and that was nowhere. So I had to go out there and get the odd job and I worked several jobs at the same time, and I got myself there to Hawaii, and Mark Richards got himself there, and Shaun Tomson, we all got there, and so we embarked on our careers.

'Times were kind of tough but at the same time there was a lot of incentive. I don't think there's any greater incentive than arriving in a foreign country with a one-way ticket, with barely enough money to get through a couple of weeks. There's no better incentive to try to succeed and win some prize-money and get yourself back home. I remember very clearly in a supremely grand gesture, I went into the Turtle Bay Hilton, to the all-you-can-eat smorgasbord, with my last ten dollars and I ate up big, and the next day the surf came up big. It was about 25 foot by Hawaiian standards, which is pretty big. And all three of us, Mark Richards, Shaun Tomson and I, we all made the final, and I ended up coming third, and I won something like $1500. To me, I was like a millionaire. I couldn't believe it.

Bustin' down the door

> *'So we returned home, and the right thing to do next was to get fair dinkum and establish a business, and I remember filing my first tax return and I duly put down all my earnings and my expenses and I signed it at the bottom, "Wayne Bartholomew, professional surfer," and about a month later, after the Australian taxation department had processed my return, I received a letter in the mail, and it started out: "Dear Mr Bartholomew, there is no such thing as a professional surfer." Basically, get a real job, mate.'*

THE DEVIL CAME TO COOLANGATTA

While I'd been forging my destiny in Hawaii, things had not been so rosy back home. I returned from that Hawaiian trip to discover that four of my old school friends had overdosed on heroin while I was away — two of them on the same hit. They were so strung out, someone had sold them battery acid and they shot it up. Battery acid, straight in the veins and dead.

I still hear old shopowners talk about the day the devil came to Coolangatta. I know exactly when he came. It was in 1975 and he was standing on the hill at Snapper Rocks, with a big Grim Reaper's overcoat on, calling guys in from the surf with these pockets full of smack. When I came home in '76, heroin really had a grip on the town. If you owned a TV set it wasn't safe. I moved out of town, to a place out the back of Currumbin, and no-one except a couple of close friends knew my address. There was no way I was going to live in that town. I didn't want to have anything to do with it.

An entire generation of healthy, young surfers were cut down by smack — mainly because no-one knew about the effects. We knew if you took too many mushrooms you ended up like one of the zombies we'd seen walking around. We knew if you took acid 300 days in a row that the Summer of Love was never going to finish for you. We knew that pot wasn't that bad — you smoked it and got a bit high but it wasn't going to kill you. But no-one knew what heroin did to you. They'd tried to tell us smoking pot would drive you crazy and we'd seen that wasn't true so there was a lot of scepticism about the official warnings against heroin. And there were a few pied pipers — really well-respected surfers who used huge amounts of smack and kept surfing as well as ever. I remember standing on Kirra Point and watching one of the great surfers of the day absolutely ripping, and guys were standing there, going, 'See, how bad can it be for you? Look, this guy's surfing better than anyone.' The police had cracked down on marijuana. The frequent Gestapo raids had just about wiped out pot — so the climate was perfect for the Grim Reaper.

Crime went through the roof in Coolangatta, businesses moved out of town, and there was hardly anyone surfing. The only surfing partner I had left in '76 was my old mate Mont, we were surfing by ourselves again. I decided for myself that this drug was anti-surf and anti-life. I made my mind up then and there — I know that it's the enemy, that ain't no soft drug. I remember walking up to Point Danger one morning to check out the surf and seeing a dozen of the hottest surfers in town lining up to go into this house and shoot up. All of them became addicts and gave up surfing.

The heavy thing is, surfers have always had such strong constitutions, they became really flippant about the effects of the drug. It became like a competition to see how many times you could OD and come back to life. But the strong lead the weak, and the weak died.

I'd come home and Mont would give me the latest toll. 'Noakesy ODed, and Peter Evans, he's gone,' — and these were incredible guys, good friends. The town was insane. I called it the invasion of the bodysnatchers, because one day you'd see someone and they'd be fine and then the next time you saw them, they'd have beady little eyes, the pinners, and they would kill you for $200. They'd rip your TV off, they'd steal everything in your house, and if you got in their way they'd fucking kill you. It was the scariest town. I went down to the surf shop one day and half of my trophies were there for sale!

Bustin' down the door

The dealers moved in and they were selling the stuff on the beach, virtually calling guys out of the surf. At first they were giving the shit away — but once they had 'em, they had 'em. The second half of the year was the worst, when the northerly winds kicked in and the surf might stay flat for weeks and weeks on end. That's when the smack would really flow, and that was easily the most dangerous time of the year. My whole schedule was based around leaving home in June and coming back in January. I just did not want to be anywhere near that town from July to December.

MONT: 'It was a heavy era. You'd get out of the water and someone would just offer you smack the way someone might offer you a mull today. Someone would say, "Do you want some smack? Here you go." It was almost like they were just giving it to you. And then you had cops coming down and raiding everyone, just jumping in your window, 20 narcs, ladders up on the wall, crowbars at the door. And full beatings. They cleaned out the whole town and they did it with violence.

'I made my mind up once and for all when I ODed. I was just having another hit and didn't even know what happened. I was just lucky there was a guy there and he knew mouth to mouth. Next thing I know they've got me out in the yard walking me round. That was it.

'There were a lot of really big drug runners in town involved in overseas importation. Full-on. They were dealing in pounds and pounds of the shit, and making phenomenal money, then coming into town ... and they had all this money and they were making out like they were giving everything away to all the local crew. But really they were working you because they took something good — a good town, a good surfing town — and turned it into something evil, and because we didn't know any better it was just like we were getting experimented on. The guys that dealt it, they weren't like hard-core surfers. They tried to surf.'

THE AUSTRALIAN CIRCUIT

MP dominated the Australian contest scene from '74 to '76 and that dominance was never more evident than at the '76 Pa Bendall. He virtually had the contest won before a heat had even been surfed. Most of the competitors had moved into the local caravan park and MP arrived, with all eyes on him. He pulled his latest surfboard out of its cover, and it was all over. The 'moon rocket', we dubbed it. It looked liked something from outer space, with six stingers stepped along the tail. Right then and there he freaked everyone out — the competitors, the judges, everyone. I tried to shape my own board too that year, paddled out in my heat and … well, it made a good submarine. It promptly sank to the bottom of the ocean and that was the end of my shaping career.

Early in my pro career I came to prominence as an eater of some ability. I guess it stemmed from the days when we didn't have a lot of food. When I first saw those American smorgasbords I just ate until I couldn't eat any more — because we didn't always know where our next meal was coming from. So I became known as an eater, and an important part of the fledgling Australian pro surfing circuit was the eating tournaments. There was a big eating event at Bells that year, at this health food restaurant called the Summer House. *Tracks* editor Phil Jarratt organised it and had a book going and I did alright for my first start — even though I got disqualified for throwing up. But the big eating event of the year was at the Coke contest. I had a bit of a reputation as an eater but they were getting the big guns out for this one. Gerry Lopez was my manager, and Nat Young was my trainer so I had the right men in my corner. Jarratt was running the book again and all the heavyweight eaters were there — there was Maurice Cole, Kanga Cairns and Midget Farrelly had this big guy entered — all serious eaters. And there was a lot of grandstanding and showmanship going on. As the book went around Midget got up and had a talk about how his guy could eat anyone under the table. Then Lopez got me up and said, 'Look at Rabbit, he's all skin and bone, no chance,' and this was our little bit of hustling and I shot out to eight to one. When I got out to eight to one Nat, and David Elfick from *Tracks* magazine both put 25 bucks on me and I put 20 bucks on myself, and we were the only three people who bet on me.

We each got to choose our meals from the menu and it was simply a matter of whoever ate the greatest weight of food would win. Midget's downfall was that he ordered this big French flambé, and his man was never going to last the distance. Kanga Cairns was never going to make it on steak, you can only eat so many steaks. Maurice went for Mexican food, which was a bad decision. I ordered rice and vegies, and they brought me out this mountain of rice with a few stray pieces of carrot in it. When I'd polished that off I ordered two pounds of grapes, whipped them down, and then ordered bananas, oranges, all this healthy stuff that's quick to digest. Jack McCoy was doing the commentary and I was still chowing in as the others started to collapse in their food. In one hour I ate seven pounds of food, won the contest and broke the bank. Nat and Elfick won 200 bucks each and I won $160 plus the first prize, and that led to my first acceptance speech. I was standing up there going, um, er, and Nat was beside me and he started feeding me lines — 'Unaccustomed as I am to public speaking,' — and he put the words in my mouth and I said word for word what he told me to say. That was the beginning of my public speaking career.

The next day at the Coke Classic everyone was waiting to see if Rabbit could still surf after all that food and I came from like seventh to third place in one surf because of that eating contest. I realised by drawing attention to myself before the event I was not only psyching out some of my opposition, I was also being watched more closely by the judges. It was all part of the proud Australian surfing tradition of pulling radical stunts before a contest. Even if it didn't always work, we were having fun, and creating the legend of Australian surfing.

SHAUN TOMSON: 'Easter at Bell. The only restaurant in town is Jack McCoy's Summerhouse. McCoy is suffering from amnesia and thinks he's an Aussie and I'm hanging there on a regular basis with the late John Pawson (a respected local surfer who drowned in big surf at Bells Beach) and the rest of the surf crew.

'Someone comes up with the idea of an eating contest and the game is on. As far as I remember Rabbit chooses enchiladas, Ian Cairns gets stuck into meat, Maurice Cole is into pasta and Ray Thomas picks vegies. Bets are laid and my money is on Bugs. Even though he's the smallest he has the biggest competitive heart.

'The boys start grinding and when they hit 6 pounds, the wheels start coming off. Maurice is very, very quiet for the first time ever, Kanga nauseously contemplates a rotund future and Ray is still chugging. Bugs starts going green but just keeps powering. At that moment he rushes for the dunny and does a good Aussie spew. Then the true nature of Bugs' competitive persona is revealed. He returns a few pounds lighter after unloading, takes his seat and tries to get back into it and keep going. He gets disqualified — there's a no spewing rule.

'I'm blown away and think, how will it ever be possible to compete against such mindless determination.'

MARK WARREN: 'I remember in the final of the '76 Australian Titles at Point Leo (Victoria) Rabbit screamed he saw a shark. Because he wasn't doing any good he convinced everyone that he'd seen a shark and we had to come in and re-surf it. He was quite adamant that he'd seen a shark, so they re-ran it. He had this real aura about him. As a competitor he really could build a fortress about him that I found quite intimidating ... You'd look at him and try to have a chat and he wouldn't even talk to you, and you'd go, shit he means business here.'

Bustin' down the door

The Coke Surfabout that year was a points-for-manoeuvres system and by the end of the sixth or seventh round MR and I were so far ahead of the field that it was a two-horse race. I drew a heat with five Hawaiians in it — BK, Gerry Lopez, Rory Russell, Michael Ho and Jeff Hakman. BK was sitting out there waiting and waiting for a decent wave and I was the only one who could catch MR. At last, this wave came, it was a heat-winning wave, it was the best wave that I'd seen all day — finally there was a wave that BK liked the look of. He turned around and stroked for it like he was out at Sunset, taking these big, deep, double-armed strokes. I was on the inside, and I started frantically paddling for it. We both took off and I called out, 'Hey, Barry.' He went up and did a little snap, and I went up and did a snap behind him, desperate to rack up my points. He finally flicked off and as I went past him I yelled out in frustration, 'Ah, fuck.' I didn't think too much more about it because it was all in the heat of competition. Later, in the car park at Narrabeen, the results came through and I hadn't caught MR, I'd finished second, but I was still pretty stoked. I'd won three grand, enough to get me back to Hawaii without having to work a part-time job. I was talking to Kanga when he glanced over my shoulder to indicate there was some cause for concern behind me. It was a look I came to know all too well before the year was out, but I wasn't familiar with it then. Next thing I knew BK had me in a headlock and he was saying, 'When you come to Sunset Beach, you tell me to fuck off then.' I instantly dropped to my knees. He was shaping my boards at the time, he was my hero, and I tried to explain how sorry I was and how much respect I had for him, how I didn't say, 'fuck off,' it was just an expression of frustration. He didn't say much, just released his grip and walked away, and even after that I didn't think too much of it. I said to Kanga, 'Gee, that was close,' and never gave it another thought all year.

NUDE SURFING

My growing fame was greatly bolstered by an historic photo spread in *Tracks* magazine. Under editor Phil Jarratt, *Tracks* had earnt a deserved reputation as a truly subversive journal of surfing counter-culture and they were always dreaming up new and outlandish stunts to pull. Jarratt and Paul Neilsen got together and decided they were going to do something crazy — and they decided I was going to be the bunny. We drove down the coast, found an isolated stretch of beach and performed the first nude surfing photo shoot ever. I ended up on the cover doing a forehand off the top that only just preserved my modesty, but there were several pages of fairly revealing action shots inside. This was pretty radical stuff for 1976 and we were prepared to milk the resultant publicity for all it was worth.

A mate from the Gold Coast, Dave Cross, appointed himself my manager and the first-ever in-store promotion and autograph signing was organised in this big surf shop in Brisbane to coincide with the release of the magazine. But none of us were prepared for the reaction it caused. They were lining up down Queen Street and I spent the day signing these posters of myself surfing nude. They advertised it over the top radio station at the time, 4IP, and hundreds of people turned up. It was all time. There had never been anything like it in surfing before and I was pretty overwhelmed by the spectacle of all these teenage girls wanting me to sign nude photos of myself. I could sense things could get a little outrageous in the fallout to this thing, so I adopted the old strategy of jumping on a plane and staying away until the storm died down.

I spent a few months in California prior to the Hawaiian season. We did a run down to Mexico to finish filming for the movie *Free Ride* and got hit by a hurricane, nearly got killed, and got completely skunked for surf. But in California I was a superstar, being lauded and given the full treatment everywhere I went, living the life.

TV network CBS was staging this series of sporting events called the 'Challenge of the Sexes', pitting top male and female athletes against each other. I was invited to take part against the women's world champ, Margo Oberg, but with this ridiculous handicap system. It was something like a 10-point handicap over the best three waves. The winner was going to get US$2500 plus $1000 just for turning up and we were accommodated in the best hotel in town. I thought they were trying to set me up to have this woman beat me and I put everything I had into it. I really went berko.

Bustin' down the door

I think I even hassled her. It was perfect Trestles, just made for my surfing, and I came in and knew I'd beaten her by a huge margin. There were three judges, two men and a woman. The female judge told me, 'That was the most fantastic hotdog display we've ever seen.'

'How'd I go?' I asked.

'Mmmm, on my sheet you got second,' she replied. But the other two had me first so I won it. I won US $3500 for half an hour of surfing. It was all happening.

It was amid this mood of adoration that I was asked to write a piece for US *Surfer* magazine, about myself and the new crew of surfers coming to prominence. In hindsight, the name alone — 'Bustin' Down The Door' — got me into hot water before anyone even read the story, but in fact the article was totally respectful to Hawaii and Hawaiian surfing from start to finish. However, I did document in quite glowing terms the great surfing feats of myself, Kanga, MR and Shaun, and it was all adding fuel to the fire. But I was still happily ensconced in my bubble and I turned in my article and jetted off to Hawaii to meet my destiny.

EXTRACT FROM 'BUSTIN' DOWN THE DOOR', US *SURFER* MAGAZINE 1976:

'The fact is that when you are a young, emerging rookie from Australia or Africa, you not only have to come through the backdoor to get invitations to the pro meets, but you have to bust the door down before they hear you knockin'. I mean, it was left up to people who weren't even into surfing to say who was hot, and who was not. Our situation was that we had read about and seen photos and movies of all the established stars, for years and years, and then we'd travel to Hawaii as total anonymities, or nobodies, and literally cat shit each session, each day, each season. The pro contests were already full of super-hot surfers, and there was already

a giant queue waiting to get in, so our only alternative
was to surf each big-wave session with total abandon ...

'There was no real need to have young blood in the circuit
because the old guys were still red-hot and to put some
unknown Aussie kid in the lineup meant that some guy who'd
put in maybe eight or ten seasons had to be put out, and
understandably no-one was keen for this to happen, except
us. And so to gain both media and competitive recognition,
we had to paddle out on the gnarliest days at Pipeline and
Sunset, and literally attempt impossible manoeuvres. This
situation set the stage for the introduction of the hard
rock-ripping, full-tilt boogie band, which in true "Story-of-
Pop" fashion, has for its first time climbed to the top of the
hit parade, and now band members such as Shaun, Kanga, and
Mark Richards are top-billed features at many inside-out,
upside-down jam sessions.

'For sure, Gerry and Rory still provide the most in-tune
sessions at Pipeline, and BK, Hakman and Reno are always the
showstoppers at Sunset, and their past notoriety is directly
responsible for the emergence of the new boys, but this new
band is developing the ability of versatility, in that they
are displaying the same explosive intensity at 12-foot
Pipeline and Sunset as they do at six foot V-land and Off The
Wall. The already established surfers like BK and Hawk were
into such heavy directions on our arrival that we were forced
to delve into certain subtleties which they found
unnecessary in their flights to the heights. Some people are
either introducing original theatrical moves, or adding
flash to already established body English cliches, although

Bustin' down the door

some of Owl's and Fitzgerald's are patented, and increasing degrees of stylish statements, even the odd Jagger or Bowie oriented moves are being witnessed on both large and small waves.'

Letter to Betty, from Mexico, September, 1976.

'We were caught right in the middle of the most intense hurricane to hit Mexico this decade. I don't know if you heard about it but the death toll reached well over 1000. We were positioned on a cliff which overlooks the surf spot called Rattlesnakes, and as the wind grew wilder we drove into the fishing village to see what was happening because the only radio was in town and we witnessed 44 gallon drums being thrown around like soft drink cans and the rooves of some of the more flimsy buildings beginning to lift off so we moved back to the cliff where we made our stand. The wind ranged between 95 and 110 mph and buffeted us for at least 12 hours and there was a really wild dust storm preceding the rain. I could go into other incidents involving scorpions and rattlesnakes but I'll just say that Mexico has definitely left its mark in my memory banks.'

HAWAII 1976-77

I flew into Hawaii on October 1 and for some reason, the rest of the Australians didn't arrive until November 1. Maybe they'd heard something on the grapevine. Jack Shipley, from Lightning Bolt Surfboards, picked me up from the airport and straightaway he was trying to tell me something, but I still didn't get the message. He was saying, 'Oh, I don't know if you'll be getting that many boards this year.' That was another one of our crimes in the magazines — we'd bragged about how we were getting 33 free boards a year from

Lightning Bolt. No-one was getting that many free boards then, so that upset the locals. I was just like, 'Yeah, no worries Jack, we'll give a few back or whatever,' but there was a weird vibe.

I spotted Owl Chapman and he called out to me, 'You don't know what's coming down man.' I remember saying to myself, fucking Owl, he's still tripping out. Owl was almost screaming, 'You don't know what's coming down. It's all coming down,' and I called back, 'Yeah, it's all coming down.' I ran into Ken Bradshaw, a big-wave rider who'd moved to Hawaii from Texas, who'd never liked me, and he started giving me a really hard time, but I still thought nothing of it.

Two days after my arrival, I paddled out at Sunset and saw BK out there, and I still thought, 'Unreal, there's BK, there's my man.' I paddled over and asked if he'd shape me a board and he just looked at me and said, 'Get Geoff McCoy to shape you a board.' I thought, ah, he's still a little mad at me. I'll soften him up with a couple of jokes later on and everything will be sweet. Then the water started clearing, guys just started paddling in. Unreal, I thought, I've absolutely killed it here, timed it to perfection, I've got Sunset Point all to myself. That's when I looked in and saw about 30 Hawaiians lined up on the beach in front of this house, and I wondered to myself, what's going on here? I could see they were pulling these big old boards out from under the house, two guys started paddling out from one direction, then one other guy paddled out from another direction — I could see the whites of their eyes as they started converging towards me. Then, in one terrifying instant, the penny finally dropped: 'Oh fuck, they're coming for me.' I had pretty long hair at the time and this guy grabbed me by the back of the hair and said, 'Are you Rabbit Bartholomew?' I actually hesitated, and thought about saying, er, no I'm not, never heard of the guy. But it was too late for any amount of fast talking. I got totally pounded. I was held under water, pounded round the back of the head, then pulled up and pounded in the face. They knocked all my teeth out and just flattened my nose, I had cuts all over my eyes and lips. I finally blacked out and that's when one of them gave me a giant backhander and brought me round and ordered, 'Swim to the beach,' and I just said, 'Ah, that sounds like a good idea.'

Bustin' down the door

I don't know what happened to Captain Cook but the scene that confronted me on the beach always reminds me of Captain Cook, but Captain Cook with tourist buses. There were all these Hawaiians, still standing in a line, and there were the three guys who got me standing in front of them, and there was my board at their feet. I was totally dazed, and then these tourist buses pulled up. Tourists started shooting snapshots and the Hawaiians didn't move. It was like a ritual of manhood, a full public display of anger. I had no idea of the history and heritage of Hawaii and how everyone — from the early traders, to the missionaries, to the modern-day real estate developers — had always come and taken from them. But I must have appeared as the absolute enemy trying to steal the last vestige of their heritage — surfing. I didn't know any of this at the time — I was just a naive kid. I looked at them, looked at my board, and I just turned around and walked along the beach towards Rocky Point. I was waiting for them to come for me, but something told me, don't run, just don't run. So I walked and walked, not daring to look back.

As I approached Rocky Point, I heard someone calling my name from up amongst the houses, and there was Owl Chapman, lying in his hammock. His prophecy had proved correct — it was all coming down, and it wasn't over by a long shot. He saw the blood and he invited me into the house, put a steak on my face, and told me the whole story. 'Hey man, when I was 20, I came over here and said, "I'm the best goddam big-wave rider the world has ever seen," and they beat the shit out of me,' Owl said, 'but you guys, five of you done it.' And he told me a bit of Hawaiian history and I began to understand.

I was only staying a couple of houses away and I made my way home as night fell. Some time during the night Ken Bradshaw came over with my board and said, 'I want you to know that I had nothing to do with this,' which was kind of weird. I got up the next day and slowly it became apparent that things were only just starting to boil. It wasn't going to be as easy as copping a thrashing and all would be forgotten. I was living with this South African guy and he told me, 'Look Bugs, I feel sorry for you, it's really fucked what they're doing to you, it's just really heavy shit, but can you move out straightaway? Otherwise they're going to burn the house down tonight.' So I said, 'Yeah, I'll move out now,' and I got my bag, left my boards there, and I pitched camp in the foreshore bushes in front of a little surf spot called Kammieland. There was nowhere else for me to go.

It's amazing I didn't come out of this completely and utterly paranoid. It took a few years to get over this, it really affected me for a long time. My surfing suffered for a few years, I felt it made me a little bit hesitant, and a bit paranoid on land. After this glorious roll I'd been on, the whole experience just totally took the wind out of my sails. I'd hang in these bushes all day long, hiding out and watching. I didn't know if they were searching for me. I didn't know what the fuck was going on. Kammies Market was where all the heavies would meet, I'd watch them from the bushes and when I saw a clearing I'd make a dash over to the shop with an old floppy hat on, and buy some food. One time I'd made a run to the shop and as I came out this carload of Hawaiians pulled up. They were looking at me and I could read their lips as they talked to each other. 'There's that Rabbit,' someone said. 'I'm going to kick his fucking ass,' someone else said. I didn't even look for traffic, I was gone. I ran all over the neighbourhood until I was sure I'd lost them, then snuck back into my hideout. I figured if they found my spot it was all over for me.

I was pretty beat up and most of my teeth were gone, but a couple were trying to hang in there. When I ate I had to try to hold my front teeth in with my tongue. It was ridiculous. I must have been a sorry sight. For some reason I never considered just getting on a plane home. I knew that this was the biggest crossroads of my life and if I disappeared off the North Shore it would be very hard to come back, ever. After everything we'd done there was no way I could go, oh well, that's over, I'll go home and work in the pub again. I knew I had to stick it out and ride through this storm. The airport was always there, but it wasn't an option this time. I *still* didn't realise things were getting heavier and heavier.

Finally, some of the other Australians turned up, they took me out to the Kui Lima Estate, the quite flash hotel at the eastern end of

Bustin' down the door

the North Shore (home of the $10 all-you-can-eat smorgasbord). This became our sanctuary, surrounded by enormous gardens, a golf course, and security guards. I was so relieved to move in there.

I rang up surfboard shaper, Tom Parrish, to see if I could get any boards and he said, 'Sorry Bugs, no-one's allowed to make you a surfboard on the North Shore. They're going to burn factories down.' This one guy came out of the blue and befriended us: 'Look, I'll glass your boards for you if someone will shape them.' So secretly Tom Parrish made us a couple of boards, with no writing or identifying marks on them, and this guy glassed them up for us, in the knowledge that his time in Hawaii was over if he got caught. So there was some underground support, but the word was filtering around the Island and heavier and heavier elements were getting involved.

One night a muffled phone call came through to our condo and a mysterious voice warned me, 'Don't go to the Proud Peacock this Thursday.' I thanked him very much and assured him I wouldn't. Thursday was a big night at the Peacock, the restaurant at Waimea Falls, and a bit of a tradition for me. I stayed away, but some hapless Australian film director on holidays, who'd never surfed in his life but bore a passing resemblance to me, was found face down in a glass ashtray and a pool of blood. He was taken to hospital with a huge gash in his face.

Kanga Cairns turned up and they were after him too. Mark Warren and MR had to go on record as saying they disowned me, or they weren't allowed on the North Shore. Mark Warren came out with this quote: 'Rabbit's a monster, he deserves everything he gets.' It took me a long time to forgive him — that was really heavy for me, after all the camaraderie between us. But it became dangerous just to be an Australian on the North Shore. This is when we started doing shifts with tennis rackets, standing guard in case they came for us during the night, huddled in this little condominium. We started surfing Kui Lima Point, a fairly soft wave right in front of the hotel, and somehow some locals heard about it and came out there after us. I was sitting under this tree on the beach and Kanga was out in the surf waving at me furiously. I looked around and saw this mob heading towards us. I had to run over lava rock and cut my feet to ribbons, then cut across the golf course back to our condo to lose them. Nowhere was safe. It was like they were tracking our every move.

A few days later, there was a big rap on the door of the condo, and we tentatively opened it a few inches, Kanga standing behind me, tennis racket at the ready. It was Eddie Aikau, the legendary big-wave rider and one of the most respected surfers in the Islands. He came in, sat down, and said, 'I don't dig what you've done. I'm a proud Hawaiian, but it's gone too far. My family, we're trying to intervene, but we don't know if we can. It's out of control. There's contracts on your lives. You either go home or stay put and don't move until I come back.'

We didn't need convincing. We had visions of snipers taking pot shots from the Kam Highway. For three days we sat in that condo, not daring to leave. Finally, Eddie came by again and said, 'The family's cooled things off a bit, pending the outcome of this trial.' He was serious. We were to be tried for crimes against the Hawaiian people. They booked a conference room at the hotel, came and got us, and took us in to face the court. Eddie was up the front, he made MR come up and chair the meeting with him. All the heavies were there, they read out some charges, and presented evidence. They even had people in Australia sending newspaper and magazine articles that incriminated us further. Somehow they'd gotten hold of a personal letter I'd written to PT from America, saying, 'We're hot as shit over here, Australians are the biggest thing in surfing, they're looking to us for inspiration.' That nearly had me convicted then and there.

CLYDE AIKAU: 'I was in school then. I was all over Waikiki, chasing all the haole girls, partying. All I know is that Eddie and this family have always tried to help out everybody on the North Shore. We have a saying in Hawaii, "Ho'o anu nui" which means gathering all different people together who are having a problem and you sit down and solve the problem so that we can all go on with our lives happily. With Rab, it was basically the same thing. In those years those guys came over here from Australia, they were young and spunky and I think the thing that really hurt a lot of Hawaiians was not exactly what they did when they came here. When they came out to the North Shore they were pretty cool guys. If they were in the best part of the waves, we'd let them go. The problems were in the magazines, when he would give interviews and he would say something about the North Shore or the Hawaiians and then some of the Hawaiians would say, "Wait until you come next season." I guess it was a media thing. It was just that this family has always tried to help out. And Eddie got along with them, they were always nice to Eddie. The Hawaiians have always been proud people, they don't like people saying bad things about us ... The main thing was we didn't want to see everybody fighting around the surf so we did what we could.'

At the end of this trial, the verdict was that Kanga and I could surf in the contests. But I was pretty keen to know if we were allowed back on the North Shore to surf and prepare for the events. The response to that was, 'Well, yeah, sort of. You can go back on to the North Shore and train. We're going to call the dogs off, but just be prepared. There will be some random violence. We can't stop individuals coming out of the woodwork and punching you out.' And that was really all we could be guaranteed.

For me to say I wasn't paranoid in some way would be a lie. I was scared. I still clearly remember going back to Sunset and gingerly walking down that beach to the scene of my public flogging. To walk back down that beach and surf 10 foot Sunset — it was nerve-racking. I really couldn't concentrate on surfing. I mean, tennis and Kui Lima Point ain't no preparation for the Smirnoff and the Duke, where they're going to wait for 15 to 18 foot radical Sunset.

Kanga really bounced back a hell of a lot better than me, but he's got a lot thicker skin. He had arrived there a month after me, and he was a couple of years older, he kind of thrived on the situation. The whole experience really spelt the end of our partnership. We sort of hung together for the rest of that season, but we were heading in different directions. He was already planning the formation of the first professional surfing team, the Bronzed Aussies, and I decided to go my own way. I wanted to repair my relations with the Hawaiians, to get back to the fun times when I used to have dinner with the Ho family and go surfing with all the hot, young local guys like Buttons, Bertleman and Mark Liddel. I just longed for those days and realised how much I'd taken for granted the hospitality I'd been shown.

To do this I felt I really had to distance myself from Kanga. I'd been standing next to Kanga as a junior partner in crime — he'd been saying, 'We're going to show you all how to surf,' and I was quite happy to go along with that because I still thought, naively, that it was all fun and games. Sledging was a new thing in sport in the 1970s, in men's tennis and heavyweight boxing, and I just thought that was what you did. Muhammad Ali was writing off Joe Frazier before the Thriller in Manila. 'I'm going to beat up the Gorilla in the Thriller in Manila,' he told the world. Anyone who could deride their opponent like that and pull it off, I thought that was the ultimate in sports psychology.

Kanga still managed to do well in the contests that year but my confidence had really been shaken. I went out in the Duke contest at big Sunset and just got thrashed. I took off on this huge west peak and I made the drop, but because I hadn't really done my time out there, I came skittering off the bottom and I never really got a solid edge in. This rearing peak just doubled up and kept coming through to the inside section. It didn't back off from the outside to the inside, it was one of those west swells that just connected. The wave barrelled over me and because I never really got my edge in properly I went down the face belly first and just got slammed by the lip. It was one of the worst thrashings I have ever had. It was as if the ocean had to administer a thrashing of its own for my misdeeds.

MP turned up briefly in Hawaii that year, and he was already kind of invisible. But just to add to my troubles, I got to the semi-finals of the Smirnoff and MP was in the same semi. We made a pact on the beach not to work each other over but, predictably enough, on the first wave we faded each other, and both ate it. MP beat me in a swimming race to where my board was floating in the channel, paddled my board into the beach where his board was, left my board on the beach and paddled his board back out. Unbelievable. Real 'Spy vs Spy' stuff. But I can't say I wouldn't have done the same. I really can't.

The other bodyblow waiting for me when I came out of my exile at the Kui Lima was the fact that pro surfing's first governing body had been formed and the first world champion had been decided retrospectively in my absence. Two Hawaiian contest organisers, Fred Hemmings and Randy Rarick, had formed International Professional Surfing (IPS) to administer a world circuit. With a fair bit of input from PT and his meticulous book keeping, they'd gone back over the major contests of 1976 and calculated points and ratings and, lo and behold, PT was announced the inaugural IPS world champion. There's a pretty classic story about PT doing a media interview and photo shoot at one of the outrigger canoe clubs in Waikiki and, when it was realised he didn't even have a trophy, they discretely borrowed a rowing cup from the trophy cabinet. PT turned the inscription away from the camera and proudly posed for photos cradling the cup. I doubt if he's even got a trophy — or anything — to commemorate that first World Title to this day.

While I was holed-up in the Kui Lima, the surfing world had changed dramatically. Aside from the IPS being formed and PT becoming world champ, this South African guy who I'd been living with had gone out and got a footwear company, Beachcomber Bills, to sponsor a circuit. The Beachcomber Bill's Grand Prix was already laid out for 1977.

It was a real blow to Kanga too, because he'd been anticipating all these events and had set his heart on winning the first World Title, but he finished second to PT. He made the best of it, however, by teaming up with PT and forming the Bronzed Aussies, so he was still able to stand alongside PT and declare, 'We're number one.' In a way, PT really deserved that first World Title, because his vision for professional surfing was so strong, in some ways even stronger than mine, he had almost willed it into existence.

The heaviest thing for me was when the invitations to the Pipeline Masters went out. Because I hadn't done the whole circuit, I wasn't in the top 16 of these new ratings, so I didn't get an invite. After leading the backside attack at Pipe in '74 and '75, when I came down the beach to go in the Pipe Masters in '76, Randy Rarick looked at this new ratings list and said, 'Um, you're not in the top 16. You don't get a start.' I had still never been in the Pipe Masters. All my sparring partners were in the Pipe Masters — MR, Shaun, Kanga, PT, the whole blooming lot of them — more foreigners than had ever been in the event before. That was the one of the biggest frustrations of my life. I'd led the charge at Pipe the year before for four months straight along with Shaun Tomson and pushed everyone.

When you go back and look at those first ratings from '76, I'm nowhere. So in the course of my Hawaiian season, I'd been beat up, banished from the North Shore, I didn't make the top 16, and I didn't have a high seeding for '77. It was devastating — my dream was finally being realised and I wasn't invited. Meanwhile, PT was world champion, he'd been able to surf the whole North Shore season, Kanga had finished second, they'd formed the Bronzed Aussies, and were on their way to superstardom. I was the black sheep left out in the cold.

The only saving grace for me was Peter Drouyn's return to the North Shore. Peter Drouyn arrived on the North Shore in '76 for a comeback. He was staying at Randy Rarick's house when I was already in hiding at the Kui Lima. Drouyn came out one night to see me, and decided the only way to fix my paranoia was to get me drunk. So he dragged me to the hotel bar and bought me White Russians all night. At this time I didn't even drink. And there I was, holding up the bar, drinking White Russians, while Drouyn tried to convince me that there was nothing going on and I was imagining the whole thing. 'It's just like old times,' he said, not having been to Hawaii for a few years. 'It's so much like the old days,' he said, 'I had a hassle with some guy and I told him to paddle in and we went in to the beach and duked it out like the old days.' This had happened

Bustin' down the door

down at Laniakea, not at Sunset. If it had happened at Sunset he probably would have got killed. But he was convinced. 'Bugs,' he said, 'we duked it out, shook hands and went surfing.' He almost had me convinced. That same night I actually met my future wife Toni. It was just a conversation in a bar, but we got on fabulously and I told her I'd meet up with her somewhere down the line. 'I'm not really supposed to be on the North Shore. I'm in hiding,' I explained. And somehow we did meet up again. When I was allowed back on the North Shore I managed to find her and I remember talking to her, trying to hold my teeth in with my tongue.

Drouyn kept coming out to the Kui Lima every few days, and I kept trying to tell him, 'This is for real, I'm scared for my life.' One night I actually got up all my dutch courage and went, 'Yeah, I'm going back to the North Shore,' and the next morning I woke up and just went, 'I'm not going back out there, I know what's going on.' Finally, Drouyn came to the Kui Lima one night, and he was looking over his shoulder, totally paranoid. 'I went home and they've axed me boards,' he said, 'there were axe marks and knife marks and they've dragged 'em out in the alley.' Now I was the one trying to comfort him. 'It's okay Peter, you'll be okay. You're down there staying with Randy, you're going to be okay,' I told him. He went home that night, walked up the driveway to Randy Rarick's house, heard a rustle in the bushes, and he was so paranoid he turned around and punched out a telegraph pole. Broke his wrist. He went inside, packed his bags, drove straight to the airport, got on a plane, and flew home. I heard the next day, 'Drouyn's gone, he's back in Australia.'

About two weeks later, there was a launch for the Beachcomber Bill's Grand Prix — a big lavish party on the North Shore. And suddenly, out of nowhere, Peter Drouyn marched into the place, marched through the crowd and marched on to the stage and announced, 'Everybody, I'm here to tell you about a revolution. I'm here to tell you about the future. It's called professional surfing. I'm here to announce that in March 1977 man-on-man surfing is going to happen at Burleigh Heads, Australia.' And there was the most uplifting feeling in that room that night. It really felt like Drouyn was our saviour. He had gone home, invented man-on-man surfing, found a big corporate sponsor in Stubbies, marched into their Brisbane boardroom and convinced them to put up the money, and triumphantly returned to the North Shore to the launch of the new circuit, at the last big gathering of the season. It was inspired. And we all felt so buoyed. We'd been under siege that year on the North Shore, but at the end of the season we were coming home to the biggest event in pro surfing history, and they would all be coming over to our shores. And Drouyn was up there, like Moses handing down the ten commandments. 'There's another front for professional surfing. It's called Burleigh Heads and it's called man-on-man surfing, and I want to see blood in the water. This is gladiators.'

PETER DROUYN: 'I know that deep down he was probably pretty fearful but, it's like any warrior worth his salt, and Bugs was a true warrior, unless I was talking to him in hospital I wasn't altogether that concerned for his safety because he could obviously handle himself. He was obviously holding his end up. I also knew once an Hawaiian hits you for any reason, they don't hit you again normally. Once you've proved you can take it, and I think that what I'm saying was proven afterwards, that he gained respect out of all that. I know he did, by actually sticking up for himself, and by the time I got there he'd done all the sticking up for himself. So I thought it was very similar to my initiation into the Hawaiian scene, particularly Makaha, through a couple of fisticuffs and sticking up for myself and then you're one of the team.'

Bustin' down the door

the birth of pro surfing

W hen I came home to Australia, my Hawaiian ordeal was big news. Little things happen over in Hawaii and somehow they get back here and get blown out of proportion, but this was a big thing. It had been on the radio news and in the papers. My family didn't have a telephone so I hadn't spoken to them, but they'd heard all this, and were starting to wonder if I'd make it home alive.

I was trying to play it down, going, no, no, no, nothing much happened. There were a lot of gnarly old characters around Coolangatta, coming up to me and saying, 'So, they mistreated you Bugs, those boys really did you in, ay? Well, the old gang's here boy — as soon as you snap your fingers, we'll go.' I had to really go, hang on here, this is not my vision, this is not what I'm about. 'This is not a tit-for-tat thing,' I told them. I could have made a war out of it, but I wanted professional surfing to prosper and I wanted the Hawaiians welcome out here, and I wanted to go back to Hawaii and make my peace with the Hawaiians.

And they did come out here for that first Stubbies. The Aikau brothers, Barry Kanaiapuni, they all came. And they came, I think, wondering what was going to happen, with a bit of apprehension. They knew that surfing was big in Australia and that we were idolised, and they wondered if there was going to be a backlash, but I quelled it. I had to go round and pull guys up and tell them to back off.

THE FIRST PRO TOUR

In the lead-up to that first Stubbies I had a personal tragedy to deal with. My old surfing mate, Bucky Perriot, crashed his fishing boat into the rock groyne at Duranbah and went into a coma. This was unfathomable for such a great waterman. He was cleaning fish and thought his mate was steering, but his mate was doing something else and thought Bucky was steering.

Bucky had the respect of all the hard-core old fishermen round here. He was into fishing, diving, surfing — anything to do with the ocean. He knew as many reefs out there as my old man. And if something went wrong with any of the fishing boats, Bucky would just dive over the side and fix it for them.

He started surfing late but just picked it up instantly. Within six months of starting he had mastered the roundhouse cutback.

I was surfing Duranbah on that morning in February '77 when his trawler came in through the Tweed River mouth. They went up onto the Duranbah wall and Bucky got thrown out of the boat and landed on the rocks head first. He was in a coma for about six years before he died.

Mont used to go into the hospital and sit with him, tell him how perfect Kirra was, to try to snap him out. Mont really nursed him for years. He dedicated years of his life, attempting to bring Bucky back. I couldn't handle it. I couldn't keep going in there and doing it. Mont would drag me to the hospital, sit me down and say, 'You've got to tell him how perfect it is, how he's missing it, how good you're going,' and I'd sit there and talk to him. It was gut wrenching.

THE FIRST STUBBIES

In the weeks leading up to the Stubbies I was just stoked to be home. Toni, the lady I met in Hawaii, had come back to Australia with me and we moved into this fantastic house right on the beach at Bilinga. I spent my time preparing for the Stubbies and competing in a few minor events — I wanted to be ready for the showdown I was expecting with my old foe MP at the Stubbies.

This was really the last year I went in anything other than the pro tour events. I went in the first round of the Queensland Titles, at North Stradbroke Island, and blitzed it — but this was a total juncture in my career. Here I was still going in the Queensland Titles and a month later international pro surfing was going to kick off in such a big way with the Stubbies that I would walk away from those Queensland Titles forever.

After the trauma of the Hawaiian season, I was just totally stoked to have a major professional event on my home turf at one of my favourite waves. As far as I was concerned, there was only one other person in that event, only one guy who could beat me — MP. We went through like a heavyweight boxing psych out for months leading up to that event.

First there was the Pa Bendall Memorial up on the Sunshine Coast. We'd both won it before, and I expected to meet him in the final. I won every heat I went in, and he won some heats, but he was really just doing enough to get through. We both made the final and I'd never felt more ready for him. I even had the red singlet for the final, MP's superstitious favourite … but he didn't show.

Then we went down to Burleigh for the Chris Doulas Memorial, two weeks before the Stubbies. Chris Doulas was a well-known surfer, originally from Manly in Sydney, who lived in Surfers Paradise and had ODed on heroin. It was really good Burleigh and MP and I both made the final, along with top local guys Craig Walgers and Ross Phillips. Once again, MP didn't show for the final and again I went on and won it. For some reason, MP didn't want us surfing against each other until the Stubbies.

Drouyn had pulled off an amazing coup with that first Stubbies. He went to Brisbane to a company called Efco and sold them surfing. Here was a top-level competitive surfer, who not only invented a revolutionary contest format that has not been bettered to this day, but also went out and convinced a major sponsor to back it. His is one of the single greatest contributions to the evolution of professional surfing ever, yet surfing history has all but ignored his achievements.

Prior to this, heats contained four, six, eight, up to 15 surfers at a time — confusing judges and spectators alike. Man-on-man was cleaner, simpler and made for a more exciting, head-to-head battle.

The draw for the Stubbies was announced amid great anticipation and ceremony and it looked like MP and I were going to meet in the semi-finals — if we both made it that far. There were some incredible surfers in that event — one of the heaviest international fields ever assembled in Australia at that time — but all the way through I was anticipating that clash with MP.

The psych up was unbelievable because he and I had been at battle stations for years, and everyone in town knew it. There was a real buzz about all these international surfers coming to the Gold Coast for the first time, but everyone wanted to see the High Noon showdown between Bugs and MP.

My first heat in the Stubbies was against an American, Randy Laine, and I won comfortably. Then I drew, of all people, Barry Kanaiapuni. It was perfect five foot Burleigh and Barry surfed really well. He really gave me a run. People were going, 'Ah, he can only surf 10 foot Sunset,' but at five foot Burleigh he surfed brilliantly, with a lot of down-the-line-speed and style. I had to surf

Bustin' down the door

really hard to beat him. In the quarter-finals I was up against PT, and I wasn't going to let him deny me my showdown with MP. I beat PT on pure tube-riding. And on that final morning of the Stubbies, the Sunday morning, you couldn't have asked for a better scenario. Perfect Burleigh for the semi-finals, MP and I in one semi-final, and MR and Shaun Tomson in the other.

The semi-final between MP and I was one of the all-time heats of man-on-man surfing. We both got numerous perfect 10s, and we outstripped the other semi and the final by a mile. That was virtually the final right there — I had no doubt that whoever won our semi-final would win the contest. My performance in that semi would have won the final. We really pushed each other to the limit.

I rode 10 waves and didn't fall, getting plenty of barrels and some big moves on the face. MP rode 10 waves and fell on three but he was pushing it and got deeper than me on a few; he fell because he was too deep and was really going for it. The semi ended with this incredible climax. As the final seconds ticked away, MP got a good set wave and a long barrel, and I got the wave behind it, which was even more perfect, and got a full-on, hands-behind-the-back barrel right across Burleigh. Just as I came out and straightened out the hooter went.

Under Drouyn's system each judge awarded you a score out of 10 for the whole heat. You were allowed to ride a maximum of 10 waves, so 10 perfect rides would give you a perfect score of 10. One of the judges, Randy Rarick from Hawaii, gave me 10 out of 10. He said I gave a perfect surfing performance. One of the other judges gave MP a 10. It came down to averaging out 9.5s and 9s. It was heavy because at that point I surfed for Darby surfboards and Geoff Darby was a judge — he gave it to MP by 1.5. On the master sheet we actually tied but his 1.5 difference gave it to MP. I ended my sponsorship with Darby Surfboards that day. He was in a hell of a spot because he had his sponsored guy to judge, but at the same time he loved MP. He didn't want to appear biased in my favour but even years later he admitted that he did over-compensate.

The MR and Shaun semi-final was pretty good but it wasn't as good as ours. MR narrowly defeated Shaun to go into the final against MP. MP then went on to beat MR handsomely in the final, the tide had gone out and he really did some tube-riding. His confidence was supreme. The Great MP ensured his all-time legend status by coming out of his hazy shadow world and taking on the new breed of surf stars on the eve of the big-money era of pro surfing. It was his last hurrah — as if to say, I could beat you guys if I wanted to, but I can't be bothered. I'm not interested in playing this respectable, mainstream sports star game, and I'm out of here.

PETER DROUYN: 'The big focus seemed to be on Rabbit and MP. That seemed to be the really big focus and, you know, sure, MP was starting to show the shell-shocked look and didn't want to talk to anyone ... the nervy, twitchy look, sort of trying to remain stable through a pretty stressful situation. And Bugs in his own way had that evaporated look, you know, withdrawing all the nerves into his toenail, forcefully, and putting on a brave face, you know, a wry cracked smile. Showing the determination more than, say, MP would show determination. Rabbit shows that look of fierce determination probably without him even knowing it ... They went helter skelter from go to whoa, there was no easing up on the power, the energy. Probably more so than any heat in the whole contest, they espoused the man-on-man tradition — well, they probably created it right there ... I remember too, every manoeuvre was done precisely, there were no half manoeuvres in that heat. They were all done carefully, with precision, timing, they were done deliberately and to me that's the trademark of man-on-man, when they're done precisely for effect on the audience. And I think that's when we saw some of the incredible advantages of man-on-man, when they were doing these deliberate manoeuvres ... it was like manoeuvre for manoeuvre, function for function. Right there I knew it had worked, right through that heat I knew man-on-man had done it.'

Bustin' down the door

We didn't see much of MP after that, except for the occasional, spectacular appearance at Kirra when it was firing, and at the Bamboo Flute — a health food restaurant on top of Duranbah Hill. The Bamboo Flute was run by the Hare Krishnas who, at that time, were just a bunch of well-known local surfers like Brian Cooney and John Mantle, who had turned to Krishna. Or they were the Pigabeen Valley gold top mushroom connection, the fallout from the Summer of Love, who wound up finding Krishna.

We ate up there all the time. It was the best feed in town. You could eat your brains out for about five bucks. Tuesday nights they had the free Hare Krishna feast, which was unbelievable. We'd just wail on it. But of course they expected you to hang around afterwards and do a few chants. We'd just eat the food and at the end of it, we'd just go, 'Yeah, it's time for the chants, check ya.'

MP would go in there every night and so would I. It was weird. We had the fiercest rivalry in the surf, but at night we'd go to this place and they'd play really peaceful music, exuding calm and tranquillity. It was a pretty awesome atmosphere. This went on for years. MP would sit there with his hand over his face, eating his food, and never say a word. I wasn't about to let my guard down either, so for years we'd eat at the same place every night and never speak a word to each other.

I'd learnt that MP either got completely on top of you or you stood up to him, and I decided on the latter option. If he called me a kook, I called him a kook. We hated each other's guts at that point, but I still really respected him, and if he were to have offered a sign of peace I would have taken it. But I'd been burnt by him so many times, when he'd offer the olive branch before a heat then just go out and work me. And I was thinking about the world by this stage, I knew that I could perform on an international level and he couldn't it. It was advantage Bugs. He'd made me stronger —

between the Hawaiians and MP, I was a product of the school of hard knocks. MP couldn't handle travel. He was outrageously eccentric. His mum later revealed that he was suffering from paranoid schizophrenia, there was no name for that then. We thought he was just incredibly paranoid.

The early years of the tour included some obscure little ports. Phillip Island in south-east Victoria is a pretty sleepy place most of the year but in April '77, just before Bells, the world's touring pro surfers headed to Phillip Island for the Alan Oke Memorial, in memory of the well-respected local surfer and surfboard maker.

Phillip Island on a sou-wester is not a lot of fun, so we'd hold these marathon card games to while away the inevitable, stormy, onshore days. There'd be Terry Fitzgerald, Paul Neilsen, Fatty Al, Phil Jarratt and me, all playing cards for hours and sometimes days on end, for about 20 cents a hand. If we were lucky, there might be a local party to liven up the cold southern evenings.

MP's trip south for the Alan Oke and Bells, after his Stubbies win, was like something out of a Hunter S. Thompson book — the full fear and loathing trip. MP teamed up with the colourful big-wave surfer Owl Chapman and the details remain blurry to this day, but it took them a couple of weeks to drive from the Gold Coast to Victoria. They rolled cars, got thrown in jail, everything that could happen happened to them. They hadn't surfed since the Stubbies — just careered down the east coast of the country flirting with disaster.

The contest had already started and there was no sign of MP. The only reason he didn't miss his heat was because for three days the sou-wester howled at Phillip Island and we were inside playing cards. We were getting pretty restless. At last, the swell came up, the wind swung offshore, and they started the event at perfect Express Point — an abrupt right-hand reef. It was a solid eight feet with some bigger sets, as big as you could ever see the place. There were no legropes allowed and it was just a big, ledging barrel — we were loving life. I went out and won my heat, but everyone was wondering the same thing — where's Michael Peterson? He'd just won the last event and no-one had sighted him since.

MP's heat was getting closer and speculation was mounting about what hideous fate had befallen him and Owl. To get to Express in those days, you had to park your car a mile or two away, and walk through a few paddocks. It was wet and muddy, and MP's heat was only a couple of heats away, when this figure appeared, trudging through the fields. As this dark silhouette got closer, you could make out a big black trenchcoat and a matted mess of long, straggly hair. He had a surfboard under his arm with a wetsuit draped over it, and that was it. He looked like the prince of darkness. God knows what had happened to Owl by then. MP marched right past the contest judges and sat next to me. He sat for a while without saying anything, but the vibe wasn't bad. It was incredible actually, I was blown out. It felt like old times. He opened up the trenchcoat and casually pulled out a foil of buddha. He then proceeded to roll up a joint, and smoked it. I was freaking. This was not the done thing in this new era of slick professionalism. By now, they were calling his name for his heat. 'Michael Peterson, Michael Peterson, come and get the red singlet.' And then it was, 'Michael Peterson, your heat's paddling out.' I finally had to go, 'Ah, Michael, you're in this heat.'

'Ah, am I Chine?' he muttered.

I've gone, 'Yeah, there they are, they're paddling out now.'

And he went, 'Oh, alright,' and he casually looked around, got himself together, got changed, and collected the red singlet. By the time he paddled out, the heat was well under way. He got out there just as a 10 foot wave reared on the reef, trails of seaweed being sucked up the face from the shallow bottom. He paddled up the face as it pitched, turned around three-quarters of the way up, and executed a no-paddle take off. He freefell top to bottom and just got destroyed … then proceeded to win the heat. It was as if he was just waking himself, feeling the power of the ocean again and washing the dust off after his wild road trip. He went on and just destroyed his opponents. Even I was sitting there scratching my head. That really was his last great contest performance.

Peter Drouyn's man-on-man system had been a huge success at the first Stubbies and everyone was keen to see it adopted throughout the tour. But individual events still persisted in coming up with their own, peculiar systems. At Bells, they decided to have two rounds of man-on-man, two entire tournaments, and then add them both together and calculate the placings on points.

Incredibly, the first man-on-man final at Bells was between Peter Drouyn and I. The surf was brilliant, and we hugged each other on the beach before we went out. I tried everything, but I was nearly hoping he'd win. And win it he did. If it had been a regular man-on-man contest, he would have been the '77 Bells champion. In the second round though, Drouyn went out early and I went out in the quarter-finals. They worked out that only Simon Anderson could overtake me and Drouyn, and Simon ended up winning the second final and winning the '77 Bells.

The next event, the Coke Surfabout, I got a fourth. At the end of the Australian leg, they used to have a thing called the Australian Professional Championship — what they call the Grand Slam now — for the surfer with the best results over the Australian leg. Simon won that, I got second, and Shaun Tomson got third. The race was on — we finally had our circuit and something to aim for.

PETER DROUYN: 'Bells was my first man-on-man contest. I didn't go in the Stubbies for obvious reasons but the world tour was happening, pro surfing was starting, and I wanted to do as well as I could. And I found myself in a final with Wayne, and the one thing that we were all stoked about was the new fairness in judging, the new fairness in the format. You could actually turn on and get a fair result nine times out of 10. It was amazing. The odds were so far in our favour that we took on this almost swashbuckling attitude to the final ... It was a good 10 feet that day and we were just like bloody rashes all over the wave and we were actually — it was almost like an exhibition session in a heat. You had the creator and the original master of it really showing it off. It was a showpiece for man-on-man ... The whole thing was beautifully in concert, that whole heat. I think we were sad to see it end. It was remarkable and I don't think it mattered who won.'

Bustin' down the door

MR TUBE (FROM AN INTERVIEW WITH RABBIT, *PIX/PEOPLE MAGAZINE*, 1977): 'The basic breakdown of human beings has to do with cycles ... emotional, mental, physical and intuitive. I've been studying these cycles and learnt to conserve and balance outlets of energy. Through the study of numerology I've learnt that I'm a high physical number and a high emotional number and that's why my surfing is my art ...

'The lifestyle around surfing is a much more natural relationship with the world than just about anything else going. Surfing can be used as a vehicle to get an appreciation and understanding of our natural environment. Not only the physical but also cosmic environment. I would dig to see a surfer interviewed by *Time* magazine, for example. I mean, why not?'

BAND ON THE RUN

Timing is a funny thing. After dreaming of this circuit for so long, once it materialised another opportunity came along that clouded my pro surfing vision. 'Hollywood Harry' Hodge was a former journalist and surf shop owner from Frankston, Victoria, turned filmmaker. He had a lot of style and the silver tongue; somehow he managed to get funding for this incredibly ambitious surf movie project. He persuaded companies like Quiksilver and Rip Curl to invest in his project and he got the Australian Film Commission and Coca-Cola to back it as well. I think he did a bit of romancing of a girl that worked at the

AFC, and that certainly hadn't hurt his application for a grant. *Band on the Run* was going to be this fabulous, big-screen surf movie and Harry recruited me, Bruce Raymond, Paul Neilsen and emerging pro surfer Brian Cregan to star in it. It was going to make us all movie stars and be a fantastic career move, the way Harry told it. And so, all of a sudden, we were embarking on this giant, round-the-world film shoot, as well as trying to follow the pro circuit. This is my one major regret in pro surfing. I must have had stars in my eyes, because I allowed this to get in the way of my pro surfing dream.

After the Australian leg I didn't really have a sponsor to pay my way round the world. Because of *Band on the Run* I was indirectly getting some support from Quiksilver, and I was sponsored by Rip Curl, but there was no money, only free wetsuits. The only way I got to South Africa was on my *Band on the Run* world ticket. Here I was coming second in the world, and I still didn't have enough to buy myself a world ticket.

First stop was South Africa to film at Jeffreys Bay, and I was able to compete in the Gunston 500, in Durban. I finished seventh, and Simon Anderson made the final against the local hero, Shaun Tomson. All the Aussies were together cheering Simon on, because Shaun had won something like four or five Gunstons in a row. But this was the first year Shaun had been up against a really international field. We all thought Simon won it, but they gave it to Shaun. Another local surfer, Gavin Rudolph, got second and Simon ended up finishing fourth. We were outraged. They threw this giant party after the contest and all the Australians corralled around and started up a chant during the presentation. It was the first time I'd ever heard this chant — 'BULLSHIT, BULLSHIT, BULLSHIT.' We got ourselves so worked up with the injustice of it all, and then word came through that Shaun Tomson was having a victory celebration and we weren't invited — in fact we were banned. That was it, the final insult! Andrew McKinnon had a hire car, and somehow 17 of us, including this enormous Hawaiian guy Big Byron, squeezed into that car and we drove to Shaun's house. We piled out of the car and marched up to the gate, where Shaun had a bouncer on duty. We could hear the party going on, and the bouncer told us, 'You can't come in, you're not invited.' Byron picked this guy up, hurled him into the swimming pool and I led the charge up the driveway and into the party. The South Africans were horrified. I ended up having a major confrontation with a local guy. I just about had him by the throat, telling him the Gunston was a rip off, and they were all cheats. It turned out to be Peter Burness, the guy who ran professional surfing in South Africa — not a good career move. The next minute, Shaun's girlfriend came over to me and said in her plum, Afrikaans accent, 'Rabbit Bartholomew, you are disgusting, you do not deserve to be a professional surfer.' I considered how to take this for a moment, then I grabbed her by the hand, took her over to the record player, put the Rolling Stones on, and started dancing on the sofa. Things could have gone either way at this point, but for some reason she liked it — and the party went off. I'd broken the ice and suddenly we were all mates.

The next event was the Umhlunga Rocks. We thought this was an hilarious name and Drouyn and I used to stand there and go, 'Umhlunga', in German accents giving the Nazi salute, much to the disgust of the locals. It was the first man-on-man event in South Africa, and I was starting to warm to this new system. I tore through the field and blitzed 'em all. I won my first event, my maiden victory, at Umhlunga Rocks.

I won US$3000, which was a Godsend, considering I only had an air ticket to my name. I'd taken the number-one ranking, I'd won my first event, and I had money to do the rest of the tour. I still find it unfathomable — what happened next. Somehow Harry Hodge talked me into handing over that $3000 cheque, investing it in his movie, and going down to Jeffreys Bay to continue filming — instead of going to Brazil for the next leg of the circuit.

So we went to Jeffreys Bay. It was an incredible trip, J-Bay is one of my favourite waves in the world. We got good surf and footage for the movie, but meanwhile my closest rivals were at the next event in Brazil, trying to eat away at my lead. Finally, while I was down at J-Bay I've gone, 'Hey man, I am going to Florida. I am flying to Florida and I'm going in the next event.'

So off I went by myself to Florida. My strategy was to travel the world with one surfboard — naked, no board cover. My theory was that airline staff would go, 'Look at this idiot's surfboard with no protection,' and put it somewhere safe, and it worked ... most of the time. But this time, not only did my board go to Houston, but by the time it arrived in Florida it was flattened. Destroyed. So I arrived at the Florida Pro without a surfboard. I stayed with top local surfer Jeff Crawford and I had a local shaper Mike Tabeling make me up this incredible surfboard. A great, little 5'10" — a real Florida, small-wave model. I went on to make the final against my friend and host Jeff Crawford. It was the most bizarre end to a contest I'd ever witnessed. The final was nearly over and I looked in to the beach and the officials were pulling the contest structure down. The tents were gone, the scaffolding was gone, the event had disappeared off the beach. And there was one guy, Gunner Griffin, one of the heavies that used to run the contests over there, and he was up the top of the sand dunes going, 'Crawford first, Rabbit second. If you want your money it's at my house.' And he was gone. That was the end of the 1977 Florida Pro.

So me and Kanga Cairns decided, under the circumstances, to team up again and go collect our prize-money, just in case there was any trouble. Kanga told me, 'These guys are heavies. We've got to get round there quick smart and get our money.' So we found out where Gunner lived and we went round to his house. We didn't quite know what to expect, we found ourselves sitting round with all these gangster types, but fortunately they liked me. They thought I was a bit of a rough diamond. We got our money without incident and split. Three hours later, someone else arrived with an iron bar, knocked them all out and stole the rest of the prize-money.

This was the style of the pro tour in those days. Half the events were run by criminals or gangsters or businessmen whose sources of income were more than a little dubious. But the infantile IPS tour couldn't afford to be too precious in its choice of sponsors.

After the Florida Pro, I shot straight back to number one. Shaun had taken number one in Brazil but after Florida I suddenly had a

Bustin' down the door

700-point lead in the world rankings. I was still cursing my decision not to go to Brazil. I went straight from Florida to France to meet up with the rest of the *Band on the Run* crew. They got stuck in London for a few weeks with no money, and I had a solo adventure through France that blew my mind.

A FRENCH DEBUT

In 1977, not much was known about the surf in France, but it sure sounded like an appealing reconnaissance mission. I made the necessary connections to get from Miami to New York to Paris and on to Biarritz. It was lucky I'd won that prize-money, because nobody was there to meet me at Biarritz airport. I figured I'd catch the crew at the surf so I booked myself into the Biarritz Hotel overlooking Grande Plage, which roughly translates as 'Big Beach.' I walked down to the beach, wrapped my gear in a towel, and left it within eyeshot of my debut French surf session. What I failed to account for was the massive tides in France. Within half an hour I'd completely lost my bearings, my gear had disappeared, and it wasn't until I noticed my leather jacket going over the falls in the shorebreak that I realised what had happened. I made a hasty retreat back to the hotel, minus a Stones world tour T-shirt but with the trusty and sandy leather jacket intact.

The following day I walked to the Côte de Basque, a gorgeous little beach with a nice pavilion above the high-tide mark. It was here that I noticed that not too many people wore clothes — at least not on the beach.

I surfed for a couple of hours and couldn't help noticing a crowd building on the beach. Why were there 100 or so naked people standing in front of the bank I was surfing? Was there a shark in the lineup or something?

I lost my board after a deepish barrel and swam in to find a perfect 10-out-of-10 naked nymphet with her foot on my board waiting for me to retrieve it. I had to crawl up the beach on my belly to hide the bulge in my wetsuit.

After the session I walked up to the pavilion, got changed with a towel modestly wrapped around me and lapped up the beautiful

September rays. It was weird. All these people were definitely watching me surf but when I walked up the beach they pretended not to notice me. Suddenly, someone tapped me on the shoulder, I turned around and instantly recognised François Latigau, a dear French friend with whom I'd shared many glorious hours at Burleigh in '73 and '74. He'd returned to France earlier in '77 and was already ruling the surfing roost with the skills he'd honed on the Goldy during that golden era.

François wanted me to meet the girl he had been sleeping with. They were his exact words. This was the '70s when love was free and safe and everyone was pretty open, especially in France. But I was still a little shocked when I spun round to see this gorgeous blonde squatting down beside me, totally naked. I completely forgot to ask François the whereabouts of Hollywood Harry and Co. At that moment I couldn't have cared if I never saw another Aussie again, or at least till the weather turned cold and the girls had to put some clothes on.

Anyhow, the next three weeks were quite blissful. I was still pretty self-conscious, so the first week was strange. I'd go surfing with François and friends, they'd all arrive at the beach and immediately shed their gear. The girls would start doing stretches and I'd try to look the other way.

The swell absolutely pumped that September. I thought Grande Plage was good until I discovered Laffitania, a right-hand point that held an eight to 10 foot swell. I was shown the sacred spot where Nat Young surfed solo in 1970. Over the mandatory bottle of rouge, I gradually picked up on the history. Nat and Wayne Lynch had come here in the early '70s, Lynchy forging a legend at the now extinct La Bar while Nat enhanced his own legend by surfing this massive left peak in front of an inaccessible cliff on his own without a leggie.

The Hawaiians followed in '73. Stories unfolded — about Jeff Hakman and Gerry Lopez surfing a crazy beachbreak to the north and some wild characters who besieged the hotel overlooking the Côte de Basque. What finally struck me was the fact that I was the first modern surfer to step foot on French soil since Hakman and Lopez in '73. It was only four seasons, but a lot had gone down in that time.

Bustin' down the door

I was befriended by an eccentric French surfer, Yves Bessas. He and his girlfriend, Marichoo, lived in a 17th-century farmhouse in the Biarritz Hinterland. They took me in.

Three back-to-back 10 foot swells poured into the Bay of Biscay. I'd heard of a legendary left-hander, Mundaca, in Spain, and on the second swell Yves took me down there and promptly blew my mind. You needed 7'6" to 8' boards in Europe — that really stunned me. Next on the hit list was Guethary, a reef that broke similar to Hawaii's Sunset Beach. When I pulled into the lower car park, near Alcyon, a perfect left on its day, I couldn't even see the peak at Guethary. One, because it was so far out, and secondly because a deep sea mist had surrounded the outer peak. I knew it was huge. 12-foot mounds of whitewater were roaring out of the mist.

A guy whose French name translated into something like Peanut Brain accompanied me out there, both of us on 8'6" boards. Peanut Brain wasn't scared but he couldn't surf either. I hesitated on the edge of the mist and Peanut disappeared into the shadows. I could hear a set lurching on the outer reef and suddenly, there was Peanut Brain, in the lip of a 15-foot ball of whitewater. It was unsettling enough for me, let alone El Nutto, who disappeared for 90 minutes. I gingerly paddled into the mist and as the curtain slowly faded I got to ride a couple of monster peaks on my own.

A few days later Yves and Marichoo took me to a beachbreak called Hossegor. The swell had dropped at Guethary but this beachbreak was still three to five feet and insanely good.

That same day I met Arnauld de Rosnay, a colourful surfer/skater/skier/sailor who had, at one stage, surfed with Nat and Wayne. Arnauld, or the 'Baron de Rosnay', as he was affectionately known, promptly whisked me up to the Pyrenees Mountains and I watched him literally fly down the side of a mountain on what looked like an oversized skateboard with a sail. I had some new friends to play with and got lost for a further week.

When I returned from the Pyrenees, my friend Yves received a phone call and he frantically indicated to me to lift the other receiver to my ear. He whispered to me that it was Mickey 'da Cat' Dora, a truly legendary Californian surfer who kept up a mad

The birth of pro surfing

surfing circuit all of his own around the world. The first words I heard were, 'I went to J-Bay and those fucking Aussies were there shooting some god-damn movie so I packed up and left.'

'Where are you now Mickey?' enquired Yves very tentatively.

'I'm in India but I'll be by to see you next month.' Mickey hung up and Yves buckled with laughter. I thought Mickey had sounded quite intimidating, particularly as I was very recently at J-Bay being filmed.

'Oh, Mickey is such a chameleon. I know he is close by, he'll be here soon,' predicted Yves.

How soon, I wondered? Tomorrow, next week or in a month's time as he'd stated? An hour later there was a knock on the door. Yves pulled the ancient, refurbished barn-door back and promptly had a large case of wine thrust into his stomach. It was the one and only Mickey Dora — he definitely wasn't in India.

Over a bottle or two of the finest, Mickey's story unfolded. Yes, he had been in J-Bay and, yes, we had inadvertently upset him. On arriving in France, da Cat had been taken in by the largest grape growing family in Bordeaux, after making contact with the heiress on his trans-Atlantic flight.

Somehow, Mickey already knew that I could play a decent set of tennis and for the next week we waltzed into the finest country clubs in the region, posing as snotty-nosed aristocrats. When the club secretary would enquire as to why I was wearing black socks, the story of a family tragedy sprang forth from Mickey, and we would brush past the front desk and order ball-boys, fresh balls and Perrier to be delivered courtside.

Before I knew it, I'd been in France for over four weeks and had completely forgotten why I was there. Mickey and I started surfing Guethary together, I was amazed by how perfectly Mickey's style fitted into the wave and the French countryside — and the entire European scene. We returned to shore one day to find Hollywood Harry and Paul Neilsen waiting for me. It seemed the lads had been stuck in Chelsea living on fish and chips while I'd been courted by the French aristocracy. However, I managed to deliver such a hard-luck story that Hollywood actually felt sorry for me and it was on with the show.

HAWAII 1977-78

Returning to Hawaii that year was a mix of excitement and trepidation. I didn't rush over there on October 1. I definitely didn't want to be the first one over there again — I just didn't want to chance it. I was pretty sure it was all cool — we'd all travelled together from the start of that '77 tour and I was pretty close to all the Hawaiians. Buzzy Kerbox, Hans Hedemann and Michael Ho were really good friends of mine.

I was also still embroiled in the *Band on the Run* shoot and there was a major Hawaiian segment planned. The Australian Film Commission's money had come through, and we moved straight into the Kui Lima Estate. It was an interesting group: Bruce Raymond, Paul Neilsen, Brian Cregan, me and Toni, and Harry Hodge. It was just so completely different from the year before, it was ridiculous. Paul had a great rapport with the Aikaus, so I felt the heat was off a little. I was just trying to concentrate on the contests — I was still ranked number one in the world.

But Hawaii has a way of always dealing up the unexpected, no matter how low you try to lie. It was blowing kona winds in late November and the surf was junk so Toni and Bruce Raymond and I decided to go and see a movie in town. I had this all-time classic car, with the power steering, and this incredible transmission system where you just pushed a button to change gears. Classic '50s American automotive engineering. And it was all mine — I'd won enough money to actually buy this thing — I was so proud of it.

Bruce and I were really close friends from the old schoolboy days and our early Hawaiian seasons. He was one of the major go-for-it guys. He was on the next-to-be-dead list. November 30, 1977, it was my 23rd birthday, so the three of us cruised into Honolulu to watch a movie. I loved driving this car so much, I decided, 'Let's go the scenic route,' and we set off down the east side of the island, taking the slow road to town.

It was a winding old road in those days, until you cut through the mountain to get down to Waikiki, through the Like Like (pronounced Licky Licky) tunnel. We were about halfway through

The birth of pro surfing

the tunnel, in the fast lane, when I started noticing this horrible screeching, but because all the noise reverberates through the tunnel, I didn't know where it was coming from. But it wasn't long before I realised that we were losing speed — I had it flat to the floor and we were slowing down. I started revving it more and more, until finally the transmission just blew up. The hood flew up, we came to a complete stop and actually started rolling backwards.

I put the handbrake on. There were no hazard lights, I glanced in the rear-view mirror and all I could see was this stream of traffic roaring up the tunnel. They weren't slowing down and I could tell they didn't realise I'd stopped dead. We clambered out and the carbon monoxide was so thick we were almost passing out. Bruce and I just looked at each other, wondering what to do, and all we could find to flag down the traffic was a pair of red board shorts. So we started madly waving these shorts. One of the first cars that came towards us was a big pick-up truck — it came roaring up alongside us, with this big Hawaiian guy behind the wheel. He leant out and handed me these two stick-like objects. I didn't know what they were at the time but I realised later they were distress flares to stop the traffic. But this was where the old paranoia kicked in. I took a quick look at them and went, 'Nah, not this time buddy,' and threw them into the back of his truck. I actually thought they were sticks of dynamite.

The cars were getting closer, and thankfully there were a few big trucks in the slower lane, but that still meant the cars in our lane couldn't get across to miss us. The front car hit its brakes, and a deafening squeal of screeching tyres started up. The car behind it went sideways, nose first into the side of the tunnel and all the cars behind started locking up. The front car stopped about two metres from us, and the rest of them ran up its arse, eventually shunting the front car forward until it came to rest inches from our bumper. The noise was unbelievable. Trucks roared by, everyone madly tooted their horns — it sounded like there was a B 52 bomber coming down the tunnel.

I suddenly thought, where's Toni? I spun around and there she was, passed out on the road, overcome by the fumes. I said to Bruce, 'I've got to go. Take care of things.' I picked up Toni and started running out of the Like Like tunnel with her in my arms. When I reached the end of the tunnel, I laid her on the ground and revived her — she was okay. I peered down the tunnel, wondering what was going to happen next. Soon after, the police and tow trucks began arriving. I didn't have insurance, I didn't even have a licence. I had nothing. Bruce staggered out, all wide-eyed, 'It's just unbelievable down there.'

'Look,' I said to Toni and Bruce, 'sit down in the gutter here. This is the strategy. We're in shock. We've got to be in total shock. Maybe they'll feel sorry for us.' And so we went into shock, which didn't really require much acting. Cars were being towed out, four or five in all, scattered around the mouth of the tunnel. The traffic hold up must have been horrendous. The police started going round and checking insurance and registration and getting everyone's version of events. Amazingly, my car never got a scratch. Finally, the head cop made his way over to us, and just said, 'Well, what are you going to do?' I was imagining being thrown in jail or lumped with a damage bill of $100,000.

'We're just trying to get in to Waikiki to see a movie. We're Australian tourists,' I said, doing my best to appear on the verge of a nervous breakdown.

'Well, what are you going to do with the car?' he asked.

'I don't know,' I answered blankly, bowing my head in anguish. This cop was incredible. He lined up a tow truck driver and had my car towed to the nearest garage. Then he told us to get in the police car and he drove us into Waikiki — we got there in time to see George Burns in *Oh God*. And we had just walked away from the whole thing.

About four days later, safely back on the North Shore, I rang up the garage, and they said, 'Oh yeah, brah, you owe us for a bottle of transmission fluid, come down and pick it up.' I went and got my car and happily drove back to the North Shore.

The birth of pro surfing

The first event in Hawaii was the Smirnoff Pro at Sunset Beach, I was having a pretty good tournament in solid 12 foot surf. I got a screamer early in my semi-final, pulled in and it was just too hollow. I was really deep — I ate it and landed on the face of the wave. I didn't even penetrate the water, I just skipped along on my belly. The lip caught me ... I just got pulverised. The force of the lip actually snapped my ribs. I surfaced, unable to breathe properly and I had this burning pain in my chest. I said to the water security, 'I've hurt myself,' and the guy just stared at me and said, 'Your board's out at Kammieland,' and that's all he said. I thought, well Rabbit, you're still on your Pat Malone. I swam out with the rip and retrieved my board, it was way out past Kammieland. I tried to lie on it but I couldn't because of the pain in my chest. So I knee paddled all the way from out past Kammieland across the channel back to Sunset. My semi was still going, so I tried to knee paddle on to a 10 foot wave. I'd never done this before in my life, and I struggled to my feet too late and got pitched. I decided to call it quits then, swam after my board once again, and paddled in. I staggered up the beach and was put straight in an ambulance and taken to hospital.

Shaun got a third, he made a lot of ground, but the real problem was I had broken ribs and the Pipe Masters was in a couple of days. The doctor said six weeks till I could surf — I gave it four days, at which time they were actually worse. I got to know rib injuries pretty well, they get worse for a while before they get better. I got a sponge and taped it around my ribs and put a wetsuit over that, I found I could actually lie on my board. I went out at Pipe and got the most insane barrel, got through my heat and managed to get a 10th in the Pipe Masters with broken ribs. Shaun got second at Pipe and took over the lead.

The next contest was the Duke; I was trying to hold my act together, but my room-mates weren't making things any easier. Hollywood Harry was unbelievable in Hawaii. It all went over his head, the lingering sense of menace and the need to tread softly. It was just a big fun park to him, and he found an ideal playmate in Paul Neilsen. All I'd known in Hawaii was surf, surf, surf, and

Bustin' down the door

I rarely left the North Shore. They discovered Waikiki and started going into town to all the clubs.

It was the night before the Duke Kahanamoku Classic, and all was quiet on the North Shore. Suddenly, Paul 'Smelly' Neilsen turned to Hollywood, with that unmistakable mischievous gleam in his eye, and declared, 'TOWN!' That was it, they were spruced up and gone before they'd downed the first beer. Next morning, Sunset was 10 to 12 feet out of the west — real solid Duke stuff. Smelly had jagged heat three with Reno Abellira, Clyde Aikau, Sam Hawk, and several other heavies. Halfway through heat two, a black limo pulled up in the official area. The back door opened and amid raucous laughter, out stepped Paul Neilsen and Hollywood Harry. They were still in their *Saturday Night Fever* clobber. Paul shed his nocturnal gear for his Duke boardies, grabbed an 8'0" Brewer and paddled out blind, literally. We all watched, waiting for him to fall on his face as karma should dictate at this point. The hooter went, Smelly jagged the first wave, a 12 foot peak way outside. The wave in front obscured him momentarily. The beach was hushed. Then suddenly a great whooping hoot went up as Paul carved under the lip. He advanced to the semi-final with room to spare.

The '77 Duke final, however, was a one-man show. Eddie Aikau dominated the larger sets. He caught at least a dozen 12 footers, taking off deep on the north peak and backdooring the west bowl at incredible speed. As far as I was concerned, the Aikau brothers — Eddie and Clyde — were direct descendants of the Duke, not in bloodline but definitely in tradition.

Eddie dwarfed us in that final. I remember Michael Ho and I paddling up the west peak as Eddie came flying past on his yellow gun. It seemed so meant to be. I was just stoked to be out in a final with the great Eddie Aikau. Unbeknown to Michael and I at the time, we were witnessing the great Hawaiian's farewell appearance. Three months later, Eddie was lost at sea. A team of Hawaiians were attempting to retrace the maritime journeys of the ancient Polynesians when their giant outrigger canoe, the Hokule'a, became swamped. Eddie tried to paddle his surfboard to shore to raise the alarm but never made it.

The birth of pro surfing

So it came down to the last event, the World Cup. If Shaun won his semi-final, he had the World Title, while I had to virtually win the event to have any chance. It was man-on-man at Haleiwa and he won, I finished third. Shaun was world champion. I ended up only a couple of hundred points behind him but at that point I completely rued the whole *Band on the Run* thing and missing Brazil. That was the only thing that I was really dirty about in my entire career. But Shaun was a worthy world champion and I didn't begrudge him for a moment.

Still, *Band on the Run* had taken me all over the world and helped finance my travels — and it had given me some fantastic experiences. After the contests we went to the outer islands and had a beautiful time surfing some incredible waves in the most idyllic tropical settings you could imagine. I washed off all the contest stress and came home really refreshed.

1978

Finishing second in the first professional World Title race in 1977 ignited something inside me. I felt ready to be world champion. I made up my mind that nothing was going to get in my way this year. I was going to go to every event. I felt like everything was in place: I was number two in the world, the number one contender. I was super fit — I could out-paddle anyone, my stamina was phenomenal. I came home to good waves at Kirra leading up to the events, and just paddled up and down that Point, all day, every day, readying myself.

I went into the '78 Stubbies full of confidence. It wasn't classic Burleigh like the year before but there were some great confrontations. I had my first great clash with MR, the first of many over the ensuing year. I'd beaten MR in a heat at Bells the year before and this time we met in the semi-finals of the Stubbies at three to four foot Burleigh — I really waxed him. In the final, I was up against Micheal Ho. We both had a great final, but I experienced that magical sense of being on an inevitable path to the winner's dais. As I accepted the over-sized winner's cheque and trophy in front of my home crowd, I felt like no-one was going to catch me all year.

MARK RICHARDS: 'When the Stubbies was on in '78, the year he beat me in the semis, I remember Bolman (contest director Bill Bolman) had this gig on the stage where they did an introduction, and I was a bit nervous. There's thousands of people basically staring at us and Bugs was actually jumping up and down on the spot and sort of shadow boxing. It was just bizarre. And psychologically he probably beat me right there. He was arguably the best competitor ever on a psychological basis. He scared people. It was like he was jumping out of his skin to get me.'

Next it was down to Bells for the Rip Curl Easter Pro, by now the grandest tradition in Australian surfing contests. I sailed through the early rounds, and then beat Shaun Tomson in the semi-finals, in good six to eight foot surf. That win meant a lot to me. I met MR in the final and started out okay, but the turning point came when this one set swung through wide. MR just picked it up and on the way back out he picked up another one, and on the way back out from that he picked up yet another one, and he just did major damage. But I was still happy. I'd got first in the first event of the year, second in the second event, and I was thriving on the level of competitiveness between MR, Shaun and myself.

I was starting to make pretty good money, too. That's when retainers came in — companies actually started paying us to go surfing and endorse their products. I was on a retainer with Hot Stuff surfboards of around $90 a week, and I finally got on a retainer with Quiksilver board shorts and Rip Curl wetsuits. Quiksilver was $3000 a year and Rip Curl was $2000, but it was still a breakthrough. It was just unheard of at the time. Airfares gobbled most of that up pretty quickly. I was still going to all these places with no money in my pocket, sometimes with Toni, sometimes on my own. She didn't really like the cold, and she loved the Gold Coast so she'd stay there and I'd go down to Bells and come home with a couple of grand. I'd always pick up a few special awards, I'd realised they were easy money (at $300 a piece) and not many guys specifically targeted them. I'd go out and try to get the best tube, and do the most radical re-entry.

This was a really happy time. We were living in a beautiful, old house right on the beachfront at Bilinga, with my sister Wendy. I had a clear view of Kirra and I could walk to the airport. I could have a shower, grab my board and my bag and actually say, 'See ya honey,' and walk across the Gold Coast Highway and walk onto a plane as if I was just another commuter going to work. And I had this incredible car, that I bought for $50. I was walking down the hill at Burleigh one day and this guy said, 'Do you know anyone who wants to buy a car?' and I said, 'How much?' and he said, '50 bucks,' so I said, 'Yeah me, I'll buy it now.' I gave him the money and drove the thing away. It was an EH Holden and it would only ever work for me. I would leave the Gold Coast in June to follow the circuit and come back in January, and I'd store the car under the house while I was away. All through the northerly season my Holden EH just got worked by the wind and salt and seaspray and people would try to drive it while I was away, but it would never start. I'd get home and friends would say, 'Sorry about your car, Bugs, it's not working,' and I'd go, 'Bullshit.' I'd just turn the ignition, you didn't need a key, and it started first time. I'd drive it around and never check anything. It was a bit of a Fred Flintstone car — I was taking my sisters to school at Miami one time and Heidi actually put her feet through the floor and the road was visible, racing by beneath her feet.

THE MAN IN THE WHITE SUIT

Befitting my international sports star status I took on a manager — Ken Brown, who now does the 'Coastwatch' fishing, boating, and surfing reports on the tele. Somehow, we got together and decided he was going to be my manager, and again this was unheard of at the time. Together, we marched into the board of directors of Smirnoff Vodka in Sydney and convinced them that they should pay me money to go surfing. These hard-nosed business types sat there and told us how their sons played rugby and in the summer their boys were surf lifesavers. 'Why would we be giving money to a surfie?' they asked. They didn't like me, they didn't like my kind. But unbelievably we got 20 grand out of them, and the deal was I was going to be the man in white. I had this $2500 wardrobe of Smirnoff gear and had to travel the world in a white suit, spats, and a Panama hat, all emblazoned with the Smirnoff logo.

My cheque from Smirnoff was actually signed in New York by this giant corporation that owned Smirnoff, so it was a world-wide deal. It was all linked up — there was the Smirnoff Pro in Hawaii and I was to be Smirnoff's man in white, their surfing ambassador around the world. Unfortunately, the Hawaiian contest director, Fred Hemmings, had a falling out with the Smirnoff people soon after and the Smirnoff Pro ceased to exist, so that put my deal on shaky ground.

Ken and I had to go back in and try to salvage the whole deal. We were driving in from Whale Beach in Sydney and we were having this all-time barney. We were really pissed off with each other and it came to a head on the Spit Bridge, Mosman. He pulled over and said, 'Let's get outside and have it out now.' In the middle of the Spit Bridge he stopped his four wheel drive and we got out and duked it out. We fought in the middle of the Sydney morning traffic. We landed a few punches, soiled our clothes, rolled around a bit, then got up and both said, 'Well, let's get into that meeting.' We went in there a bit dishevelled, but we actually pulled if off. We had a plan to save the deal. We were going to propose a new drink to go on the market called 'the Bugs' — vodka and carrot juice. The first one we tried curdled but we told them we'd persevere and refine it. And they thought it was fantastic, just what was needed. But it was really only a band-aid measure and my Smirnoff deal was always on shaky ground after the Smirnoff Pro fell through. Sad to say, 'the Bugs' never made it on to the market.

The birth of pro surfing

That year I had a shocker in the Coke Surfabout in Sydney. I took out too small a board at good-sized Narrabeen in the second round and my good mate, Bruce Raymond, took me out, I had to be content with a ninth. That was the only time I really stumbled that year. A cocky young Australian, Larry Blair, went on to win the Coke from Wayne Lynch — who had staged a sensational comeback to competition — in perfect barrels at Manly.

But I'd done enough to win the Australian Professional Championship as the best-performed surfer over the Australian leg of the tour. I had a bit more time at home after the Coke, just hanging out with my girl, surfing really good Kirra and Burleigh, and training pretty heavily with my old mate Mont.

Mont was a major factor in my success, he'd come by every morning at 5 am and get me going and we'd go surf Burleigh — we were always the first ones out. Mont would be on my doorstep every morning without fail. He was the keenest surfer in town. I also spent a lot of time with my shaper Gill Glover going through boards, trying to get the magic board for the next all-important leg, South Africa, which I saw as being absolutely crucial.

SOUTH AFRICA

Shaun Tomson had such an advantage in South Africa it was unbelievable. He had incredible support there, he was actually a better surfer when he competed in South Africa. There were half a dozen of us Aussies trying to share the limelight at home but over there it was all Shaun — he was their only surf star and the locals adored him.

Shaun hadn't had a great start and I felt like I had to drive the advantage home on his turf at the Gunston 500. It was at Nahoon Reef in big surf and I drew this incredible succession of accomplished big-wave surfers. I beat Kanga Cairns, and two hot locals, Gavin Rudolph and Jonathon Parrman, before I finally met Shaun in the final ... where I lost the most controversial decision of my career. I still feel that I was robbed of the Gunston 500. It was a big event, with a lot of history and tradition, like Bells. I came out of the water knowing I had won — but the judges gave it to Shaun.

The pain was eased by the traditional stint at Jeffreys Bay for a bit of free surfing. South Africa was revealing itself as one of the most surf-blessed stops on the circuit. I was hanging out with Peter Drouyn and one of the South African judges who I'd become firm friends with, Mike Ginsberg. We'd do the first contest, then roar off along the Natal Coast on the full surf safari, then at the end of the month there'd be another event to bookend the trip.

So we were back at Umhlunga Rocks and that was where I started to really see the dangers associated with being the number one seed, which I was for many events that year and throughout my career. In those days, the number one seed would compete in the first heat of the day, sometimes at 7 am in the morning. If there was going to be any skulduggery, it would happen then, with no-one else around except you and the judges. Sometimes it felt like you were being executed by a firing squad at dawn, with no witnesses. There was nothing the local judging panel liked better than packing off the number one seed in the first round, to make the way clear for their boys. I knew I had to be so on my toes.

In '78 I came straight up against Californian Joey Buran, who'd recently done well in the World Amateur Titles. I went out and did pretty well, and my camp said, yeah, I definitely waxed him. I came in and I'd lost 3–2. It was the first time I'd ever lost in a first round, but they had a losers' round so there was the safety net. I ended up working my way out of the losers' rounds and finally met Joey again in the round of 16 in broad daylight and this time I made sure of it. I ended up going on and placing a 5th, which was an okay result. With a second and a fifth I ended up top scoring in the South African leg and held on to the number one spot.

The Title race was hotting up — and all of sudden there was a new contender. Cheyne Horan, a Bondi teenager in his first year on the tour, or 'the blond bombshell' as the tabloid press dubbed him, made his first final at Umhlunga Rocks. I was accustomed to jousting at the top of the ratings with MR, Shaun and Dane

Kealoha, but all of a sudden everyone was looking over their shoulder at Cheyne Horan. He just came out of nowhere and started getting great results. Michael Tomson, Shaun's cousin, beat Cheyne in that final at Umhlunga, which really helped me out. It ended up being the only tournament victory of his career but it was one that I was really happy about. Michael couldn't believe it — he put together the finest hour of his competitive surfing career, and I was going, yes. Thank you!

BRAZIL

Cheyne got a real boost when the tour hit Brazil. They went crazy over him. He was everything they loved — the cute, blond, freckly, new upstart kid. We were already the established guard. We'd been big names in Brazil for five years, and the way they went crazy over Cheyne made us feel like we were almost over the hill. It was heavy — only the second year on the tour and it felt like our time was running out.

The latter stages of the contest were held at Aprador, a left-hand point at the northern end of the famed Ipanema Beach. When Cheyne Horan came up against young Wollongong surfer, Chris 'Critta' Byrne in the quarters, thousands upon thousands of excited Brazilians were screaming for Cheyne. And because Critta had already knocked out one of the local heavies in quite ruthless fashion, the crowd were heckling him with just as much passion. At one stage, Critta was running around the headland to paddle back out after a wave, and the crowd started hurling things at him — bottles and food and stuff. Critta was just copping this barrage of abuse and missiles and suddenly he stopped in his tracks and just flipped off the whole crowd — which is very nearly an act of suicide in Rio. Sure enough, this one crazy guy decided Critta had directed it at him personally and chased him round the point, threatening to kill him. Critta had to be escorted by security guards out of the water, while the crowd bayed for his blood. He was escorted off the beach, back to his hotel and went straight to the airport.

Cheyne went on to win the tournament, I got another fifth and suddenly he was *really* catching up — within 200 points. It was a race between me and the super kid. It really felt like this kid might take over and relegate all of us to history in one go. It was radical.

FLORIDA

The east coast of the USA was beginning to feel like my leg of the tour. I had done so well in Florida the year before and I just felt comfortable there. The first event was the Seaside Pro in New Jersey and it was pretty classic — we all stayed on this crazy boardwalk inhabited by all kinds of colourful and eccentric locals. They held the contest on the Labor Day weekend, which was just the biggest weekend of the year, when millions of people from inland cities descended on the beach. It was one big carnival.

The locals were all raving about this kid from Florida, Pat Mulhern. They were saying this kid was going to wipe all of us out of the contest. But in fact, he ended up being my greatest ally in the World Title race. We were on opposite sides of the draw and Pat came up against Cheyne early in the tournament. It was a super-exciting match between the two hot rats and Pat beat him. He went all the way through and I met Pat Mulhern in the final. They moved the contest down the beach a bit to this little running right-hander and I just looked at it and went, oh, this is exactly like home, like small Greenmount or something, and I went out and stomped on him. I really ate him for breakfast and widened the gap between me and Cheyne, and the rest of the contenders.

But then one of those things that I tend to do happened. I flew back to California to be with Toni and had a great time, just relaxing between events, feeling on top of the world. I was riding my bike down to Newport Beach, when I got clipped by a car and sent head first over the handlebars and landed face first in the gutter. I re-did my whole face. All my teeth got knocked out, I dislocated my shoulder — I was really messed up. The Florida Pro was on the next week and I didn't have time to get my teeth fixed or anything. I turned up at the Florida Pro looking like Leon Spinks, the toothless contender for Muhammad Ali's heavyweight title at the time. Here I was — the number one seed, the heir apparent, and I just had a mouth full of gum. It wasn't a pretty sight. When I slept my lips would stick together and my face scabbed up — it was a shocker. And to make matters worse, I could only paddle with one arm. But somehow I got through a few heats. I was doing the one-arm paddle and struggling to my feet, but once I was up and away I surfed like a maniac because every wave counted and I knew I might fall apart at any time. I ended making the semi-finals and lost to Dane Kealoha in a super-close heat. My man Pat Mulhern took Cheyne out again early in the event. Despite my condition, I widened my lead even further.

I headed back to California to recuperate and prepare for Hawaii. I also got the chance to fulfil a lifelong ambition. Muhammad Ali, my all-time hero, was fighting Larry Holmes at Caesar's Palace in Las Vegas. I drove out there, determined to see Ali in his last hurrah. I managed, at considerable cost, to get great seats.

It was the first open-air World Title fight in Las Vegas, a real glamour occasion — the crowd acknowledging Frank Sinatra, Gregory Peck, Sammy Davis Junior, and a real who's who of Hollywood.

The undercard featured Leon Spinks versus Hector Comachi, this brute from Peru. Spinks annihilated Comachi and the scene was set. The anticipation was overwhelming. They introduced the challenger, Holmes — a mean-looking bastard, and then Ali came dancing on to the stage. He'd already predicted a series of miracles, the first being a return to his prime fighting weight.

Unfortunately, the weight loss program combined with the dry desert air dehydrated Ali and the champ spent most of the night covering up. We diehard Ali fans thought it all a ruse, like the George Foreman rope-a-dope in the Rumble in the Jungle in '74. But no, sadly, there was no sweet victory, and Ali got beat up pretty bad.

I waited around as the crowd dispersed. A sadness hung in the air. Hundreds of women had congregated outside Ali's trailer. They were crying, some openly wailing. It was like a wake.

Bustin' down the door

Soon after, I got an unexpected call from my manager, Ken Brown, in a state of high excitement. He wanted me to up-end my whole World Title campaign and Hawaii preparation and fly home to star in a Julie Anthony Christmas Special. Toni wasn't too stoked about this either — the demands of my pro surfing career were starting to put strains on the relationship.

THE JULIE ANTHONY CHRISTMAS SPECIAL

I was a bit dubious about the Christmas special idea, but Ken convinced me it would give me great mainstream exposure and would lift my profile immensely on the eve of my anticipated World Title victory. So home I flew, to join the cast of soap opera stars and English comedians to help Julie Anthony sing Christmas carols. This was all going to coincide with the grand opening of the Gold Coast International Hotel, so I dutifully donned the white suit and headed uptown.

But first I'd heard that an old surfing friend, Joe Engel, was having a party to raise money so he could go to Hawaii, and I thought I'd better support that. So I headed down to Joe's party first, driving my trusty old EH Holden. I didn't touch the drink in those days — I just turned up, said g'day to Joe and a bunch of people I hadn't seen for a while, and gave him 20 bucks towards the airfare. I tried to make a discreet exit to slip up to Surfers for the gala occasion, but a mate who I hadn't seen for a while nabbed me and wanted to hitch a ride up with me. Craig Walgers was a good surfing mate but he had these two quite worrying, punk-looking characters with him. So I drove them up to Surfers, parked the car, and started walking down Cavill Mall to the Gold Coast International. It was Saturday night in Surfers, and I felt more than a little conspicuous in my white suit, spats and panama hat. Next thing, the two punks started getting real rowdy. They were kicking garbage cans over, and uprooting pot plants. Craig was walking with me and I said, 'Let's get out of here. Let's walk a bit faster.' The next minute the guys started throwing these giant pot plants and rolling garbage cans down the Mall. I just went, these guys are bad news, I'm out of here, and I broke into a run. As Craig and I started running, three cops came round the corner, saw the debris, saw us running and shouted, 'Freeze.' By this time I was late, and I thought, there's no time to explain here, it's time to run. As we started sprinting this other plain-clothes policeman came out of nowhere and grabbed Craig, who was only 14 or 15, and Craig just went, 'whack', and decked him. The other cops were chasing me through Surfers and I thought I'd almost shaken them. I rounded the last corner towards the Gold Coast International Hotel, and I could see the bright lights and all the glitterati. I was sprinting for the line when one of the cops pulled out his gun and yelled, 'Halt or I'll shoot,' at which point I stopped dead in my tracks. 'Put your hands over your head,' he commanded, and I did. There I was, hands on my head, being handcuffed and dragged away down Cavill Mall, in front of the cream of the Gold Coast social set. They made Craig and I clean up all the mess the two punks had made, and I was down in the gutter in my white suit picking up garbage cans and pot plants. Then they threw us in the back of the police car to take us down to the station to book us.

One of the cops asked me, 'What's your name?'

'Wayne Bartholomew,' I told him.

They didn't believe me at first. 'The surfer, the champion surfer?'

'Yeah, really.'

'No wonder we couldn't catch you.'

Craig was being charged with aggravated assault for punching the cop and they had all these other charges they wanted to lay on us, but we kept protesting our innocence. They took us to Southport Police Station and threw me in the watch-house for the night with all the drunks. They took Craig home to his parents because he was a minor. By this time, the white suit was brown, and I got in a fight in jail because some drunk came in and booted me in the head and stole my pillow.

They let me out Sunday morning, when I was supposed to be on location for the Christmas Special. I was a mess. I hitchhiked back to

Bustin' down the door

Surfers and got to the Gold Coast International at about 7.30 am. Shooting was supposed to have started at 7 am. There didn't seem to be anyone around so I figured I could sneak into the hotel and at least clean myself up a bit. I tip-toed through the lobby and hit the elevator button. The doors opened and out stepped Julie Anthony and her husband, and the director. They looked me up and down and all I could think of to say was, 'I went jogging early this morning and fell over.' That's the best I could come up with. 'But I'm here to drive you to the location,' I continued, just trying to fill up the awkward silence. So, reeking of gutter and jail, I drove them all in the old EH up to Seaworld. They thanked me very much and said I had the morning off — they wouldn't be needing me until the afternoon. I made my get away, wondering if that was the end of my TV career.

I still remember the last thing that policeman said to me when he let me out — 'Son, go and win the crown for Australia.'

HAWAII 1978-79

I flew straight back to Hawaii, eager to prepare for the World Title showdown and to see Toni, who had stayed on in Hawaii when I flew home. But, in my absence she'd decided she'd had a gutful of this whole lifestyle of me gallivanting all over the world. I was one of the only guys with a girl on tour, if not the only one. We didn't have enough money to do the whole tour together, and I often had to leave her for a couple of months at a time. She was questioning if this was going to be her life and when I got to Hawaii she was pretty keen to call the whole thing off. I was devastated. I was trying to prepare for the World Title and I suddenly had to try to repair my relationship with my girlfriend, who I loved very much. It was a difficult time.

The relationship status went from one of mild concern to red alert the evening Toni walked out of the bathroom, looking a million dollars and declared she was going out with friends. The World Title, my guiding light and irrepressible life goal since the age of 12, was suddenly relegated to the secondary rung of priorities. Toni had finally jacked up. The minor rumbles had gone virtually unnoticed by me and now she had literally walked out on me.

I was fortunate to have my good friend, the late Col Smith, from Newcastle, at my side to help me through. It's always good to have a mate giving you a bit of support when your relationship's on the rocks. We were staying out at the Kui Lima Estate again, and after that year I came to really despise the idea of living out there in an artificial resort environment, because you're so removed from the real North Shore. You go out and do your surfing and come back to this sterile, middle-American country club environment, nothing like the real Hawaii. I kind of wanted to be down there in the jungle (as we called the North Shore) with everyone else, but I was still wary of the local ill-feeling towards me. I thought maybe I hadn't given the whole healing process enough time, so Smithy and I played it safe and stayed out at the Kui.

Col was in the Pro Class Trials, the qualifying event for the major Hawaiian contests if you weren't in the top 16. The trials always featured a very strong local contingent and Col had his work cut out, so I decided to have my first foray into the world of coaching, and I ended up coaching him all the way through the trials. We became so close that year and we helped each other through some pretty radical situations. He was still a bit edgy in the big stuff but I pushed him into some solid days at Sunset and he started to get more comfortable.

Incredibly, he made the final of the Pro Class Trials, held on a small day at Sunset Point, also known as Val's Reef. I helped him devise this plan where he could go out and surf away from the other competitors on this one part of the reef — where he could utilise both his forehand and his backhand attack, and do these kind of floaters that he'd perfected. I thought this was the best part of the reef to do that and he went out there and did some amazing surfing. He did this one layback and got in the barrel, came out, did this amazing backhand smack and a floater over Val's Reef and won the Pro Class Trials. That was really uplifting for both of us. I'd helped him through the trials, and I knew he wanted to pay me back by supporting me through my own emotional trials.

It was really hard to focus on surfing and the job before me. Even though I realised it was the final test, the last hurdle before the winner's tape, I couldn't do much about the descent. I was

Bustin' down the door

unaccustomed to these emotions. I did not know how to deal with a bust-up.

At one point in the lead-up to the contests, Toni and I jumped on a plane and flew to Maui to try to rekindle the magic. We stayed in the beautiful, little town of Lahaina and went on a bit of a shopping spree during the day and at night had cocktails and just forgot about everything else. It was weird doing that in preparation for a World Title, but it was something I had to do. It was probably the most difficult time of my life — I couldn't walk away from the World Title and pro surfing, but I felt that to keep the relationship with Toni, I might have to. I was just trying to hedge my bets and keep both — win the World Title and end up with the girl.

We returned to Oahu. I felt I'd made up a bit of lost ground, however it was clear there were no certainties. Toni, realising I was showing huge cracks in the armour, urged me just to concentrate on winning the Title. There were three events in Hawaii and I had a fairly commanding lead, but only the sort of lead I'd had the year before when I broke my ribs and lost, so nothing was certain on that front either.

The first event, the Jose Cuervo Pro, was held in really good Sunset and I got through the heats and quarter-finals. The semi-final was crunch time. All the contenders were still in it. I was buoyed by the fact that Toni came down and watched me go out in my semi-final. I completely went off at 10 to 12 foot Sunset, won my semi-final and advanced straight to the final.

I kissed Toni before I paddled out for the final. I really wanted to impress her and went for it hard. This cavalier approach rewarded me with some great rides, but then I got just a bit too cute. In the closing minutes I got caught out by a huge west peak. Diving underwater attached to my board by this fancy, new big-wave leash, I felt smug. The wave cracked right on the board, pulling the rope-based leash taut and flinging me upward into the lip. I travelled underwater towards shore for hundreds of metres, attempting to penetrate the whitewash and reach the surface three times without success. I'd just about given up when at last the wave let me go and I rose up to hear the final hooter. I was still in the race.

I got back to the beach only to hear that Toni had just bailed with her new friends. I snapped, went straight to the liquor store and bought whisky. I'd gone so hard at Sunset I'd nearly died — I just drank myself into a stupor.

Col Smith found me in a bad way. I'd smashed up the apartment and had broken one of my boards. It took him hours to bring me round. 'You've beaten them Bugs, all the contenders, you beat 'em today, you're going to be world champion.' I settled down and went about fixing things up.

A top–10 finish at Pipeline could seal my World Title, even before the final event, and I got through my heats without a problem. I then drew one of the heaviest semi-finals you could ever face at Pipe — I was up against Gerry Lopez and Rory Russell and some other really hot locals. All the calculations had been done — if I got through that semi-final, I would be the world champion. But the other World Title contenders saw who I was up against and figured this was their one chance where I might stumble and they could overtake me.

It was an epic semi-final at 10 foot Pipe and Gerry and Rory were getting some good rides, just falling into the natural, easy rhythm they always seemed to find out there. It was a six-man heat and only three got through, and it looked like Gerry and Rory had first and second sewn up. I took off on this set wave and dropped to the bottom, did a bottom turn, pulled in standing bolt upright, didn't grab the rail, and got shunted through this enormous barrel. The next section looped over and I was about 10 or 12 feet back inside the tube. The wave had actually twisted round a bit of a corner, and I couldn't even see out of it. It was such a critical wave and at this point it was kind of beyond my control. As long as I could just hold my line, it was up to the wave whether I was going to come out or not. I kept going and going and finally got spat out. At the time it was considered one of the longest backhand barrels ever, and I'd done it with the World Title at stake at Pipeline. I came out of the barrel and knew I'd won the World Title.

I think Gerry won the semi, Rory got second and I got third, and they announced the results as I walked up the beach. The first person I saw was a friend from Wollongong, surfboard shaper Phil Byrne. 'How'd you go in that? Alright?' he asked me.

'Yeah, yeah, I won the World Title,' I told him, as casually as I could manage in the circumstances.

It was the most victorious feeling I'd ever had in my life. Better than everything I'd ever done to that point. First place in the semis went straight to the final, and second and third went into a repechage, and I didn't even make the final. But it took the wind out of everyone else's sails and none of the other contenders made the final either. It was over. I was world champion.

There weren't any celebrations though, because I still hadn't won the girl. I remember coming in and going, 'Hey honey, I've won the World Title,' and she was all stoked for me but I still felt that she wasn't quite with me yet.

I was a million miles away from the last event, the World Cup. I didn't even try to get through a heat. I rode a board that was about two feet too small on the day. The waves were terrible, this north wind had come through and destroyed the surf, and they finally held the early rounds in small beachbreaks at Ehukai Beach Park. But the Title was in the bag, and none of the other contenders did any good anyway. It ended up being won by Buzzy Kerbox — his maiden victory.

There was quite a bit of time between clinching the World Title and the presentation banquet. It was an agonising few days because my relationship still hung in the balance. Winning the World Title had meant everything to me all my life, but now I needed to win the girl more than I had ever needed the World Title. The whole winter was an emotional roller-coaster ride for me.

Finally, the day of the awards banquet arrived. Everyone knew we'd had problems and rumours were circulating. On that very day Toni decided that she'd thought it all out and she wanted to be with me — she wanted to come back to Australia. Everything came in a big rush — that I do remember as the happiest day of my life. To walk into the awards banquet with my girl and collect the World Title ... that was the sweetest moment of elation I could ever imagine. I was inspired that night to deliver a pretty classic speech that ended with a warning to all competitors to expect a bit of a party when they came Down Under for the next year's Stubbies. 'You better wear your dancing shoes when you come to Burleigh,' I told them.

The next day I thought, I'm leaving nothing to chance. I packed my World Title trophy, grabbed Toni and I drove straight to the airport.

MIAMI HIGH SCHOOL HEADMASTER BILL CALLINAN, *SUNDAY TELEGRAPH*, 1978: 'Rabbit was a good athlete. It was only that he settled on surfing that precluded him from being a top-class rugby league winger, a quarter-mile runner or anything he set his mind to. His studies suffered a bit because of his surfing but it's excellent he's reached the top.'

Bustin' down the door

the dream come true ...

I had everything I'd ever wanted in life — the World Title, the girl, and an incredible lifestyle as a professional surfer. Suddenly, after all those years of dreaming, I was finally living the reality and it felt like time to grow up and start planning a future.

Toni and I travelled to California and went skiing for a week or so before returning to Australia. I really wanted to show her that I was willing to do things together away from surfing. I felt like I had matured in a lot of ways when I won the World Title and that the whole experience of that Hawaiian season had taught me not to take anything for granted.

Of course, I felt super ready to walk in the shoes of the world champion. I was so proud to have won the World Title leading the ratings from wire to wire — from the start of the season to the finish. I really wanted to soak up the sense of achievement and enjoy every moment of it. I arrived home to a hero's welcome. We were met by a chauffeur-driven Rolls Royce at Coolangatta Airport, the mayor had organised a bit of a reception, and the famous Gold Coast meter maids formed a kind of guard of honour for me.

The bad news when I got home was that our beautiful little house at Bilinga where I'd lived with my sister Wendy in '77 and '78 had been sold and the new owners were going to tear it down

Extract from Tracks magazine, December, 1979.

HEROES, AUSTRALIA'S 10 MOST INFLUENTIAL SURFERS OF THE '70S, BY PHIL JARRATT:

'Rabbit Bartholomew -- Simply the best and fiercest competitor to emerge in the 1970s, Bugs is a wonderfully flamboyant surfer whose personal development over the decade has been as astonishing as his contest record. When *Tracks* first got on to his case in 1974 he spent most of his time mooching around the Gold Coast with, oh, anything up to 10 cents in his pocket. He hitchhiked around the place with young Guy Ormerod, and he had a board at Burleigh and one at Kirra. He'd turn up at the right time, surf his heart out, and then mooch off again. But he was a thinker. In quiet moments you'd see him sitting in somebody's car, chewing on the end of a towel, and working out the master plan. Muhammad Bugs in his own mind. In six years most of Rabbit's dreams have come true.'

and build units. Despite the fame and glory, we had basic things to tend to like finding a place to live. That was a real bummer, but in a way it was fateful, because it forced Toni and I to go out and find a place of our own. We moved into a fairly plain little unit in Bilinga and I settled into what felt like a prelude for the calm domesticity of married life. But, somehow, things never remained calm for too long.

Soon after, I went surfing at Snapper Rocks and a stray surfboard came exploding out of the whitewater and stabbed me in the front of the leg. I looked down and the skin wasn't broken so I didn't think too much about it, but what I didn't realise was that I'd herniated the calf muscle. About a week later there was still a lump there and it showed no signs of going down; so I went

Bustin' down the door

to the doctor and he opened it up, drained the lump and sewed me back up. Another week later the lump was still there so I started wearing one of those elastic muscle supports and that allowed me to surf.

That season we got the best swell at Kirra since they built the Big Groyne. For the first time since '72, not only was it as good as it got, but it was holding six to eight foot. On the best day of the swell it was the most perfect Kirra I've seen there since the Big Groyne to this day. I had this beautiful Tom Parrish board and I felt so in control out there that on one wave, as I did my bottom turn I shuffled into a parallel stance, like a skier. I got a barrel from in front of the Kirra shed all the way down to Little Groyne in a parallel stance. It felt insane and I just squatted lower and lower as I rode higher in the face of the wave. It was one of the longest barrels of my life but finally I got sucked too far up the face and the lip just took my head off. My old boyhood hero Nat Young had been watching and told me it was the closest thing he'd ever seen to a marriage between skiing and surfing, so that was a stoker. It was the first day I'd surfed on my injured leg and it held up no problem.

As the first contest of the new season approached I was in a supremely confident mood. When asked if there would be a lot of pressure on me as defending world champion, I replied, 'I am the pressure.' I changed my surfboard designs a little bit but I knew I didn't have the absolute magic board. My first contest as defending world champion was the Stubbies at Burleigh Heads. I got through the early rounds with ease and came up against a red-hot MR in the quarter-finals.

It was really good Burleigh and it ended up being a super close heat but MR won and went on to win the Stubbies. That was enough for some people to start declaring a changing of the guard. MR was surfing brilliantly and it seemed like he'd really come of age. MP beat him in '77, I beat him in '78 and now it was his turn. His surfing in Hawaii during the winter of '78–79 had been phenomenal. He was definitely doing the best surfing at Off The Wall on his new twin fins and we all knew he was going to be hard to beat in '79.

The dream come true ...

After the Stubbies I went to work with my shaper Gill Glover and we came up with a better board. And with my new board in tow, I flew down to Bells to prepare for the second contest of the season. I went for a surf a few days before the contest at Jan Juc, a little beachbreak just east of Bells, and as I was getting ready to go out MR pulled up with his parents. We were both in the car park getting our boards out, and we looked over at each other and as if we were just saying hello, we both went, 'See you in the final.'

Sure enough, we met in the final, though we both took very different paths getting there. Yet another new system had been introduced, with a losers' round. I had a habit of seeing losers' rounds and just diving in headfirst, figuring I had a safety net if I blew it. The organisers took the first round down to Johanna and, sure enough, I lost straight up. Then, the contest was moved back to Bells, and they completed the winners' heats like they would in a normal contest, and us losers had to wait our turn to battle our way back into the draw through a gruelling series of sudden-death repechages. They completed the winners' rounds right through to a quasi final to determine who would meet who out of the losers' rounds — MR and Dane Kealoha made the winners' round final with MR just beating Dane. If there hadn't been a losers' round, if it was a normal contest, that would have been the final. But instead, MR and Dane had to sit it out after their battle and see who they'd draw out of the losers' rounds.

I had to surf something like 11 consecutive, sudden-death heats if I was to claw my way into the final. I got through about four of them, but then the surf went flat and time was running out. Back in those days the Bells presentation night was such an institution, people just wouldn't tolerate missing out on a preso night. So the organisers decided, bugger it, we'll have the preso night anyway. So they held the preso before the competition was over. Everyone was getting into the spirit of it, dancing and carrying on, and at some point during the evening they just decided to accept the results as they'd fallen in the winners' round and scrap the rest of the losers' round. Despite the party atmosphere, I was devastated. I accosted Rip Curl boss Doug

'Claw' Warbrick in the midst of the partying and said, 'You can't finish it like this.'

'Ah well, we'll just have to accept the results as they are,' he said.

'Nah, you've got to have the losers' round. You've got to have it. Just have it tomorrow.'

Somehow in the course of the evening I managed to turn things round and the announcement was made quite late in the evening: 'The final day will be tomorrow. We're going to go through with it.'

That brought a fairly abrupt end to the partying for those still in the event. The next morning it was still small and they moved the contest just down the beach to Winki Pop, a quality reef/point set up just east of Bells. I was the driving force in having the contest called back on, so maybe I had something to prove, because I just had the most unbelievable run that day. I was in every heat, coming from the bottom up and my opponents read like the who's who of surfing. I had Cheyne Horan, Larry Bertleman, Hans Hedemann, Col Smith, Bruce Raymond and finally Dane Kealoha. By that stage, Dane was just coming down the hill for his first surf of the day and I'd already had five heats. We got out there and I just had an insane heat. Not only did I win the heat, but I took the front running in a bunch of special awards — the most radical manoeuvre, the highest scoring wave of the tournament, all those special, cash awards.

So, true to our prophecy, I was in the final against MR. As I prepared for my seventh heat of the day, MR came trotting down the hill, fresh as a daisy, and we paddled out for the final. We had another really close heat, but with a minute to go I knew I had an edge on him — I knew I was just in front. The best set of the final came through wide in the dying moments, and I was sitting wide and we were both paddling for it, desperately trying to make position. I got onto the first one and he was too far inside. I hotdogged it all the way down the point, finished up way down past Lowers, at the very end of the break, and just went, unreal, I've won Bells. He'll never get one that goes this far. I turned around and saw MR in full flight on the next wave but it had a little double up in front of it. He did a bit of a snap, and I thought, there's

The dream come true ...

no way he can get over this double up. He's history. But somehow, he skated over the double up — he was still a good 150 yards away from me — and proceeded to do 15 snaps all the way past me. I was already standing on the beach and went from elation to despair. Not only did he take the Bells Title off me in the last 20 seconds of the final, but he also did a clean sweep of all the special awards with that one wave.

But the second placing at least put me back on track. I'd had a fifth and a second in the first two events, which wasn't too bad, except that MR had scored two firsts.

MARK RICHARDS: 'We had some pretty epic tussles at the Stubbies and at Bells. We just kept bumping into each other. We'd always seem to meet in the finals or the semis. We had some pretty intense heats, jockeying for position and bumping rails, a bit of push and shove. This was all before the priority buoy (which largely eliminated hassling in the surf) and it was nowhere near as polite as it is these days.'

DOUG 'CLAW' WARBRICK: 'When we had those losers' rounds and repechages, if Rabbit lost a heat he'd come back bigger and brighter and better the next day and he was always there. He never won it but I think he came second to Mark Richards three or four times, when MR was obviously the dominant surfer of the day. But they were epic encounters. Mark never got over the top of him, he never swept to victory. He'd look like he was just starting to dominate Rabbit or he'd get a couple of great rides and you'd go, "No-one can come back from this sort of assault." Logically, you've just been smacked. But Rabbit would just pull out a great ride and always the final would go to the last five minutes, because the pattern was the same every time. They'd jostle wave for wave, Mark would change gears into championship form, he'd make a big break on Rabbit and you'd think it would be all over. And then Rabbit would just chip away, get a great ride, work the thing over, and

Bustin' down the door

then in the dying seconds Rabbit was right there and the final was in the balance again. Every time Mark had to pull out something great, like truly great, to hold off Rabbit's charge. He was going for the win, he's a winner, he knows how to win, and he didn't lose by coming second to Mark Richards.'

GILL GLOVER: 'I can remember spending nights in the shaping bay and in the glassing room and actually making a board overnight for Wayne to surf a contest, and he'd ride it the next day. What the hell, we were out there to win. All those things we did, we didn't question them. We wanted to do them because we were on a mission. You'd wake up bleary-eyed the next morning or didn't even go to sleep and he'd be down at the contest and I'd rock up with a board. They were good highs. You go to your grave remembering those ones.'

Next, it was up to Sydney for the Coke Surfabout. It was good Narrabeen and I came up against my old mate Bruce Raymond again in the second round. This time I thought, right, I'm going to really give it to you. My first two waves, I went berko and got two big scores. This is fantastic, I thought, I've got him on toast. My third wave, I took off, came off the bottom and as I went up the face, the lip hit me and I heard my ankle just go, 'Snap!'. My ankle just completely went on me. It was the same leg that I'd injured previously. I didn't realise it at the time, but wearing the muscle support all that time had weakened the ankle. No-one on the beach realised, and I tried to keep surfing, but I only had the use of one leg, and Bruce beat me. That was the year they air-lifted the whole contest down to Bells and Cheyne Horan went on to win the Coke. I always wondered what would have happened if I'd got through, because I loved surfing Bells, and

The dream come true ...

MR had gone out early too, so I could have really got back into the hunt there.

Instead I headed back to the Gold Coast to recuperate. This was the first year the tour went to Japan and it went without me. Every result counted towards the final world rankings, so I was desperate to get fit as quickly as possible. For the first time since pro surfing began, I was in the agonising situation of awaiting the results from the other side of the world. MR won the first contest in Niijima (a small fishing island off the mainland), and then Mark Warren won the next event. It was too much for me to bear. The ankle wasn't really ready but I just decided I had to get over there and do the best I could.

This year there were four Japanese events over about a six-week period and I got there in time for the third event, the Japan Cup, at Shonan Beach, the closest surf beach to Tokyo. I was so hungry I forced my way into the final on sheer strength of will, and met Dane Kealoha. I really hassled him in the final, and we ended up having a huge scene in the water. I came in from that final and realised — to my horror — that our hassling out in the water had totally polarised the competitors on the beach. All the Hawaiians were on one side of the beach and all the Australians were on the other side. There was very nearly a major flare up. Dane completely blew up at me and was ready for a bit of biffo. Fortunately, by the time the presentation was made we'd both cooled down. But, importantly, I was back on tour with a win under my belt, and my leg was getting better all the time.

Japan was a real culture shock for everyone. The diet, the lifestyle, the rigid politeness and regard for protocol sat uneasily with the wild surfing mindset of the day. And it was starting to take its toll. It was the first and last time they had such a long Japanese leg.

The last straw came at the launch of the final event. This was the end of the real crooked contest systems and things blew up so spectacularly that I think it actually helped usher in a fairer era. The mayor was at the contest launch, local dignitaries, all the officials, they were all there to see the formal announcement of the contest draw. It was such early days in pro surfing that no-one really agreed on how the contest draw should be done and a debate began over which of two rival methods should be used. One, which I considered to be the proper way of doing things, involved combining the current ratings with the previous year's ratings to come up with seedings for the event. The other, which PT and Kanga Cairns were backing, just went on current ratings and it was the chosen method. Basically, everyone supported the system that gave them the easiest draw. After the Coke event and missing the first two Japanese contests, I'd dropped down in the ratings, but as reigning world champion I believed I was entitled to a higher seeding than the current ratings would have given me. As it was, they had me up against MR in the second round. I just completely called bullshit on it. I argued that there was no way, even in the interests of spectator appeal, that you could have the world's number one and number two meet so early in the event. But they wouldn't budge, and I totally spat the dummy and went off at PT and Kanga.

'You Bronzed Aussies, you're a bunch of wankers, I'll have you right here and now,' I blustered, and we started shaping up. This was the first blow-up me and my old mate PT, the Coolangatta kid, had ever had and before we knew it we were throwing punches at each other in front of the mayor and all these people. I realised this wasn't a good thing for pro surfing but I was so angry, I called them outside.

'Right, Bronzed Aussies, I'll have you all on. Outside. Kanga, the lot of youse,' I repeated. I was fuming. I stormed out of the place and started pacing back and forth, hoping that big Kanga wouldn't actually accept the invitation.

The next minute, two young Hawaiian guys, Louie Ferraria and Vince Klyne, came out all ready to back me up, 'Yeah, we're going to help you out. We're going to hide in the bushes here. We're going to fuck the Bronzed Aussies up. When they come up we're going to beat the shit out of them.'

Hang on, I thought, I don't really want this to happen. I'm ready for a bit of a stoush, but I don't want to start a major incident here. But it was too late. Mayhem had already broken out inside. All the pent-up emotions, the anger and frustration of the previous weeks just spilled out. The doors swung open and out staggered Pat O'Neill, the owner of O'Neill wetsuits, with blood running out of his head. He'd made the insane mistake of pinching Hawaiian Brian Surratt on the bum to try to introduce a bit of levity to the proceedings — but Brian didn't see the funny side of it and he just turned around and clocked Pat. And then it erupted.

I couldn't believe it. I had Hawaiians hiding in bushes, I'd called out the Bronzed Aussies and one of the captains of the surf industry was bleeding from the head. It had just turned into a full-on brawl. There were fights breaking out all over the place and I'd been the catalyst.

But at least it showed everyone that you couldn't get away with these rinky dink systems, changing them every event. We didn't know what rating system was going to be used from one event to the next, who was number one, when you'd meet who in the contest. It was a joke. It took that blow up to make them say: Firstly, we'll never have four events back to back in Japan again in the history of surfing (and they never have). And secondly, we've got to get it right.

PT and I shook hands later on, and agreed, let's just get it right. Let's get in there and have the surfers involved, let's get this whole thing right and running according to some set rules so that we've got some credibility as an organised sport.

MR and I met in the second round and he beat me. It was in small surf, and he was just all over it on his twin fin. My ankle just wasn't ready for a major showdown like that and he went on to make the final, where Shaun beat him.

MR opened up a huge lead. From Japan, we went to South Africa and, sure enough, MR won the Gunston 500. I got a third so I was staying in touch but I needed a big result. The second contest was in Durban and the surf was huge. It was a solid 15 feet at the Bay of Plenty and guys weren't even getting out in their heats. I went out there and had a pretty good go and got through, dodging clean up sets to pick up the rideable, smaller ones. We were all riding our little boards in this huge surf because no-one travelled with a comprehensive quiver of boards in those days. Finally, it settled down to six to eight foot and I beat Jonathon Parrman, one of South Africa's best big-wave riders ever, in the semi-finals. My opponent in the final was none other than PT. He got on the microphone before the final and announced, 'If I win this I'm going to retire. I've never won a major contest, I just want to win this one and retire,' which made him sentimental favourite right then and there. It was a best of three final, and I came in from the first one pretty sure that I'd beaten him, but he got the nod. I just thought, well, bugger it, I don't care. I'll go out there and beat him in the next two. We went out in the second heat and I knew I beat him in that one. We came in — and the judges had scored it an unbreakable tie. I said, 'Okay, okay, we'll go out there again.' So, PT had won the first heat, we'd tied the second, and if I won the last heat it would be a draw — and, I presumed, there'd be a surf-off. But they decided there was no time for a surf-off in the event of a draw, so they declared PT the winner. Yet another example of dodgy contest systems. I just copped it and tried to focus on the positive. I'd got a third and a second in South Africa and I was on the comeback trail.

There were two big events on the east coast of the USA that year, and for some reason MR decided not to go. The East Coast had always been a happy hunting ground for me, and this was my chance to catch up. I got second to Dane in the first one, the Seaside Pro. Then, on the eve of the Florida Pro, Hurricane David began hovering just off the coast — the biggest hurricane of the century, at that time. I was staying with Jeff Crawford again, along with Critta Byrne and Mark Warren, and on Jeff's calm insistence, we didn't evacuate along with the rest of the population. Instead, we ripped down his fence and nailed the palings up around the windows and sat it out. David hit with full force and stopped just over nearby Cocoa Beach. Trees were snapping and debris was flying through the air. Jeff lived on a narrow peninsula, with ocean in front and a river behind, and the waters were rising on both sides and nearly linking up in places — it was terrifying.

Then, all of a sudden everything was calm. The eye of the hurricane had stopped right over us and we ventured outside to inspect the damage. It was the most eerie sensation. We got in the car and drove down to the local surf spot, Sebastian Inlet. There were power lines down, trees ripped out by the roots, and the surf was huge, perfect and completely empty. We could hear the other side of the hurricane coming and jumped back in the car and drove back to Jeff's. The second half of the hurricane hit and blew all night, and the next morning we picked our way down to the beach through all the debris and surfed Sebastian Inlet by ourselves, as good as I've ever seen it, before or since. We surfed by ourselves all morning, now with our minds firmly set on the contest, due to start the next day. By lunch-time people started returning to their homes. By the afternoon, we were starting to wonder where the rest of the competitors were. The next morning, there was still no sign of a contest, and it was only through luck that someone came by the beach and told us, 'Oh, the Florida Pro's not on here, it's on at Canaveral Pier.'

'What?' we bellowed in unison. We jumped in the car and high-tailed it down the coast — it was about a 20-minute drive — only just getting there in time for our heats. And the waves were terrible.

Cheyne Horan was right in the World Title race again, and once again, my little buddy Pat Mulhern came to my aid. Pat knocked Cheyne out early, and Pat and I met in the final again. Pat was my greatest ally in those years. For some reason, he had Cheyne's measure, yet I would absolutely wail on him when we met up. Pat's dad wasn't totally delighted with this arrangement and hurled abuse at me from the pier throughout the final, but that only made me more determined. I won the Florida Pro and, suddenly, guess who was number one in the world? After falling out of the top 16, the ankle injury, having the Coke taken out from under me and missing two major events, I'd made it all the way back to number one.

I was going into Hawaii, the next leg of the circuit, with a similar lead to the one I'd held the previous two years, around 800 points — I felt on top of the world. I'd made nearly every final since returning from injury. MR had missed two events as well, and he was in second place, with Cheyne Horan and Dane Kealoha also in contention for the Title. Cheyne was unproven in Hawaii but the

Bustin' down the door

other two could be counted on to get some big results in the Islands. It was going to be a great winter.

THE MIKE BOYUM EXPERIMENT

There was quite a break before Hawaii so Toni and I went to California to hang out for a while. I hooked up with the Quiksilver crew, and stayed at Bob McKnight's place, the president of Quiksilver USA at the time, right on the beach at 56th Street, Newport.

That was where I got to know Mike Boyum, the archetypal hard-core, travelling surfer — one of the first guys to discover Grajagan (the epic left-hand reef in Java) and set up a camp there. I'd met him in Indonesia before and had admired his boundless spirit of adventure. The guy had learnt to surf at eight foot Grajagan at the age of 40. But I really got to know him that autumn in California. He turned me on to this incredible, macrobiotic diet and we did a lot of surfing together.

I didn't realise at the time, however, that the other reason he wanted to get to know me was that he knew I came from south-east Queensland. As a serious connoisseur, Mike had done his homework, reading up in books and *High Times* magazine, and he knew that the number one magic mushroom in the world was the Queensland gold top. I used to tell him all the stories from the early days about crew going out into the valleys and picking mushrooms, and how people who'd never taken drugs in their lives would unwittingly fry up a few gold tops in their omelettes. He loved these stories. Mike had lived a pretty radical life, not always on the right side of the law but, at 42, he was so fit and healthy and so full of life, he had a real energy I was drawn to. He suggested we go surfing together and I thought that was a great idea. There was only one small complication — he was currently a resident of a low security Long Beach correctional facility and I would have to pick him up from there at 5 am. He was paying his debt to society for some past, murky misdeed I never inquired about, but he wasn't considered dangerous and was on a day-release scheme. So I'd drive out to Long Beach Prison and sit outside and wait for him each morning — we'd go down and surf Newport together. Afterwards, he'd train me in the finer points of the macrobiotic diet, teaching me how to make brown rice sushi rolls and all this incredibly healthy food, and then I'd drop him back at the facility.

But Mike's eagerness to sample the Queensland gold top got the better of him. Unbeknown to me, he'd sent away to *High Times* magazine and got the spore of a gold top mushroom and he started cultivating it in these big glass jars at Bob McKnight's place. His little experiment remained a closely-guarded secret, until one evening when Bob threw a huge party. Mike must have been out on weekend release, and he chose this night to bring his experiment out of the closet. Late in the night, a guy came up to me wearing an expression of great alarm. 'There's a guy down on the beach and I think he's dead,' he stammered. Bruce Raymond and I bolted down to the beach and there was Boyum, definitely not dead, but not quite of this world. His hair was actually standing on end as if there was electricity surging through his system. He claimed later that he had left his body and was floating above us.

When he finally came back to earth, he confessed about his experiment and had no hesitation giving the brew the double thumbs up. He'd nearly died, he'd thrown all his clothes, watch, jewellery and other valuables into the ocean, and that was enough for him to declare proudly, 'They work!'

We got Mike inside, got some clothes on him and released him back into the party when we felt it was safe. He quickly regained his composure and we never heard another thing about it.

Not long after, Mike finished serving his time. He decided to head to Hawaii and I drove him to the airport. Little did I know that he'd packed his experiment kit. He issued me with a warm invitation to join him over in Maui before the contests and I agreed, thinking it would be a great way to relax and surf it up before the big Title showdown. I told him I'd meet him over there.

A few weeks later, Mike collected me from the airport in Maui and drove me back to his place. Halfway up this winding mountain road, he pulled over, got out of the car and marched off into the hills with a big green garbage bag, ordering me to follow. He got me to hold open the garbage bag while he shovelled cow manure into it, then lugged it back to the car, threw it in the boot, and drove on. When he got home he threw it all over the garden.

He never offered any kind of explanation, and I didn't think too much of it at the time. We just got into a cruisy routine of surfing all day and eating really well. A few days into my stay, he announced that he was going to take me to this secret surf spot, this really special little bay on the other side of the island. But first he was going to make us a special protein drink. He made up this abomination — there was pawpaw and protein powder and all sorts of healthy things in it, but what I didn't know was that it also had a huge amount of Mike's personally cultivated gold top mushrooms in it. And these drinks were black. Black smoothies.

'What the hell are these?' I protested.

'It's the spirulina,' Mike told me, 'it makes them turn out black.'

And I thought, alright, and chugged it down. 'It better be good for you, it tastes pretty revolting,' I said. Mike gulped his down happily and off we went, along this beautiful, winding coastal road. While I marvelled at all this incredibly lush, tropical scenery, I started experiencing a strange light-headed sensation.

'Oh yeah, by the way, you're my latest experiment. I've just given you a massive dose of gold tops,' Mike told me casually, as they started to kick in.

I was speechless, way too freaked out to formulate any kind of reaction. We turned off down this dirt road and pulled into a small car park. Spread out before us was the most magnificent bay I had ever seen in my life. My senses were on a roller-coaster ride and there was no getting off. The waves were good and Mike hurried me into the water. We paddled out and I was barely holding myself together. I couldn't feel the water as I paddled through it. My hearing seemed so acute, I swore I could hear a bee buzzing in the next valley. Colours and smells were all outrageously vivid and I was starting to actually see things that weren't there.

Somehow I found my way out the back, where two local Hawaiian guys were sitting waiting for the small, clean waves that ran down the flank of the bay. Instantly, I became convinced they were leering at me. Every time I looked at them their faces would change and I imagined they were licking their lips and drooling as they looked at me. Then the penny dropped —they're cannibals! It seemed to make perfect sense. They're going to eat me, they're sizing me up for dinner. And it seemed like they were edging closer to me.

I had to escape. I saw a set of waves approach and I paddled out past the Hawaiians, turned and swung on to the first wave and headed straight for them, trying to show them that I wouldn't be easy prey. I slashed and sliced my way in between the startled locals, only missing them by inches, cackling madly to myself. I surfed the wave all the way on to the rocks and did one last massive re-entry in the close-out on to bare rocks. My board hit me in the chin and the wave just splattered me all over the rocks. I had blood and scrapes all over me, but I didn't care. I had to make good my escape. I ditched my board and scrambled into the undergrowth.

For the next four hours I tramped through the jungle, bleeding and cutting myself to pieces as I tore through the vegetation. In the meantime, Mike and the local guys found my board smashed on the rocks, saw the blood and feared the worst. I must have circumnavigated that entire valley before I came staggering out into the car park later that afternoon looking like a road accident victim. By this time I was starting to come down and, oddly enough, I felt profoundly at peace. I walked into the car park as calmly as you like and just went, 'Good afternoon gentlemen, how are you all today?' The same local guys were there, but they no longer looked like cannibals. Things started returning to normal and Mike looked exceedingly pleased with the results of his experiment. Then the great Hawaiian surfer Gerry Lopez turned up and Boyum opened up the back of the car and turned to Gerry and said, 'Here Gerry, have one of these,' and pulled out, to my absolute horror, another milkshake container with a lid. He pulled the lid off and held out the appalling black smoothie.

'Gerry, please, don't take that,' I begged him.

He just laughed. 'Rab, I'm too smart for that. I know what would be in that.'

Bustin' down the door

'Well, I didn't,' I said, and everyone enjoyed a hearty laugh over it. Another guy did turn up soon after, the full space cadet, and he was only too happy to accept Mike's offer, knowing full well what was in it. As I watched in horror, he just tipped the thing down his throat and sculled it.

I'd had enough. I had to get off the island and away from this guy.

That night we all went out to dinner in Lahaina and as I walked out of the restaurant I could hear the voice of the guy who'd sculled the last smoothie. He was delivering what sounded like a stirring sermon but I couldn't for the life of me figure out where it was coming from. Then I looked up and there he was, standing on the roof top, telling all and sundry to repent or burn. I just went, oh man, that's it, that's the final chapter. Time to go.

HAWAII 1979-80

Toni was having trouble getting a residency visa from the Australian Consulate. It was pretty difficult back then — if you weren't married — to have a partner who was a foreigner and be coming and going from Australia all the time. We had pretty well decided that we were going to get married eventually and in the end, I just thought, let's bring the wedding forward. And I proposed to her while I was in Maui and she was in California, over the phone, and she said yes. I flew back to California for the wedding, so her family could attend. It was a pretty low-key wedding — put it this way, the only other Australians in town, Harry Hodge and Bruce Raymond, couldn't even find it. We had a brief honeymoon on the Queen Mary docked in Long Beach Harbour and then we flew back to Hawaii to prepare for my World Title defence.

This was an Hawaiian season of quite some controversy, and I've heard passionate arguments over the years about who most deserved the Title in '79. It was true that there were five Lightning Bolt judges on that panel. You can't deny the fact that five of those judges were directly involved in the biggest surfboard label of the day, which also happened to be MR's main sponsor. The other fact you can't deny is that MR was doing the

217

The dream come true ...

best surfing all around the world and the best surfing in Hawaii that year.

There were three events in the Hawaiian contest season — the Pipe Masters, the Duke, and the World Cup. Myself, Cheyne Horan, Dane Kealoha and MR were all still in contention for the Title and the mathematics of who had to do what to whom to become world champion was mind-boggling.

First up, in the Pipe, Cheyne had a close heat and was knocked out early. He thought it was a rip-off, but I thought he simply hadn't done enough time out at Pipe. I was confident I got through my heat, but I was eliminated early too, so we both felt like we were being rubbed out of the World Title race. It got really big and perfect for the middle stages of the contest and MR kept getting through. For the final, Pipe was small and MR won the Pipe Masters on the Backdoor rights, which was a real break from tradition. Suddenly, he'd made up a huge amount of ground and was right back in the hunt.

Then came the Duke Kahanamoku Classic and Cheyne, MR and I all made the final. MR and Cheyne surfed more up the Point on the north peak that runs down the Sunset reef, whereas I paddled out and waited for the big, A-frame, west peaks. In all my years of surfing Sunset, I'd always considered that to be the winning formula out there: to sit and wait and ride the biggest west peaks that came through, just like I'd seen the great Eddie Aikau do in '77. When I came in to the beach, Reno Abellira shook my hand and said, 'You definitely won the Duke. You rode the biggest waves, you took the greatest drops. That's what the Duke is all about.'

But that particular year the panel thought differently — MR was announced as the winner, Cheyne got second and I got third. That was a real blow to me. I was counting on winning that. I felt I'd won it, and I needed to win the Duke to get some momentum going for the last event.

Going into the World Cup, the last event, I was still leading. I'd been the number one ranked surfer for five months now. But my lead was being whittled away. The scenario was unbelievable. I was only seven points ahead of Dane Kealoha, and Cheyne was another 13 points behind him. Only 20 points separated the top three, and

MR was still 100 points behind me. Less than one placing separated us from first to fourth.

The World Cup was at good-sized Haleiwa, but I already felt things weren't running my way. Sure enough, in the early rounds I broke my legrope and my board got washed up on the rock wall east of the break. I had to swim in, retrieve my board off the rocks, run along the beach and paddle back out, and I still only lost on a 3–2 split decision to Ken Bradshaw. But that was it for me, I was history, out of the Title race. I was devastated. I'd lost a shot at the World Title because of a broken legrope.

Then, in the very next heat, the unthinkable happened. Dane Kealoha lost to this almost unknown Puerto Rican guy called Edwin Santos. You would have got 100 to 1 on Edward before the heat. He was quite a competent surfer but not in the same class as Dane.

That left it down to Cheyne and MR, and they both made the semi-finals. MR had to win the event, and hope that Cheyne got knocked out in the semis, to win the World Title. All Cheyne had to do was beat PT in his semi, and he was world champion. Just to complicate matters, Cheyne had just quit the Bronzed Aussies and wasn't PT and Kanga's favourite person right then. PT openly bragged later that if Cheyne had been a Bronzed Aussie, he would have thrown the heat for him. But PT was bent on revenge. Cheyne was still inexperienced in Hawaii and PT worked him, just shadowing him, holding the inside position and trying to stop him getting waves. But when Cheyne managed to slip away, he was surfing really well. His Hawaiian surfing came of age that day at Haleiwa. There was nothing in it, as a beautiful set approached in the dying moments of the semi. They both looked at the first one and neither of them took off. Cheyne started paddling for the second one but PT had the inside and also went to paddle for it, but they both pulled back at the last moment and scurried for position for the third wave. There was only about 20 seconds left and PT took the third wave and a got a good ride right through to the inside. Cheyne was left alone out in the lineup as the final seconds ticked away and the last wave in the set approached. Cheyne started paddling for it as they started the countdown.

5, 4, 3, 2, 1 … the hooter sounded just as Cheyne stood up and no-one was sure if the wave would count. Regardless, Cheyne surfed the wave of his life. He came hard off the bottom, snapped under the lip, and pulled into the barrel. I'd never even seen him do any of this stuff before. He came out of the barrel and did a big roundhouse cutback to finish off, just as the commentator announced, 'That wave does not count.' It would have easily won the heat if that wave had counted, and Cheyne missed out on the World Title by a fraction of a second.

MR still had to win the final to become world champion, and at that point PT decided, bugger it, I'm not going to lay down just to stop Cheyne from winning the Title, I want to win this thing. And PT set about trying to do to MR what he'd done to Cheyne. But MR was just that bit more worldly than young Cheyne, and he managed to slip out from under PT's grasp. MR won the contest and the World Title, launching the longest World Title reign in pro surfing history.

THE MR ERA

So began what has become known as the MR era of pro surfing — an incredible four consecutive World Titles from '79 to '82. But he didn't have it all his own way, and I spent plenty of time in the number one spot. Going into the final event of '79 I'd been number one, and two months later I'd won the first event of 1980, the Straight Talk Tyres at Cronulla, and was back at number one. But MR had clinched the number one spot when it counted. I was always in the top five, within striking distance, and I remember it as a great period of really high performance, competitive surfing with a fantastic spirit between the top surfers.

I look back on this time with a kind of wry amusement, because I can't help feeling like we were pulling off a bit of a confidence trick. The fact was, none of us had much money. Here we were, the first generation of professional surfers, travelling the world, living like kings, being lauded and just buffed out wherever we went. But, basically, we were living on our fame, relying on the hospitality of friends and strangers alike to get by.

I also look back with a fair measure of pride, because we were pioneering the new surfing world. I felt like we were the modern day Marco Polos of surfing. We were among the first international surfers to go to Japan and Europe and all the other non-traditional surfing frontiers where people had never even seen surfing, or at least not top-level surfing. I think that instilled in me an understanding that the lifestyle was way richer than any financial rewards could ever make it. In a way, we were being paid in priceless experiences. I really saw us like Vasco Da Gama and Bartolomeu Diaz (no relation) and Christopher Columbus and Captain Cook, pioneering new territories in the name of surfing. We were in uncharted waters and sometimes we found ourselves sailing up the Magellan Strait.

MIKE GINSBERG: 'They were setting the ground rules for the kids today. They deserved to make more money but they didn't and they're not complaining about that. They don't have any sour grapes about it. That's the way it was. They had experiences that those kids today will never have. Those guys were real men, and money would have distorted their potential. Bugs and those guys with lots of money — they just wouldn't have been the same people.'

South Africa became one of my favourite parts of the tour. Despite the country's well-documented racial tensions and political unrest, I loved the place and made a lot of good friends. We didn't like the Apartheid system and made sure we registered our own protests in our little rebellious ways.

The dream come true ...

But, more than anything, I just fell in love with the South African coastline. The free surfing trips to the southern Natal Coast in between contests were always memorable. My good friend Mike Ginsberg would take us to the most amazing surf spots in the middle of nowhere. Myself, MR, Cheyne, Mike Tomson (Shaun's cousin), Marc Price and photographer Aaron Chang were regulars on these idyllic trips.

On the morning of a surf run down the coast, we'd get up half an hour before the dawn, at 5.15, when they were just getting the smorgasbord breakfast ready at the Maharani Hotel on the beachfront. We'd go in there and just rip through the place in about two minutes flat. We'd fill the napkins with buns and muffins and the finest danish pastries and smuggle them out. Then Michael Ginsberg would come by and we'd head off down the coast and as the dawn approached we'd be at some unbelievable empty point break. We'd open the napkins full of the finest fare in the world, and all the local kids would come down from the tribes and they'd be eating the mulberry muffins, the banana–nut danish and the chelsea buns. It was awesome. And then they'd all sit there and watch us surfing.

It's such raw coast, it's got a reputation for being really sharky, and not many people surf round there. There's a wave down there like Kirra Point and it just runs straight across the mouth of this river — completely shark infested. The locals stand on the bridge and shoot them. So we never surfed that particular spot.

MIKE GINSBERG: 'We used to go surfing at Green Point early in the morning, dawn patrolling, and just before Green Point there was a little pastry shop — I think it was called the Cabin — and this place used to make the best chelsea buns. So we used to finish surfing and we used to hit the Cabin for the chelsea buns and it became an obsession with us ... And I credit Bugs, and I honestly believe this and I spoke to Bugs about this, we believe that it's the truth, that that's where the word "filth" derived from. We used to have these steaming buns in our faces and be waiting to pay for them and Bugs

Bustin' down the door

came up with, "These things are just filthy," and the lady behind the counter didn't know how to take it ... We had some really, really hysterical times. Just like, God, I'm hanging round with the four best surfers in the world (Shaun, MR, Rabbit, Cheyne) just going to the best surf spots and seeing the best surfing, and just seeing the guys as they were ... They were so competitive but they were only competitive when they needed to be competitive. They were just like buddies, just like surfing partners on a surf trip and that's when you saw the true side of those guys, and I was fortunate enough to see that side, and when they went to contests people saw the other side.'

In Durban, we stayed at the Mentone Mansions, the last of the old, derelict hotels in town, surrounded on all sides by modern, high-rise, luxury hotels. It was fantastic — cheap and right on the beach, we could watch the surf from our balcony. A few times, I shared a flat with Cheyne Horan, which always proved to be quite an experience. Cheyne was the full, good health guru of the tour and he'd declared any room he stayed in a total smoke free zone as part of his health regime, which was fine with me. This particular day, I'd had a surf and decided to take a nap. Cheyne had been threatening to make these kiff scones, and while I slept he arrived home with this enormous bag of mull and embarked on his scone-making experiment. As part of his anti-smoking campaign, he'd decided to ingest the stuff rather than smoke it. He stuffed all this mull into a giant pressure cooker and turned the heat on full power. Soon after, someone came round to tell Cheyne there was an international call for him at a friend's house. Cheyne was doing radio reports in Sydney and he'd forgotten to file a report, so he raced over to his friend's house to take the call. He left the pressure cooker on and, of course, it just about exploded. I woke up to this outrageous whistling noise and all this commotion in our room. I stuck my head

The dream come true ...

into the kitchen and there were five African hotel staff trying to figure out how to approach this possessed pressure cooker. I guessed what must have been in there — the whole room was reeking of the stuff — and did my best to cover things. 'My friend has burnt the breakfast. No problem. I'll fix it,' I told them. As the words came out of my mouth, the cooker started blowing black soot all over the kitchen, coating the ceiling and walls. The hotel guys were getting more and more agitated and decided they wanted to open the cooker up and look inside. It took all five of them just to prise the lid off and when we peered inside all you could see was this thick, black gunk. Cheyne finally turned up and we managed to convince the hotel staff that it was all under control, but I don't know how the police weren't called. The whole floor of the hotel stunk of burnt mull. It was a really putrid odour, not at all pleasant. You could smell it as you came up the stairs from the floor below. I'm sure it must have stunk for the rest of the building's existence — it just completely contaminated the building. They actually pulled it down the following year.

When all the commotion had died down, Cheyne continued on with his cooking experiment quite happily. He scraped all this black gunk out of the bottom of the pressure cooker and mixed it with flour, milk and eggs and whipped up the most foul-tasting scones you could imagine. You couldn't even swallow them. It was a hold-your-nose job. He made a batch of about 20 scones which had the resin of about six ounces of mull concentrated in them. He convinced me to have a nibble on one and it was so potent it was unbelievable. I just put up the crucifix and went, 'Keep those things away from me.' They were scary.

Cheyne had already been knocked out of the contest, and I made it through to the final. Just as I was about to go out for a best-of-three sets, man-on-man final, Sydney pro surfer Richard Cram called round to wish me luck.

'Do you want to stay and watch the final with a cuppa tea and a scone,' Cheyne asked. Now, you've really got to know Crammy to imagine his reaction. He loves a cuppa, and he loves scones, there was nothing in the world he'd have liked better than to sit down with a cuppa and a scone to watch the final.

The final went the distance and I lost in the third and deciding set to Hans Hedemann. It had taken hours to complete. I picked up my runner-up trophy and cheque and went back to the hotel room ... and there was Crammy, seated at a desk, facing the wall, gripping the edge of the desk until his knuckles went white. He was hanging on for dear life. 'How many scones did he have?' I asked Cheyne.

'Aah, he went back for seconds,' he said.

He must have had some outrageous amount of THC in his system — he didn't recover for hours and never touched anything like that ever again in his life.

But the final chapter of the scone saga was played out 30,000 feet above the earth. At the end of the Durban contest, we all arrived at the airport to fly on to Brazil for the next leg of the tour, and Cheyne whipped out a few remaining scones. There were three or four of us sitting around, word had spread about these scones so no-one would touch them. They were abandoned on a table and we boarded the flight. Unbeknown to us, two of the straightest guys on the tour came by, Joey Buran and David Barr, and helped themselves to the scones.

During the flight, Joey and David decided they wanted to get off the plane. They hit the panic button, and were frantically telling the flight attendants that they had to be let off. I heard the commotion and came down the aisle and recognised the symptoms straightaway. They had their meal trays down and were gripping them with the white-knuckled death grip, hanging on for dear life, and just blubbering like babies. They really thought they were dying. I figured I had to do something.

'Here's the deal boys. How much did you have?' I asked them.

'We ate a whole scone each. Are we going to be alright?' they stammered.

'Look, you're going to be okay but for the next four or five hours you're going to get higher and higher and higher and higher — and then you should level out,' I explained.

This didn't do much to calm them and they just became more hysterical. The experience probably changed their lives. I don't think Cheyne realised just how strong those scones were.

RETURN TO FRANCE

France also became one of my favourite ports of call, and there was a distinct buzz in the air about returning to Europe in 1980. I hadn't visited the continent since my cultural sojourn of '77. Once again I was to rendezvous with Bruce Raymond, this time in Biarritz. I flew solo from New York to Paris.

En route to Paris I experienced the strange sensation of overhearing my name being spoken in whispered conversations on the plane. I wheeled around in my seat to see where it was coming from, and saw the entire US amateur team seated in the rows all around me. I was seated in 48E, and in 47E directly in front of me was a 15-year-old Tom Curren. We acknowledged each other with a casual nod. They were heading to Biarritz for the 1980 World Amateur Championships.

Charles De Gaulle Airport in Paris is a labyrinth of escalators encased in perspex tubing, like a scene out of 'The Jetsons'. At one stage, I was happily cruising up one tube on my way to a domestic connecting flight to Biarritz, when I spotted the US amateur team going past me down the wrong tube. I had to literally fight my way against the flow of humanity to rescue the American team, who appeared to be on their way to Abu Dhabi. I managed to get this brilliant young team on their correct flight, which just happened to be the same flight I was booked on to Biarritz.

TOM CURREN: 'I remember the first time I saw him was on the plane going to France and I didn't know he was going to be on the plane or anything. We were going to the World Championships and he was there just travelling or something and I had a little ghetto blaster. I put it on, I think I had the Who or something. It was kind of loud, you know, and I was looking around and I looked back between the seats and I just saw his eyeball looking through and so I turned the music off. He didn't like it, you could tell. I remember the first thing he said to me was, "Oh, you're the son of Pat Curren." I pretty much looked up to him a lot.'

Bustin' down the door

The World Titles were staged at La Grande Plage, usually a magnificently hopeless beachbreak under the shadow of the equally magnificent Napoleonic structures ringing the Bay of Biscay. But with unusually defined banks, La Grande Plage threw us up excellent six foot barrels, and Bruce Raymond and I were invited to put on an exhibition in front of 20,000 bewildered Frenchies.

Tom Curren made both the junior and open final. He took out the juniors decisively and acquitted himself well in the opens against seasoned Aussies Mark Scott and Glen Rawlings. In a split decision, Scott took the crown over my future brother-in-law Rawlings.

We then headed to Hossegor. John Law, from Quiksilver in Torquay, had rented a beach house at La Gravier in central Hossegor. Bruce and I met up with Victorian surfer Maurice Cole and we did a bit of surfing. After a run of fairly average surf, Maurice came flying in the house one morning — speechless, gesticulating wildly. Fearing some maritime disaster, we ran to the top of the sand-dunes. The sight was beyond our belief. Overnight, La Gravier had transformed itself. Brisk, offshore winds fanned the most beautiful six to eight foot groundswell one could ever imagine. The ocean was corduroy. Concealed sandbars exploded into life. A galaxy of perfect surf lay before us — with not a soul out.

The frenzy was unnecessary, it was only 8 am and it didn't get dark until 10.30 pm. The wind puffed offshore and the swell pumped without another surfer in sight all day. What ensued was the most perfect day of surfing any of us had ever experienced. There was Bruce, Maurice, John Law, myself and local pro Frank Gomez. We could have had our own peak each and surfed in solitude all day. But perfection of this magnitude deserved to be shared and together we settled on the most epic bank of all, conveniently located directly in front of our house.

We surfed our brains out. The tube-riding got deeper and deeper as the afternoon wore on. A Paris-based film director who had been searching for me for days found me that day. He set up his camera and made *Wayne Rabbit Bartholomew — the Movie* in one day. Take one.

That day had a profound effect on all of us. In our wildest dreams we couldn't have imagined such perfection in Europe. The

September warmth, the beach culture, the waves. Maurice was so moved he stayed there for 14 years. And I have no doubts that Quiksilver Europe was born that day — sewing the seeds of the huge European surf boom of the '80s and '90s.

I moved on, richer for the experience, but with contest points and prize-money to chase. Europe's first international pro contest was being staged 200 kms up the coast at Lacanau and I was keen to win first up. It wasn't part of the IPS tour at that stage, but I sensed France was going to come to play an important role in world surfing and I wanted to be there from the start. My lasting memory of that Hossegor stay was driving out of town, seeing Bruce Raymond sipping a fine red wine in the evening of that brilliant day.

I was the top seed for Lacanau. They seemed pretty chuffed to have one of the 'big three' in attendance. Most of the Aussie team entered, as did a smattering of the top 16 professionals.

The day before the tournament, a huge swell hit. Being a relatively straight section of coastline, there was no chance of Lacanau handling the swell. Nobody could believe that 12 to 15 foot surf could be generated in Europe. The first two days of scheduled competition were abandoned. On the next-to-last day of the waiting period, worried officials approached me. Would the great Bugs be willing to surf? I felt obliged to say yes.

That was all the encouragement they required to begin the contest. Within the hour I found myself paddling out into the maelstrom alongside my opponent, Robert Wolfe, a Queensland amateur. My troubles began when he got out to the second layer of swells while I got caught by a huge set of close-outs. There I was, the former world champ, and number one seed, disappearing down the coast under an avalanche of whitewater, while my amateur opponent plucked a couple of open-faced waves in front of the judges.

I returned to the beach thoroughly humiliated, a score of zero next to my name. My only consolation was that I was in the losers' round and only 12 heats away from being back in the main event. I hid in a friend's Kombi for the rest of the day. I finally drew strength from an overheard conversation between Australian pro surfer Derek Hynd

Bustin' down the door

and a couple of British lads. 'Don't count Rabbit out,' Derek advised them knowingly, 'he'll be back, you watch.'

The final day saw the swell drop to six feet with excellent conditions. With a resolve to atone for my fall from grace, I began my campaign. Terry Richardson and Glen Rawlings had qualified for the three-man final and they sat on deckchairs high atop the promenade, smugly watching proceedings. I got on a roll, and each time I dragged myself up the long stairwell from the beach to the promenade I'd look at them and say, 'I'm starting to get angry,' or 'I'm coming for you guys.' I was knocking them down, heat after heat. My sixth round opponent packed his van and headed back to England before the heat even began. I finally met Robert Wolfe again and despatched the talented goofyfooter in his prime conditions — four to six foot lefts.

I was in every heat from lunch-time on. I continued to drag myself up the stairs, glare at Richo and Rocky Rawlings, change singlets, and charge out into the fray again. My last hurdle was to beat newly-crowned World Amateur Champ Mark Scott. Having done that, I was in the final. By late afternoon the tide had dropped. Suddenly, what had been a left-hand bank all day turned into a hollow right-hand barrel. At last, the gods had smiled on me. I wreaked my revenge on my goofyfooted opponents in ruthless fashion.

I could barely paddle, I had an insane wetsuit rash after a dozen heats, and all I could do was take off and lean into the barrel. After half a dozen classic tube-rides, I knew it was over. The top seed had prevailed. The Lacanau Pro officially went on the circuit soon after and has been a fixture as a World Championship Tour event for many years.

Postcard to Wendy and her husband, Wayne, from Tahiti, November, 1980.
'This trip has turned into one of the best of my life. The Tahitians have really made me not only welcome, but they treat me like some sort of king. I've been on television, front page newspapers, I've done two exhibitions to which the whole island turned out to watch, and last night I presented their champions with trophies.

The dream come true ...

'They have asked me to coach their national team. We're staying at a mansion with a swimming pool and I have a new car to drive. I just can't believe how friendly and genuine they are. Hope you're well. Love, Rab and Toni.'

I remember those years with Toni, when we were able to travel together in style, as one of the happiest times of my life. The following year in France, 1981, the Quiksilver house was moved to Seignosse, another beach suburb of Hossegor. I took my wife over and we had an absolute ball, surfing and lazing in the beautiful northern sun by day, and then eating out at the sidewalk cafes and sharing the odd bottle of beaujolais at night.

One morning there was a knock on the door. I opened it, and to my surprise Tom Curren was standing there, suitcase and surfboards by his side. 'Um, er, can I stay with you Rabbit?' Tom asked coyly.

'Yeah, sure Tom, you can stay in that corner over there,' I replied, a little bemused.

This was odd. He'd just flow from LA to Paris, trained it down to Bayonne and somehow found my residence. Toni and I went out dancing that night at a typically cool, French, open-air disco and came home kind of late. We were only lightly merry from a few wines but I was a little bleary-eyed when, sometime around dawn, I was awoken by young Tom shaking me.

'Bugs, you should see the waves in front of the house. I've never seen waves so perfect,' he babbled, and with that he was off.

I clambered up the sand-dunes, wiping the sleep from my eyes and, lo and behold, there it was again. Perfect Hossegor. Only this time, instead of peaks, it was one long, Kirra-like sandbar. Tom was the only one out and had his pick of the insanely long barrels.

As I raced up the sand spit with my board I witnessed the young Curren get a mindless barrel, get spat out the end and hurtle through the air over the back of the wave. What followed was a tube-riding orgy. The master and the apprentice — Bugs getting

Bustin' down the door

barrelled off his nut as if he was back home on the Goldy, and Tom displaying tube-riding skills way beyond his years.

Nearly every time I pulled into a deep one, Tommy would scramble into a position where he could check out my style and technique without interfering with the wave. And I found myself checking out his style — I couldn't believe the way he maintained edge control on his little twinny. The kid definitely had an affinity with the tube.

Tom ended up marrying a French girl, Marie, several years later, and spent many great Septembers at his beloved Hossegor, yet he maintains to this day that the session we shared at Seignosse was the best he'd experienced.

On the last day of our stay, Tom urged me to swap boards with him. I was off the idea of twin fins but reluctantly exchanged boards. To my surprise, I had a ball. In fact, I enjoyed watching Tom ride my Gill Glover single fin even more. Tom insisted I take his Al Merrick twinny to California. Something told me to do it, and when I arrived in Cal I had Bob Hurley do me up something similar, only to my dimensions.

Bob rushed it through and presented the board to me at Malibu Point on the morning of the US Pro. It was a huge gamble. However, the double-hulled twinny loved Malibu. I tore through the field and just as I was about to paddle out for my semi-final Curren appeared on the beach. To his delight, I went completely off. I probably peaked in the semi, as I only managed third behind MR and Buzzy Kerbox in the final. However, a first up good result on the twin fin buoyed me as I prepared for the inaugural Marui Pro in Japan.

In what would become my migratory pattern for the next five years, I went to Hawaii in late September and rode the first winter swells as a prelude to the season proper. In between swells in that early October of '81 I whipped out my twinny and fine-tuned my hotdog surfing at Sunset Point and V-land.

The 1981 Marui Pro was held in two to three foot surf at Hebara Beach in Chiba. In the man-on-man semis I posted one of my strongest wins against MR, then met another twin fin maestro, Dane Kealoha, in the final.

The dream come true ...

Dane and I were to wage some intense battles throughout our careers. I'd beaten him at Cronulla in '80 and in the Japan Cup final in '79. He'd done me up in New Jersey in '79 and in Florida in '78. We both blitzed the field at Hebara and went into the final of the Marui Pro as equal favourites.

Halfway through the final I hassled Dane on the inside and took a vital wave, slashing my twinny to the beach. Dane blew up, began abusing me, paddling at me and splashing water. I could see that he'd lost his composure and I remained calm. While he was regaining his concentration I snagged the winning wave. I was relieved when Dane shook my hand on the podium, conceding that my tactics had won through on the day.

As fate would have it, young Tommy Curren had given my career a second wind by introducing me to the twin fin. I headed to Hawaii happily ensconced in the top 3.

HAWAII 1981-82

All the hassles of the '70s were so far behind me by the winter of '81, that I really loved going to Hawaii again. I'd made a lot of dear friends over there and my surfing at Sunset Beach had really matured. The first half of the '80s was the peak of my big-wave surfing. I gained the confidence in big waves that can only come with years of experience, and I lived for big Pipe and Sunset. Even more than the World Title showdowns and the contests, big-wave surfing was now what I went to Hawaii for.

But I'd also just fallen in love with the twin fin, and this led me to start going back to Velzyland. V-land was the last spot in Hawaii where I was forgiven. It is such a stronghold of Hawaiian surfing, I was actually banished from the break for five years. I'd tried to surf there again in '79 and was literally chased out of the water. I tentatively ventured there again in '80, just to check the surf one afternoon; when I got back to my car there was a brick sitting in the passenger seat. It had arrived there through the windscreen — I figured I still needed to give it a bit more time.

But by '81 I'd served my five years and it was at last behind me. I'd finally buried it, and so had everybody else it seemed. So I returned to Velzyland on the twin fin and started having an absolute ball. It's one of my favourite waves in the world and I'd really missed it. It was a beautiful reunion and, of course, I returned a lot wiser.

The highlight of that year was making the finals of the Duke and the Pipe Masters. The Duke was held at Waimea and on the day of my semi-final I caught my best wave ever at the Bay. It was basically a 20 foot day, but swells of that magnitude fluctuate a lot during the course of a day. They peak, then back off, sometimes quite quickly, but I think the swell peaked in my semi. On a 20 foot day, you are guaranteed there will be some bigger sets, every couple of hours one humungous set will come through. I remember paddling back out after a wave and there was only Larry Bertleman and I in the lineup. A set approached and as we paddled over the first wave, we could see the second wave was a solid 20 feet and the third one was already towering over the top of that. Larry just went, well, 20 feet's good enough, and swung and took the second wave. It's the strangest feeling paddling over a 20 foot wave at Waimea Bay, knowing you're the only one in the lineup. There is a gigantic gallery of people watching and they know you're there, in the spot, and it is there for all the world to see whether you really want to catch the big one. I paddled over the second wave and there was a perfect 25 foot wave. Absolutely perfect. It was a crystal clear day, a nice, light offshore wind blowing, not a waterdrop out of place, but here was this huge wave. And there's nowhere to hide if you discover you don't want to take off on the thing. But this day I felt so in sync there wasn't a moment's hesitation. I found I really wanted that wave and I remember just taking a beautiful, clean-as-a-whistle drop. There was no drama halfway down, there was no skittery board, just a pure adrenalin pump. It was a very special wave for me — I'll never forget it. It was in front of a big gallery and it was in the Duke Kahanamoku Classic, which honoured Hawaii's greatest surfing legend. That wave was every inch of 23 to 25 feet, and I won the semi and advanced to the final. I ended up coming fourth in the final, but I'd peaked in that semi

The dream come true ...

— that moment was enough for me. The swell had backed off in the afternoon for the final and I sat out there waiting for another one but it never came.

New Zealand-born surfer/shaper Alan Byrne, Darrick Doerner and I had become very tight in Hawaii, doing a lot of surfing together at big Sunset. Al and I had been friends for years and he had recently started shaping my boards. Doerner, a North Shore lifeguard, was really ruling at big Sunset, and he was also riding AB's sleek, channel bottom surfboards. We all had a lot of respect for each other's surfing and Darrick and I regarded AB as one of the master big-wave gun shapers in the world. When you are surfing big waves together on a regular basis, there's a definite bond. There's sort of an unspoken agreement to push each other and test your limits. AB's got one of the biggest hearts I've ever seen and he's got elephant balls to go with it, so I was stoked when AB and I both made the Pipe final. Also in the final was big Simon Anderson, from Narrabeen, doing a pretty remarkable job of proving his revolutionary thruster design in big waves. He'd already won Bells and the Coke in Australia on the three-fin board, and Hawaii was the final test for the design. Hawaiian great Buttons Kaluhiokalani completed the four-man final and we had an epic heat. AB and I pushed each other like there was no tomorrow. I pretty well shot myself in the foot by going right on a big set and getting cleaned up with about two minutes left. It was a desperation move because I knew AB and Simon had the front running. I decided, bugger this, I'm going to try to paddle back out through Backdoor.

This is always a sketchy move because you're right in the impact zone, it's super shallow and you're asking yourself that age-old question: What is behind that next wave? You've only got a short area to cover to get to safety, but it's a terrifying place to get caught inside. I put my head down and started paddling furiously through the bubbling foam, desperate to get to the safety of the open, blue water outside, as a set reared up on the reef. I got over the first one, scratched up the face of the second, and I could already see this thing towering out the back. I could hear the other guys, AB and

Simon in the Pipe lineup, just screaming and hooting as this wave approached. It just sized me up. It didn't matter if I paddled to the beach, to the horizon, or sideways, it didn't matter. It had claimed me, big time, and the best I could hope for was to miss the actual moment of detonation itself. I got totally flogged by that wave and the hooter went as I was getting thrashed around in the whitewater.

AB very nearly won, but Simon got a clincher in the dying moments, won the Pipe Masters — proving the thruster once and for all — and changed the face of surfboard design for ever. Buttons got third and I got fourth. But AB and I were pretty stoked — it had been a good showing.

That night AB and I thought, let's do the right thing. It's the old tradition, up to the Kui Lima for a few celebratory drinks. Let's do the sporting thing and stop in at the condominiums and congratulate Simon Anderson, let's go and have a beer with the big bloke. Al, myself and my wife Toni went up there clean, and sober as a whistle, freshly showered, neatly dressed, ready for a civilised night out. We walked into the condo where Simon and his crew were staying, and there was a room full of men in various states of undress, towels wrapped round waists, or still in their boardshorts from the surf, playing this notorious Narrabeen drinking game called 'animal thumper' with Wild Turkey. Somehow, we became embroiled in the game and between 7.30 and 8 pm, AB and I went from sober human beings to raging, drunk maniacs. Beds were being thrown off the top level of the condo and a general mood of crazed excitement prevailed.

I delivered one of my first great emotional sprays to the young guys that evening, which I was to become famous for in later years. For some reason, I became incensed that some of the young Australians hadn't charged Pipe in the proud tradition of the fearless wave hunters from Down Under. I accused them of piking out and honed in on one poor unfortunate, Mark Scott from Maroubra. I actually chased him around the Kui Lima Estate on foot. I have no doubt that he could have gone toe to toe with me and done very well, but that night he knew that I was serious so he ran from me. We never made it to the hotel itself for our civilised celebratory drink. By 8.30 pm Toni

The dream come true ...

had got us out of the condo, and AB was unconscious. We were just a blithering mess. I still wasn't much of a drinker, particularly hard liquor, and I spent the rest of the night with Toni walking me around our yard down at Log Cabins — me just dribbling and babbling on about how I was going to go back and get 'em all. But that was the way we celebrated Simon's win — with a game of animal thumper. I don't know what the Australian cricket team or rugby league teams get up to when they celebrate a big win, but I suspect it isn't a million miles away from the scene in Simon's condo that evening.

Simon's win at Pipe really gave the final stamp of approval to his new three-finned thruster design. Simon is a great Australian surfer and one of the best backhand surfers of all time, and winning at Pipe on the thruster, after winning at big Bells earlier that year, was his finest moment. I think winning the Pipe Masters made him a very satisfied man.

Of course, MR won the World Title again, this time over Dane Kealoha. As for me, I was just stoked to be back in the jungle, happily residing in the Log Cabin (where the surf spot Log Cabins takes its name from). There was just a great vibe that year in Hawaii and we did a heap of surfing. I was really focusing on my tube-riding at Sunset. It's a difficult wave to tube-ride, and it can also be a very painful wave to tube-ride. When Sunset Beach slaps you, it hurts. I copped the chop one time really badly that season and it remains one of my worst wipeouts ever. I came around the bottom at Inside Sunset and lined up the barrel. As arrogantly as I could, I just stood there and tried to do this soul-arch bottom turn into the tube and, as Sunset will do, the lip threw violently and unpredictably and caught me by the head. My feet went out from underneath me and my head swung straight down and hit the water so hard that I beat the lip to the bottom of the wave, and then the lip hit me again. Simon Anderson saw it as he paddled out and when I finally came up, he paddled over to make sure I was okay, he could see what a heavy wipeout it was. I'd been trying to be a bit too cool. That wipeout sent me in with a migraine. No matter how much you thought you'd mastered Sunset Beach, it was always the king. It would always remind you: don't get too cute.

NICK CARROLL: 'I remember Rabbit going off once, it was '81 and the Pipe contest had been on; all the young Aussies went in it and some of us did a bit better than others. One of the Aussies, I think it was Mark Scott, Scotty from Maroubra, kind of wimped out in his heat. It was about eight to 10 feet Pipe, pretty good, pretty easy to surf and he sat right over on the shoulder, just caught a couple of little end sections and later on in the contest Simon Anderson won. There was a big party round the Kui and Rabbit was there and we were all there carrying on, throwing shit everywhere, when Rabbit just suddenly turned fucking mean. It was insane, he just fucking turned mean and he got hold of Scotty and he just started abusing the shit out of him, just going, you've fucking got no pride, just going off. He really meant it, it wasn't like stage acting, like a lot of what Bugs does is stage acting, he was fucking dead serious.

'He was just furious that a young Australian had gone out at Pipeline and wimped out — that's 'cause for Bugs it was such a defining moment coming here and defying nature and the odds and doing well; it was obviously like the big achievement of his whole life, and he was kind of disgusted that people would let down that legacy. That was a really heavy moment. Prior to that I'm sure none of us had thought of ourselves as part of a real tradition at that level, and that really brought it home that, fuck yeah, we're all part of Australian surfing and we should try hard to support that tradition because it is so important. Before that, despite bravado and all that, we thought we were just groms compared to Rabbit and MR and the rest, but seeing Rabbit go off like that made me and a few other people there aware that no it's not like that, we've got to kick a bit of arse here.'

237

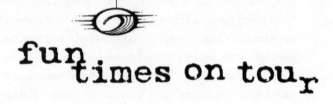

fun times on tour

1982

Cheyne Horan came out of the blocks firing in '82. He won the first two events of the year: the Stubbies and the Straight Talk Tyres in Cronulla. MR struck back to post his fourth Bells win, and I was feeling a bit left out of the action. But then the Coke Surfabout made history by offering the biggest purse ever in surfing — $70,000 total prize-money. The thing that got me fired up was that first place was worth $30,000, almost half the total purse.

The Surfabout was a magical event that year, in the true Surfabout spirit. We travelled all over Sydney in buses, chasing waves, and went right up to the end of the two-week waiting period. Autumn in Sydney was a beautiful time of year and there was a great vibe between the competitors. The amazing thing was, Dane Kealoha and I just kept bumping into each other — it was similar to the feeling I'd shared with MR at Bells. Dane and I were in different halves of the draw and when we'd cross paths we'd just look at each other and go, 'Yep, see you in the final.' After our earlier blow-ups, it was the tightest we'd ever been and we started hanging out together a bit away from the contest. Toni got sick of the waiting and she flew back to the Gold Coast, so I was left to totally focus on the contest and that 30 grand first place prize.

The swell finally came up on the second last day of the waiting period. It was eight feet and for the first time ever they moved the Coke to Dee Why Point, on Sydney's Northern Beaches. For the third year in a row I drew Shaun Tomson in the quarter-finals. The previous two years he'd knocked me out of the Coke, but this year, from the quarter-finals on it was the best-of-three sets. The first set stuck by tradition with Shaun dusting me, but I got to love this best-of-three sets deal. It was like the losers' rounds. I just thrived on comeback situations where I got to show my strength of will. I never quit and I was a fighter. I took the second set convincingly and we were both really fired up for the decider. In the third set I'd made up my mind — if Shaun Tomson could take off deeper inside than me at Dee Why Point then he could have it, because I was hell bent on taking off as deep as humanly possible. I was inside the Chair, a local lineup spot right outside the Point, and I dominated the lineup and won my way through. My sister Wendy, and brother-in-law Wayne, drove down from the Gold Coast so they were there to see that win, I really got a boost out of that. It was also the day a 16-year-old Martin Potter came of age and beat MR.

The next day the swell was still up and the competition went to Cronulla Point, on the south side of Sydney. There'd never been an event at good-size Cronulla Point either. In the semis, Dane Kealoha came up against Martin Potter and beat him two sets straight up. I was up against local favourite, Jim Banks — of all the places, Jim Banks at his local spot with all the local support. Even though he was on his backhand, he was pushing hard and we went all the way. Again I lost the first one, but I came roaring back and just out-gritted him. At that point I brought into play the run — which no-one had done. I figured out that you could ride a wave all the way and come in on the rocks and then run up the Point over these really sharp rocks, rather than having to paddle back out. I actually cut my feet to ribbons but I was beyond pain. I knew that if they really wanted to follow my path they were going to have to sacrifice their feet too. Even a few gobs of spit from the Cronulla locals who wanted to see me lose couldn't phase me. I beat Jim and came in exhausted.

Fun times on tour

Contest director Graham Cassidy gave me my singlet and said, 'Right then, here you are, back out for the final.' And I said, 'No. I'm not paddling straight back out there. I demand a 30 minute break.' I stood my ground and I got a 30 minute break, which was only fair and is standard practice between the semis and the final these days. Deciding to make the most of the break, I went into the competitors' tent and had a massage. Unbeknown to me, Dane was out in the water, waving his arms, wanting to know what was going on. Finally he came storming in, stuck his head in the tent and there I was getting a massage, listening to this beautiful relaxation music. You could almost see the steam coming out of his ears. I had a major psychological advantage before we'd even got in the water.

I won the first set, but Dane came roaring back and just whopped me in the second one.

$30,000 was a lot of money in 1982, and second prize was only $6000. The way I saw it, coming second wasn't a matter of winning $6000, it was more a case of losing $24,000. And we had a rip-roaring final. The tide had come in and the swell had backed off a bit and it was a little inconsistent. It got to the point where I wasn't just riding these waves to the death, I was riding them up the rocks. I was so keen for that money that I was cutting back in between rocks and doing little floaters on to bare rocks, and then running back round the Point. Dane was in the lead with a couple of minutes to go and I picked up a solid set wave and rode it to the best of my ability all the way through. I got to the beach, looked at my watch and decided, I can't get back out there. I walked to the top of the cliff with a minute left in the final and I could see this wave coming. It was the biggest wave of the whole three-set final. It was about a five to six foot wave and Dane saw it too, he sat out there patiently as the final minute ticked away. He let go a couple of waves that he might have been able to get enough points on. There was only 20 seconds left and this wave was just beyond the break. He paddled over the wave before it as they started counting down, and turned and started paddling for it with all the strength he had left. He was paddling for his life as they counted down and he got to his feet just after the

Bustin' down the door

hooter. He got up and just terrorised this wave to the beach. Absolutely tore it to shreds, but it didn't count.

It was one of the greatest moments of my competitive life, standing on the clifftop at Cronulla Point, suddenly $30,000 richer — the biggest payday of my career. I came straight home and spent it in a week. I bought a block of land for $20,000 in these beautiful hills (that I'd dreamed of living in since childhood) up behind Tweed Heads, and I bought a Mazda RX7. In another stirring tribute to the persuasive powers of my old mate Hollywood Harry, I also bought shares in the *Band on the Run* movie soundtrack. I duly received my contract, which is still in a bank vault to this day, and is yet to yield any sort of dividend.

> ANDREW MCKINNON: 'Rabbit won the 30 grand and they gave him champagne for winning and he nearly sculled the whole bottle. Then I've got to line him up for an interview with Sydney radio station, Double J. I've got him in the phone booth and he passes out. He passes out and so I've had to grab the phone and go, "Sorry, Rab can't do this interview, he's won the final against Dane Kealoha but he's passed out." ... And as we drove back from Cronulla across the Sydney Harbour Bridge — me, Rabbit and Peter Crawford — Men At Work came on the radio, "Down Under", and we just sang it at the top of our voices all the way across the Harbour Bridge.'

SOUTH AFRICA

I was starting to get pretty theatrical in my contest preparations by this stage. I'd become good friends with Hawaiian Buzzy Kerbox and at the Gunston 500 in '82 we decided to make a video of my contest psych up. I'd just beaten Tom Carroll in the semi-finals and I was about to go out against MR in the final when Buzzy walked into my room with a video camera and asked if he could video me. I was feeling so confident, I said, sure, why not. This was when that Rocky movie came out with the theme song, 'Eye of the Tiger'. Buzzy's playing this song over and over as I'm getting ready for the final, filming the whole time. He followed me down to the contest and before the final they'd introduce you to the crowd up on the presentation dais. They were all there waiting for me, MR and all the officials and about 20,000 spectators. I came striding out of the crowd with this cape on and Buzzy behind me with the 'Eye of the Tiger' playing and the video camera going. I just leapt up on stage and went, 'AAAAH! I'm going to kick your arse.' And Buzzy was filming the whole thing. He still has this video. It's hilarious, it would make a great motivational video … It was unfortunate I didn't win that one.

BRAZIL

By the time the tour got to Brazil everyone was starting to get a little tense from the travel and keen for any form of entertainment that was going. The Hawaiians used to come by my hotel room when they were bored — Michael Ho, Hans Hedemann, Buzzy Kerbox, all of them — just for a laugh. They'd heard that I'd thought up these nicknames for everyone on tour based on the top tennis players of the day, and I used to make up these elaborate contest commentaries using everyone's tennis nicknames. Michael Ho got on to it and he used to tell the other Hawaiians, 'You've got to come by and hear Bugs.' MR was Borg, I was Jimmy Connors, Cheyne was McEnroe, Michael Ho was Ile Nastase. It went on and on. Hans had heard that I'd given him a nickname too, so he came by to check things out because he thought I was writing him off. But the fact was, I just had this classic name for him — Heinz Gunthans. Heinz was the main Swiss player at the time, who ended up becoming the coach for the Swiss Davis Cup team. I had to put it all in a story for Hans to satisfy him that I meant no offence, and the other Hawaiians all ended up on the floor. I'd weave this whole commentary together and every time I saw Michael Ho all he wanted me to do was say, 'Heinz Gunthans', and he'd just crack up.

We had a classic trip to Brazil that same year. Everyone wanted to hang out with the pro surfers and all kinds of characters radiated towards our hotel — and I'm talking, all kinds of characters. Rio is a wild city — radical people. It was an easy place to get yourself into trouble.

One naive tour rookie thought he'd play a practical joke on some of the other surfers one day. There were all these people in this particular hotel room and he banged on the door and yelled, 'Federais, Federais, Policias, Policias.' He didn't know at the time, but the crew in the room had all manner of drugs and some heavy Rio coke dealers visiting. They started furiously flushing thousands of dollars worth of cocaine down the toilet. One of the guys was so scared he stepped out onto about a six-inch-wide window ledge six storeys up and edged his way along to the next window with all kinds of drugs strapped to his body. The crew had guns at the ready, the full bit, when they opened the door and the rookie went, 'Ah, just kidding.' They weren't impressed and he had to give them five surfboards and get the next flight back home. That's how it worked over there. Someone was always getting into trouble.

I was sharing with Wollongong goofyfooter Terry Richardson and he went on to have his maiden victory — it was fantastic. He was over the moon, and in classic Richo style he was ready to cash in on the win in any way he could. Not only had he won the tournament but he decided to sell everything he owned, expecting to command a healthy price for the contest winner's boards, boardshorts, clothes, the lot. So he got it all lined up in the room ready to receive prospective buyers, when he had to step outside to do an interview. I left the room for a minute to go and see Michael Ho, and in that short time our room got ransacked. They stole everything of Richo's.

You had to go into the black market if you wanted to change your money. It was outrageously dangerous. You had to go in there with your big bundle of cruzeiros — which weren't worth the ink they were printed with outside Brazil — and haggle with a black market money exchanger to get US dollars out of him at some funky rate, and then get out of there alive with hundred dollar US notes. It was scarier than surfing big Pipe. How no pro surfers got murdered I'll never know. The better you did in the contest the more dangerous your predicament.

THE OP BOARDSHORTS SHOWDOWN

The tour went from Brazil to California for the inaugural OP Pro at Huntington Beach. Kanga Cairns, recently retired as a competitor, was in his new guise as a contest director, but we ended up in a confrontation just the same.

Kanga had spent his whole time on the tour as a surfer representative and in that time, he and I had waged some great campaigns together to knock the tour into shape. Together we'd had full stand-up screaming matches with the contest directors, who wanted to run things their way and maintain all their lurks and perks.

The most heated issue for me was the boardshort rule. If a contest was sponsored by a clothing company, the contest directors wanted all the competitors wearing the sponsor's brand of shorts in the event, regardless of individual endorsements. But if I surfed in any other brand of boardshorts, my sponsor, Quiksilver, fined me $1000 an event. If you came third in those days you won $1250, so I had to finish third or better if I got fined, or I was losing money. It was insane. Finally, at the big end-of-year meeting in December 1981, Kanga and I presented the most comprehensive case against the boardshort rule and, to my utter astonishment, we won and had it overturned.

But when we got to the OP Pro the rumour was going around that now that Kanga was a contest director, he was going to make us wear the OP boardshorts. I was incredulous.

They held a big function at this swish hotel ballroom to launch the contest and, sure enough, Kanga got up there and started telling us how we must wear OP boardshorts. Before I'd even had a chance to object, he singled me out in the crowd. 'Bugs, you have to do this or the event won't be on. You've got to make this concession.'

'But we won the victory. The rule was overturned,' I argued.

Kanga is a magnificent public speaker and he rose to the occasion, just haranguing me, trying to humiliate me in front of everyone. 'Why don't guys like you Bugs, you rich guys, who are up there making a good living, why don't you think about these poor guys out here who've got nothing,' he hollered, suddenly turning the tide of opinion against me. 'Why don't you take your money and piss off, Bugs.'

The other surfers got up and clapped him. I was so devastated. He was such a brilliant politician. He had them convinced that I was the troublemaker, impeding the progress of professional surfing to protect my own interests. I walked out of there, shaking my head, just going, 'You fools.' I had no choice but to wear the OP shorts and cop the fine. I lost the first round of that OP — in five years, I'd never had a 17th place before — those kind of placings did not exist for me. In the whole history of the circuit the lowest I'd finished was 9th. I came in from my heat pretty confident that I'd won, but lost it to a local Californian guy, Todd Martin. I really felt the knives go in then. Kanga had humiliated me in front of everyone, I'd been rubbed out of the biggest event ever in mainland USA, and my World Title hopes plummeted. I'd come into the event seven points behind MR for the World Title race. I admit that at that point, I actually hated Kanga. Not only did I bomb out, I copped a $1000 fine from Quiksilver.

Tom Curren had inspired me to win the inaugural Marui Pro back in '81 by turning me on to the twin fin. By the Japanese leg in '82, he'd won the World Amateur Title and turned pro. He got an interference call against Cheyne Horan at the OP Pro and Cheyne went on to win it. But at the Marui, Curren caused a sensation. He and I were staying at the Rip Curl house together, and every one of the established pros became acutely aware of him as he quietly worked his way through the field — it was almost scary. Here was this quiet, humble young kid who'd just go out in the water and eat you alive. Curren beat another young sensation, Tom Carroll, in the final of that Marui Pro and, of course, those two went on to dominate pro surfing throughout the rest of the '80s.

It was a pretty sobering turn of events for the established guard; there was a sense that we'd better knuckle down and hold down the fort here, because they were about to inspire a whole new generation to come up and stomp all over us.

> **TOM CURREN:** 'We stayed together in Japan one year and one time he put a whole bunch of that wasabi stuff in my food. He went, "Look over there," and he put it in and I was, like, stoked because it was Rabbit.'

MOVIE TIME

Surf movies have always provided great historical records. I grew up spellbound by them and when I had the opportunity to actually appear in surf movies myself it was an even greater buzz. The first two surf movies that really depicted the new age of surfing were *Free Ride* and *Tubular Swells*. Before that it was *Five Summer Stories* and *Sea of Joy* and they always featured Pipeline, Lopez, BK and Hakman. *Free Ride* and *Tubular Swells* really ushered in the Shaun, MR and Bugs era and they came along at a great time. Those movies, particularly *Free Ride*, really buoyed our careers and ran as a parallel to the whole birth of professional surfing and the world circuit.

The next major movies that I worked on were *Storm Riders* and *Kong's Island*. *Storm Riders* was made by Jack McCoy and Dick Hoole but I particularly worked with Jack. We started *Storm Riders* in '81 and it came out in '82 to a thunderous reception. There's a sequence of me surfing perfect, winter Burleigh with almost no-one else out, and great footage of young Gold Coast hotties, Thornton Fallander and Joe Engel at Nias, and Wayne Lynch

246

with dolphins out at Monkey Mia, and a really good soundtrack. It set a benchmark for surf movies at the time. It was kind of the last of the great 16 mm movies. My sequence was set to 'Down Under' — that song became a bit of an anthem for me.

After I won the '82 Coke Surfabout I came home and started another project with Jack McCoy, and two dynamic, new talents — Gary 'Kong' Elkerton and Chappy Jennings. We made *Kong's Island* in 11 days in June 1982. It was a remarkable time — easily the most fun, raucous project I'd ever been involved in. Kong and Chappy were unbelievable characters and the three of us just seemed to produce a special chemistry together. Jack captured it perfectly and the movie remains a cult classic to this day.

I'd been watching Kong coming through the ranks on the Sunshine Coast for a couple of years. He was just this young kid who was a powder keg of natural ability. He oozed this raw, unbridled power and a real carefree attitude. He was a bit overweight — his mates called him Fatboy — he wasn't an athlete, but he was just this super talent and you knew there was something special about him. I hooked him up with my old mate Paul Hallas at Hot Stuff and soon we were both riding AB channel bottoms.

Chappy had moved up to the Gold Coast from South Australia in about 1980 and he was this skinny little kid who lived at the top of Duranbah Hill. I took him under my wing and we'd go surfing together during the day. At nights he was a waiter at the Bamboo Flute, so after surfing we'd go into the kitchen there and growl out. He was an unbelievable character — the Little General, we called him.

Jack had the vision of just depicting the three of us as we were, surfing and carrying on together. I felt like a teenager again, hanging out with these super energetic young guys.

JACK McCOY: 'Al Green came to me and said, make something for kids, make it for kids. So my whole line of thought then was to make a little fairy tale. Rabbit was the figurehead of Quiksilver at that time so I wanted to use him ... He was like the Peter Pan and Kong and Chappy were his little apprentices, so to speak ... This was the period of time when Kong was just going to the pub and staying out all night, and then he'd come and get me in the morning and we'd go and get the others and just go off all day. Every day was an adventure. I had an idea of what I wanted to do — Rabbit was going off with Chappy to try to find Kong — but we made a lot of stuff up as we went along. We were all really inspired by the concept of what I was trying to do.

'There was a *Kong's Island 2* that was going to be released and we shot a whole segment of that in Hawaii when we were doing *The Performers* in '83, and it was just magic stuff, man. We just took it further. We just set out to do really amazing things. One shot that comes to mind was, I had them in this old car up in the canefields. They were coming down this really long hill, this dusty hill through the canefields, taking turns driving while one guy climbed out of the car, over the car, and back in the passenger window. And the three of them were doing this continually in rotation.

'I shot some footage of Rabbit at Sunset one day, shot it from the water, 15 to 18 foot Sunset, with this huge, sucky, animal bowl on the outside there. Rabbit and Darrick Doerner were trading off, going tit for tat. Rabbit really blew my mind that day, aggressively attacking these 15 foot waves. The footage was never put in the movie. It just sort of vanished. I had a little bit of a falling out with Quiksilver after that.'

Toni and I had already begun to grow apart and the constant travelling had begun to take a toll. She was pretty keen for me to give up the pro surfing lifestyle and settle down. I was reaching my

Bustin' down the door

late 20s and not only was I showing no signs of settling down, I began showing signs of doing the exact opposite. I was re-discovering my youth, or actually living my youth for the first time, because all throughout my late teens and 20s I'd been totally dedicated to competitive surfing. I rarely drank, I went to bed early, I trained, I didn't even have a 21st birthday party.

So when Kong, Chappy and I got together, something was awoken within me, something that I'd managed to subdue all this time. My life was really on track for me to settle down, but suddenly I dug my heels in and refused to grow up.

The *Kong's Island* project was a canny bit of marketing by Quiksilver, eager to launch their new wild child, Kong. That's when Quiksilver came out with that poster, 'If you can't rock and roll, don't fucking come,' the star boardshorts, and this whole rock 'n' roll image.

But there wasn't any image-making required with Kong, Chappy and I. The three of us together were larger than life. Something opened up inside me. The key was turned and I felt like one of them, running wild, having an absolute ball.

After being crucified at the OP Pro, the wind really went out of my sails as far as chasing the World Title went. I just basically went, bugger it, and went to Hawaii with Chappy and Kong. We stayed together out at the Kui Lima Estate again but for some reason being stuck out there didn't seem to bother me. I was having too much fun. We were going out surfing at dawn every morning all over the North Shore. It was Kong's first trip to Hawaii and he was completely under my wing. I introduced him to the local boys, like Darrick Doerner, and young Pipe chargers Mickey Neilson and Marvin Foster, and he got off on the right foot straightaway. Kong and I were both riding Alan Byrne's boards for the Hot Stuff label and Kong was my boy.

I introduced him to Sunset because that's where I surfed all the time. His first session, he was like anyone else, he was a bit scared. Little Chappy was getting air on every wave he took off on, it was unbelievable. The wind would get under his board and he didn't mean to, but he was doing these incredible air drops on every wave, just flailing his arms and legs to the bottom of the wave, and making it. I used to be so scared for him. I thought, he's either going to get broken in half, blown out to sea, or just killed on impact, but he was a lot harder than any of us realised.

Toni came out to visit us and didn't know quite what to make of my new playmates. Kong had introduced me to serious drinking, even though he was about 10 years my junior. He was the son of a fisherman and he loved his tequilas and his rum, but I rarely drank spirits. Kong introduced me to the Long Island Iced Teas at the Kui Lima and I fell in love with them. They are an amazing mixture of alcohol. If you want to know what goes into an Iced Tea it's quite simple — everything. And just at the top they put about a quarter of an inch of Coca-Cola for colouring, and the rest is pure hard liquor. The most vicious drink you could ever come across in your life.

One particular night, Kong, Chappy, Toni and myself went up to the hotel cocktail bar for a few quiet Iced Teas. Kong drank about 10 of the things — enough alcohol to kill a man — and I had about six. I was absolutely delirious but having a blast. Kong was dominating the whole bar, as he was wont to do, charming the barmaids and other patrons with his rough Australian charisma. We stumbled out of the place at closing and, foolishly, I decided to drive us all home in my car. It was only a few hundred yards back to our condo and it was within the hotel grounds so I figured it was pretty safe. But as I approached one of the security gates, Chappy and Kong climbed out the windows and started dancing on the roof of the car. Suddenly, Kong climbed back in through the window and knocked me clear over to the passenger's side, seized the wheel and accelerated straight towards the security gates. Chappy wasn't even in the car at this point, he was still trying to climb back in through the window, hanging on for dear life. Toni was just sitting in the back seat while all of this was going on. The security guards saw us coming and realised there was no way Kong was stopping, so they raised the gate to stop it from being smashed.

The security guards jumped into little golf buggies and gave chase. They were these big Samoans, like 300 pound men. I was

Bustin' down the door

trying to settle Kong down, and I was sobering up fast, trying to figure out how we were going to get out of this one. We pulled up out the front of our condo and the security guards must have been using walkie talkies because they were converging on us from all directions. It must have looked like a scene from *Keystone Cops*. All four of us went running into the condo, then decided that that was a bad idea, so Toni stayed behind and the rest of us went running out the back door towards the golf course. We were still blind drunk, half laughing but also terrified because we'd heard some gnarly stories about what these guys did to troublemakers.

We were cackling to ourselves, running down the middle of the golf course, and looking back down the fairway of the 14th hole, all we could see were these lights coming over the greens and fairways. The security guards were out on the golf course in their buggies with spotlights. We decided to split up. Kong went straight up a tree and Chappy took off in another direction. I went running around and around in circles and couldn't find anywhere to hide, I ended up hiding behind a tree about six inches wide. This buggy pulled up right in front of me and I was cornered like a bunny in its headlights. A Honolulu Police patrol car cruised by, saw the commotion and came to investigate. I couldn't believe it. I was being shunted along by this golf buggy, that constantly nudged me in the back of the legs, with my hands up in a full arrest position.

'It's over Kong, come on down, it's over,' I called out as I was being shunted along, eager for a bit of support to share the guilt. But he wasn't budging. And Chappy was nowhere to be seen. The owners of the place were already on the scene outside our condo. They were already convinced there were all kinds of despicable evils being perpetrated in our condo, just because there'd been a bit of noise and a few complaints from the neighbours.

So I was on my own, facing the owners, the security and the Honolulu Police Department, racking my brains for a plausible explanation.

'I'm sorry, just a couple of young guys mucking up. They're a bit out of control. It's nothing really, it's just a lark,' I tried to tell them. 'Terribly sorry, it won't happen again.' The police said to the security, 'Ah, it's nothing, we'll leave this up to you. Just a few tourists going stupid,' and they left.

The owner wasn't so easily pacified. 'I want to inspect your place. I think there's something very funny going on in there,' he commanded.

'There's nothing going on in here,' I told them, and took them inside. What I'd forgotten was that Kong had ripped out the centrespread of a *Penthouse* magazine and stuck it on the fridge door. The owner took one look at it and went, 'I knew it, there's pornography in here.' He looked around the room trying to spot other evils. 'What's in that room?' he barked, indicating my bedroom.

'Nothing really, just my wife,' I said calmly. I opened up the door and there was Toni sitting up in bed trying to read a book and at the foot of the bed there was this conspicuous lump.

'What's that?' the owner demanded, and ripped the sheets back. There was Chappy Jennings cowering at the foot of my wife's bed. It was an unbelievable scene. I was flabbergasted. There was nothing I could say. All of this guy's worst fears seemed confirmed. It took some real fast talking to avoid getting evicted and we ended up being given one more chance.

But that was enough for Toni. We both decided just to shake hands and go our separate ways. There were no tears. Of course, all these things take a long time to settle in, but at the time we both went, well, we're obviously heading in different directions, and it looks like all the struggle, all the patchwork and the good intent, wasn't enough. We realised that we'd just grown too distant. We walked away from our marriage.

I started hanging out with some pretty colourful local characters that Hawaiian season, like Marvin Foster, Tim 'Taz' Fritz and Mickey Neilson. They were guys I'd known just to say hello to, but now that I was back on my own, they started coming by with beers and drinking them in front of our condominium. One time Taz and Marvin came roaring into our car park on two wheels and went straight through the car park, through the bushes and up this embankment that led to the swimming pool. The car was half

Bustin' down the door

hanging over the pool, and we had to very carefully reverse it back down. Afterwards, the owner came by, he'd apparently heard about Taz and Marvin's detour. I said, 'No, no, no, sir, nothing like that happened at all,' and he went over to the bushes and said, 'Well, can you explain these tyre tracks?'

And I had to say, 'No, I really cannot explain them.'

Our condo became a real social centre that season and it was booked in my name. I got barred for life from the Kui Lima Estate. The final straw out there was when Hurricane Iwa came, it was massive. It really wiped Kauai out and it hit Oahu pretty hard too. We decided at the last second to go for a surf out at Kui Lima Point just before the hurricane hit, and the wind came up to about 70 miles per hour. Chappy Jennings nearly got blown out to sea. He just could not get onto a wave and we thought he was gone. By the time we all got safely back to shore we decided it was time for a couple of Iced Teas. So we went up to the cocktail bar and everything was blacked out, so we sipped Iced Teas by candlelight.

After a few Iced Teas we completely forgot about the hurricane and stepped outside into the night. The wind just picked up little Chappy and rolled him down the road like a tumbleweed. Kong and I were in hysterics. Anyone else would have been killed, but by this time we'd begun to realise what a tough little bugger he was and we were laughing our guts out.

We decided to throw a hurricane party and the concept quickly caught on. The party spilled out from our condominium to another condominium and things did actually degenerate a little bit and some furniture got broken. There was a bit of hurricane damage. Chappy was pretty mindless and every time I let him loose he'd run outside into the hurricane. There were trees bent over parallel to the ground, there were coconuts flying through the air, and Chappy kept flying out there on some kind of crazed death wish. After dragging him back inside three times, the next time he did the bolt I just walked over to the back door and threw his blanket and pillow out into the hurricane and that's where he stayed the night. We found him in the morning in the foetal position, bathed in his own vomit. This was the nature of our Hawaiian season.

Taz, Marvin, and Mickey lived in Hawaii Kai, a beach suburb just beyond Honolulu on the other side of the island, and this gave us an excuse to start hanging on that side. We started going surfing at Sandy beach and meeting some of those beautiful Hawaii Kai girls. And on Friday nights all roads led to Waikiki — that's really when the trouble started. There were guys like young Ronnie Burns and Noah Budroe, a big crew of surfers who were going in every Friday night to a nightclub called Club 3Ds. It was the wildest nightclub in the history of nightclubs. It was on the second floor of this building overlooking Kuhio Avenue and it had this giant window which was always open and that's where troublemakers went — out the window, splat, onto the streets of Waikiki. Taz despatched people out that window several times. In this nightclub you would find an amazing cross-section of society — marines, black disco dancers, Hawaiians, surfers — and we were accepted as part of the cool crew. It was a phenomenal time.

I remember coming home from Hawaii that year for New Year's Eve and getting together with all my sisters. We were all partying and having a good time, and then one of them turned to me and said, 'When's Toni coming out?' and I've looked at them, sculled my beer and just gone, 'She's not.' And that finished the night. My sisters were absolutely distraught. But I was too far gone. I'd already started to live my lost teenage years — I'd decided to become a teenager at the age of 29.

Bustin' down the door

the warrior

983 began with an incredible challenge looming in pro surfing. There was no doubt that Tom Carroll and Tom Curren were doing the most progressive surfing in the world. MR had collected his four World Titles and retired. Cheyne Horan was still only young and was in there fighting. Shaun and I were getting towards the end of our competitive careers, but that World Title hunger was still alive within us. The question was: Who was going to ascend to MR's throne?

There was also a major upheaval in the administration of professional surfing in '83. Kanga Cairns formed the Association of Surfing Professionals and overthrew the IPS, winning the support of the surfers with promises of more events and prize-money, greater media coverage and more professional administration. He argued that the governing body of world surfing could not operate out of Hawaii (as the IPS had done under Fred Hemmings and Randy Rarick), and expect to win over middle America. That became Kanga's shining goal — to awaken the inland American masses to surfing and usher in a new era of big-money competition.

Central to the ASP plan was moving the season end away from Hawaii, and instead finishing it in Sydney, where big on-beach crowds and mainstream media coverage were almost guaranteed. This required changing from a calendar year to a May-to-May season and in the transition period there would be no world champion in 1983.

Just before the '83 Australian circuit began they announced that it wouldn't count towards the World Title at all and the new World Title season would start at the end of the Australian leg.

Ironically, the ASP, and new director Cairns, finally ratified the boardshort rule once and for all, and Kanga and I settled our differences. He had a vision and an incredible drive to really turn the world on to the wonders of surfing, and I supported him in that. Kanga was based in Huntington Beach, California, and he and PT had been involved in coaching junior American surfers through the National School Surfing Association (NSSA). He was squarely in the American corner and eager for a new American world champ in NSSA product, Tom Curren. But finishing the circuit in Australia was contest director Graham Cassidy's vision and together they became the two most influential administrators in professional surfing.

That Australian season, the new guard totally dominated and I was thinking, thank God this isn't counting towards the World Title. Tom Curren just blitzed the first event, the Straight Talk Tyres at Cronulla, Tom Carroll won his first big tournament at the Coke Classic, and Martin Potter won the Stubbies. The new kids had cleaned up the Australian leg.

But then the new circuit began in earnest, in South Africa, running from June '83 through to May '84, to decide the first world champion under the ASP. I used that whole Australian circuit in '83 to get myself ready for this big charge at the World Title, but I was still stunned by the form of the young guys. My own poor results in Australia gave me bit of an insight into my competitive make-up. Unless it was the real thing, unless there was a World Title at stake, I just didn't seem to be able to awaken my competitive energy. And the kids did take over, but it was almost like a ruse by us wily old buggers. Let 'em think they've taken over, we were telling ourselves, because we were ready to pounce when the circuit really began.

I badly wanted to perpetuate the old guard. I'd won the Title back in '78 which seemed like a lifetime ago, then MR had won his four World Titles, and I wanted to win one more before relinquishing the tour to the new guys. I liked the idea of book-ending MR's reign and wrapping up our whole era neatly like that.

ABOVE: Feeling very comfortable at beautiful Backdoor in '85, after a solid decade of surfing the place. Jeff Hornbaker, *Surfing* magazine.

BELOW: Setting up my bottom turn at Sunset ready for the sling-shot through the inside. Jeff Hornbaker, *Surfing* magazine.

ABOVE: A classic big Sunset drop in '77. Jeff Divine, *Surfer* magazine.

INSET: My World Title-clinching tube-ride at the '78 Pipe Masters.
Peter Crawford.

ABOVE LEFT: The first Billabong Pro, and the contest director takes a breather between waves, '92. Lee Pegus, *Surfing Life* magazine.

BELOW LEFT: On the job at the Billabong Challenge at Jeffreys Bay. Chris Van Lennep.

BOTTOM LEFT: Carving it up on a fun day at Off The Wall in '94, 20 years after first surfing it. Sylvain Cazenave.

ABOVE RIGHT: MR and I await the result of another keenly fought Bells final. Peter Crawford.

BELOW RIGHT: Cruising at Burleigh on the last day of a 28-day swell. Jack McCoy.

BOTTOM RIGHT: One of the first good days at Kirra when the banks finally returned after the big groyne went in. Jack McCoy.

ABOVE: Having a blast with the kids at Velzyland, Hawaii, in '95, still one of my favourite waves. Ted Grambeau, *Surfing Life* magazine.

BELOW: All-time Duranbah in the late '80s. *Surfing Life* magazine.

TOP LEFT: Racing past the camera in the heat of competition at the Stubbies, '82. Peter Crawford.

TOP CENTRE: Honolua Bay, in Maui, one of my favourite getaways. Peter Crawford.

TOP RIGHT: In the zone at Sunset in the mid-'80s, trading waves with Al Byrne and Darrick Doerner. Aaron Chang, *Surfing* magazine.

ABOVE: A welcome-home swell at Kirra in '93, straight off the plane from Hawaii, on my big board, in the Queensland colours. Joli.

LEFT: The backhand attack at Big Pipe in '75, during the filming of *Free Ride*. Dan Merkel, *Surfing* magazine.

ABOVE LEFT: Me and my namesake at Movie World for the launch of the '96 Billabong Pro.
Lee Pegus, *Surfing Life* magazine.

ABOVE RIGHT : A birthday hug for mum in '95.

BELOW: Taking the drop at Waimea in the '86 Billabong Pro. I ate my lunch so heavily just after this shot was taken, the other surfers in the water didn't expect to see me come up.
Dan Merkel.

I got to the number one ranking through a series of consistent placings. I got a second and a third in South Africa. In Atlantic City I had my first heat against Tom Curren, scored a perfect 10 by catching this freak wave that went from pier to pier, and beat him. We went on to England for the Fosters Surfmasters, and I got a third and Tommy Carroll made a bit of a move by winning that one. It was looking like me and Tommy from that point on.

We came through to the OP Pro and that's where I really had a chance to get on top of things. But in my semi-final against young Californian Joey Buran, I broke my favourite twin fin in half and just missed out on an opportunity to meet Tom Curren in the final, which would have been fantastic. But that third placing put me about 800 points clear in the number one spot ... and then came the critical Japanese event.

The Marui Pro changed pro surfing. In those days, the number one seed would surf against the hottest home-seeded guy, and first round I drew the local champion, the best surfer ever from Japan, Shuji Kasuya. I went out there and I dusted him. I knew I did him up, everyone knew I did him up, but they gave it to Shuji. It was the last time they ever let three local judges dominate a five-man judging panel. The three Japanese judges had him first, and the two international judges had me first. For about the only time in my career, I completely and absolutely lost it and just blew up.

I was told later that the Japanese officials had actually met the evening before to discuss this heat. The Japanese are sticklers for protocol and ceremony and the contest judges and officials would meet each evening, have a traditional Japanese bath, change into their robes, sit down to a Japanese banquet and then very seriously discuss the next day's events. They were desperate to have a local surfer finish in the top placings of this contest, and the two international judges were actually told that their presence was no longer required at the meeting — they could go to bed — while the rest of them stayed up into the night and discussed this sensitive topic. I have no doubt it was basically decided that it didn't matter what happened in our heat, Shuji was going to advance.

Graham Cassidy said to me after the heat, point blank, 'You were ripped off. That was completely unfair.'

'I've got to be able to do something about it,' I said, but there was no avenue of appeal. I totally blew up at the Japanese officials and made a real scene. Little did I know that Tim 'Taz' Fritz, my friend from Hawaii, had also seen this travesty of justice and dealt with it his own way by climbing up the judging tower and hauling one of the Japanese officials down and punching him out. I didn't realise at the time, but between the two of us we really did some damage. I was inconsolable. It was obvious to me that the ASP were pushing the young guys, like Tom Carroll and Tom Curren, and if a few bad decisions hastened my departure, no-one was going to shed any tears. They'd just decided I was over. Tom Carroll went on to win that event and drew within 100 points of me. I was still number one by the end of it but I wasn't going to stick around ... because this is when the infamous trip to Tokyo went down.

When word got to me that Taz was going berserk in the judges' tower, I thought, hang on, maybe that's a little bit over the top, and I tried to calm him down. He took one look at me — saw how devastated and riddled with anger I was — and he just said, 'Let's get the fuck out of here. Let's go to Tokyo.' And I'd never heard a better idea in my life. I had to leave that contest.

Taz was this blond-haired, blue-eyed Hawaiian of German descent. He was just this radical kid who'd been brought up in Hawaii, he did it tough as a haole boy coming through the school system and he became a real tough nut. He was a fanatical surfer and what really caught my eye was that he wasn't scared of Pipeline — he'd do barrel rolls at Pipe. It was phenomenal, he was completely unafraid. One time in 1981 he came round to my place and climbed this tree to try to get a pawpaw and lost his footing. A branch snapped and, from a height of about 30 feet, he fell down and landed on his head. He should have been paralysed but he just got up and went looking for the pawpaw. He was an absolute maniac, but one of those kind of lovable rogues. He was a good-time guy and he wasn't scared of anything, he instilled this fearless attitude in you. If you ran with him you had to be pretty

Bustin' down the door

tough, you had to be very mentally tough. He was a very unique human being.

So we headed into Tokyo on a search-and-destroy mission. I had my own range of clothes in Japan at the time, the 'WRB' range, produced by a local surfwear label. Part of the range that I'd helped design was this unbelievable evening wear, called the 'After Five' range or something like that. So we got decked out in all the gear, with our own peculiar sense of style. We had our collars up, and we were the first ones to wear these long shirts untucked, hanging out. No-one did that. We'd been shopping in California when we were there for the OP Pro, and I'd bought these dungaree kind of pants, and army boots. It was a look before its time. So off we ventured into the nightclub district. We went to this club, Club Tokyo, in the Rapongi district, and to get in there you really had to be someone. Taz introduced me as the owner of a clothing range. I showed them my shirt label, showed my ID and explained that Taz was my top model, and we were in — they loved us. The club was full of western models from all over the world who were in Tokyo doing their gig and we just instantly hit up a great rapport with them.

The contest seemed a million miles away, we were having such a great time. At some point in the night Taz just disappeared. The stories that he brought back later were unbelievable. He'd scaled an apartment building to about the seventh floor to get up to this model's room — an unbelievable Spiderman feat.

Meanwhile, I'd become totally entranced by this beautiful model and she suggested we head to another late nightclub called Club Cleo. It was sprinkling rain outside and the lights of the Tokyo night shimmered off the wet road. To cap off the magical scene, my new friend had a big, beautiful motorbike.

'You get on the back and I'll drive,' I told her, feeling like I'd walked into a movie set. So this beautiful model climbed on the back and we rode through the rainy streets of Tokyo. I was just reflecting on this magnificent turn of events when … a police car pulled us over. I thought nothing of it, figuring, in my euphoric state, that it would only require a bit of smooth talking, smiling, and bowing.

'I think you're meant to wear a helmet,' she said.

'Pfff, I'll blow this away, no worries,' I chuckled.

The police got out, with their white gloves and immaculate uniforms and they were incredibly polite. Even as they ushered me into their police car and drove me away, they remained polite. My friend just went, 'See ya,' got on her bike and roared off. I watched out the back windscreen as my dream disappeared into the night.

So, I was sitting in the back seat of the police car in my flash WRB gear, with a policeman either side of me, and two policemen in the front. There wasn't a word spoken as we pulled into the back car park of a big, inner city police station through an archway and big double gates. They shepherded me into the station and presented me at the charge desk. I was still expecting to talk my way out of trouble but it wasn't long before I realised I was actually being charged. I started freaking, these guys were going to throw the book at me! They weren't just going to write me out a ticket — I was going to jail.

'Look, I'm a world champion. I'm the number one ranked surfer in the world. I'm here for a big international tournament,' I protested. I carried on like this for quite a while but it was getting me nowhere. I had my passport and about US$200 on me and I was just about to lay my belongings on the table and go to jail when, just on the spur of the moment, I said, 'Please, could I go to the bathroom?' And I was given permission.

I was standing at the urinal having a piss, just thinking, this is an unbelievable predicament. Bugs, you've really done it this time. I could look back through these thin, rice paper walls and see the police standing round the charge desk. In front of me, above the urinal, was a closed window, and just on a whim, I opened the window — there were no bars. I knew that I was in the back of the courtyard and I also knew I was more than a floor up, because we'd gone up some stairs. Without even thinking about it, I shimmied out that window. I wriggled out on my stomach — I couldn't make a noise so I wasn't really able to position myself for a fall — and I dropped straight down and did some sort of tuck and roll and just landed in this big puddle in the car park. My adrenalin was

Bustin' down the door

pumping so hard by now. I'd had a bit to drink but this had sobered me up pretty quickly. I had hit the ground running and as I rounded the corner I thought to myself, if they have locked those gates that we drove in through, I'm history. You can't just explain away falling out a second-storey bathroom window. To my enormous relief, the gates were open.

I just sprinted through those gates and out into the night. I was running wild through back streets and laneways, not knowing where I was. Finally, I thought, I've got to get out of this outfit. I was soaked through and covered in dirt, a million miles removed from the dapper figure I'd cut earlier in the evening. I walked into this clothes shop and bought a black leather outfit, and they even threw in an on-the-spot haircut — they cut my hair really short, into a slicked-back style. I was a different person when I walked out, dressed in a black shirt, leather vest, leather pants — even new shoes. I strode out into the Tokyo night in my new guise and found my way to Club Cleo, where I reunited with my model friend. When I'd told my story, she and her girlfriends thought I was a super hero. I'd pulled off the great escape. We partied into the night and I even moved into their apartment for a few days. We went out eating sushi, shopping, and clubbing — the girls treated me like a king. I was a completely new person leading a new lifestyle.

Finally, after a few days of this, I suggested we go back to Club Tokyo to try to meet up with Taz. So we went back to Club Tokyo and, sure enough, there was Taz.

'You won't believe what happened to me,' he gushed, always one to revel in a good story. But this time I knew I'd trumped him.

'No, you won't believe what happened to me,' I told him. So we exchanged stories and he conceded that I'd bettered him. His story about climbing the apartment building was good, but even he was impressed by my escape from the law. That bonded us big time and he decided I was pretty radical after that. But he had one more bit of news for me.

'Bugs, the presentation for the Marui Pro's on in Tokyo tonight.' The contest had finished the day before and Marui always held a big party in Tokyo the night after. We just looked at each other and went, 'We're there.'

I marched into that preso in the black leathers with the slicked back hair, and I even had a little pencil-thin, Rhett Butler moustache. I walked in and I'll never forget the way fellow Australian surfer, Pam Burridge looked at me that night. She couldn't believe me — her jaw dropped. The person she'd seen a few days ago at the contest with the mop of sun-bleached hair and the person who walked into that presentation night were two completely different people. Everyone was in absolute shock. I remember Graham Cassidy coming up and going, 'Bugs, that is absolutely fantastic. You've floored 'em all.'

I wasn't aware, but the alarm had been raised a few days earlier and my Japanese sponsors had gotten word that I'd been arrested, they'd been searching for me for days. They were so relieved to see me — I just walked back into my pro surfing lifestyle and left this whole other world I'd briefly lived in behind me. Taz went off on his way back to Hawaii, and it was like stepping out of a bubble. I went back home after that fateful Japanese trip and rumours had drifted back but no-one knew the real story and I never told anyone, I just denied the whole thing.

I was still the number one ranked surfer in the world but there was a big break in the tour and I slipped back into a pretty social lifestyle. I started hanging out with young Kirra surfer, Sean 'Reg' Riley, a pretty wild guy. He really impressed me with his surfing at Kirra, and on land he was another one of those people who attracted me with his energy. Ross Clarke-Jones, another radical young surfer from the NSW Central Coast, had just moved up to the Gold Coast and the pair of them had this little unit at Kirra. I started spending a lot of time there, surfing and hanging out with those guys, still feeling like I was a teenager again myself. And I started going out in Surfers Paradise a lot, probably a bit too much.

ROSS CLARKE-JONES: 'One day I just had enough of Terrigal and just said, I want to go surf Kirra. I've had enough, I've seen photos, I want to get up there, so I'm leaving school. I'm leaving home Dad, you know, like, I'm going to go on the dole.

Bustin' down the door

My parents weren't too impressed. They tried to talk me out of it but I didn't let them. I just went for it. I went up there and met Sean Riley and he moved in with me and he introduced me to Rabbit and we were hanging out, the three of us, for a couple of months. Seeing the lifestyle of a pro surfer attracted me more than anything else. Like, what do you want to do after you finish school? I thought, fuck, this is what I want to do. Elko was coming round, just like a screaming maniac. They were the biggest influences of where I wanted to go, those two, for sure. Rabbit was just so high on life because he was going for the World Title, and he had his RX7 sports car and he was feeling pretty groovy. He had chicks after him, he was feeling like hot shit, and I was getting some of that energy. Like, this guy's on fire, I want to be close to this guy. Nick Carroll (surf journalist) came up and did an interview. That was all part of it. I thought, interviews, fucking nightclubs, you know, this is the life for me. Rock 'n' roll, money — he was having a ball. He thought he was David Byrne (from Talking Heads). He had the hand signals going. He was ripping. I've got a lot of respect for Rabbit. He's a classic.'

Soon after I got home from Japan, my old friend Denis Callinan told me there was a 10-year reunion on for the Miami High class of '73. I couldn't believe it had been 10 years since I'd been hitching up and down the Gold Coast Highway, skipping class to go and surf Kirra. So along we went. I'd been away from Australia for so long that when I started guzzling a few Australian beers I was quite drunk before I knew it. I'm not trying to justify what happened next, but drink driving and the whole .05 awareness just wasn't an issue back then. The deal was that in Queensland you could drive round drunk as a skunk but you couldn't smoke pot. Those were the unofficial rules. So the next thing I knew I'd driven up to Fisherman's Wharf with a few friends and met this great girl, and I was just having a ball. I decided to give this girl a lift home and we took the back road that wound round Burleigh Hill in my new RX7. It had just started raining and as I came down the hill towards a hairpin bend I knew I was going too fast to make the corner. I tried to take it but the car just spun 360 degrees, then skidded over to the wrong side of the road and straight off a cliff, backwards. We hit a tree, the car was sliced in half. We slid down the tree in the remaining front half of the car, it was about 40 feet down. I got thrown forward on to the steering wheel and smashed my face up a bit. I looked over at the girl, expecting to see her dead or maimed, and she didn't have a scratch on her — she didn't even seem to be particularly perturbed. Our only problem was: we couldn't get out of the car. Some local residents arrived at the scene and forced the car doors open with crowbars. You could see our flight path from the cliff where we'd knocked over a few smaller trees before hitting the big one. We both should have died, there was no doubt about it. I must have still been in shock because I grabbed the girl by the hand and we just took off into the bush and, somehow, we found our way to my place at the back of Currumbin. The next day, I reported the accident to the police and explained that I'd been in shock and left the scene but no-one had been hurt, and no more was ever said about it. My family went and saw the wreckage of the car and were absolutely horrified. You took one look at the wreck and assumed that no-one could have survived such a crash. It seemed like I was doing my best to kill myself, but someone upstairs was definitely looking out for me.

Again, rumours about the accident spread quickly and people were even saying I'd killed someone. I bailed up to the Sunshine Coast and hung out with Kong to let it all die down before flying out to Hawaii in November.

HAWAII 1983–84

I don't know if I was just starting to feel immortal, or whether I harboured some kind of death wish, but the precarious path I was on continued that season in Hawaii. I think I actually did my best surfing in Hawaii around this time. I was definitely at the peak of my fearlessness in the big stuff and I was surfing and hanging out with guys that really instilled that reckless, go-for-it attitude in you.

There were no Hawaiian events as part of the world tour that year. The new ASP administration, under Kanga Cairns, and the old IPS administration who ran the Hawaiian events, Fred Hemmings and Randy Rarick, hadn't made their peace. The Hawaiian contests were still on but they refused to pay ASP sanction fees and the ASP slapped a boycott on the events, threatening to strip points and ratings from any ASP surfer who took part. I badly wanted to surf in those Hawaiian events and I always felt a bit cheated that we were forced to boycott them. I was confident I could have widened my lead over the young guys over there. I was opposed to the boycott but my hands were pretty tied. If I surfed in them I'd be out of the Title race. I was a surfer representative on the ASP board and felt like I should hold rank with the rest of the ASP surfers. Hawaiians Michael Ho, Dane Kealoha and Bobby Owens defied the boycott and surfed in the events, and were duly stripped of their points. They dominated those Hawaiian events, which were held in really good surf that year, but it cost Dane a shot at that year's World Title.

With the World Title on hold, and no events to focus on, I had a wild season in the Islands. We made a movie called *The Performers* with Jack McCoy, for Quiksilver, which still stands up today as pretty cutting edge. I don't remember surfing better than that in Hawaii. From the start of the season to the finish, I felt absolutely fearless. I was running with Taz, Marvin Foster and Mickey Neilson again and was feeding off that energy. At big Pipe and big Sunset I really felt on top of the game.

I was staying at the Keiki Hale, the traditional Hawaiian abode of the Quiksilver crew, with Kong and Chappy — some pretty wild stunts were pulled in and around that compound. The most radical shorebreak on the North Shore just happened to be in our backyard and it provided an effective release for our excess energy.

Tommy Curren and his wife Marie came by for Christmas dinner and must have wondered what they walked into. Just as they arrived, I came screaming out of my room, Talking Heads blaring from the stereo, and went running down to surf this enormous, close-out shorebreak. You know how in the cartoons the waves come up and crash right on to bare sand? This thing was doing just that at about 10 feet. So right before Christmas dinner I took off on this wave and it just sucked dry and slapped me on to the sand and drop-kicked me up the beach. Halfway up the beach my board speared me in the back of the leg and opened up this gaping wound. I just laughed, bandaged it up, and sat down for Christmas dinner.

We were surfing hard all day, every day, charging big Pipe and Sunset and every Friday night we'd go in to Waikiki to Club 3D. I was seeing this beautiful Hawaiian girl.

I was also giving Kong and Chappy a bit of guidance in the surf. We were on the beach at Pipeline on a huge day when two surfers, Beaver Massefeller and Chris Lundy, nearly died. Chappy had to go out in his heat, he was freaking out and I helped him through that. That same day I took Kong down to Sunset and it was just huge and mean, straight out of the west. It was a really windy day and Kong paddled late into this big west peak, freefell out of the lip and landed on the nose of another guy's board. He completely ripped his leg open behind the knee and the guy was ready to throttle him until he saw how badly injured he was. From the look on Kong's face, I knew it was bad. He swam to the beach and I paddled in after him. Somehow, he beat me in and some hippy on the beach put him on the back of his horse and started riding off with Kong down the beach. As I gave chase, Kong fell off the horse and got sand all through the wound. It was such a radical day, there had been sirens wailing up and down the Kam Highway all day, and the last siren of the day was for my young buddy Kong. He had to sit it out for six weeks and spent his convalescence gorging on chocolate choc chip Haagen Daaz. He got back in the surf later that season and absolutely blazed for the filming of *The Performers*.

But it was Taz who was really setting the pace in the danger stakes. I'd give him my old boards and he'd go out and surf big Pipe on my 6'1" twin fins. If you got in a car with him it was pretty radical. He'd go, 'Hey man, you want to see me do a reo?' This became famous. He'd be driving along, see a bus coming the other way, and as he passed it he'd swerve into the bus and bounce off the side. That's how radical he was.

So it was really tempting fate for me, Kong and Chappy to drive in to Waikiki with Taz on Friday the 13th. Taz got in a fight in the traffic in the middle of Waikiki. The fight stopped the traffic and the cops turned up on these little moped things and Taz took off on foot. We abandoned him and headed into Club 3Ds and he turned up there later, just snapping. It looked like he was going to punch us all out at one stage. I figured it was time to go back to the North Shore. We'd borrowed Mickey Neilson's North Shore Cruiser, and I figured it was safer for me to drive home, even in the slightly inebriated state I was in, than hang out with Taz any longer. Kong and Chappy very sensibly refused to get in the car with me, so I took off on my own, winding my way down the road through the old canefields. Just as I came off the Wahiawa Plateau I must have decided to take a nap, because I woke up in the middle of the canefields. I'd left the road, side-swiped a tree and ploughed through several rows of pineapples before I came to rest. Mickey's car was a mess. I'd taken out one whole side and the tyres were all blown, and I limped into Haleiwa on the rims. I wasn't in Mickey's good books for a while after that.

That one finally made me realise I'd joined the next-to-be-dead club and it was time to settle down a bit. The Karmic odds were stacking against me, plus I realised I didn't want to be a potential liability to the sport.

It's not a lifestyle I'd ever recommend to anyone but I don't regret a moment of it. I made a lot of great friends in Hawaii during that time and I think they appreciated an overseas pro surfer who'd get down and dirty with the boys, rather than hiding out up at the Kui Lima. It was a great bonding time and the Hawaiians loved Kong and Chappy, so there were a lot of fun times — parties, surf sessions and practical jokes. I remember the boys coming round to our place one day and just as they came to the door, a gust of wind caught it and slammed it shut in the face of Titus Kinimaka, a well-respected Hawaiian. Once upon a time, this might have caused a major incident but I just told Chappy he'd better open the door. And there was this bunch of Hawaiian heavies confronted by little Chappy and they pretended to give him a hard time for a few moments and then all just cracked up laughing. I suddenly realised how much things had changed since the '70s, when I'd been opening the door of our Kui Lima condo with Kanga behind me, tennis racket at the ready. It felt like us Australians and the Hawaiians had finally got to know each other and learnt how to get along.

> MICK O'BRIEN (NORTH SHORE LIFEGUARD): 'His surfing at Sunset spoke for itself, and the Pipeline, and he earned his respect by coming back here year after year and bringing Kong. Kong was a hit over here, even though he was brash and everything. Kong and Chappy came over with him and they got in with the right boys right off the bat ... They would party with us. That's all the Hawaiians wanted, they didn't want you hiding up at the Turtle Bay, they wanted you to be their friends — "Come on and party with us." ... I think he learnt how to do it, how to be friendly with the Hawaiians, to share with them and be their friends. Nothing an Hawaiian likes better than to have a famous friend — you know, we're at the end of nowhere — and maybe go travel and go stay with that guy some time.'

THE WORLD TITLE RACE

I stepped out of that crazy Hawaiian season and re-entered the World Title race. I was able to put all that wild living back in its box and focus myself on reclaiming the Title. Unfortunately for me, while I'd been honing my big-wave surfing and fitness, Tom Carroll had stayed home and single-mindedly trained in small waves for the final stages of the world tour. Tom had a really high-powered manager at the time, Peter Manstead, and they embarked on a full-on training routine, surfing Sydney summer slop in preparation for the next event in Florida.

I, on the other hand, went straight from surfing big waves in Hawaii to the Florida Wave Wizards, the history-making event where it got so flat the organisers actually drove a launch up and down the beach to try to generate little wake surf. I'd teamed up with an American surfer, Dave Kennedy, who kind of became my training partner, and Tom had his good friend Mike Newling in his corner. It was like a full, head-to-head showdown. But the waves were unbelievably bad. We were both in such a state of super-alertness we could surf anything. If they wanted to put us out there in wake surf, we'd damn well surf it.

There was a great vibe between Tom and I though. We were stoked just to see each other in Florida and we embraced, he wanted to know all about Hawaii. He was super fit, you could see how sharp he was. They eventually found some surf at this remote beach down the coast, and the Wave Wizards was completed in reasonable two to three foot surf. I went out in the semis and Tom won the event, I retained only a slender lead in the ratings. Before the OP, my lead had been 850 points and now Tom had whittled it down to just 60. Even though he was breathing down my neck I returned home very triumphantly with a really good attitude. I was number one and the next event was at my home beach, Burleigh Heads.

I got home on the last day of January, 1984 and I had until mid-March to prepare myself for the Stubbies. There were three events left — the Stubbies, Cronulla and Bells. I totally dedicated myself to the Title race.

In the lead-up to the Stubbies, there was a lot of publicity focused on this two-horse Title race, billed as a battle between the old and the new. We played up for the media, posing for photos arm-wrestling and stuff. It was like a heavyweight title fight and we got right into the spirit of it. Tom and I are both Sagittarians so there's a great deal of mutual respect there.

I had a fairly good draw in the Stubbies compared to Tom, who drew Tom Curren in the second round. It was only two to three foot Burleigh and I expected Curren, on his forehand, to beat him. If Carroll went out early and I went on to win, I could open up a commanding lead. But Carroll was just so determined, gouging these incredible hooks down the point on his backhand, he beat Curren. In the end, Carroll and I met in the final and he won on a 3–2 split decision. I thought I'd won — and I felt the crowd on the hill thought I'd won — but it was really tight. In fact, one of the judges was overheard saying during the event, 'We can't let Rabbit win, we can't have him as world champion again. It would be the worst thing for surfing.' There was no question Tom Carroll was surfing incredibly, but when I realised that kind of sentiment existed within the judging panel, it didn't do much for my Title campaign.

We went down to the Beaurepaires (previously The Straight Talk Tyres) in Cronulla and who should I draw first round but Tom's brother, Nick. I beat Nick pretty well, but in the next round I went down to Glen Winton from the NSW Central Coast in a really close one. Tom just got of jail against Jim Banks and then kept just getting through, all the way to the final, where he met Barton Lynch. I thought Barton had his number, but Tom got the decision, won the tournament and took over the number one ranking.

This is where I believe a real travesty of justice occurred. There were only two people in contention for the World Title, with Bells still to go and I got in my car and headed back to the Gold Coast. Meanwhile, Tommy got bundled onto a plane back to Florida where there was a small, lower-rated event that I didn't even know was on. The newspapers reported that I'd given up the ghost and 'got in a car with a mate and gone soul surfing up to Angourie.' In reality, I drove home to the Gold Coast to prepare for Bells, unaware that Tom was on his way to winning this obscure little contest in Florida. I didn't hear anything about the Title race all week, and the next Sunday night I was sitting in my lounge room eating a bowl of salad and watching the evening news, when up came a picture of Tom Carroll, with the headline 'World Champion' emblazoned across it. I just looked at it and went, how can that be? The showdown's at Bells. Tom had won this event in Florida and even though it was only worth 100 points or something, it was enough to give him an unbeatable lead going into Bells.

I completely hit the roof. I rang up Graham Cassidy and Al Hunt at the ASP and told them I could not believe that they didn't tell me about that event. To this day, I still feel I was really wronged. Tom deserved that World Title, he was taking surfing to the next level with that low-centred, gouging style of his. But I was number two in the world, and there was an event I didn't even hear of. And I'd found out the Title had been decided on the evening news!

270

I went to Bells and I couldn't mathematically win the World Title but I decided to give up my spot in the main event to go through the trials (the qualifying rounds for the unseeded surfers). I knew that if I came through the trials I'd meet Tom Carroll in the first round of the main event. I wanted to at least do that and hopefully knock him out and walk away from the World Title race with a bit of dignity. I got through my first two trial heats no problem, but it was a long time since I'd surfed four-man heats. In the third round I got starved of waves and came to grief. And that was it. Tom was world champ, the new generation had moved in and I knew then that I wasn't going to win another World Title.

I went to the World Title presentation awards in Sydney and made a pretty dignified speech and gave full credit to Tom Carroll, and that ushered in the new era. He went on to win the World Title again the next year, and Tom Curren won it the following two years. I put so much into trying to win that World Title, I felt that something had kind of left me after that.

I kept up a brave public face and, typically, in the midst of my despair I came up with the bold new mission to run for mayor of the Gold Coast. The media lapped it up and to the outside world I appeared as the mighty sporting champion already confidently planning his political career. But those close to me knew how bad I was hurting.

HEIDI: 'I'll never forget the night after the '84 Stubbies. If he'd won it, he had a plan. If he won the World Title in '84 he was going to ask Toni to come back to him, and that was the only thing he focused on and it didn't happen. I'll never forget that. I was living with him at the time and he came back to the house, and I was crying, it was shocking. We were living at the back of Currumbin, and it had been their home. They were dark times.'

271

The warrior

SUNDAY SUN, MARCH 25, 1984: 'I really believe the Gold Coast needs a young energetic mayor, someone in the thick of things, someone who can relate to people. The Gold Coast is one of the most beautiful places in the world but there have been a lot of blind decisions made. I have visions of how I'd like to make things better. One thing that surfing does teach you is a respect for your environment.'

CAREER CRISIS

For a decade I'd been considered to be in the top three in the world. At any point in time from '75 to '84 I felt I was seen as one of the best surfers in the world and I thought that was a pretty good innings. I had to accept the fact that I wasn't going to come back and win the World Title. But I wasn't prepared for what awaited me as I began the painful passage on the downward curve of my competitive career.

I received a phone call from Quiksilver within a couple of months of finishing second in the world saying, basically, that I was sacked. I had seen that coming for a while. For one, I was being fined $1000 a contest in the old boardshort days. And at the board of directors meeting held every Easter, Alan Green and I would go at each other's throats over our differing philosophies. I was totally into the pro surfing vision and they were totally into the rock 'n' roll image. I argued that one was good for the other. I was totally at odds with him about Gary 'Kong' Elkerton. He wanted him to be this wild, free surfer and they basically offered to buy him a house and set him up for life if he stayed amateur and just went on this free surfing program. I knew that he was competitive and that he wanted to be world champion. Al Green was saying, 'No, you're steering him down the wrong path. You're going to be responsible for ruining his career.' In the end that really was the straw that broke the camel's back. They wanted me off the tour and out of Kong's ear.

After finishing second in the world, Quiksilver's only career option for me was to go to work for them in Torquay and, at the time, that was the furthest thing from my mind. Walking off that World Title runner-up's dais straight into some office job. 'What are you going to do?' I asked Al. 'After 10 good years, put me to work packing boxes out the back?' And he said, 'Yeah, well, if it comes to that then we will.' And they wanted me to spend 12 months in Torquay finding a niche for myself in their operations there. I jacked up and said, 'There is no way, I am not doing that.' I knew that I was on very shaky ground and, basically, that was the parting of the ways.

I was earning about 25 grand a year from Quiksilver, which was pretty decent money for the time. But it wasn't long before Tommy Carroll came in on the huge million dollar deal with Quiksilver. Things were happening so quickly then, the surf industry was really starting to boom. Rip Curl, who were still sponsoring me for wetsuits, kept saying, 'Don't worry Bugs, you're on the small money now, but we'll look after you.' I was only on 10 grand a year from Rip Curl then, and I started hearing that they were about to sign Damien Hardman and Tom Curren to these big deals. And I'd think, gee, what happened to me? And they'd go, 'Don't worry. She'll be right. We'll look after you.' But all they did was dwindle me down to such negligible money and I became so disgusted that I just had to walk away. After 17 years with Rip Curl, I just got faded out the back door.

BRUCE RAYMOND: 'Quiksilver created a position that I could step into and the next opportunity was for Bugs, and we made a position for Bugs. And the year would end and he would go, "No, I want to do it one more time ..." We did this for, like, three years and it was always the same thing. He wanted to avoid making that step into what he saw as corporate life. He'd go, "Well, I want to look after the team." ... There was a pro event at Bondi Beach and his own personal competitive drive overrode that again. He bombed out in the quarters or semis and Kong was in the semis, but as soon as Bugs bombed out he bailed ...

The warrior

'At the bottom line, I think he's a wimp but on the other hand I really respect him because he's stuck to his vision. He was going to maintain true to that grommet vision and just keep surfing. I say a wimp, because I believe he didn't grow up, but when you look at Keith Richards or Mick Jagger, you could say the same thing about them. That's when I fired him. That was probably very hurtful for him, and me. He might have thought there was more to it but it was out of frustration ... What we required was for him to give something back to us. He'd gone a year longer and finished second and then what a great way to walk into a situation where he was going to bring that to the table.

'Rabbit framed something that is still Quiksilver policy to this day. Al Green said, "Where do we stand Bugs? Is it important to have a surfer in the top of the IPS?" And he said, "Yes, I believe it is," and that's kind of been stamped as company policy ever since. We refer back to that policy, that it is important to keep someone in the top five. It's weathered time.'

I was left with virtually no livelihood. I felt the cusp of the new, big-money era. I felt slighted, of course, because I figured I'd invested all this time and energy into these companies and at the end of it all, in the twilight of my career, I was left out on the sidewalk with no future. No-one was going to sign up a 31-year-old pro surfer who was now number 15 in the world and on the slide. What future was there in that?

I couldn't envisage a future for myself at that point. It seemed like a miserable predicament to be in. I hadn't made the big money, I couldn't just retire on my winnings. Anyone who spent 10 years in the top three or five these days would be set for life. I was paying off my house and I owned my land, and that was it.

274

But, I was still better off than a lot of guys who did the tour in those days and squandered all their money. At least I'd managed to put a bit away.

I really did bottom out there for a while, I just couldn't see what my next step was. So I adopted the philosophy, when in doubt, go out — and I started going out a lot.

My quiet, little home town had changed a lot in the 10 years I'd been travelling the world. The Gold Coast tourism boom had turned Surfers Paradise into the nightclub capital of Australia, and in the mood I was in I was all too easily swallowed up in the party scene. Without the athletic commitment and focus I'd had all through my 20s, and having been awoken to the pleasures of partying by my friends in Hawaii, and Kong and Chappy, I went off. A lot of people around the Gold Coast had never seen this side of me and I think I really tumbled off my pedestal in their eyes. I was partying hard and going out nearly every night, drinking too much and making a bit of a spectacle of myself.

They used to have this dollar night every Thursday at the Coolangatta Patch and it became famous all around the surfing world. We used to muck up quite a lot down there, me and my mate Reg Riley. He became famous for stuffing cigarettes up his nose, or putting one end of a condom up his nose and pulling it out his mouth. And it seemed like the whole Gold Coast used to converge on the Patch every Thursday, so our misbehaviour was well-witnessed. I know there were plenty of people who thought I was heading to the pro surfing junkyard of burnt-out ex-surf stars.

WENDY: 'That was Rabbit's heaviest crossroads in his whole life, apart from his marriage finishing. He'd reached the peak of the sport, he'd got to number one and he was having this big career crisis and things were going to change for him. He was dedicated to his health and so disciplined. Rab never drank much. You'd invite him to a party or a barbie and the guy'd arrive with one beer or something. He was so dedicated. He wasn't number one any more and it was all changing and so he started going out — okay, he went off, over a five-year run there. It was a heavy time for him. I mean, okay, he went off the rails for a little while. It was public and it was back home and people had never seen it before and people were pretty horrified.'

ROSS CLARKE-JONES: 'I had this little motorbike and I was driving around Bombay Rock, Surfers Paradise, and I see Rabbit on the steps, inebriated, wasted — I think this is after he'd lost the World Title to Tom, it was around that time — and I just saw him hanging on this step, and I go mate, you remember me, and he goes nah, and I said look, you need some help, and he just looked at me and said, can you drive, and I went yeah, I've got me motorbike here but I can drive and he said, look, take me to my car and drive me home. So I found his car, he didn't even know where his car was, put him in the passenger's seat and drove him home to my place, picked him up, put him to bed and then took off in his car and went for a drive in the RX7, gave it a fucking good workout, went off in it like two in the morning, he never knew that, I never told him. But in the morning he woke up all stoked and then Sean Riley fed him and praised him.'

GORDON MERCHANT: 'You can watch them go through it but I think he was one of the hardest to watch. He didn't want to let go and he was trying so hard, but in desperation more than anything. It was just sad to watch. He couldn't relax, he was always so tense in a heat, and always over amping, rather than take a little time off and try to sort the forest out from the trees ... But it's just one of those things that the person ultimately has to ride out themselves. You can be there and you can talk to them, but words don't make up for their reality of what they're seeing and what they're doing and whether they'll apply it. You can only try to plant the thought but they're just lost for a while in their own bewilderment. They just want to try to regain what they had but ultimately you know that you're never going to do it.'

276

ISRAEL

One of pro surfing's least likely stops around this time was Tel Aviv, and it provided a perfect opportunity for me to let off some steam and forget my worries in a truly alien environment. There was a fair bit of hijacking going on in the Middle East at the time and a lot of surfers were a bit hesitant about going to the first Mediterranean Pro. Shaun Tomson was the only surfer I knew who had been to Israel, and he told me, 'You've got to go to Israel Bugs. It's incredible.' So off to Tel Aviv I flew. The night the pro surfers arrived, there was a giant party organised for us on the roof of this building. We could look out over the whole city — it kind of resembled Surfers Paradise, except with about 300,000 guns in town. We heard that the local surfers had actually taken leave from the army to come and run this event and they were intent on a big night of partying with their surf heroes.

I was still in my Taz-influenced fashion phase and I fitted right in because I was already in the camouflage gear, from the Greenmount army disposals. My favourite group at the time was the Clash and the number one hit around the world was 'Rock the Casbah'. I walked in there looking like Joe Strummer from the Clash and I really felt like I'd wandered into the film clip for the song. The party raged well into the night and then we were dragged along to a disco, full of the most beautiful women I'd ever seen in my life.

Our night ended around 5 am and I woke up later in the morning in the hotel room I was sharing with Michael Ho, a little bleary-eyed and not sure what the program was. Little did I know that there was an official orientation meeting and civic greeting that morning where we were to be given the keys to the city. The next minute there was a knock on the door and it was one of the officials. 'Rabbit, Rabbit, they're waiting for you at the podium,' he barked through the door. I was supposed to be making a speech on behalf of the surfers.

So Michael and I ran out into this huge open air reception and just went, whoops! The whole side of the hill flanking the hotel was covered with soldiers. In front of the contest site there was a gun boat. There was an official stand with wreaths and ribbons and the whole bit, and lined up were all the local dignitaries … and I was the main speaker. I was escorted to the podium by armed guards, I was starting to wonder how safe this was. I'd seen the footage of Anwar Sadat getting blown away. I just remember getting up on that podium and being completely over-awed. So began my international public speaking career. It went over well — I was very eloquent and to the point and waved to the gunboat. Despite a seriously foggy head, I pulled it off.

We had already struck up an incredible rapport with the youth of Israel in that one night of partying. I'd met the Israeli junior champion and he'd told me, 'Oh Rabbit, next year I want to do it all,' and I really saw a sense of urgency about the kid. I went, 'Hey, you're young, you've got your whole future in front of you. Do it in your own time.' And he went, 'No, no, Rabbit, next year my parents are sending me to go surfing all around the world. It's going to be incredible. And the year after that when I turn 18 I go to zee battle.' It suddenly hit me that a few years in the army was an inescapable reality for every young man in the country. The local surfers were so cool. For them to take 10 days off to run this contest, they had to do an extra three months on the front.

It was an incredible event. A heavy social schedule, combined with surfing in 100 degrees Farenheit heat through the day, and all this amazing sightseeing around the city. We went on all these tours accompanied by high-level government officials to Jerusalem, Bethlehem and the ancient city. We went through the old city that hasn't seen sunlight in 2000 years. We visited the wailing wall where you can slide a wish on a slip of paper into the crevices in the wall, and I slipped one in on behalf of the Bartholomew clan. We started mucking up a bit, running through all these tiny alleys and laneways and the officials were constantly trying to corral us together. One

Bustin' down the door

night we saw a BB King concert in this natural amphitheatre at the side of the old wall of Jerusalem, and Michael Ho and I ended up meeting some of the guys in the band and jumping on their band bus with them. Me and Michael Ho jiving with all these black guys — we broke down all barriers and just had a ball.

This hectic schedule went on for 11 days and nights. I got a second in the contest, and I'd been asked to come back and coach the Israeli team. There was a farewell ceremony to bookend the whole thing, and I was the guest speaker again. But the social schedule and the heat had started to catch up with me. I was talking away, telling them what a magnificent time we'd had, when I started hallucinating on the podium. I'm talking and talking away, trying to maintain. 'I'm going to have to continue my speech on my knees, I'm sorry ladies and gentlemen … Thank you very much, it's been great, see you all next year,' and with that I collapsed and they could not revive me. There was this major scene. They took me to Tel Aviv hospital and the local doctor's diagnosis was, anything from acute exhaustion to a minor stroke. I was completely gaga for days. By the time I finally came good the rest of the tour was long gone, en route to France, and I was wheeled onto my flight out of Tel Aviv alone.

Postcard to Betty, July 31, 1984.

'At the moment I'm flying over the Mediterranean en route to Paris. I had a fantastic time in Israel. They had a smaller event than expected but I got a second and a nice trophy. I toured Jerusalem by day, seeing all the holy sites and then I saw a great open air concert at night. An unbelievable experience.

'I have some new friends in the Middle East and the young people of Tel Aviv asked me to come back and teach them to surf. It was exciting being in such a radical spot. You know how I love being amongst the action. Anyhow, take care.

'Love, Rabbi Bartolomeo'

THE LAST HAWAIIAN HURRAH

Looking back, I definitely went through a bit of a crisis in that period, and about the only meaningful thing I could find to cling on to was the old tradition of going to Hawaii and charging like a maniac. I remember those next few Hawaiian seasons from '84 through to '86 as a block — I really committed myself to the task of big-wave mastery in Hawaii in those years and had some fantastic surfs at big Pipe and Sunset. I went to the Islands with a real axe to grind with life, and it actually worked for me. The whole big-wave thing really moved in to fill the vacuum left by no longer being a contender for the World Title. I was still a contender on the North Shore; I was doing my finest surfing, and I really matured into an accomplished Sunset surfer. Despite the loss of sponsors and world rankings, my career still had life in the Islands, where the great Hawaiian big-wave surfers were still considered at their peak well into their 30s.

Big-wave surfing is something to be mastered over many years, more like a martial art, where elders are revered for their experience and wisdom. It's far removed from the shooting star fame of small wave, pro surfing. I went to Hawaii in '84 with no sponsors, no World Title campaign to wage, no surf movie documenting my heroics, or photographers targeting me. I went with the pure goal of surfing big waves as well as I could. Stripped of all those surf star trappings, suddenly it felt like it was just me, Rabbit, surfing for myself.

It was weird for me at first because I was no longer part of the Quiksilver crew, I had no accommodation at the team quarters at Keiki Hale, and didn't even feel comfortable calling by there to see my friends. Kong and Chappy were staying at the team quarters and they had to pull their heads in and dissociate themselves from me. I never called by there. I didn't want to put them in a compromising situation with their sponsors, but when I saw them round the traps they'd tell me they didn't feel right not having me round. I'd tell them, 'Don't worry about it, just carry on. I'll be right,' but I missed that camaraderie.

I hung out with a great local surfer Mike Latronic, who'd been a good friend for years, and Mark Occhilupo, an exciting young surfer from Cronulla, up at Sunset, and we all prepared for the contests together. I took Occy under my wing a bit and he became my new Hawaiian sparring partner. He was the new young turk really making a big charge in Hawaii and he was a great energy to be around.

There were still problems between the ASP administration and the Hawaiian contest organisers. Randy Rarick decided to keep the Pipe Masters out of the world championship tour and ran it as a specialty event, with only the most respected Pipe riders invited. It was like the old days of invitations being sent out at the discretion of the organisers, and everyone who deserved to be in it got in. To me, those Pipe Masters were the most fiercely fought out events in the modern era because of the prestige attached to them. The heats were just awesome. Every one of them, from the first round, were full of legendary names.

In '84, Pipe was 12 to 15 feet for the contest and Occy and I both made the final, along with Hawaiian Max Madeiros, and Californian Joey Buran. I went straight to the outer reef and caught some huge ones. Jack Shipley, who's the longest serving judge in Hawaii, if not the world, actually scored me first. He said he thought I'd got the biggest waves and went for it the most. But Joey Buran won it riding the eight foot inside waves and getting these really deep barrels. Occy got second, Max got third, and I ended up coming fourth, but I was really satisfied with my surfing at big Pipe.

Letter to Heidi and her daughter Cristel, December 3, 1984.
'It sure is a radical time for this Sagittarian. The Quiksilver massacre was brilliantly timed. I picked up all my new boards with Quiksilver emblazoned over top and bottom and I get a message to ring Quiksilver. Bruce Raymond gets on, tells me that he hates to be the one, but that I'm fired.

'Bruce is over here now and he told Kong that he knows they were wrong. Kong said that it finally came down to me being out of the top 16 and not wanting to quit and come work for them. They didn't have the guts to tell me in Sydney, but made the decision in Fiji, where they all headed after Sydney. Therefore they hadn't heard of my third in the Billabong and return to the 16 … I'm really going to show those guys. Here comes the cavalry, sweet pea …

'Now, on to the social rounds. The North Shore for years has been a boystown, but now a crop of hot, young girls has sprouted. On Saturday night there was a party for this girl's 18th and my 30th. It went off really well. I've now got a couple of new friends. Then I met these three Mormon girls at the Kui Lima disco. There's a Mormon college close by and all the pretty Mormon girls come from all over America. All the little angels want to live in Hawaii. I pretended to have never heard of their religion but I said in Australia we drink beer and have lots of girlfriends and they loved it. The little angels all loved me and now I'm going down to the College to run around the dormitories and hide from the wardens.

'At least I won't be going to Honolulu this year. I made quite a reputation for myself as a 3D rager last year. Every time people see me in the night they ask me if I'll go to Honolulu with them. But I'm not going for a few weeks at least. I'll just stay out here and surf, go to schoolgirl parties and run wild through girls' dorms. Of course, I'll have to heal my leg first. I'll just lay down for a few days and take stock of my life …

'I've decided to do the tour for a few more years …

'Please take care, lotsa love, Aunt Buggy, alias Bunny Boodle.'

In '85, I remember getting up one morning and checking Sunset, and it was just so huge, 15 to 18 feet and a really west swell. I looked at Occy and said, 'I don't know what Pipe's going to look like but I bet

Bustin' down the door

it's on.' They used to wait for like a month and a half until it was the biggest, most radical day of the season before they ran the Pipe. This morning it was 15 to 20 foot, really huge Pipe, bordering on out of control. The draw had been decided weeks before, and in my first heat I had Derek Ho, Mickey Neilson and John Damm, a very respected Pipe surfer. I'd known for weeks that I had this heat and I kept thinking, 'How the hell am I going to get through this one?'

I remember standing on the beach, lined up with the other competitors and our caddies. My friend Dave Kennedy, a pro surfer from Florida, was caddying for me, and it felt like everyone was waiting for someone to make a move. I decided to lead the charge and before any one of us knew it we were paddling into battle, about to try to negotiate a massive, 10 foot shorebreak. I remember looking at Dave as this thing was about to land on our heads, and somehow Dave and I got through.

I paddled straight to the outer reef again. It was so big that John Damm didn't even catch a wave in this heat, and Derek Ho only got one or two waves. They were ducking in and out of the take-off zone trying to pick off the cleaner, inside ones, in between clean-up sets. Mickey and I went to the outer reef and I caught two huge ones, and then ducked inside and got a clean 10 footer and that was enough to get me through.

> DAVE KENNEDY: 'Paddling out with him at the Pipe was unbelievable. I was the only guy to make it out. Everyone else got washed down to Rocky Point. The reason I got out was that just as this wave was about to break on us Rabbit fixed me with an icy stare and said, "That board goes to Darrick Doerner after this heat. Don't let go, don't let go." He had the ability to make himself feel ice cold and make you feel all the pressure.'

My next heat was just about my finest hour in Hawaiian contests. I was against Michael Ho, Ronnie Burns and Mickey Neilson. Ronnie and I paddled out the back and got a 20 foot set on the head and both got washed right in to the beach. I paddled back out and caught another huge one and rode it all the way through. They were

45 minute heats, 28 minutes had already passed before I caught a wave so I was coming last. I paddled back out knowing I needed to do something special, and I just kept paddling further and further out, and then paddled deeper and deeper, until I was so far out to sea that the Pipe Masters contest site was just a speck on the beach. I was sitting at outside Rockpiles, a gnarly reefbreak west of Pipeline, when this huge swell, I swear it was 20 feet, came marching down the coast. This thing was still travelling parallel to the coast when I paddled into it. This still stands as the best wave I have ever ridden in my life. I paddled onto this thing sideways as it started wrapping towards the coast and as I took off the wave lifted up and I just dropped and dropped and dropped for what seemed like forever. By the time I began my bottom turn I was directly in front of the judges' tower. I'd travelled about half a mile while I took the drop, and my heart was in my throat. My surfboard felt like a toothpick as I tried to set an edge in the wave face. I knew that the course I set then was a life-or-death course as this thing began to pitch over the inside reef. As I traversed this huge, dredging wall of water I realised that, even though it had taken half a mile before I'd done a bottom turn, I'd still done my bottom turn a fraction too early. I had to release my edge and do a minor snap halfway up the face, and then I freefell down the face of this wave again. My arms went up over my head as I dropped down the face and the whole thing just threw out as I pulled into the barrel. If this thing had got me it would have deadset thrown me up on to the Kam Highway. It was the hugest wave I'd ever caught at Pipe and the whole beach was roaring. I just held my line and rode the barrel and it spat me out. That wave actually felt better than winning the World Title — it was the biggest Pipe I'd ever surfed, the biggest wave I'd ever ridden, the biggest barrel I'd ever stood in. I came out of the barrel and just thought, well, I won that.

Occy, Max Madeiros and I all made the final again, along with Michael Ho. People were right on to my strategy then and Michael and I went straight for the outer reef. We made it out the back and promptly got caught by a 20 foot set right on the head. I got pushed all the way to the beach by about 10 whitewater waves. I came straight in through Off The Wall and got washed up on the beach.

Michael got swept down past Ehukai Beach Park and the lifeguards finally hauled him out at Rocky Point where he'd begun to disappear out to sea. I paddled out again and got cleaned up again. The gods just destroyed me. I finally got back out and got two huge waves. Throughout the whole day I knew that I'd ridden some of the biggest, most gnarly waves and enhanced my reputation at big Pipe and that was good enough for me. I thought that was my crowning achievement in Hawaii. I didn't win it, young Occy had that honour, signalling his arrival as a major player in Hawaii. But it really bonded all of us — Max Madeiros, Mickey Neilson, Michael Ho, Occy and I.

Then in the World Cup at Haleiwa I won every heat I went in, right through to the final. It was Michael Ho, Californians Richard Schmidt and Dave Parmenter, and I out at perfect, 10 foot Haleiwa. Michael and I had the full tube-riding duel and I pulled into a couple of huge ones that would have won me the final if I'd come out. But I got swatted by those big ones and Michael was flawless, I had to be content with second. But it was still a really solid Hawaiian season for me. I got invited to the Eddie Aikau contest and I felt like I'd finally earnt my membership in to the elite, big-wave club. I remember the day Darrick Doerner actually came up to me and shook my hand and said, 'Bugs, you are officially a North Shore veteran.' After more than a decade of going there, that was the highest compliment I could ask for.

DENNIS PANG (HAWAIIAN SURFER): 'I remember one time (Denis) Callinan and I were going into town. We had a date each and we were going to see a movie. And just by coincidence Rabbit rang up and went, what are you guys doing? Callinan, being the gracious man that he is, told him to come along. He didn't have any money so Callinan had to lend him 20 bucks. We were running late and the theatre was really full and somehow Rabbit ended up sitting with the two girls. There were, like, these three empty seats in a row and Rabbit got himself in between the two girls and me and Callinan had to go sit by ourselves somewhere up the back. He borrowed 20 bucks and he got to sit with the girls.'

IRONMEN

Back in Australia, the whole ironman movement was just taking off, and the top competitors were starting to make some pretty good money. The cultural split between boardriders and the surf lifesavers from the '60s and '70s had never been fully healed, but I had a healthy respect for the top ironmen. I was invited along to the launch of one of the big competitions, and they showed some footage of me surfing big, outer reef Pipeline, which kind of blew everyone's minds. I was asked to make a speech and I couldn't resist the opportunity of chalking one up for the boardriders.

'The difference between ironmen and surfers,' I told the assembled lifesaving elite, 'is that you blokes paddle out there through the impact zone and keep going. We live in the impact zone. When it's 15 to 20 foot Pipeline, we're the ironmen.' That was the last ironman function I was ever invited to. But since then, I think we have healed some of those old wounds, and I reckon guys like Grant Kenny and Trevor Hendy are deadset legends. They are true watermen and real surfers in every sense.

1986 was the last Hawaiian season that I felt like I was really pushing the limits. Again, fittingly, my most memorable moment of the year came at big Pipe. It was the first day I'd seen anyone tow-in surfing. Herbie Fletcher, a very colourful Californian surfer, was out there on his jetski, towing Kong into a few huge outer reef waves. It was 15 to 18 feet and really nasty looking, and I watched it for hours before paddling out. I got down there at about 8 am and I didn't paddle out until 1 pm. I was just watching how the handful of surfers out there were going, and trying to figure out how to pick off the big, clean, makeable ones. In those five hours I only saw two other surfers get waves.

Then I saw Kong paddle out and that was enough for me to figure that it was time to get out there. So out I went. I didn't even stop at the normal Pipe take-off zone. I just kept stroking to the outside, where there was a pack of about a dozen guys. And then I kept stroking past them, further out and further inside, and waited on my own. Within minutes, Kong had broken from the pack and joined me, just the two of us sitting out in the middle of these huge swells. Next thing we knew, this huge set roared through and a perfect, big A-frame peak just bobbed up in front of us. 'Go!' I screamed at Kong, and he turned and paddled for his life. The wave behind it was just awesome, and I paddled into it, completely alone out there. Guys had been out there for hours without getting a wave, and within five minutes of paddling out, Kong and I had both ridden these big, beautiful waves all the way through to the inside. That's the way it is out there — like some massive, over-sized shifting beachbreak — you've just got to be in the right spot. You're either getting them on the head, or they're missing you entirely, or you're missing them, or you don't want 'em, or you just zone in and get 'em. Two hours into the surf, I snapped one board in three places on this ridiculous late take-off, swam in and got another one and paddled back out. I was feeling that magical rhythm kicking in and there was no way I was going to sit on the beach.

I was out there for hours that day and then, finally, this huge clean-up set marched through and washed everyone in, except for me and Shaun Tomson. We looked around and there was only he and I sitting out at Pipe. 'Hey Bugs, it's just like old times,' Shaun said to me. We paddled over this wave and the one behind it was this solid, most beautiful, 12 foot A-frame. And for some unknown reason, I don't know how or why this happened, but those words of Shaun's just sparked something in me and just for old time's sake I took off on this wave … and … went … right.

It was the only right-hander ridden all day and as I was dropping down it drew off the reef so violently, just the look of it horrified me. I was going, well, you've done it this time Bugs. I remember coming off the bottom and going into this full death stance and it threw so hard, I was so deep inside this thing, travelling so fast, and I realised that the face of this wave was so taut, that my surfboard was not going to handle it. I decided, I want out of this thing and

I don't care, surfboard, I'm leaving you behind and I am going out the end of that tunnel. I just abandoned my board, and started clawing my way through mid-air. The next second I felt this thump as my surfboard came up and hit me in the leg. The impact of the board just seemed to halt all my forward momentum and I fell into the trough of this tube, got sucked up the wall, went over with the lip, and got slammed into the bottom at Backdoor Pipe. I was getting too old for this shit. I smelt something that day, I reckon I smelt death, because I honestly thought I'd gone too far. I got rolled over, slammed again, and came up just in time for the next wave to slam me. I finally just drifted in to the beach like a limp rag doll and started kissing the sand. I was so exhausted, so injured, and so throttled that all I could do was just lie there. Martin Potter and Gotcha clothing boss Marc Price came running down from their house. They'd seen the whole thing. Pottz says to this day it's the most insane thing he's ever seen in his life. They came running down and carried me out of there, completely destroyed.

And that, in all honesty, is the last great thing I ever did.

DARRICK DOERNER: 'He was the best tube-rider in the bowl at Inside Sunset for years ... I remember one day in the mid-'80s he came down with an 8'6" at big Pipe. He paddled straight to the outer reef. He was too far inside and he went anyway, and all we saw was (stands up with arms above his head on tippy toes, miming a late, freefall take-off). That was the last big Pipe contest he ever was in. He snapped his board in three pieces and came to the beach happy. I never saw him in a bad mood. He's my hero. Guys like Rabbit opened the door for professional surfing ... When I think of Bugs I see him as the main inspiration of Australian surfing.'

DOUG 'CLAW' WARBRICK: 'His attack on the North Shore was the thing most significant of all in his surfing ... At all those classic power breaks, he just attacked them with that enthusiasm, and he took some terrible poundings, in free surfs

Bustin' down the door

and in contests, some hell poundings. And he wasn't always received well by the locals. When the Australian charge came Rabbit probably wore the greatest brunt of it because he was brash and outspoken and well-spoken. It was probably Rabbit that wore most of the flack but, like I say, he doesn't go away. If he went out and took a pounding at Pipeline he'd be back the next day. If he had a disagreement with the locals, and he had a couple of serious ones where I think he was quite heavily beaten, he'd paddle right back out there the next day. Even they had to respect that in the end. They just went, "Shit, this guy's committed." They'd physically and verbally given him the word. "This is it son, pack your bags and leave." And they'd paddle out the next day, and there he is large as life, in the lineup hustling for the biggest and best waves. In the end, they just had to go, "Well, Rabbit's here to stay."'

EXTRACT FROM AN ARTICLE WRITTEN BY RABBIT IN THE *TRACKS BOOK OF BIG SURF*, DESCRIBING HIS PREPARATION FOR THE '85 PIPE MASTERS FINAL:

'I am a viking warrior king about to conquer a new world. I am Alexander the Great leading my horsemen over the plains of Sidon. I have the expert cunning of Rommel leading his tanks into another desert foxtrap. The power and the glory pulsate through my veins. The great prophecies resound deep in my soul. "Live your life like a warrior, as if every day were your last." This is truly Being. I AM the legacy to all ancient warriors and kings. I've passed through the dark caverns of fear, I've overcome the pain barrier and fully acknowledge my ability to fly through cliffs and shoulder the mountains themselves. I lust for the cherry blossom moments of today. I stand on the edge of the universe. This is the meeting of the minds. I take a handful of sand and feel each grain squeeze through my clenching fist like the sands of civilisation. A primeval scream from deep within is silenced by the master.'

chaPTeR 10

preparing for civilian life

hose last few years on tour were confusing times. I couldn't make sense of just being there to make up the numbers, just going along for the ride. My time at home became a kind of desperate, ping-ponging search for something to fill up the void. There was a lot of extremism going on in my life. Over a period of four or five years during the second half of the '80s I bounced between various, seemingly incongruous guises — from environmental warrior to party animal, from born-again Christian to aspiring rock star.

I was living off my name a fair bit, just trying to piece a livelihood together. What was amazing through those years is that whenever things got really desperate financially, some kind of windfall would come my way. I did an ad for Japanese Kellogg's, I wrote articles for the surf magazines, I was paid appearance fees to go on a couple of TV shows.

I had no form of sponsorship whatsoever for nearly a year and I was really starting to doubt my own worth. I was lucky to be picked up by Billabong in mid–'85, who sponsored me for those last few years on the circuit. It wasn't a lot of money but it was enough for me to get myself around the world.

The first time I rode for Billabong was at the Kirra Team's Challenge in '85. It was perfect Kirra the very first time I wore Billabong gear out, I ended up getting the barrel of the

290

tournament and perfect 10s. I thought that was a good omen for the new relationship. I'm not even sure how they came to pick me up, I think Occy made an approach on my behalf; he and I had become friends and he could see how tough I was doing it. Occy and I drove all round the Australian circuit during 1985 in my RX7. We became quite a successful partnership — I was no longer a contender but it felt good to be putting a bit of energy into someone who was. It was quite amazing — in '84 I had finished 2nd in the world and he'd finished 15th, and the very next season, he came 2nd and I came 15th. Having swapped places in the ratings, and seeing him vie for the World Title eased the pain of that transition for me. I learnt a lot about myself through that and I got to taste the satisfaction of performing a coaching or mentor-type role. I realised I could let go of the World Title race and not become embittered about no longer being a contender. I think Billabong boss Gordon Merchant could see the value of having that tour experience on his team. Soon after we returned from Bells that same year, Billabong signed me up for something like $20,000 a year. Most of that was gobbled up by airfares and travel expenses but I was out of financial dire straits.

GORDON MERCHANT: 'When Rab had a fall out with Quiksilver he was kind of shattered. It was a big blow for him. Everyone really felt for him ... Guys who are that totally involved in professional surfing, being a part of it and going on the circuit for that long, suddenly find that they've lost their main sponsor and they're too old for anyone else to really pick them up and put them back on the circuit. Their professional career's now over and what do they do? It's a really hard adjustment, and Rab found it quite difficult over those next few years. He was still value and so I sponsored him. We always knew it was going to be tough because he had such a strong image with Quiksilver; to bring him across to Billabong was going to take years. But he had a lot of respect, especially in Australia and on the Gold Coast. It was good because even though it did take a while to

Preparing for civilian life

change him across, he still contributed a lot as a spokesman for the company and in lots of ways, when I needed feedback from him. And he has always been into coaching kids and giving hints to anyone who he'd like to see do well in a contest.'

EXTRACT FROM TOM CARROLL'S SURFING COLUMN, THE *SUN-HERALD*, AUGUST, 1985: 'The Gunston 500, Durban, South Africa: Occy snapped his centre fin out, changing it from a tri fin to a twin fin. The soothing influence of Mark's coach, former world champion Wayne "Rabbit" Bartholomew, was a major factor in the win. He took his young charge in tow and re-built his shattered confidence, telling Occy that the crippled board would work ideally in the inconsistent one metre waves. I would like to see Bartholomew made national coach.'

Postcard to Heidi from Cape Town, South Africa, September 7, 1985.
'I'm standing on the top of Table Mountain overlooking Capetown. I've witnessed the meeting of the Atlantic and the Indian. It's six feet on the Indian and 10 feet on the Atlantic. That's the surf report from up here. Really an amazing high. I'm going to attempt to walk down a goat trail next, so have a Heineken for me and I'll see you all soon after this arrives. I'm sending it via the Roaring Forties Express.

'Regards from the deep dark jungle, the Bugwhan.'

Through '85, '86 and '87 I quite comfortably followed the tour. I was having plenty of fun, trying to help out younger surfers on tour who caught my eye as possessing something special, and diving into the Gold Coast social whirl, or some noble cause or another, when

Bustin' down the door

I came home. Wavelength wetsuits also picked me up and paid me a small retainer, so I was doing okay. But I was never going to set myself up for life on these modest earnings on the tailend of my competitive career, and I was still baffled by the vexing question: How would I support myself once I retired from the tour?

I did a lot soul-searching and I felt the first stirrings of an inner calling. I knew the career I wanted within surfing didn't exist, and I was going to have to will it into being with the same conviction I'd applied to my pro surfing dream. I'd led the high life, travelling around the world for 10 years, but now I had to start from absolute scratch again. It felt like time to get right back to the grass roots of the sport, as if obeying some kind of natural cycle.

I decided to establish the Wayne 'Rabbit' Bartholomew Surfing Academy to teach young kids to surf, from beginners to elite competitors. Fittingly, I went into partnership with my old mate Mont, who'd introduced me to the surf in the first place, and Denis Callinan, another great friend and son of Miami High headmaster Bill Callinan, who'd given me so much support when I was a kid. Another mate, Johnny Charlton (young Johnny Charlton from Burleigh, not old Johnny Charlton from Kirra), acted as a consultant for us.

It was an exciting undertaking — Australia's first surfing academy — it was a novel concept, but perhaps a little ahead of its time. We were the first group to approach the local council for permits to use the Gold Coast beaches for the purposes of surf coaching. I think we paid a fee of something like $1000 a year, to use any beach between Snapper and Main Beach. The council were right behind it and thought it was a tremendous development. We also had to draft the first comprehensive insurance cover for such a project, which was quite a feat in itself. Insurance companies become a little nervous when you take groups of young children beyond the high-tide mark.

Unfortunately, Australian parents absolutely refused to pay money to have their children taught how to surf. 'I'm not giving Rabbit 10 bucks for little Johnny to go surfing. I'll just go down there myself and throw him into the shorebreak and push him into a few waves myself,' was the prevailing attitude among surfing fathers.

So all those barriers had to be broken down. We got ourselves up and running and held plenty of classes but we just didn't make a cent. It ended up being like a sponsorship program, and we'd stage these little contests for promising youngsters — like Shane Bevan, China O'Connor and Jason Buttenshaw — at Greenmount Point and not even charge them. It wasn't providing a livelihood for any of us but, without us realising, it was providing a good foundation for things to come.

For a while there I became immersed in environmental issues. At one time or another I was a founding member of the Group Against Sewage Pollution (GASP), a spokesman for the Kirra Environmental Protection Trust (KEPT), a spokesman for the Surfers Against Nuclear Destruction (SAND), I got involved with the Gold Coast Protection Trust, and I was a founding member of the Surfrider Foundation. I had high hopes for the Surfrider Foundation, perhaps a group that could embrace all the environmental fronts. The most meaningful contribution I could think of was to raise funds, so I went out to the surf industry, hat in hand, and established a financial platform from which the foundation could operate. Billabong were first in for $5000, closely followed by Quiksilver, Rip Curl and then the smaller labels.

My pet environmental project, though, was SAND. Formed by my old school mate Denis Callinan, SAND campaigned for a nuclear-free Pacific and raised money for worthy local charities. The highpoint of its activities was the annual SAND surfing contest, and the first contest in '85 was a huge success, tapping into a latent environmental streak in Australia's youth, surfers in particular. It was Denis's vision, he was really the prime mover, and I was his counsel, his lieutenant.

The first SAND contest was on the Sunshine Coast just after Easter in 1985 and I had this incredible timetable to try to meet. I was down at Bells Beach in Victoria for the annual Bells Easter contest, and I had to get from there to the black tie ASP Awards night in Sydney and then on to the Sunshine Coast, all in a matter of days. I was in the RX7 and I actually made the papers for picking up speeding tickets in all three states.

Peter Garrett, lead singer of rock band Midnight Oil, was a guest speaker at that first SAND contest and commanded an awesome respect when he addressed the crowd. He gave SAND his full support and extended an open offer to have the Oils play free of charge the next time we held a major event.

Two years later in '87 we held the second SAND contest on the Gold Coast, with a huge presentation night starring the Oils and Spy vs Spy at the Patch. It was a brilliant event, we had perfect weather, and top international surfers like Vetea David and Nick Wood competing. The man-on-man final was between myself and my old mate Chappy Jennings, and Chappy won. In fact, the only problem with the whole project was that it was supposed to be a fundraiser and somehow we clocked up $12,000 worth of debt just in the staging of the event and the presentation night concert. Denis was horribly nervous before the preso night and we all knew we needed a huge crowd just to break even. The night was so successful, we raised $17,000, cleared our debts and were able to donate $5000 to charity.

I began to see the potential for surfers to be at the forefront of the environmental movement. It seemed natural for us to be the watchdogs of the coast, on the frontline, the first to feel the effects of beach pollution or insensitive development. And so I entered my phase of voluntarism. My mentor in this new crusade was a great, old guy by the name of Don McSween who, at the age of 92, was the driving force behind the Gold Coast Protection League and the Group Against Sewage Pollution. I became a spokesman for both groups and I could often be found roaming the streets of the Gold Coast with groups of retirees doing letter box drops. Or, I'd spend my Sunday afternoons outside Fisherman's Wharf handing out pamphlets and getting people to sign petitions, where once I would have been inside breasting the bar. Don McSween was an absolute champion with amazing drive and commitment, and our protests were being heard in the corridors of power. We had meetings with the Gold Coast City Council and their engineers, and foreshore committees, pushing for the upgrade of sewerage plants from secondary to tertiary treatment. When plans for an ocean outfall at the Southport Seaway were put forward, we dropped hundreds of oranges into the ocean at the Seaway, to demonstrate that the sewage field would extend southwards to the Gold Coast's prized beaches. Sure enough, oranges washed up all along the coast.

It got to the point where I had meetings almost every night of the week, when you include my local boardriders club, Snapper Rocks. Monday night was the Snapper Rocks Surfriders, Tuesday night was GASP, Wednesday night was SAND, Thursday was Kirra Environmental Protection Trust, and on the weekends we were doing all sorts of community projects. It was pretty full on.

I had plenty of free time and at least it was keeping me out of the nightclubs, but one bit of partying endured right through the '80s like a religious ritual — dollar nights at the Patch. I'd often attend the KEPT meeting on a Thursday night, already dressed in my going out gear, and head straight to the Patch afterwards — making sure I had a written copy of the minutes so I could remember what we'd discussed the next day. Those Thursday nights were brutal — a thousand people from all over the Gold Coast just binge drinking every Thursday. Thank God those nights finally ended.

All of this time I was putting in to these causes was strictly voluntary and, in fact, was actually costing me money — because there was always some raffle or fundraiser, or a few bucks needed here and there for photocopying or printing. I enjoyed contributing to the cause but people seemed to be making endless demands on my time and finances; and whenever a prominent talking head was needed to front the media, they'd ring me and out I'd go to face the cameras. I realised that people must have thought I was just a wealthy philanthropist, already set for life financially and able to afford the luxury of devoting all my free time to these noble environmental causes.

Just to compound my shaky financial situation, my own surfboard model, that had been produced through Hot Stuff surfboards, came to grief in '86. We'd been marketing the Wayne 'Rabbit' Bartholomew model for close to 10 years. Way back in the uncomplicated '70s, I'd been looking around for a logo for my own surfboard label. I remember actually going to the movies thinking, what would be a cool logo to pick up on the 'Bugs' theme? Sitting in the cinema, watching the cartoons before the main features, the big 'WB' Warner Brothers logo flashed onto the screen, with the lovable, carrot munching Bugs Bunny slouching over it. WB! Wayne Bartholomew! Bugs! It was too perfect. We adopted a slightly modified version of the WB shield and the Bugs caricature on my surfboard stickers, and happily marketed surfboards and T-shirts around the world. Mark Richards had the 'MR' Superman shield, and I had the 'WB' Bugs logo, and none of us ever thought for a second about international copyright laws.

MR was the first to get a letter, demanding he cease using his adaptation of the Superman emblem or face legal action. Mine was an even more blatant rip-off, and it wasn't long before Hot Stuff received a letter too. Hot Stuff boss Paul Hallas was pretty relaxed about it and kept up a volley of correspondence with Warner Brothers' legal department for years, while still using the logo. Japan in particular loved the logo, but they were the first to back off at the whiff of legal action. We tried coming up with alternative Rabbit caricatures, but they either wound up looking more like donkeys than rabbits, or they weren't different enough from the original for the lawyers' liking.

I had some old surfing friends in California, the Paskowitz family, who were actually related to Mel Blanc, the creator of Bugs Bunny. They related the whole story to him and Uncle Mel thought it was fantastic, but there was nothing he could do once it was in the hands of the lawyers.

In the end, the whole saga reached the highest levels at Warner Brothers and they decided to get heavy. One of the directors of Warner Brothers was having this big Hollywood pool party, and his kid came downstairs wearing the Wayne 'Rabbit' Bartholomew T-shirt. He was horrified, seized the offending T-shirt and immediately placed it at the top of the agenda at the next board

Preparing for civilian life

meeting. Once you get on the agenda at the Warner Brothers board of directors meeting, that's it. The gig's up. The T-shirt came out at the board meeting and they just said, 'Nail him!'

Our distribution man in California was in the middle of a big local trade show when he got a phone call at home one night. I don't know what was said but he shut up shop the next day and vanished. Within days the Wayne 'Rabbit' Bartholomew boards and T-shirts had disappeared off the market worldwide. They'd finally sent Elmer Fudd in to ferret out that wascally wabbit.

THE OP PRO RIOT

I had the occasional earn as a contest commentator or interviewer for the TV crews in these twilight years on tour, but it wasn't close to a living. In fact, I was lucky to escape from one particular commentary job with my life. The '86 OP Pro, at Huntington Beach, Southern California, was held over a holiday weekend and local radio personality D. David Moran and I had the job of entertaining 60,000 sun-baked Americans over the four-day event. On finals day, a beach girl quest, although rather tacky, was part of the on-beach format and a rowdy mob of pier-dwellers, 'valley' surfers and bikers descended on the event. When a couple of busty girls in the grandstand flashed their assets to the rowdies, the mob lost control. Topless bathing is illegal in the US and that glimpse of breast was the catalyst for a full-scale riot. They set fire to the lifeguard towers and began beating up anyone who strayed in their path. The police intervened but were quickly overpowered. Caught unprepared, two police cars were rolled over and set alight. Smoke billowed into the sky and the mob formed a front as a legion of baton-wielding riot police launched a pitched battle. This riot was happening just behind our position in the commentary tower. Co-commentator Joey Buran went up for a look and returned ashen-faced. 'I'm outta here,' were his parting words. D. David also went missing and I was left to hold the fort

Bustin' down the door

while finalists Mark Occhilupo and Glen Winton tried to concentrate on surfing.

The police used the public address system in the main lifeguard tower on the pier to order me to shut down our PA and cancel the final immediately. Tournament director Kanga Cairns ordered me to ignore the police and carry on commentating the final, as if nothing was wrong. He was concerned that if 60,000 surf fans left the beach and walked into the riot, casualties would only mount. I agreed with his position and disobeyed the law. We knew we had to stall the crowd, who were largely unaware of the scale of the trouble going on behind the bleachers. Occy had just demolished Winton in two straight sets, but Kanga told me to announce that Glen had won the second set and a third-set tie-breaker would proceed immediately.

The cops then announced that we were in violation of their authority and demanded an immediate end to the event. Kanga leant over my shoulder and ordered me to carry on. A bewildered Occy and Winton paddled out again. I ducked up to the top of the tower to take a peek at the action. The riot squad were advancing in a line, shielding themselves from a constant barrage of bottles, rocks, cans, and even shoes. The mob would retreat, take a stand and then repeat the cycle.

I knew my goose would be cooked if Winton clearly beat Occy in the third set. I'd be there in front of 60,000 people crowning a bogus winner. I privately asked Occ to try his guts out before he paddled out, and he did, taking the third set easily. While that dilemma was averted, I was still waiting for the riot squad to charge our position and shut us down, if not arrest us, possibly with a beating thrown in for good measure.

Miraculously, as the final presentation wound up, the riot squad had the last of the mob corralled up in the car park. For a short while the riot had moved into the main street of Huntington before coming under control, just as 60,000 happy surf fans dispersed from the beach.

Surfing finally hit the six o'clock news that Sunday night and the front page of the *LA Times*, but for all the wrong reasons. Kanga Cairns resigned as ASP Executive Director, his dream of awakening the American masses to the wonders of pro surfing in tatters. Graham Cassidy took the helm of the ASP with the sport in damage control mode.

THE RABBIT WHO FOUND GOD, *Sunday Telegraph*, 1987.
'I have always believed in a higher order of things, a universal order. In Japan I had an overwhelming vision of what I should do with my life. It was something pounding away inside me. I could feel it on the waves. I felt it all the time. I was getting these really strong visions in my dreams. It seemed overwhelming that someone was calling me ... It's a personal thing. I'm not going to stand on a street corner pushing my religion down people's throats. But it's right for me.'

After all the wild living of the mid–'80s, I felt a calling in the Hawaiian winter of '86. Christianity had come to the North Shore like the second wave of missionaries and I decided to make my peace with the Lord. I began going to church every Sunday of my six-week Hawaiian stay. It was a cleansing experience and I began fellowship. As in all things I undertook, I became fanatical and was attending *Bible* study five times a week, plus two prayer sessions on Sunday. I had a lot to be forgiven for.

I set out on my walk with Christ with incredible vigour and conviction. On my return to Australia, I summonsed my beautiful, young girlfriend at the time and informed her that I no longer believed in sex before marriage. My old Burleigh buddy Guy Ormerod baptised me in the surf at Miami and I roamed the coast with *Bible* in hand.

My testimony was quite colourful — in fact, I could fill a hall with tales of my former sins. Only thing was, my testimonials were soon in demand and I was being summonsed by one church after another to speak. I really only wanted to sit up the back and take in the gospel, but I'd always be called upon to speak.

The armour cracked in spectacular fashion. I won a local surfing tournament and was presented by, and with, this beautiful model who was quite keen to make my acquaintance. Six months of celibacy had taken its toll and when Suzy turned up for dinner in the leopard skin mini-skirt I knew I was a goner.

SNAPPER ROCKS SURFRIDERS

As my pro tour commitments and my life as an international surf star began to wane, I started putting a lot of time into the Snapper Rocks Surfriders Club. As the pro surfing system spat me out at the end of the tunnel, my local club and old surfing mates were still there for me, ready to welcome me back into the fold. My competitive drive remained strong and I was able to direct it into the club. We had launched a junior development program way back in the early '80s before junior development programs even existed. I became president of the club in '86 and have remained so ever since. I've put my heart and soul into the club, along with dear friends like Mont and his wife Lorraine, Wayne Deane and Bruce Lee.

The boardriding club tradition is one of the great strengths of Australian surfing. All our world champions have come through the club system — MR and the Merewether club, Tom Carroll and Newport, Damien Hardman and Narrabeen, Barton Lynch and Queenscliff. Australian surfers are blooded into the competitive spirit at a young age through their local club, and no other surfing nation has a system anything like it. PT, Shaun Tomson and myself tried to introduce club surfing into America in the early '80s when we were spending a bit of time in California. We formed clubs at Huntington and Newport but as soon as we left town it just fell on its face. I think Americans' sense of individualism is just too strong and they're less accustomed to the kind of voluntarism needed for a successful club. It just seems to me to be a very Australian characteristic: to form these sporting/social clubs that run largely on volunteer labour and are dedicated to the nurturing of the next generation.

We really dedicated ourselves to the concept of creating a champion club and we created a 10-year plan to nurture the young talent in our local area. The Gold Coast is a bit notorious for producing brilliant surfers who don't always make the most of their potential. We had the twin goals of establishing ourselves as the premier boardriding club in Australia, and helping prepare the elite surfers in the local area who wanted to make a career in pro surfing. We attracted a lot of great, young surfers to the club — Shane and Dean Bevan, Will Lewis, Jay Phillips, Mark Rawlings, Trevor Gleave — and I knew if we could just hold it together that success would come.

It's a beautiful thing coming home from a world tour environment — where it's a very individual pursuit and you're there without any real support structure — to the club atmosphere. I'd come home on a Friday and hear that there was a club contest on Sunday, and go down to Snapper and there'd be the club. And I'd be back in the club tent exchanging smart-arse remarks with all the crew, surfing in a heat against all my friends and they'd all be trying to knock me off.

I remember Reg Riley coming down late for his heat after a big night out. He turned up on the beach with the full camouflage gear on and the army boots. On the way through from some nightspot or party, he'd grabbed his board and come straight to the beach and he surfed his heat at Snapper Rocks in the full regalia, army boots and all. He rode a wave right to the beach, and on the way back around he grabbed a beer out of the esky (because some of the older members used to like having a beer while the club contest was going on), sculled it, and went back out and won his heat. He then went on to win the club round that day. After gallivanting round the world, stuff like that really let you know you were home.

PAT RILEY: 'Rab had come home at Christmas just before the club broke up in 1983 and we had the Snapper Club Open Championships on. We took them round to Duranbah and we

Bustin' down the door

surfed them and I had the results. Rab decided that he didn't surf any good and he started a thing on the beach, telling the guys, "Club championship? That wasn't it? No. I thought we were just mucking around." He kept going until he got Bruce Lee on his side, he got all these people on his side, and they declared it null and void. At the club meeting they'd all said that was going to be the club championship, but on the beach Rab managed to turn them around. And I went, "Okay, fair enough, it's not the club championship." But what I knew and what Rabbit didn't know was that he had won it. I was a stickler for rules — if there's a rule, just stick to it. That shuts everybody up, otherwise you've just got a never-ending argument. I thought, "No, I'll let this go this time if you want to change it." I think he had to leave after that for a pro contest so he never got his club championship.'

THE DREADED FIREWALKERS

I guess my partying days reached a bit of a crescendo in '87 at my mate Reg Riley's 21st birthday party. I'd never had a 21st because I just wasn't into partying at that time, so Reg was determined that his 21st was going to be a big enough night to retrospectively celebrate mine as well. I was about 33 at the time, but that didn't seem to matter. People came from far and wide — even MP turned up for a while. Somewhere during the course of the evening, I decided I was going to fulfil a long-held ambition to perform a bit of firewalking. I was always a great believer in the powers of mind over matter and was convinced I could pull this off, although the tequila might have had something to do with it. There was half a 44-gallon drum full of hot coals, white hot in parts, and in hindsight, there was probably still a bit too much flame to attempt a walk. But a crowd had formed around the coals and I wasn't about to back down. I got about halfway and decided to stop and have a bit of a chat to a quite attractive girl I noticed in the crowd. We started talking away, getting along famously, when there was a bit of a shift in the load — I looked down and my leg was on fire. I lost my balance, fell down in the middle of the coals and gashed my leg on the edge of the drum. Some guys dragged me out of the smouldering mess and actually had to hose me down. My leg was still smoking and I had this giant black hole in the back of it. I still bear the scar to this day.

But that didn't dent my party spirit one bit. There were quite a few injuries this night and it just seemed to add to the sense of occasion. To make sure people earned their beer, the keg had been set up on the edge of this steep slope, so that pouring yourself a beer was quite an athletic feat in itself. There'd been a bit of rain and you had to hang on to the keg while you poured to stop yourself from sliding down the hill. As the night wore on there was a growing pile of casualties at the bottom of the hill. Sure enough, I came to grief and slid down the hill, and somehow the keg came tumbling down after me. I was just trying to collect myself at the bottom of the hill when the keg took me out and went right through the back fence.

I was so injured that night it was unbelievable. There was a bit of clothes line surfing going on too. The police turned up just as I was simulating a late Pipeline take-off on top of the Hill's Hoist. Reg's long-suffering dad Pat was yelling out, 'Get Rabbit off the clothes line before' ... but just as the words were leaving his mouth, the whole thing collapsed under my weight ... 'he breaks it.' I ended up being taken to hospital: burnt, bruised and scarred from head to foot. It even made the national news — 'Former world champ injured in firewalking mishap.'

The next day was the Stubbies Legends, an event for surfers over 28, a new concept in pro surfing. I was a mess, but true to the old warrior spirit I still went in it, and ended up coming second to Hawaiian Hans Hedemann. I left for Hawaii soon after that but I departed with an ominous threat hanging in the air — when I returned, Reg and I were going to get a band together.

Inspired by the events of Reg's 21st, we called ourselves 'The Firewalkers'. I'd always fancied myself as a potential rock star and I idolised Mick Jagger and David Bowie, so this band became my

Bustin' down the door

new mission. Reg and I were the lead singers, a mate of ours called Hoppy was on lead guitar, a guy named Big Eddy was on bass and my old mate from the Tweed, Spook Corowa, was on drums. We had our first performance at a place called the Jet Club, which is now extinct. There was a band on before us and we retired to the band room to prepare for the show. We opened the bar fridge and it was full of the other band's booze and, unversed in the protocol of such occasions, we just hooked in. By the time the other band came off, we'd completely emptied the fridge. Understandably, they weren't impressed, and it didn't do much for the quality of our performance either. I actually came on a song early and started singing 'Satisfaction' while the band was playing something else altogether. We did a lot of Rolling Stones and Sex Pistols covers, but we'd only ever get through about four or five songs in a show, and at times I swear each band member was playing the song list in a different order. But it was quite a show just the same. At one stage local pro surfers Munga Barry and Jason Buttenshaw jumped on stage with us and I think it was Butto who decided it would be a good idea to throw a bottle into the crowd. Next thing, we were getting pelted with anything moveable that was in the place.

It was on the verge of a riot when the bouncers moved in and tried to shut us down. Hoppy bopped one of the security guys over the head with his guitar, and then it was on. We became the only band in the history of the Jet Club to get evicted through the back stage door mid-performance. Unperturbed, I wandered round the front and sauntered through the main entrance as a paying punter to watch the mayhem.

We had a band meeting afterwards and decided it was such a successful night that this would become part of our stage show. Whenever possible, we would get thrown offstage mid-performance, and in this way we would carve out a unique niche for ourselves. At our next performance we appeared as 'The Dreaded Firewalkers', but our musical careers were short-lived. I had trouble getting Reg away from the bar and up on stage. I'd see him in the crowd having a beer and announce his arrival on stage and he'd just go, 'Up yours,' give me the finger and keep drinking.

One of our original songs was called 'I don't like drinking, drinking likes me', and Reg was too busy living it to get up and sing it. One time Hoppy took 20 minutes to plug his guitar in because he'd had a few too many beers. In the end, we just kind of imploded.

WALKING THE PLANK

Things didn't get really tough for me financially until '88, when I officially retired from the tour. All through our careers we were heading into uncharted waters, at all times, every step of the way, and of course the final step is walking the plank, walking into retirement. In surfing, retiring was like walking the plank into oblivion — the world was flat and you sailed right off the edge when you finished your competitive career. From the very beginnings of my dream of becoming a pro surfer and actually seeing my dream happen, living an idyllic lifestyle and going to all these places, pioneering new frontiers, ushering in professionalism — it was hard to accept that you'd come to the end of the line. There was nothing set up, there were no cushy jobs to walk into that would keep you involved in surfing in a very real way.

My first foray into the world of business was an unmitigated disaster. Billabong couldn't justify paying me the same wage after I quit the tour, but I was given the opportunity to buy into Billabong Europe, which looked like a great investment, with the French surf market booming. I still owned some shares in Quiksilver so I sold those to go into Billabong Europe, in partnership with two other guys. I spent a lot of time in England and Europe over the next few years trying to get this thing off the ground. It was always a pleasure for me to spend time in Europe, but I was never as comfortable in the business arena as I was in surfing competition. Without going into the messy details — we came to grief in spectacular fashion. There were some embezzlement charges laid against one of my English partners, and the upshot of it was: Billabong Europe wound up bankrupt and owing Billabong Australia about a quarter of a million dollars. Billabong boss Gordon Merchant very charitably waived me of any debt, but it wasn't a terribly fun introduction to the world of commerce. I'd done my dough and this venture that I'd hoped would set me up for retirement fell to pieces. That's when I really did bottom out. I was no longer involved in the surfing industry on any level. I was completely out of the loop.

Over the course of four years, I'd gone from being the number two rated pro surfer in the world, to a retiree with no source of income — not even so much as a gold watch. In 1987 I was inducted into the Surfing Hall of Fame, and received quite a handsome plaque to hang on my wall, that was a proud moment for me — but it still felt like the end of the road, like I'd been officially relegated to the pages of history. I finally stepped off the end of that plank I'd been reluctantly shuffling along for the past few years into the unknown.

```
RABBIT RETIRES
EXTRACT FROM THE DAILY TELEGRAPH, BY RAY
KERSHLER, 1988: 'Surfing owes a lot to Wayne
Bartholomew. The sport wouldn't have the respect it
has today without him. When Bartholomew decided to
become a professional surfer in 1972 the popular
image of a surfie was a cross between a dole
bludger and a junkie. That the sport today enjoys
such a clean, healthy image is in great part due to
Wayne Bartholomew. "In a way we virtually created
the world surfing circuit," said Rabbit. "There was
no circuit -- we just kept travelling round and
round until we made one."'
```

THE BIG C

With exquisite timing, fate handed me another test in '88 — the news that I had a malignant melanoma in my back. Ever since the dermatologist warned me in 1973 that I was topping the

Preparing for civilian life

endangered species list, I'd got into the habit of caking myself with zinc cream whenever I was in the sun. 'Listen pal,' he told me, 'when your friends are walking down the promenade with their girlfriends, you won't have a nose. And by the time you're 30, if you keep going this way, you'll be dead.' That made quite an impact.

I've had a skin cancer specialist for many years, Dr Morgan O'Brien. He is an Irishman with a classic sense of humour and I'd walk into his surgery with a troubling sunspot and he'd just laugh, 'That little thing, that's nothing,' and get out the blowtorch.

On the day before I was due to leave for a 10-week tour of Indonesia and Europe, I pulled into my osteopath's studio for a tune-up and manipulation. My osteo, Jeff Hale, had an assistant prepare my back and neck for him. She advised me to get my back checked as there was an irregular growth on it. I asked Jeff about it and he also used that dreaded word, 'irregular'. My survival instincts were alerted.

I made a beeline to Dr O'Brien and instead of his usual offhand manner, he admitted that it looked like a 'nasty'. Morgan took the knife to me, then informed me that I wouldn't be catching my flight the next day. It would take 48 hours for pathology to test the growth and if the news was bad they'd have to operate immediately.

Only the day before I had hired a pager and I awoke at 7 am to my first message: 'Ring Morgan O'Brien immediately.' Shit, it had only been 16 hours — the news must be bad.

I was informed that I had a superficial, spreading malignant melanoma on my back and a further, deeper cut would be needed. Only then did I postpone my Bali trip. I was well aware that it was a rarity to eliminate the malignancy before it reached the lymphatic system and riddled the body with cancer. I'd been to Morgan in March for a burn-off and it was now early August, so the thing could only be months old. Fortunately, the surgery confirmed that the melanoma was in its infancy and they'd been able to get it all.

The whole experience had a profound impact on me — I had a new mission. At all junior events since then I've had a free screening clinic for competitors and the general public. Over a dozen potentially deadly melanomas have been discovered and, to my knowledge, all competitors have survived.

Bustin' down the door

I gave a testimonial in an item on skin cancer on the final edition of '60 Minutes' for 1994. The segment hit home hard, featuring survivors like myself, as well as people with terminal cancer. There is still a lot of work to be done educating people on the subject. Perhaps I was spared to carry on with the mission.

THE FIGMENT

Just like melanomas, past misdeeds have a disturbing way of catching up with you in the end. Now that I was spending more time at home it was probably inevitable that my rather colourful driving record would bring me to the attention of the authorities. There was a period of time there in the RX7 days when I did get a few speeding tickets and other traffic infringements. But I was on the move so much that I'd successfully dodged paying them or having my licence taken from me. I'd come home from my travels and my sister Heidi would say, 'Oh, the police came by again but I told them you were out of town.'

Years later, I was down the pub having a beer with a football mate of mine, Neil Pringle, and he introduced me to a few people. And this one guy just looked at me with disbelief. 'You're Rabbit? I finally meet you in the flesh? Rabbit Bartholomew?' he asked incredulously.

'Yeah, why?'

'We used to refer to you as "the Figment", because you didn't exist. I'm the ex-police chief of Coolangatta and I used to send my best men out to bring you in and take your licence off you. Six years and we never found you. I would read the papers to see when the surfing tournaments were on and I would send my men down there and they still never found you.' It was like I was this guy's great white whale. Of course, the circle of us had the biggest belly laugh of all time. He went on and on about it. Finally, I did get tracked down and there were so many tickets, there was a booklet of them, and I had to go through each ticket and show cause as to why I should keep my licence. As I went through them, I made up all these incredible stories like, 'Oh, I ran that red light because I was having lunch with the mayor … I had a coaching class here … I was late for a heat.' In the end they had to take my licence off me, so I learnt my lesson. Fortunately, I was overseas for the duration of the suspension.

GOING TO WORK

I'm not exactly sure when it happened, but gradually it dawned on me that it was time to go to work. I'd been bobbing around between all these different things, searching for that sense of mission and purpose that I'd always thrived on. And, quite apart from anything else, I was watching the bank balance going down and down, I still didn't have any real income. The environmental campaigns gave me a lot of satisfaction and I felt like I was making a worthwhile contribution, but eventually I realised they were also sending me broke.

I decided I was going to have to start looking out for number one. I knew that I could achieve results in whatever I did. Once I made up my mind to do something I was totally committed to the cause; I just needed a cause I believed in, one that would provide me with some kind of income and still involve me in surfing in a meaningful way.

I remember reading an interview with Damien Hardman around this time and he was asked what he was going to do when he retired. 'Well, I don't want to do what MR and Rabbit have done, which is nothing,' he said. That felt like a bit of a kick in the teeth, but I realised I wasn't forging any kind of new path for myself. Being the first guys to walk that plank of pro tour retirement, I think we all felt a bit lost for a while — I know I did.

At this point, I'm sure there were those who wouldn't have been a bit surprised to read about Wayne Bartholomew departing this world by wrapping his car round a tree, or to find me seeing out my days in the front bar of the Patch, reminiscing into a beer glass.

But I knew I still had more to offer surfing. I knew I was intelligent, I'd acquired a lot of life skills, and I was determined to find my next true calling.

Even though my own competitive career was at an end, there was still a lot of work to be done to realise my vision of how pro surfing should be. Pro surfing had grown in such a random, haphazard fashion, and the sport was still so young. There was nothing in place at the end of your career, and there wasn't much in place at the beginning of your career either. The new crop of pro surfers like Tom Carroll, Tom Curren, Barton Lynch and Damien Hardman were doing pretty well. They were starting to get big retainers, big incentives, multiple sponsorships and better prize-money. But I could see that there were a lot of kids really struggling, and there were a lot of mistakes being made. There were no career paths established for young surfers. Some kids were being given too much too soon, while other kids were getting nothing.

Ironically, it was the ravages of economic recession that provided me with my new career direction. We'd already decided we were just a bit ahead of our time with the WRB Surfing Academy but, at the same time, I was watching the virtual disintegration of Australian pro-am surfing, and the disappearance of an important career stepping stone for aspiring professional surfers. Since its inception in 1974, the Australian Professional Surfing Association (APSA) had been a growing force and had come to provide an important pro-am circuit, or domestic competition for surfers preparing to make the leap to the ASP world tour. As the '80s came to a close, Australia was feeling the painful grip of economic recession and promotional budgets for pro-am surfing contests seemed to be one of the first things to dry up. The APSA had imposed ambitious new, minimum prize-money requirements and sanctioning fees, and potential sponsors just weren't coming to the party.

No-one seemed too perturbed about the imminent collapse of Australia's pro-am circuit. But without a domestic circuit, young Australian surfers would have to make the leap straight from the amateur ranks to the world professional tour, where they were in danger of being eaten alive by contest-hardened older competitors, or the eager new talents emerging from the USA and Brazil. I sat down and talked to a few of the young guys in Hawaii one year and they were all pretty anxious about their future. I mentioned that I'd thought about organising a few small events at home to help fill the void left by the collapse of the APSA and they just urged me to go for it.

Mont and I had already been discussing the idea of shifting the operations of the WRB Surfing Academy into staging local surfing events — so the timing seemed perfect. We decided to strip away the administrative costs of staging events and give local businesses the opportunity to get behind surfing for a fairly modest investment. We jokingly referred to our planned contests as 'the Jack Slasher Recession Buster Budget Circuit'.

The entire thing was a bluff because we only had one confirmed event, backed by Montezuma's Mexican restaurant, but we were already calling ourselves a circuit. The first event went off really well with great waves at Snapper Rocks. The Gold Coast's own, new FM radio station, SEA-FM, got right behind us and the surfers couldn't have been more stoked — there was obviously a need for more events to keep the momentum going.

I kept telling people there would be four or five events, but it got down to within 36 hours of the alleged second event and we still didn't have a sponsor. It looked like our bluff was up and the 'Rabbit' Circuit was going to fall on its face before it had barely got off the ground. Then, miraculously, this group of Christian surfers who ran Hydro Cool Surfboards came to my aid and put up the prize-money. We had incredible waves at Duranbah for the second event, and this reputation for being blessed with good waves for our events started to develop. Unfortunately, it bucketed rain all weekend. The surfers were happy, but we didn't have much of a crowd on the beach. In fact, there was only this one, little old lady who came down with an umbrella and stood in the torrential rain, and watched the contest all weekend. And when it came time for the presentation night on the Sunday evening, the same little old lady turned up at Hill Street Nightclub, much to our bemusement. We were to learn a valuable lesson this night.

Bustin' down the door

In hindsight, we left it a little bit late to hold the formal presentation part of the evening, and in the buoyant mood of a successfully executed event we were all … well, untidy would be a nice way of putting it. The winner, Jason Buttenshaw, got up there and went, 'Ah, it was a fucking great event,' and I've been led to believe that some colourful language may have left my own lips that evening. But we were all surfers among surfers, letting our hair down after a big weekend on the beach and there didn't seem any harm in it. A great night was had by all and the event was declared a raging success, and celebrated in fine style. However, the little old lady just happened to be the sponsor of the event and she fled Hill Street Nightclub convinced that she'd stumbled upon a meeting of the servants of Satan.

At 9 the next morning the sponsors rang me and said, 'We've cancelled our cheque. We've withdrawn our sponsorship. We didn't get what we were promised. It rained all weekend and there were reports of foul language at the presentation.' With a decidedly fuzzy head I had to slip into damage control mode, and I basically had to go to the Christian Surfers on my hands and knees and just about beg for that $4000 cheque. Otherwise the Rabbit Circuit would have been bankrupt after its second event. I offered to impose a $500 fine on myself as penance for swearing at the presentation; they accepted that and I managed to smooth things over.

But I still had to find a sponsor for event number three. I went to see my old mate Paul 'Smelly' Neilsen, who by this time was presiding over the hugely successful surf shop chain, Brothers Neilsen. Always a formidable businessman, Paul insisted that our negotiations be conducted over these unbelievable lunch marathons. It would take about five lunches to finally stitch up the deal — I earnt that contest sponsorship through sheer stamina. It would always be a Friday lunch and Paul would bring in a few big hitters for the occasion. We would have to debate the whole concept of professional surfing, the philosophy behind the event, how the prize-money figures were arrived at, and most of the problems of the Western world — all over many bottles of red wine. It was hilarious, and inevitably we'd end up over at the Casino, making less and less sense as time wore on. By the next day I was never quite sure what stage the negotiations had reached. So the next lunch meeting we'd have to backtrack over the business already covered to make sure we knew where we stood. It was a gruelling way to do business, but at least we knew that we were philosophically in tune.

As this harrowing business of finding event sponsors progressed, I stumbled upon one of the great untapped contest sponsors of our times — nightclubs! The popular Gold Coast nightclubs were doing well and I'd certainly invested plenty into their businesses over the years. In a lot of ways, they were the ideal contest sponsor. The nightclubs could do a deal with a brewery as co-sponsor and get all this free product and then sell it to the surfers during the weekend, thereby recouping their prize-money through the bar takings. They couldn't lose — they got radio promotion through SEA-FM and the official contest party would be held at their nightclub, so they'd be guaranteed brisk business from all the surfers keen to celebrate, and all the young ladies eager to meet pro surfers.

Of course, this required spending a great deal of time in nightclubs myself, handling the delicate negotiations with management. I didn't like the idea of going in and having meetings in the owner's office at 11 am. I liked to go in and see them in their clubs at 11 pm, in an environment where my persuasive powers seemed to be at their peak. Discussions might continue until 2 am and, like Smelly's lunch meetings, we'd have to re-convene the following week and backtrack to work out exactly where we'd got to. This wasn't conventional surfing administration, but this was the way I was doing business and it was getting results. Soon we had the Party Nightclub, the Rose and Crown, the Surfers Paradise Beer Garden and Hill Street — all my favourite haunts basically — sponsoring events. The Rabbit Circuit was up and running and I'd finally made a virtue of my habitual nightclubbing.

We called ourselves the 'Queensland Professional Surfing Circuit', but everyone knew us as the Rabbit Circuit, and from nothing we built up quite an impressive little contest series. At the end of it we had the Montezuma's Shield, with a prize pool for the series winners. Not even the ASP had a season's end prize pool then.

This was all encouragement enough for me to recognise the beginnings of a new career — part coach, part contest director, part administrator and development officer.

Around this time, the Australian Surfriders Association (now known as Surfing Australia), traditionally the administrator of amateur surfing in Australia, stepped in to pick up the pieces of the collapsed domestic pro-am circuit. Seeing what I had achieved with the Rabbit Circuit, the ASA convened a meeting of its state representatives to come up with a masterplan to resurrect pro-am surfing in Australia and re-establish the important career stepping stone it provided. A lot of really dedicated people came out of the woodwork and stood up to be counted for the cause. The result was the Australian Championship Circuit (ACC), a new umbrella organisation to band together the fragmented series of minor contests dotted about the country. Queensland surfing administrator Peter Whittaker and I put our heads together and made the ACC truly national. He had a great rapport with Quiksilver and convinced them to stage major ACC events in each state. With the half dozen Rabbit Circuit events and half dozen Quik events, the ACC was off and running.

GORDON MERCHANT: 'He had to sort himself out and figure out, well, "What's Wayne Bartholomew do now?" and I think he just went back to things that could keep him on the beach and keep him in touch with what was going on. He enjoyed being a part of it all. All the experience he's got — he needed to be passing that on to other people, or just being a personality and being able to go out there and drum up sponsorship for a contest and get something happening that wasn't happening. Graham Cassidy virtually killed off pro-am surfing in Australia with all these high ideals and the reality wasn't there. Rabbit picked up the pieces and put it back together again and built up a little circuit, much to the amazement of the Graham Cassidys — the ones who were sitting down making all the rules and coming up with nothing.

I was blown away. From nothing, suddenly he had a little circuit going and the ASP want to talk to him. "Is this a take over or what?" It was quite amazing. That was how we actually got into the Kirra contest, because Rab was looking for a sponsor.'

Over a couple of years, our modest little Rabbit Circuit had grown to the point where I was getting the big players like Billabong to sponsor events. Billabong boss Gordon Merchant agreed to come in and sponsor an event at Kirra in '92 to the tune of something like $5000, and Hill Street Nightclub came in as co-sponsor. I consulted moon and tide charts and the existing contest schedules, and picked a weekend in March to stage the event. Kirra is one of the world's greatest waves, revered around the world as the ultimate tube, barrelling as it does along the perfect contours of the Kirra headland. But she is a fickle mistress who doesn't bestow her charms lightly. Kirra can lie dormant for weeks and months at a time. In a typical year, there might literally be only a handful of perfect days.

There was a lot riding on that first Billabong Kirra Pro. It's an anxious business awaiting a Kirra swell. Cyclones which spin across the top of our continent traditionally round Cape York, and then position themselves somewhere in the Coral Sea. They must sit squarely in a defined 'swell window' for the ocean pulses they generate to reach our shores at the right angle for classic surf. Even then, if they sit too close to the coast we get only torrential rain, raging winds and wildly unsurfable seas. It can be agonising, willing something as erratic as a cyclone to behave itself.

I felt it was important for Kirra itself that it turned it on like the Kirra of old, as well. We hadn't had a classic cyclone season for years and people were starting to forget what a special wave Kirra was. The dreaded Kirra marina proposals kept rearing their ugly heads every year or two — oblivious to the fact that one serious cyclone could wash away anything humans chose to construct in its path.

Kirra needed to remind everyone just what an incredible wonder of nature it was, and why it had to be preserved.

The week before the event, there was a lot of excitement and, right on cue, Cyclone Fran appeared on the map. In the week leading up to the contest, Kirra was about two to three feet — just really fun little waves. On the Friday, Fran moved into position, and on Saturday morning, the first day of the event, it was six foot by six foot, with corduroy swell lines to the horizon. There were hardly any breaks in the sets, and it was the most perfect Kirra I'd seen for years.

A lot of surfers had never seen Kirra like this — it was like this mythological place that people had heard about but never seen and they were surfing it for the first time in contest heats. The only bummer usually associated with contests in perfect waves is that all the non-competitors feel deprived of their surf spot. I thought, gee, some guys are seeing this for the first time, and there are plenty of waves out there. I told everyone, 'Look, if you guys are all cool, you can all just surf and we'll have a contest in amongst you all. Just don't drop in on the guys in their heats.'

So all these free surfers went out there, just surfing their brains out, and throughout the entire contest there was not one interference. It was an unreal celebration of surfing, in a spirit that sometimes goes missing in the modern era of crowds and big-money contests. Everyone went, 'Bugs is being cool about it, we'll be cool, we'll reciprocate.' I remember clearly two of Australia's top, young surfers, Brenden Margieson and Guy Walker, coming up and saying they'd just had the best barrels of their lives and they just couldn't believe how good the wave really was.

The next day the swell had dropped a bit but it was four foot and absolutely ruler-edged. There was some phenomenal surfing, particularly from some of the pros like Luke Egan and Occy. But the final ended up being an all local affair, between Munga Barry, Sean 'Reg' Riley, Brett Hodge and Darren Magee. I was so stoked, because the locals had shown that when it came to riding the Kirra barrel, they could match anyone in the world. Munga had been away on the tour and he'd got his welcome-home swell, and he just took it out over Reg.

That event really made me think that this was all a meant-to-be thing. We'd had quality waves for something like 17 of the 18 events we'd run, and that Kirra contest received coverage all over the world — way out of proportion to its actual prominence on a global scale. The world's top pro surfers at the time were starting to make rumbling noises about the poor surf on the world pro tour, and suddenly they all wanted to come to Kirra for our humble little contest. My status as an organiser of quality surf contests was established and I can't help feeling that my beloved surf spot had given the stamp of approval to my new career.

The Kirra legend was re-born from that event. Of course, Gordon Merchant was delighted. For a $5000 investment he received about $250,000 worth of publicity around the world. It caused all sorts of dramas within the ASP, however, because we weren't sanctioned by them, yet all these top pros like Luke Egan, Munga Barry, Mark Occhilupo, and Cheyne Horan had taken part in this tiny, $5000 event. Because I was friends with them, and it was at Kirra, they just wanted to go in it. In the end, Graham Cassidy just sort of had to wear it, but I assured him that we would be upping the ante and making it an international, ASP event in the coming years.

Later that year, I undertook my first coaching assignment with the Australian team at the World Amateur Titles. The World Titles were held in Lacanau, France, the scene of my miraculous victory through the losers' rounds back at the first Lacanau Pro in '81. My co-coaches were old pro surfing buddies Paul Neilsen and Bruce Raymond, we made a good team. It was huge and stormy for most of the event, similar, in fact, to the conditions that had originally sent me packing to the losers' rounds in '81. But with all this experience on our side, we knew how to send those kids out into the maelstrom and pick out the rideable waves in their allotted time each heat. The Aussies posted a glorious victory in those World Titles and I could feel the old fire returning. Nothing can match the pure rush of being a competitor at the highest level, but I could experience that heady thrill vicariously by running successful events or coaching successful teams. There was life after pro surfing!

Bustin' down the door

ROD BROOKS: 'From Rab we've seen some classic coaching performances. The most outstanding I can remember was the finals of the Lacanau World Titles, in '92. We had three finalists in the open men's, and Rabbit took them up to the other end of Lacanau, about a mile up the beach, to paddle out. The current was so strong that by the time they'd drifted down and cleared the break they were right in front of the contest area. Rab was taking the Australian finalists in a bus, right up to the other end of the beach and paddled them out there, it was like a big eight foot shore dump, and a lot of competitors never crossed the bar. Other teams were sending their surfers straight out and they were just disappearing down the coast. That was his first coaching campaign with the national team and he convinced us we had the right guy then.'

In early '93 a call came through from Rod Brooks at the Australian Surfriders Association, giving me the quiet, inside word to check that Saturday's *Australian* newspaper. I picked it up and there was an advertisement for the position of national coaching director for the ASA. I must admit, in my time as a pro surfer, I'd often regarded administrators as the crusty, old, conservatives of the sport. But this was food for thought. I talked to Rod over the phone about the position. I still wasn't comfortable with the idea of a desk job, but he explained that they wanted a very hands-on, in-the-field kind of role for the coaching director. The successful applicant would be co-ordinating the new Australian Championship Circuit, overseeing the coaching of elite juniors, overhauling the entire coaching accreditation system and ensuring the credibility of our coaches, and liaising with the ASP to help develop the Australasian leg of the world tour.

The collapse of the APSA had neatly coincided with the introduction of the ASP's new two-tiered system. In a nutshell, this meant pro surfing had been split in two with a World Championship Tour for the elite top 44 rated surfers in the world to decide the world champion, and a World Qualifying Series for young hopefuls to try to break into the top ranks. America and Brazil had seized the opportunity to launch healthy WQS legs in their regions in '92, giving their surfers the best possible chance of qualifying, without having to jet all over the world. Australia, however, just wasn't ready for the change and a generation of talented, aspiring pro surfers toppled into the void.

It was a huge job, working at all levels of the sport, and I suddenly realised — here was my new mission. I'd finally found my true calling, where I wanted to be, working for surfing. I realised later that the whole bottoming out process I'd been through had been completely necessary. It's partly about passing on the mantle and stepping aside — getting out of the way to let the next generation have its day. But also, I had to go through a metamorphosis. I had to die as a surf star to be re-born as something else. I guess I did have to declare myself dead as a surf star and totally accept that before I could move on again. For a while there I had been clinging on to the surf star status, reluctant to relinquish it and enter an uncertain future. But out of that lowest ebb, I was able to emerge as the real me — at my real age — and move on to my next life phase.

GORDON MERCHANT: 'It's funny. He came to me and wanted a job, and I said, "What do you want to do?" and he wanted to work a couple of hours a day and I said, "Oh mate, that job doesn't exist, I haven't come up with that one yet, because if you come in here it's going to be full on ... and I don't see you being able to do that." And I think he's thought about that and realised, "No, I don't think I can either." He's just had to face reality and figure out, "Okay, well, what can I do to work in with my lifestyle?" He's created his own job, and it's like nobody's done it before.'

Bustin' down the door

KELLY SLATER: 'When someone is a high achiever they don't stop achieving. Just because you might not hear about them doesn't mean they stop. Even when I play golf with Bugs he always pulls something out of the hat ... I think he wants one last hurrah, one more great achievement, like a surfing contest with all the past world champions in it.'

putting the house in order

These last few years have been good to me. We had perfect surf three years in a row for the Billabong Kirra Pro. Snapper Rocks has won the national club championship, Surf League, twice, as well as a bunch of other teams' titles. I've coached the Australian national team to two World Titles and three World Junior Championships in Bali and am still undefeated as a national coach.

I set myself a couple of goals a few years back — to win the Australian senior men's title, and to win the Snapper club championship — just to keep the personal, competitive fires burning, and achieved both of them. I finally became Snapper club champion at age 38, 15 years after my World Pro Title.

I still go to Hawaii every year and under one of the many different hats I wear these days, I manage to get myself to Indonesia, Europe and Africa most years, as well as around a fair whack of the Australian coastline. I've always loved travelling and the wanderlust remains as strong as ever.

My job as national coaching director is kind of an umbrella position, under which I am also co-ordinator of the ACC, and Australasian rep for the ASP. As well, I have been able to combine all this with my work for Billabong as a kind of special projects co-ordinator, running events here and overseas. Things have turned out pretty good for a washed-up, old surf star. I'm surfing and travelling and working in the sport I love at all levels.

They say that Sagittarius is a lucky star sign and I think that I have been pretty lucky with waves and catching good swells throughout my life. I've always prided myself on getting a good swell to leave on, before heading off on an overseas trip, and there'd always seem to be a welcome-home-Bugs swell. I guess I set things up that way. I'd be at home for the first half of the year and then leave here at the end of our surf season, and not come home all throughout the northerly months. Then I'd come back in January just in time for the new cyclone season to kick in. I'd sometimes even watch it from Hawaii and try to return just as those first southerlies chimed in and there was a big cyclone sitting off the Queensland coast. I'd shoot home and try to get that first swell, and I've done that for years.

When you get a really good run like that going, people love to tell you about it when you miss it. A lot of people went way out of their road to let me know this one time that I missed a perfect day at Kirra a few years back. They were just lining up to tell me about it when I got back. I was already distraught and they really rubbed the salt in, so that just made me more determined never to miss a good day at the Point.

As I've gotten older you'd think that finally I could get over it, but I still feel weird knowing that Kirra's breaking when I'm away. It happened again in '96. I went to Hawaii in March, happily surfing 10 foot waves with no crowds in the beautiful, late season, spring swells, and I just happened to ring home one day and a friend said Cyclone Beti was off the coast in a great position. I tried to tell myself, 'I'm not missing anything, the surf is incredible right here and there's no crowds.' But within hours I'd rung home again and said, 'Yeah, I've got a flight tonight and I'll be at Kirra in the morning.' I figured, how could I not come home for a cyclone that bore my mother's name?

A lot of people have attributed this apparent synchronicity with good surf to some kind of mystical quality. 'Rab's got a direct line to Huey (the god of surfing),' they'll say. The fact is, if I've got any sort of flexibility in my travel arrangements, I keep an eye on the world weather and try to arrive at places when it's happening. It's as simple as that.

Putting the house in order

We've had really good luck with all the events I've been involved in running. For the first three years of the Billabong Kirra Pro, we had a four-day waiting period and every year, all four days were perfect Kirra. Over three years, we had 12 days of perfect Kirra, and the odds of that happening are pretty amazing. It's not that consistent a break, and to have the cyclones just chime in at the right time makes you feel blessed. There'd be nothing on the weather map and then they'd just appear a day or two before the event.

The second year of the Billabong Kirra Pro, Cyclone Roger was just huge. In the afternoon before the event started, Gordon Merchant and I went down to Burleigh Heads to check out the surf and it was 15 feet. Just huge. I thought I'd overdone it that time, but it just mercifully moved out to sea and we got a big, clean swell off it. A lot more pros turned up that second year and it was won by '89 world champ Martin Potter. It was epic surf, Pottz was surfing at his best and I was stoked for him. I could tell he trusted me and had put a lot of faith in us, he just paddled out there and went off. And the next year we got a double swell — we had two cyclones happening at the same time and that was probably as epic as Kirra can get. Hawaiian Sunny Garcia won it that year and I felt great about that because I've always admired Sunny and we'd spent a bit of time together when he first came on the tour. I know those Kirra Pro wins are among those surfers' proudest achievements.

The only time we got skunked for surf was in '95, but that year will go down as the worst cyclone season in living memory. We actually didn't get one perfect day at Kirra in 1995 — it just didn't happen — and the contest was held in fairly mediocre waves at the old reliable fallback, Duranbah. It was an enormous anticlimax after the great run of waves at Kirra for three years, and that convinced me that the future of contests lay in being mobile. We had to have longer waiting periods and the ability to move to wherever the waves are best along a wide stretch of coast.

That's what we did in '96, as part of a general shift by the ASP to make wave quality a higher priority. The '96 Billabong Pro was a World Championship Tour event, with an 11-day waiting period to run a four-day event. This gave us the luxury of mobility — getting up each morning and chasing the day's best waves, much like recreational surfers would on a surf trip. We had some good quality Duranbah, then we moved up to Burleigh and got some great waves, and then finally Kirra came on and we had the best surfers in the world riding classic, four to five foot Kirra. That day was distinguished by Californian pro surfer, Shane Beschen, recording the highest heat score in the history of pro surfing — three perfect 10s for his best three waves. Then we went back to Burleigh and got all the way through to the semi-finals when an onshore wind came in, and we just pulled up stumps and said, 'We're not finishing this with a drop of water out of place.' Within an hour, we'd organised for the whole contest entourage to board a bus to North Stradbroke Island, and it was like the old Surfabout days. The next day, we finished the event in six foot, thumping Point Lookout beachbreaks. Hawaiian surfer, Kaipo Jaquias, notched his maiden victory, and promptly flew home and named his newborn daughter Kirra.

I've run the Billabong Jeffreys Bay event, in South Africa, for the last three years, and it's been the same deal as the first three years at Kirra. It's a four-day event, and in three years we've had 12 good days at Jeffreys Bay. And there is no Duranbah as a fall-back over there. It's either J-Bay or nothing.

At Jeffreys Bay every year a pod of dolphins swim by the Point and I always know I'm on the right track when the dolphins appear. It's always just before a classic swell and there will be two or three thousand of them, they take over the whole point. It's the longest point in the world and from end-to-end it's thick with dolphins riding waves — it's one of the world's most phenomenal sights. We had a Southern Right Whale come through the contest area one year, and there were a few thousand people standing on the point spontaneously applauding this whale as it came up the point. It came so close to the beach and then breached, came completely out of the water as if to acknowledge the applause, and just put on this huge show. It was one of the most amazing things I've ever seen in my life. We've had Thresher Sharks jumping out of the water, 10 foot Thresher Sharks 20 metres outside of the break. It's just raw ocean there, and we've had a really good success rate with all the events at J-Bay.

Putting the house in order

Last year we ran the Billabong Challenge — a new concept in pro surfing, with eight of the top surfers in the world invited to compete at two of the world's best waves. One is the 'Mystery Left' out on the edge of the Australian desert (which we don't identify to protect the interests of the local surfers), and the other is Jeffreys Bay in South Africa — considered one of the best rights in the world. We take a bunch of the best surfers in the world, a skeleton contest staff, and a film crew, spend 14 days waiting for the best waves, and make a movie of the whole thing.

The Challenge in the desert was incredibly testing. We all camped out and got hit by a desert storm which wreaked havoc for days, but we hung in there. It was an amazing experience because the challenge was just to stay put and hang in for the good surf. We had a ping pong table in one tent and held these marathon ping pong tournaments just to stay sane. It was a great life experience that we all shared. Finally, on the 14th and final day, we got perfect surf and we pulled it off. I don't like to fail and if we hadn't done it, Billabong would have spent well over $100,000 with no result.

The Challenge at Jeffreys Bay was even more radical because at one stage we were looking at perfect six foot surf, unbelievable surf, and every single person, even the Billabong people in South Africa, were saying, 'Bugs you must run the Billabong Challenge.' And I had to turn around and say, 'No, we're going to wait for bigger surf.' Only filmmaker Jack McCoy and I knew why I couldn't run the Billabong Challenge. Gordon Merchant had spent many seasons at Jeffreys Bay in the '70s and his vision was to have the Challenge in eight foot surf. He had stipulated that we weren't to run it in five to six foot surf.

Once again, it came down to the very last day of the two-week waiting period. The day before had been dead flat. There was a front coming up the coast but it didn't look like it was going to get there in time to save the event. Everyone, including all the surfers in the event, had just about turned on me, going, 'Ah, you blew it. You should have had it,' and I was telling them, 'Keep the faith,' all the while thinking, I'm a dead duck.

On the second last day of the waiting period, we went down to this place called Seal Point, about 30 minutes drive south of Jeffreys

Bustin' down the door

Bay, and had a surf in these tiny waves just as this big southerly front came roaring through. It came through about midday and I knew the latest I could start the event was midday the next day. I had 24 hours for the surf to come up. In the morning, Jack got me up, and he and Occy and I went down to the Bay at dawn: it was three to four foot J-Bay, just pathetic looking and I went, 'The project's dead in the water.' And my old mate Occy was going, 'Nah, hang in there.'

That one little bit of support was all I needed. I just made up my mind: yep, it's going to come up, and, in fact, it's going to come up in the next hour. It was only four foot surf and I pulled out my 7'6" big-wave board and my Hawaiian big-wave legrope. I went out there with all my big-wave riding gear and literally just sat out there trying to will this swell up ... and it came on. I was as amazed as anyone. I caught an eight foot wave and came running up the beach just delirious and called the event on. And the surf just kept getting bigger. We started the event at 10 am. By 10.30 it had got to 10 feet and before the first heat was over — they were 90 minute heats — the guys were completely undergunned. The surf had got to 12 feet and guys were snapping boards.

Things were so tight, so down to the last minute, that we completed the event, held a quick presentation on the beach and I had to bolt to the airport to try to make my flight — I had to get to a special meeting of the ASP in California. This is where it becomes tricky wearing all the different hats. Sometimes you've nearly got to be in two places at once, but somehow I've managed so far. We haven't had any project fall through because of me spreading myself too thin.

Another one of my major projects each year is the Billabong Junior Series, which has been going for four or five years now. It's brilliant that the best young surfers in Australia can go and compete and surf at places like Bells Beach, Yorke Peninsula in South Australia, Rottnest Island in WA, and the NSW Central Coast. They have their own mini-tour to get used to travelling and competing at these epic breaks. They're always great trips away, surfing and hanging out with all the new, young guns coming up. One year over at Rottnest Island we were visited by a pod of Killer Whales.

At one stage Mark Occhilupo was riding a wave in a free surf session and there was the two metre high dorsal fin of a Killer Whale just out to sea from him. He and the other surfers paddled in pretty quickly, just in time to witness this incredible rush of a few hundred Killer Whales pass by, like a buffalo stampede at sea. Moments like these only happen once in a lifetime, but when you spend most of your life by the ocean you get to see wondrous sights.

> GORDON MERCHANT: 'I'm always very grateful that he's there, even though he can be a real pain in the arse to get hold of at times. But he always comes through ... And the surfers can always talk to him, identify with him and trust him. That's a big part of holding things together when you're out in the middle of the bloody desert and you're battered with rain and there's no surf and it's onshore and shitty ... That's about as hard as it gets. But after all that the surfers went through, they all want to come back and do it again. I think it's nice that Rab and the rest of the crew can make it so it's like a holiday for them — away from the madness of the travelling circus and the crowds and the whole lot — and go up there and sit in the middle of nowhere and just enjoy it.'

> DAVE KENNEDY: 'He reminds me of Miles Davis. I saw this interview on TV and Miles said, "I don't have much to say to a lot of people, my friends are whoever's in the band with me right then," and that's how Rab was. He becomes incredibly close with whoever's in the moment with him.'

The other thing that means a lot to me is coaching the Australian teams. I team up with a few of my old pro surfing pals, who are also on the coaching panel, and our combined experience is pretty vast. I really put my heart and soul into coaching, especially when it's for Australia. I had a bit of a reputation as a hassler when I was a pro, but I never tell kids to go out there and be ruthless and hassle their opponents. As a pro surfer earning your livelihood, I think that's your right, but I don't coach kids that way. I just try to coach them to go out and do the best they can do, read the conditions the best they can and try to come out on top.

I've been undefeated as a national coach and it's a great feeling, and a great challenge to try to maintain that record. We won so handsomely in France in '92, but in Brazil in '94 it was the exact opposite — it came down to the last heat, the open final.

I think my greatest coaching feat occurred in the '94 World Titles in Rio de Janeiro. It was a result in the women's division that hardly anyone took any notice of but it was a magnificent personal achievement for the surfer involved and a source of great satisfaction for me as coach.

Most of our top girls were unavailable for the World Titles because of ASP commitments, so we'd had to go quite a way down the list to get our two female competitors. One of them, Phillipa Tugwood, from Margaret River in southern WA, was a totally unknown quantity. It turned out she was a real gutsy goofyfooter in the big Margaret River surf. But she was quite uncomfortable in small surf, didn't have much competitive experience and she virtually had no backhand. Her boards were completely wrong for the conditions and we actually called a coaches' meeting to figure out how to get her through a few heats. The final team standings are based on aggregate points and a poor result in the women's would have been disastrous for our hopes of coming out as the top nation. I stuck up my hand and said, 'Leave the women to me.' And Phillipa and I began this incredible campaign. I picked out assistant manager Eddie Valladares and promoted him to national coaching status for the day. Having worked with him before with the junior squads, I knew he was game.

I gave Phillipa the most explicit instructions I'd ever given a competitor in my life. She wasn't allowed to veer from these directions one iota. The surf was solid at the Barra beachbreaks just south of Rio, which was about the only thing going in her favour, but the sandbanks weren't really handling the swell. There was this vague semblance of a left-hander that really wasn't there, but every now and again, in between close-outs, there'd be this section that would hold up and reform into the shorebreak. I looked at it and went, this is her only chance. I told her, 'You are forbidden to go on those good rights with the rest of the competitors. You have to surf these lefts.' And she did exactly what I said, and got through her first heat. After that, her confidence started to build and she kept getting through heats. We'd send her out on these lefts that no-one else could see and she'd actually find them. She was taking air drops and getting around seemingly impossible sections and she always looked like she was just about out of control and about to fall off, but she wouldn't. She'd grovel right through flat sections and just burrow her way through to the shorebreak and do these amazing go-for-it manoeuvres and get washed up the beach. I was down there on the water's edge cheering and clapping and yelling, 'Go get 'em.' She got through about nine heats — it was absolutely blowing our minds.

And then she came up against Anne-Gaelle Hoarau, who was runner-up in the last World Titles. Hoarau was far and away the favourite — a super experienced surfer. Also in the heat was a fantastic surfer from Tahiti, Patricia Rossi. I figured we'd had a good run, but getting through this heat was just too much to hope for. As Phillipa paddled out I looked up at Eddie and made a sign of the cross.

But the other girls had seen Phillipa's amazing run through the day and completely threw their strategies out the window and all came and tried to surf Phillipa's invisible left. I just went, 'Oh, this is insane, they'll never find it. It only exists in Phillipa's mind. I've got her thinking it's Margaret River out there.' And she won the heat. Patricia Rossi got second, and Anne-Gaelle Hoarau went out the door, out of the tournament. Phillipa Tugwood was in the top six in the world.

When we got back to the hotel no-one in the Australian team could believe that Phillipa Tugwood was one shot away from being in the final of the World Titles. Phillipa got knocked out in the semis the next day but she'd already far exceeded everyone's expectations, including her own, I suspect.

We won the World Team's Title when gutsy Queensland goofyfooter Sascha Stocker won the open men's final, but I reckon Phillipa Tugwood also won that World Title for Australia. Those points

Bustin' down the door

were crucial. It was a real exercise in the power of self-belief and the almost unstoppable momentum confidence can generate.

Working with Bruce Raymond and Paul Neilsen at the World Titles is a real treat because we go all the way back to the '70s. Bruce and I did so much big-wave surfing together, going for it at Backdoor Pipe and Sunset in Hawaii, and Paul and I go back to the early Burleigh days and numerous surf trips together; all three of us were part of the whole *Band on the Run* thing. At the International Grommet Titles in Bali each year I team up with my old mate Mark Warren, and it's the Rabbit–Warren coaching show. The contest is held on the Kuta–Legian beachbreaks, but in the first week we take the kids out to Uluwatu and Padang to get all the reef surfing out of their system. And then a few days before the event we go down to the beachbreaks and prepare for competition. All the other teams just slog it out in the beachbreaks the whole time, and we actually cop a bit of flak for taking our kids out to the reefs. But we get the results, and the kids have a ball.

It's happening in Hawaii too — all the old boys are getting into coaching the kids. I love going to Hawaii and seeing the older guys putting all their efforts into junior surfing. I think we're all moving in the same direction now and the kids mean everything to us — giving them the good oil and the best start in life.

When you see the different generations interact so happily and effectively like that, I really feel like the surfing community has a lot to teach the rest of society. The old boys stay young by tapping into the energy of the youth, and the younger surfers benefit from the experience of their elders. It's a form of tribalism — the passing on of wisdom and the comfortable relationship between the generations.

BRUCE RAYMOND: 'Our lives keep crossing. We've shared two World Titles together, fighting to the brink for Australia, and we go, we're pretty good at this sort of stuff. We could have been enemies for life and here we are being drawn back together despite ourselves. Look at Bugs now. I think he's found his niche — What a fantastic thing. He has this dream now to be the Neil Fraser of surfing.'

Putting the house in order

DOUG 'CLAW' WARBRICK: 'He's just been so much a part of the Australian surfing culture, for a long time now. He's probably the most significant person in the Australian surfing culture. He's just had that longevity and staying power, that sort of standing and significance, and mainly that love for the sport. I think he's one of the greatest spokesmen for surfing now, because his command of the language is incredible. His public speaking and his work on the PA and all that is just amazing. He seems to exhibit a greater knowledge and love of surfing than anyone else. After all, you've been world champion, surfed all the great breaks and surfed against all the great surfers and won most of the classic events, I guess you must have just a little more insight than the rest of us. Even the way he speaks naturally you just think, I'm being exposed to something valuable here, I should sit up and take notice.'

THE SPIRIT OF CLUB SURFING

Snapper Rocks Surfriders continues to be a huge part of my life. It really meant a lot to me when one of our best young surfers, Jay Phillips, got up at one presentation night and said that since the passing away of his father he felt like the club was his family. That meant so much to me because those are exactly my feelings. I guess not having kids of my own, it's like they are my kids. The club has been my extended family. Every year I set goals for the club and right now we're aiming for the treble. The three events that we really focus on are the Kirra Teams' Challenge, the Straddy Assault and the Surf League. For the last three years we've won two out of three every year, but we've never won the three all in the same year. When we won the Surf League in '93 and '94, we won at Straddy but we didn't win the Kirra Teams' challenge for both of those years. Last year, we won the Kirra Teams' Challenge and the Straddy but we just fell short in the Surf League. These three competitions are what I consider the Grand Slam of club surfing in Australia.

I reckon there are three other super clubs in Australia — Queenscliff, Narrabeen and Merewether — and the rivalry between us all is intense. They've all got a long tradition, most of them have been round for close to 30 years and have been through the inevitable cycles that govern a club's fortunes. Merewether had the dynasty in the '80s when they had MR there as the coach and young guys coming through such as Nick Wood, Luke Egan, Matt Hoy, Simon Law and a few other really hot guys. They swept all before them. While they were doing that we were putting in place our junior development program and I knew, if we held the club together, we would be a power of the future.

There was a time when people were a bit critical of me for driving the club too hard and thinking winning was everything. But winning is important to keep the club bankrolled. It's not that cheap to galavant around this country taking 12 or 15 people with you. Winning is a means to an end, to finance these surf trips and club functions. And there's nothing like the victory cry of the club when we all get together and do the 'Snapper Rules' chant.

The competitiveness even spills onto the stage at the presentation night. If a team loses narrowly they'll still try to find a way to steal the victor's thunder on the winner's dais. The Queenscliff boys were magnificent in defeat at the Kirra Teams' Challenge this year. One of their members got up and sang the full Elvis number and brought the house down. Queenscliff got top points for that. That's part of the beauty of it because when they get back in their den they'll be able to finally go, 'Well, Snapper beat us by a point but we won the night.'

We've got a strong contingent of girls in our club too, and we've really gone out there to bolster the female ranks of the club. We can boast the likes of Trudy Todd, Lynette MacKenzie and Kylie Webb, some of the top pro surfers in the world, and some good, young girls coming through. There was even an all-girls team at the Kirra Teams' Challenge this year, and that was a great first for surfing in this country.

One of California's top surfers, Donavon Frankenreiter, was at the Kirra Teams' Challenge presentation night this year and he came

Putting the house in order

straight up to me and said, 'I can't believe that this whole vibe can exist.' He had never witnessed a gathering of surfers like it, in California or anywhere else in the world. He could see exactly where Australian surfing was at and he was envious.

WORLD SURFING

While Australia has continued to dominate the World Amateur Titles, our fortunes have declined on the world pro tour over the last few years. Personally, I think this has been a great thing for world surfing, and a really character-building thing for Australian surfing. We had been resting on our laurels. It's a shame a generation suffered because we didn't have the infrastructure here and the domestic circuit was in tatters, and when the two-tiered system came on board, we weren't as prepared as other nations. But at least it gave those other nations a chance to get up and really give us a good battering.

The Americans are dominating in a way that we haven't seen for 30 years. There are American world champions in men's, women's and longboards. The new, young American competitors are clean-living, dedicated athletes and are incredible role models for the younger generation. The Brazilians are coming out of a backdrop of social and economic chaos, hungry for success and with a real sense of mission to strengthen national pride through their achievements.

It's good for us to go back and realise what we are, and establish it all over again, to make sure we don't forget that winning formula. A lot of people analyse when you lose. I tell surfers to learn to analyse when you win because then you won't forget — but we forgot. We had a few guys holding the banner and underneath we had a void. Australian surfers had come to regard pro surfing success as a birthright.

A lot of talented, Australian surfers have squandered their opportunities and never fulfilled their potential. Once you get in the top 44 in the world, you really should give it your best shot. When I was there, I loved being a contender, and to be a contender you've got to be true to the cause. There's a place for the partying and there's a place for celebrating this incredible lifestyle of ours.

But it's not when you're in the heat of battle, it's not while you've got the chance to make something of your life — because that window of opportunity passes by very quickly.

You've got to be strong-willed and true to yourself; you've always got to relate back to the sense of mission that you walked onto the plane with. You've got to remember that there's all those people who are counting on you on the other side of the world and you can't let them down. In times of weakness or doubt, I always used to think of my sisters and my mother seeing me off as I left for the airport, I remember thinking that I just could not let them down. I've got all these people who are waiting for news of me and I'm going to make sure they get a good report.

Temptation has always been a part of the tour. You've always got the rat pack and the serious contenders. I was a serious contender for most of my time on tour and when you're a serious contender you can't stray from your sense of mission. If you lose that focus then suddenly you're in the rat pack, and then it's goodbye for that year on tour.

You can't go into a sporting career unless you're armed with the knowledge that it's a war zone and to the victor goes the spoils. You're either the victor or the vanquished. Sport loves winners and it's cruel — there are no guarantees for tomorrow. A lot of surfers don't have any fallback position, which is why you've got to be educated. There's never been a dumb world champion. You've got to be world-wise and when you've got a good, broad education base you'll pick up life skills all the way along. Your qualifications will come thick and fast just through your life experiences. That's how it worked for me. Academically, I could have gone on, but as it worked out I picked up a lot of life skills in areas that I could fall back on to make a living.

Maybe the industry has got a bit to answer for in its treatment of emerging, young talents at times too. The industry has been the backbone and the provider of professional surfing but there have been some sad instances where it has caused some casualties too. Young surfers can get carried away by their first, heady taste of surf stardom and some of the companies more or less encourage them with the attitude: there's no rules, just go off — act like rock stars. There have been top surfers busted for drugs or suffering serious personal problems and their sponsors have just dropped them. One minute they're being lauded and the next minute they're being condemned, and I think that's really sad. Everyone deserves a second chance. Guys who are freak talents are often extreme characters and they can get used up and burnt-out. We're going to have problems. The whole sport's in its adolescence and we've got to preserve the free and wild lifestyle, we've got to preserve that at all costs, but we've also got to toe the line and have these safeguards there. Guys have got to know: by all means have a lot of fun, explore the outer reaches of your character, but don't step over the line. You've got to do this all within the laws of the land.

I used to have this real fear that haunted me when I was coaching kids. Always in the back of my head, I'd think, I can't send them down the path I went. I just cannot. Because they wouldn't survive. The frame of mind that I had to get into to do some of the stuff I did is not something I'd recommend to anyone. For one, you can't coach anyone on that, it's a very personal thing. And two, it was a really dangerous attitude. When I think about that, what do I do when it comes to coaching someone in the attitude it takes to go out and ride big Pipe?

Everyone's got their own race to run. Some great surfers have only become confident in Hawaii after years of going there. You can have some horrifying experiences if you take on too much too soon, that can really put the fear of God in you. Sometimes you go in the deep end and you find out, oh, well, I can handle this okay. Sometimes you're in completely over your head and you've got to pull back and swallow your pride, and go, let's get in alive and come back to fight another day. At Pipe, it's three stikes and you're *out*, permanently.

THE BACKSIDE ATTACK AT PIPE

Ask me what I'm proudest of in my surfing career and, without question, it is my surfing in Hawaii, big Pipe in particular, from

'81 to '85. I was in the final of the Pipe Masters four of those five years and that was my time at Pipe, when I felt very comfortable and felt I was pushing things. I was really trying to explore that outside reef area. Picking them up outside Rockpiles as the west refracted into the coast was really something. A few guys had done it but I thought it was fairly new territory. That was an awe-inspiring place to surf when it got big. I spent a lot of time on those outside reefs in those years.

My inspiration to attack big Pipe was the photos of Big Monday, back in 1971, when I was about 16. I had the photos up on my wall and that was always what I wanted to do. Those images of Owl Chapman doing this incredible bottom turn and Sam Hawk pulling up high under the lip, all on their backhand, mesmerised me. It was uncanny the way Michael Peterson and I hooked up with Sam and Owl on that first trip to Hawaii in '72. I didn't realise then that I was going to be a Pipe rider, but they were part of my lineage.

I reckon Pipe's the meanest slab of water on earth, consistently. It's amazing more people don't get killed there. We learnt our trade at Pipe just by endlessly pulling into huge close-outs, I used to figure we must be doing something right because we'd always seem to come up relatively unscathed. I remember many moments of public bravado, pulling in to the barrel in front of a packed gallery, but as soon as you're in there and the north bend comes around and slams shut like Aladdin's cave, it's just you then. Bravado's pointless. They were gruesome moments. But you'd always seem to pop up and go, well, that was pretty wild, now I'm ready, and that was our training. After paying your dues on all those days of ugly close-outs, on the perfect days you could just pick the eyes out of it.

I remember staying with this friend of mine, Ray Street, and his wife Karen, in 1984. They lived right on the beachfront at Ehukai Beach Park right by the lifeguard tower. I got to know Ray really well. He was a beautiful guy and a Vietnam vet — he told me some horrifying war stories.

One morning, we were sitting at his kitchen table having some scrambled eggs and coffee. Ray and I have already checked the surf early and it's good, it is really, really good. Pipe's 10 to 12 feet,

Sunset's 10 to 12 feet, and his wife Karen's flipping pancakes and making conversation.

'How's the surf Rabbit?'

'It's really, really good today.'

'How big is it?'

'Ah, it looks great, 10 to 12 feet, west swell.'

'Are you going to Pipe?'

'Maybe Karen, maybe I'm going to Pipe.'

And she just turned to me and said casually, 'Please don't take my husband to Pipe.' And she meant it. My jaw dropped. I just thought, that's life in Hawaii. It must be an incredible situation for wives and loved ones over there — like the wives of the pilots in the *Right Stuff*, waiting to hear about the next plane crash. As all the North Shore veterans get older and start families, the wives don't want their men dying. It's like having the running of the bulls through your neighbourhood every day. It's life and death and that's why the guys who live there and surf big waves all the time are so gnarly — so intense.

I felt like I could relate to Ray Street, in my own way. I hadn't been to Vietnam, I hadn't experienced war, but I had lived in an impact zone during my trips to the North Shore. I had to get myself into a different space to even take that stuff on, and I took a lot of knocks and poundings along the way. I really think it had an effect on me, because I'd come home to Australia with all this excess energy. You don't require that kind of intensity to live day-to-day in Australia and when I had a few drinks — particularly tequila — all that pent-up, excess energy and intensity would come spilling out. I'd go into this state I called stage nine on the Richter scale. I believe it was a kind of post-battle trauma.

I have so much respect for the guys in Hawaii who continue to charge huge waves, day in, day out, year after year. To me they are the epitomy of watermen. I see guys in their 40s and 50s who are so surf fit and have so much ocean knowledge and commitment — their whole lifestyles revolve around surfing huge waves. They seem eternally youthful but at the same time they're taking on life-and-death situations that really would turn a mere mortal grey overnight.

It's no fun being out there if you're not fit and your mind's going, 'Yes, go,' and your body is not ready to go. If you start throwing yourself over 12 to 15 foot walls of water and your whole respiratory system's not up to it, you're going to die. It's heavy for people like myself to go back over there every year and face that challenge again. It's like going to the doctor for your annual check-up, and you find out how your heart is, your blood pressure, your fear level. Hawaii will let you know exactly how your health is very quickly.

MIKE GINSBERG: 'I haven't seen the old guy for so long, the young guy, and he's just surfing so good. He's still got that spring to his surfing. We're surfing the best Velzyland I've ever surfed about two weeks ago and I'm going, "Fuck, look at him." He still looks like he's 18 years old ... He still looks exactly the same. He paddles into a wave exactly the same, he stands up, does his first turn, exactly the same. He's actually surfing better now than he was the last few years of his pro career. Bugs is a guy who'll never let himself surf badly. If Bugs starts to surf badly he may kill himself. Bugs is the type of guy, if he's not surfing as good as he should be surfing he's not very pleased with himself, and that's always going to be the overriding factor with Bugs — the most important thing to him. To be able to operate properly, he has to be able to know that he can go out in the morning and rip the shit out of a wave. Even if it's one manoeuvre, even if it's 10 waves, to be able to do that, get out of the water and know that he's surfed well, everything else falls into place after that ... He's my man. I love you Bugs, you fucker.'

A FEW DOORS STILL TO BUST DOWN

Surfing is just reaching the end of its adolescence in this country and I'd like to think it's now embarking on a process of putting the house in order. And that's what I want to be a part of — looking after our own, looking after the next generation, improving the sport's standing in the general community. To foster a real awareness of this beautiful lifestyle and to maybe blunt the aggression that's out there and have surfers co-exist happily — to have the whole tribal family thing really happen. That's where I'm at. This will be my life work, my thesis, and hopefully I'll leave the sport a little bit richer for that or at least a little bit happier.

People say, 'Oh Bugs was the super aggressive competitor and the super tactician,' and all that. That was me in a contest guernsey and that was me going for the World Title. But I've been able to store that in a bottle on the shelf and, okay, every now and again I might get a bit self-indulgent and have a little whiff out of that bottle and just remember the good times, but I don't dwell in the past.

My mission statement with surfing, since I was 12 years old watching guys get run off the beach by the police, was to have respect. I've always had this vision of walking down the street and being respected for being a surfer. I accept that I've got my rough edges, that I'm not the most virtuous character, but I've always been able to draw the line and maybe even guide people to stay on the right side of that line. A lot of surfers have this fear of moving away from the renegade spirit that we started with, but I think that there's a balance we can achieve. We can be seen as a legitimate sport without losing the character of surfing. The other thing is: it's not 1970 and you can't live on 10 dollars a week any more. The surfing industry in all its forms offers career paths for people who want to stay close to the sport. Reality's caught up to a lot of surfers and they work, and make a contribution to this country, and I kind of feel good about that. It's hard to maintain that idyllic surfing lifestyle today unless you're independently wealthy.

I'd like to see surfing included in the Olympic Games in time for the 2000 Games in Sydney. The father of modern surfing is Duke Kahanamoku, who was a gold medal winner in the swimming at the 1912 Stockholm Olympics. He is a part of our lineage. The Duke was an ambassador, he travelled the world as a gold medal swimmer but he also carried his surfboard and he spread the seed of surfing in Australia and the United States. Back in the days of the

Bustin' down the door

ancient Hawaiians, surfing was the sport of kings. The ultimate for any sport is to be included in the Olympics. In October this year, at the World Surfing Titles in California, the International Olympic Committee officials will be visiting the competition. As this book is being released we will find out if we have a shot at being a part of the 2000 Olympics. I feel that we're destined to be an Olympic sport and that will be a real milestone in our development.

I remember attending a meeting down at Byron Bay a few years back to discuss a problem between surfers and dive boat operators at the Pass. The divers wanted the surfers banned from the famous right-hand point, they argued that the surfers got in the way when the dive boats were coming in and out of the water. Someone threw a barb and said, 'Oh, you're just a bunch of surfie scum,' or something similar. One of the local older surfers, a very dignified gentleman by the name of Captain Ron Bligh-Ware, just instantly rose to his feet, this elegant elder statesman of the sport, and he said, 'Sir, surfing has no apologies to make.' I really feel strongly about those words.

We've paid our dues. Surfing used to be seen as a subversive activity. Now we've got a multi-billion dollar industry; Australia's surfing products are recognised internationally as the best in the world and earn export dollars for this country. We've made a great push in the environmental movement as watch dogs of the coast. We've produced more Australian world champions in the last 30 years than any other sport. We've made Australia synonymous with surfing outside this country. People all across the world think, oh yeah, those Australians, they're surfers, they're good surfers. Our feats in Hawaii and around the world contributed to our national identity abroad. We brought the bronzed Australian to life. We were like the modern day Rod Lavers and Ken Rosewalls and Lou Hoads. When those men were first doing the tennis circuit they were broke, just tennis bums going around the world, but they just happened to be the best in the world. Surfing now has the respect of people at the highest levels of government. Surfing's administrators have won all kinds of awards for their work with indigenous people, for their work with the disabled, the disadvantaged and for the quality of their coaching and junior development programs. These are things that other sports pay lip service to. We believe in them. We nurture them and care about those things and that's our domain. In that regard we're only doing what comes naturally — turning other people on to surfing.

Surfers have uncovered some of the riches of the world, and there's not always a monetary value you can place on that. Surfers beat paths to find the most beautiful natural environments, and the rest of the world follows. It's happened in Australia from Noosa Heads, to Byron Bay, from Bells Beach to Margaret River; and overseas in Indonesia, Hawaii, Europe, Africa, South America, the South Pacific ... everywhere. There's this whole spirit of adventure, camaraderie and pioneering that is still there in surfing. We've gone into uncharted waters, to the last bastions of absolutely primitive parts of the world, and we go and just ride the waves and leave the place as it was.

MARK RICHARDS: 'I think Bugs actually believed more than Shaun and I. I think out of all those guys he was the great believer. His dream was to walk down the main street of Coolangatta and hold his head high as a professional surfer and that people would respect that. His conviction was greater than mine and Shaun's. It was something that I thought was pie in the sky. We were saying, "I hope so," and he was saying, "It will happen."'

DAVE KENNEDY: 'He was very charismatic in the real sense, and many players in his time were like that. 'Bustin' Down The Door' was for real. They were young men. They weren't kids with credit cards. I'm very jealous that they had the opportunity for those golden years. In climbing terms, they got the first ascent. By the time we came along everything had been done before.'

Bustin' down the door

RABBIT, IN *FREE RIDE*, 1977: 'Surfing's young. Professional surfing itself is really young and, like, people still see surfing as a thing for kids, a youthful outlet, you know. It's not that at all. If you can approach it as just this unbelievable artform, you're going to develop at it all the time and you're going to get more in tune to the waves because you're getting more in tune to nature all the time and you're going to be a much purer person.

The indigenous surfing movement is gathering incredible momentum, not just in Australia, but around the world. I believe surfing is one sport where racism doesn't exist. Once you're out beyond those breakers, everyone's equal. There have been Aboriginal surfers in Australia dating back to the '50s, just individuals, but the indigenous surfing movement has really taken shape this decade. As some of the original surfers, like Steve Williams at Wreck Bay, became Elders in their communities they could see what a positive thing surfing could be for their youth. Now, there's an Aboriginal Surfing Association with regular contests, coaching clinics and camps, and the simple aim of introducing more Aboriginal kids to the surf. They have ties with indigenous surfing associations in Hawaii, New Zealand and Tahiti and members have travelled to each other's countries for cultural exchanges.

As national coaching director, I've had the opportunity of working with some of the top Aboriginal surfers, to put together the Aboriginal Surfing Development Plan. The Australian Sports Commission has provided six surfing scholarships for elite Aboriginal surfers, worth $2000 each a year. The surfers can use that money to get themselves to Hawaii or pay entry fees into contests or other travel and contest related expenses. And we are running camps in each state for Aboriginal surfers to learn to surf under qualified coaches. There are already Aboriginal coaches and it's just a matter of giving the whole thing a bit of a kickstart and then they can take it up and run with it themselves.

It's great to see them come together at the indigenous contests each year and to see the rising standard and the growing talent pool. It won't be long before we have absolutely world class indigenous surfers striking out on to the world tour and really achieving a sense of pride in their own community and in the community at large. I'd like to see that happen in my time.

I think surfing and Aborigines are logical partners in the struggle to protect our environment and our coast. Our prize surf spots are like surfing's sacred sites and those that already fall inside land handed back to Aboriginal communities are effectively protected from insensitive development. We should join forces to continue to protect our coastline.

NICK CARROLL: 'He was always the spokesman for his generation to the surfing world as opposed to the outside world. Like, there were plenty of spokespeople to the outside world, some of them really horrifying, like the jumpsuited Bronzed Aussies thing, and some of them were really slick like MR and Shaun. But a lot of them should be grateful to Rabbit for being a spokesman to the surfing world. All the surfers out there who couldn't give a shit what the *Daily Mirror* thought of them, but they just wanted contact with the top surfers, but they weren't getting it from Shaun talking to *People* magazine. All that was going on there, was communication to the outside world, not to the surfing world ... Rabbit's amazingly popular in America. That's because he came across as approachable and genuine. I think the only guy who can compare with Rabbit in the Californian mind, who's an Australian surfer, would be Wayne Lynch. In the sense of being a real honest person but a really, really good surfer who didn't compromise anything of himself to do what he wanted to do.'

PETER DROUYN: 'One thing about Wayne, I think above and beyond anything else, one of the great traits about Wayne is that he has a keen sense of justice, and compassion. He has a real good understanding of what is right and what is wrong and

Bustin' down the door

therefore he has a great understanding of what human nature should be all about. In other words, he raises us all above the animal kingdom and says, no, we are something special and we shouldn't be treated badly by each other for no good reason. So Rabbit is one of those people, those very rare people.'

HEIDI: 'I think he's at one of his most peaceful times right now. The last 18 months, I just see this inner peace. The struggle's over.'

It's amazing thinking back to the early days and then looking at where everyone is today. All my old cohorts have headed in such different and varied directions, unimaginable when we were just a bunch of surf-stoked kids. Some are wealthy captains of the surf industry, some are happily married, leading completely normal suburban, middle class lives. Some have been through the wringer of drug addiction and psychiatric hospitals. Some are dead. The really lucky ones are still surfing, unimpeded by bad backs, business pressures or overbearing family commitments.

I feel like there's a bit of an unofficial, surfing old boys' club — the only qualification being a lifelong commitment to surfing. You can make all kinds of judgements about the different paths people have taken in their lives, but ultimately I think we feel like our surfing is the final barometer of how our lives' are going. When you're surfing well and often, life seems to unfold smoothly and easily. If you're surfing badly or not enough you've obviously strayed from your path as a surfer. As my dear friend Dorian Paskowitz says, 'I keep surfing because surfing keeps me.'

GORDON MERCHANT: 'You kind of wish that a good woman would come into his life and get him a bit more organised, but she'd need to be a pretty tough nut because he's got set in his ways pretty much.'

Putting the house in order

BETTY: 'He just loves what he's doing with those kids ... Age is nothing, it doesn't mean a thing, if you feel good within yourself. And to me, he's just my Peter Pan. He'll never be any different. And what a wonderful attitude to have in life ... you'll live a long time and be happy.'

There are still days on the Gold Coast, outside the tourist seasons, when I get up early and drive round the beaches and — if you can look past the high-rise — it almost feels like old times. I go and check the surf from my favourite vantage points at Point Danger and the top of Greenmout Hill, and there's barely a soul around. There are the fishing trawlers going out through the heads, and the old fishoes talking in small groups, except now they're wearing worried frowns because the mullet aren't running and their catches are getting smaller each year. But they'll happily stop and chat — imparting the most informed theories on changing swell and weather patterns you'll hear anywhere — and a few of them will still be reeking of the old port at six o'clock in the morning.

If the surf's too small to ride my shortboard I'll go down to see my old mate Billy Rak, who's set up opposite the Greenmount Surf Club, and borrow a longboard. He's still earning a modest living hiring out his battered old fleet of boards, doing the odd ding repair and charging 20 cents to use the surf club showers. He's the happiest bloke you could find to share a yarn with. Any time you're feeling down on life you can stop in and see Billy for a chat and he'll fix you right up. He'll drag out one of his dusty old relics from the boardroom under his house — one of the last of the surviving boardrooms that you used to find under every surfer's house in Coolangatta. He's got every form of surf craft down through the ages crammed in there. 'Now, don't have too much fun Rab,' he'll quip as he hands over one of those beautiful old boards, yellowed and patched up with generations of ding repairs.

Bustin' down the door

And there'll be one of those perfect, zippering little banks at Greenmount, only breaking at one or two feet, but running down the point like a miniature Honolua Bay, accelerating its way towards Coolangatta Beach, like it used to. Right where I nearly drowned, right where I first paddled out on a board for the first time, where I first discovered the secrets of generating speed. Except these days the sand build-up is likely to be a happy accident caused by the multi-million dollar sand-dredging that the council undertakes to try to replenish the foreshores from beach erosion. And I'll go out and practise my nose-riding and soul arches, just like I did when I was a 12-year-old trying to emulate my surfing heroes.

My main passion in life when I was 12 years old is still my main passion at 41 — I don't know many people other than surfers who can say that. Some might call that retarded development, but I've always believed that us surfers are on to something way more sublime than most people give us credit for. Pulses of energy roam the planet in the form of storm systems and ocean swells, and we chase them. We march to nature's drum, trying to place ourselves at the perfect interface of wind, tide, swell and coastline — to be on the spot when the magic happens. Surfing is a metaphor for life. We are tuned in to the cyclical nature of life — you ride the highs and you go through the troughs, but you always know on the other side there's going to be another high, and I think that's part of the spirit of surfing. We learn to ride life's ebbs and flows.

Surfers have always considered themselves a tribe, united by a common bond, somehow removed from the rest of society. It's a concept that's become a little lost in the modern era but it's one that we're going to have to rediscover, for the sake of surfing. As crowds escalate (and the magnetic beauty of surfing ensures they will), we must have a sense of kinship or our surf spots are going to become battlegrounds, mirroring all the ills of modern society that we want to escape. I was recently in Makaha, on Oahu's supposedly heavy westside, where 60 or more surfers can happily share the lineup because they have a sense of community, laughing and sharing waves. Longboards, shortboards, bodyboards, even outrigger canoes all co-exist with a great vibe, finding their own parts of the break suited to their craft. The old nurture the young and come to experience some of their surfing thrills vicariously, by watching the grommets develop. The young respect the old and grant them a special place of seniority in the lineup.

Surfing can show the rest of the world the way — but only if we've got our own house in order. When you embrace the act of riding waves, you are granted the key to a happy and healthy lifestyle — one that maintains a child-like sense of play, and promotes physical and spiritual well-being. If we can't learn to get along, what hope is there for the rest of humankind?

Bustin' down the door

building the dream

My whole life has been driven by the dream of professional surfing: to be able to walk down the main street of Coolangatta with your head held high and say you were a professional surfer. I've been lucky enough in my lifetime to see a lot of my dreams come true. But as the new millennium approached, I felt the dream was in danger of turning sour. A lot of pro surfers were walking away from the tour with nothing to show for all their hard work and dedication and years of struggle. And the pro tour itself seemed to have lost its spark and magic and become a chore, just another work-a-day grind for those involved. Our youthful dream of keeping the adventure alive, of not having to don suits and do the nine-to-five thing, seemed in grave danger. And my own future career path was as uncertain as ever. One way or another, I felt that old dream was going to pull me back into the engine room of pro surfing.

Maybe one reason I've always kept in touch with those youthful dreams is because there has always been a succession of grommets in my life. I've always had a young running mate, from Guy Ormerod, to Chappy Jennings, to Reg Riley, to Mark 'Baldy' Rawlings, to Dean Morrison. There's always been a grommet, some kid who wants to do well, and I've kind of taken them under my wing and either coached them or at the very least sponsored them in all their events and bought them lunch.

But Dean Morrison was special, because I became his foster parent. The first time I met Dean, it was a Sunday at a Snapper contest in '92. This kid came up and started tugging on my boardshorts, going, 'Hey Mister, I want to join Snapper.' I told him he was too little, but he insisted, so I put him out in a cadet heat. And he went out in this heat against kids twice as big as him and just flogged them. I just went, 'Wow, there's something special about this kid.' Then he asked for a ride home. He lived just down at Kirra so I gave him a ride. Then he wanted me to meet his parents but I passed on that. The next month the same thing happened, and the next month, and soon he was in the club and winning all his heats.

The next time I dropped him off, he went, 'Come up.' I could tell it was really important to him, so I did as he said. His parents, Bob and Carol, have become great friends of mine and they're lovely people, but back then they were going through a bit of a hard time. Things weren't good at home. He just wanted me to see that it was kind of hard for him. He really wanted to be a champion surfer and he was in a tough home environment. I saw all that and I decided to take him under my wing. I'd pick him up early in the morning and we'd go surfing and afterwards I'd drop him at school. We got into this routine.

They were building these units at Kirra at the time and every day when we drove past, he'd go, 'Bugs, buy one of them,' and I'd go, 'Shut up, kid, I've got my own house. I'm happy. I'm living in the country [up at Terranora].' We'd do this every day for six weeks, watching these units take shape, and finally one day I pulled in, just to shut him up. The real estate guy was out the front and it was this guy we used to call MP Lee, because he used to walk around and basically shadow MP. He did everything except surf like him. And he was the master salesman. He said, 'I've been waiting for you. There's one I've been saving for you.' It just so happened that the one left was in the middle at the front of the building overlooking Kirra Point, and as soon as I walked through the door into the place I went, 'Oh yeah, I want this.' Deano was right. His instincts got me to buy that house. I just did the quickest sale in history at Terranora and the next thing I knew I was in the unit at Kirra, and about a month later Dean moved in. When we walked in the door he walked straight through and went, 'That's my room there,' and I went, 'Oh, okay.'

There's no doubt it's the best thing I ever did. I've been so happy there. Deano swung me into that. Swung himself in too.

> DEAN MORRISON: 'I just went up to him at a contest. I was pretty young, I guess. Just went up and told him I wanted to be a pro surfer. He just tried to help me from there, got to know my family and stuff. He's like family to me now . . . Every time I go for a surf with him he's always trying to compete against me. He'll hassle me and stuff. I laugh but he's so serious, he doesn't laugh. Every time he goes past me, he's got a serious head on . . . What can I say? He's done everything for me.' *Surfing World* magazine, May, '98.

> 'Mum and dad, they're beautiful people. They split up when I was about 15. I just kind of moved in with Rab . . . We don't really get to see that much of each other any more. He always used to tell me you had to be a good traveller, and that. He gave me so much advice.' *Surfing World*, January, 2001.

THE RABBIT CAMPS

In '96, I tasted defeat for the first time as national coach of an Australian team at the World Surfing Games. After victorious campaigns in France in '92 and Brazil in '94, we went to Huntington Beach in '96 and we knew there was a bit of a Huntington hoodoo on the Australian team. A team of absolute superstars went there in '84 — Damien Hardman, Gary Elkerton, Simon Law, Barton Lynch; they were a team of winners — and they lost. In '96, the ASP had allowed the top 44 WCT surfers to represent their country. We brought Barton back, Taj Burrow was in the team, and it was a good solid team. But on the final day, the finals just didn't go our way, and the USA took the teams title.

I came back to Australia, and launched Operation Reclaim, to reclaim our position as the world's top surfing nation.

Operation Reclaim became a two-year campaign to find and nurture the best young surfers in the country. And a big part of that was the Rabbit Camps. For years, I'd overseen the MR Camps, and they were fantastic. The MR camps honour Mark Richards, the greatest Australian surfer ever. But I wanted to do my own training camp in my own style. So me and my offsider Eddie Valladares put it together. They were just fantastic, some of the most fun times of my working life. We'd go down to this little tucked-away beach resort in the forest at Broken Head, on the beautiful NSW North Coast. Deano was a fixture at all of them, along with a lot of the top juniors of the day, like Glen Hall, Adrian Buchan, Darren and Michael O'Rafferty. We'd surf our brains out all along that fantastic coast. It didn't matter what time of year we had it, we always got a great swell.

I guarantee you, the person who had the most fun was me. I used to come back completely surfed-out. Five days with the kids on that beautiful beach at Broken Head, you'd come back with this real inner glow. Their parents and coaches would get in touch with us and say, 'The kid's come back a different person, he's sweet, he's right, he's on track.' We were trying to show that this approach worked, compared to a real strict regimented program.

EDDIE VALLADARES, RABBIT'S SUCCESSOR AS NATIONAL COACHING DIRECTOR: 'Rabbit's main thing was he legitimised coaching, whereas the old crew hadn't accepted coaching. They still saw surfing as esoteric and funky ... He identified, after we suffered defeat in California, that a lot of the young crew had talent but they hadn't experienced being away from home. So the Rabbit Camps were set up to bring these young kids together who were the future champs, so they had the chance to bond together prior to them travelling, and to live in self-contained units, just as they would on the road.

'Prior to this camp, I said, "Let's set up the program." You have to have a program to give to the powers that be so they okay it.

Bustin' down the door

And Rab goes, "Hang on, what would you want to do if you were a kid going to one of these camps?" and I said, "Get up and go surfing," and he said, "Exactly, good point." And he said, "But what's the good of going surfing if the tide's low and the surf's shithouse?" So we designed the program around the tides, the winds, the swell. And we taught the kids that you've got to be considerate of the local community. Just because you're a hot surfer and you've got all the talent and you've got sponsors clamouring after you, you've still got obligations out in the broader community. And if you're going to get sponsorships and all these advantages and opportunities, then you've got some obligations back. You don't all rush out, 10 or 12 people, and take over a peak. You spread yourselves out.

'As part of the program, we'd use the latest technology and use the overhead projectors and use the whiteboard and have lectures on nutrition and sports psychology. What Rabbit would do after a really good meal, we might have the fire crackling away, and Rabbit would hold court with all these kids, about his experiences. And it would contain sports psychology, it would contain nutrition, it would contain heat strategy elements in it . . .'

THE SEEDED THOUGHT

Between the MR Camps and the Rabbit Camps, we were handpicking the best Australian team we could possibly get — not just names but people who really wanted to perform for their country. I'd been working with the juniors a lot — Joel Parkinson, Dean Morrison, Mick Fanning, Zane Harrison — a really special young crop of surfers. In '98, Dean and Zane made the Australian team and it ended up being my last national coaching assignment, which was really special for me. Deano won the world junior title in my final engagement as his coach, and we won back the world teams title. Operation Reclaim was a success.

I went straight from Portugal to Hawaii, as contest director of the new Billabong World Junior Championships. It was kind of a first. I don't remember any foreigner walking in there to run a contest. We ended up running it at Maille Point, which is a really full-on local area on the west side of Oahu. It was a neat event — well, apart from the two tiger sharks. These two tiger sharks chased the guys up on to the reef in the middle of a heat. It was really radical.

It was quite a fateful trip for other reasons, because after the event finished, I had a couple of spare days. I went over to the North Shore and surfed Sunset, and went to see Mark Occhilupo at his place at Rocky Point. Graeme Staphelberg, the ASP Executive Director, had dropped a bombshell at an ASP meeting in Rio de Janeiro two months earlier, and just resigned, out of the blue. There was a lot of uncertainty and unrest in the air. Occy was saying the surfers were copping a raw deal, that they hadn't had a prize money increase for 10 years. And he was going, 'Come on Bugs, go for the ASP job.'

I have to admit, the thought had crossed my mind. The idea had first been aired 10 years earlier, one day in the late '80s in Hawaii. I was staying at my friend Ed Clapp's house, and the surfers were having a big meeting on his verandah. I'd had a long surf that day and as I was walking up the stairs, Pottz and Tommy Curren spotted me, and Pottz yelled out, 'Hey Bugs, take over ASP!' I just went, 'Yeah boys, no worries.' Tommy Curren just looked at me and said, 'Yeah, when are you going to do this thing?' like it was somehow pre-ordained. And 10 years later, in '99, here was the newly rejuvenated Mark Occhilupo, on the threshold of his historic world title comeback, sowing the same seed.

And then, an amazing thing happened. Peter Whittaker, the ASP Tour Manager, and Interim Director since Graeme Staphelberg's resignation, just happened to drop into Occy's place while I was there.

'Bugs is going to take the ASP job,' Occy told him.

'Shut up, I never said that,' I protested.

But Peter was on to me. 'I don't want the job. I would love to work with you,' he said. 'I will be the best lieutenant you ever had.'

Bustin' down the door

I'd visited the office in California and there was something not right about it. Bad feng shui or something. It was stuck between two freeways, directly beneath Orange County airport. There was so much static electricity, when you turned on the bathroom light you got an electric shock. There were two office workers, Meg Bernado and Dori Payne, who'd been with the ASP for a long time and had done a wonderful job, but there was no captain of the ship. Peter was there under sufferance, doing a job he didn't want to do. And no one ever went down there to this office in the middle of two freeways.

PETER WHITTAKER, (ASP Interim Chief Executive Officer, Tour Manager): 'I just saw Bugs as the prime candidate. He was an ex-World Champion, he related really well to the surfers, he played golf with Kelly and Occy and everyone. I just thought the ASP needed that leadership and direction, and I started lobbying people in that direction ... Occy was thinking along the same tracks and we got Occy moving lobbying the surfers. And we got Bugs to understand that it was his destiny to do this. He had a couple of political aspirations at the time. He was talking to Nat Young and Peter Garrett and they were revving him up for a political future. But after really thrashing through it and a couple of beers, we convinced him that he had to fulfil his destiny ...

'When I was in California, I worked in a little shoebox in the middle of the road right beside the airport in Irvine, California, and in the 14 months I was there, we had three visitors. No one went there. No industry people would go there. Terry Fitzgerald came over there and I was a bit excited that I would have a bit of a chat with the old Fitz and he sent me an e-mail afterwards and said, "Sorry, you were on the wrong side of the highway."'

When I flew back to Australia, all the way from Honolulu to the Gold Coast, I started thinking it over. I didn't go into this thing with stars in my eyes. I knew this was going to be the most difficult challenge of my life. But I came to the conclusion that perhaps this was very much meant to be; perhaps this was my final calling and that maybe there wasn't anyone else who could do the job, because there wasn't anyone who loved pro surfing more than me. That's basically the premise I went on. Is there anyone who loves professional surfing more than me? I don't think so. I had the passion. I had the history. I'd been there since day one. I was a founding member. I'd been a surfer rep. I'd fought tooth and nail for every inch the surfers got. I had no vested interest.

Peter Whittaker started lobbying on my behalf, and I got some surprising support. I thought there was no way in the world my old foe Ian Cairns, ASP's North American rep, would support me. When Peter told him Bugs was running for the job, Ian thought about it and he said, 'You know what? There's one thing. Bugs knows how to win and that's what ASP needs right now.'

I was keeping my cards very close to my chest. I hadn't officially thrown my hat in the ring. It was decided ASP would advertise for the position and look outside the sport. Advertisements were placed in *The Australian*, *The New York Times*, *The Los Angeles Times*, looking for this hotshot CEO. There were over 200 applications. There were some high-flier executives used to getting half a million US bucks a year that were way out of ASP's league. When I saw the ad in the paper, I made my mind up that I was going to run for the job.

With exquisite timing, just as I was gathering myself for the greatest challenge of my professional life, I developed laryngitis. I decided to go to Tonga for a week's holiday to think about it all. I was sick as a dog and stayed in bed all week. When I got back, I never got on top of it and it developed into really serious bronchitis. I spent the whole of January in bed confined to the house, and then spent the rest of February recovering. I was so weak, and before I knew it, it was March and the meeting to select a new ASP boss was only a week away. The hidden blessing through all this was that I'd just spent two months at home by myself really thinking this thing through and preparing myself. I'd go for long walks around the beaches while I was recovering, developing my vision.

Peter Whittaker and I were going in together on the same ticket, and we had a huge supporter in Greville Mitchell, a wealthy English philanthropist who loved surfing and appeared out of nowhere in the late '90s as a kind of guardian angel for pro surfing. He's a self-made man who earned his fortune in the construction business in London and he'd just fallen in love with surfing. He had sons who surfed and they would spend their summer holidays at the Lacanau Pro in France watching all the top pros.

There's a wonderful story his wife Lisa tells of Greville stumbling into their hotel room in Lacanau one afternoon, eyes glazed over, pants soaked up to the waist, babbling about this amazing surfer he'd just seen. He'd been wandering down the beach from the contest when he'd come across three-time World Champion Tom Curren going for a warm-up surf before a heat. He was so mesmerised by Curren's graceful display that he'd waded into the water up to his waist to get a closer look — and has never been the same since! Greville has become one of pro surfing's most trusted advisers, has gotten us out of hot water and bad deals a number of times, and thrown the full weight of his world of business contacts and professional knowhow behind the organisation. Why? Because he passionately believes the surfers deserve a better deal. When one of his sons passed away tragically, Greville and Lisa set up the Mitchell Surfing Foundation in his memory and have poured hundreds of thousands of dollars into professional surfing, to fund a medical team on tour to look after the surfers, and for special expression sessions to reward the most dynamic freestyle surfing. The surfers see him as a saint, a knight in shining armour, come to their rescue. To have his support was a huge boost.

I went up to the Noosa Longboard Festival and Peter Whittaker's wedding, on the Sunshine Coast, which was huge, and I remember on the night I came back I got kind of nervous about the job. All I wanted was to get it. The applications came in and a committee was set up to review and process all the applications. There was some scepticism whether I could actually do the job. 'Oh, Bugs, he can't work in an office,' they'd say. I had to remind them I'd had an office job for seven years, as National Coaching Director.

But I also felt I had a lot of support. The committee had come down to three applicants. The other applicants were from outside the industry, the corporate world, and the US surf industry. But I felt my knowledge of how the beast of the ASP worked and the challenges that lay ahead gave me an edge. In the end, Peter and I received overwhelming support. I ended up getting in on a 13–1 vote. There was one person who didn't support me but that was only because he was adamant the office shouldn't be anywhere but California. And that was a condition of my application, that I move the office to Australia.

My initial feeling was one of relief, because I'd got to the point where it was like a world title. I really wanted it badly. I didn't want to fail. They combined the position of President and CEO, so I had both titles. The President is someone who goes out there and shakes hands and kisses babies. The CEO is an office job and you're there at the forefront of all the important decision making.

I'd been on the board for so long, first as a surfer rep, then as ASP Australasian rep, and I was always in the back stalls. And when we went back in to the meeting after the vote, they said, 'Bugs, your place is up here now.' It was really weird walking up there and sitting right in the middle, in front of everyone. I'd seen someone else sitting there for 25 years and suddenly I was sitting there, and I had to give an address. I just said I was confident we had put a good team together, and to move forward we needed a five-year business plan. And I was aware there was a lot of unrest in the surfers' camp. I was under no illusion that this was going to be a smooth ride. It was going to be a rough passage, but I could see the day when we would have our house in order. From the very first address I let them know there would be change and that change would upset some people; that they may have to give things up for the greater good. I wanted to unite the sport, no more 'us and them', and to move forward together as one.

I went straight from that meeting to the launch of the Billabong Pro at Burleigh Heads. There were lots of press there and they made an announcement introducing me as the new CEO/President of ASP International. It was really exciting — I felt a bit of a warm inner glow, but that was followed up by the cold reality of it all. It brought up a bit of a gulp. Oh, I really have done it, I thought to myself. I really have taken this on. I was acutely aware of the fact that I did not want to fail. I did not want to fall flat on my face.

> PETER WHITTAKER: 'Bugs isn't a renowned administrator for dotting his i's and crossing his t's and keeping his desk tidy, but when it comes to critical issues and actually standing up and making a bold statement or presenting a philosophy or vision, that's when he comes to the fore. He's not really a desk clerk, he's more a field man . . . Bugs is one person who can sit down and talk to the surfers and knock a little bit of sense into them about their professionalism and the need for them to take the sport forward as much as the companies investing in the events.'

THE HARDEST JOB IN THE WORLD

The first thing we had to do was go about hiring staff and finding an office.

My dream was to walk to work. When I was recuperating from my bronchitis, all through February I walked, following all my old trails through the hills and along the beaches. One Friday afternoon, I was walking along the beachfront at Coolangatta and I looked up at the Showcase shopping centre and went, 'That's my dream office, right there.' I made an appointment with the administrator and said, 'Have you got any office space? What about that up there?' and he said, 'Funny you should ask that. Here are the plans. We're just about to turn that into office space.' It had been a dance studio, a ballroom dancing school. Greville Mitchell had worked out exactly how many square metres we needed. I asked how big the space was and it was absolutely spot-on. Now I really wanted it. The centre administrator rang around for references, because he wasn't sure about us: 'This bunch of surfies came in here in boardshorts and sandals wanting office space, from ASP or something.' It was the old stigma of being a bunch of surfies. He was sceptical about us. He didn't want a bunch of blokes in boardshorts and bare feet traipsing sand through the place. I had my heart set on it, but it was far from a done deal. We had no money. We had to secure a three- to five-year lease, and we weren't even certain of getting to the next meeting.

The whole process of moving an entity from one country to another is a highly involved and expensive process. You don't just lock up and move and jump on a Qantas plane. I approached the Queensland government for a relocation assistance package. There were various other bids vying to attract ASP's international headquarters: Sydney, Honolulu, Los Angeles. I have to admit, just to get it over the line, I threw in the Jeff Kennett factor: that then Victorian premier Jeff Kennett, who was so fond of buying sporting events, was trying to lure us to Victoria, down to Torquay, with some generous business incentives. And that really got the Queensland government's ear. Between the Queensland government and the Gold Coast City Council they put together a $250,000 assistance package — $160,000 from the government and $90,000 from the council. I was able to go back to the board and say, 'The rent's paid for the next five years, it's not going to cost the ASP one cent to move from California and outfit a fantastic office.' We were able to go back to Coolangatta and go, 'Here's the rent for the next five years.' Things were starting to go our way.

Greville came to our aid again. He said, 'We're going to do this like a business,' and so he brought in Price Waterhouse to do the accounts. He also brought in Allen, Allen & Hemsley to handle our legal matters. One of the biggest accounting firms in Australia, and one of the biggest law firms, acting on behalf of a bunch of surfers! We were with the big boys now.

One of the brightest minds in the surfing industry, Norm Innes, had just resigned from his job at Quiksilver. He was a huge player in Quiksilver's expansion around the world. And he was idle. He was also a good mate of Peter Whittaker's from Noosa. Peter was able to persuade Norm to come in and use his expertise to help us hire some staff, and put together a business plan. But first of all, he had to go through our entire business history. I remember watching him locked in this room for days. He really wanted to understand ASP inside out, starting with the constitution, the rulebook, the by-laws, everything, and how it all worked. And I remember him coming out at the end of it, and Peter and I were sitting in the boardroom waiting for him to come out with the results. He looked at us and he went, 'Better you than me.' He said, 'Rabbit, you have definitely got the hardest job in the world.' This was so sobering. Peter and I were sitting there just reeling. He said, 'You've got to tear this thing down to its foundations and start again.' That was the smartest thing we ever did, getting Norm in to do that. It was meant to be. Norm didn't have to do what he did. Pete roped him in over a big night in Noosa, I reckon. It was an incredible opportunity, because it was the only lull in his career. I reckon he was sitting back in Noosa, going, 'Well, I'm retired, I'm kicking back . . . I'm bored.' Now, he's back as a director of Quiksilver, back in the thick of it, but we had his expertise at a critical time, and I'm really indebted to the guy for telling us the truth that day. He said, 'I don't know how you can survive. I can't see it.' I looked at Pete and went, 'What have we taken on, mate?' And then Pete and I went to work.

A very important position was Chief Financial Controller. It was a mess, a huge mess. We didn't even know what sort of shape we were in. We interviewed all the applicants and one guy came in, Greg Bedggood, who was one of the original members of Kirra Surfriders Club. We knew each other but we hadn't been really good mates. Greg had moved up to Brisbane for work and had been out of the area for 20 years. He quit surfing and became a suit in Brisbane, worked in Hong Kong, and at one time worked for Christopher Skase. All Greg wanted was to get out of Brisbane and get back to the beach. We all agreed he was far and away the outstanding applicant.

Karen Green was a girl I used to see out in the surf and one day out at Duranbah I bumped into her and she congratulated me on the new job. She'd just resigned from Morrison Media Services, publishers of *Surfing Life* magazine, and I told her I was looking for an executive secretary. I knew she knew about surfing. I needed people that I didn't have to start from scratch with. They needed to know the idiosyncrasies of the sport and the industry and just how surfing worked. And so Karen got the gig.

They came on for peanuts; we didn't have much of a budget, but it complimented their lifestyles. They could come to work and go for a surf at lunchtime. My deal with staff was that it was very important that they go and have their surfs. I wouldn't ever get on their case as long as their work was done. I always felt people were more productive when they were happy in their job. I'd experienced other styles of doing business, and I thought, I'm going to do it my way. Then if it fails, I'll fail my way too.

The big challenge was getting Peter Whittaker in the surf. Every company needs a workaholic and Pete is a driven administrator, the best right-hand man you could ask for. I'd just like to see him get wet a bit more often.

We started working out of Pete's apartment while we were waiting to move into the office. But the delay was starting to bring us undone. We weren't quite communicating with the world the way an international organisation should, and people were getting the shits with us. They were saying, 'Go find another office', and I went, 'No, no, it will be worth it.'

Poor Greg just got handed an absolute jumble. We just went, 'Get in there and sort it out.' He needed to be really good at his job — and he was. At the end of the wash, Greg came out and went, 'I've got the handle of the financial situation. We owe half a million dollars US.' We inherited a US$500,000 debt! That was a shock to me, to realise that I was responsible for repaying a debt of nearly a million Australian dollars.

And then we had to prepare for our first board meeting in France. It was a mid-year meeting, my very first meeting as CEO/President, and it promised to be a tough initiation. One of the items on the agenda was basically to eject me. The person who put forward the motion felt I was not going to be able to do the job, I wasn't doing the job, and I should be stripped of being CEO because I was not CEO material. I had a fight on my hands.

We went into the first meeting without an office after six months in the job. The shopping centre administrator had resigned. We had to go through it all again with a new administrator, through all the red tape with the lease, the renovations and the refurbishment. So it was pretty gnarly. I was extremely stressed. I felt like I was under siege. They could have stripped me of the job before I'd even got going. In the end though, it turned out to be a lot of hot air. The motion didn't have much support and didn't go anywhere, but it had sure put the wind up me. People could see at that meeting that we'd already started to tweak the whole thing. The change process began at that meeting and it was super-productive.

I got the job in March '99 and we actually didn't move into the office until late October. The office warming was November 5, and a cause for great celebration. Government ministers and councillors and media and dignitaries were all there, as well as the usual gang of Gold Coast surfing identities, and it was all very auspicious. Most of the politicians and dignitaries had left, thankfully, by the latter stages of the evening when Pete and I wound up dancing on the boardroom table.

But there wasn't too much time for dancing. There was the bread-and-butter stuff of keeping the tour running, from event to event, keeping the doors open by getting our sanction fees and other revenue in. Then there were the longer term tasks of enacting our plans, our visions.

One of the most important issues was shifting events to prime surf locations. This began in the mid-'90s when Quiksilver took their event to Grajagan or 'G-Land', a remote jungle surf camp surrounded by pristine national park in south-east Java, Indonesia. I recognised that as the future. We were competing against all other sports, and particularly the new age extreme sports; I felt they were leaving us in the dust. It was doing our cause no good at all to be on television in one-foot slop. The old theory was based around bums on seats, grandstand events, going to places in the middle of summer when the surf doesn't usually come. ASP was under heaps of criticism because we were holding events in poor waves time and time again. We had to be on the Formula One tracks. They were out there — we had to go to them. But that required a whole change of philosophy. We wanted the events to come with us, and reschedule to prime surf season at world-class locations. We were going into a new age, where the electronic media allowed us to go to exotic locations, the best waves in the world. We were never going to be like tennis or golf, because you can say the final is on at 2 pm, Sunday. But the surf might be onshore and crappy on Sunday afternoon. And we used to go round the world and have the finals on Sunday afternoons, at big holiday towns in the middle of summer, and often the finals were in shitty surf, because by then the onshore had come up.

It was a painful process, because people were saying that the new ASP was disrespectful to these long-standing events. But you can't say you need change and we need to be this dynamic new sport and still go to these places in the middle of summer. You can't have both. And so I said, 'I'm just going to go for it.' If enough people realised that this was the key to getting to the Promised Land, we'd make it. There were some bloody hard decisions made. We told the Japanese there was going to be no Chiba Beach in May. No more one-foot surf. The Lacanau Pro, in France, needed to move into September/October, long after the summer holiday crowds had gone back to work in Paris. All around the world, the surf pumps in autumn, and in the tropics in winter. And that was the seasonal reality. Bruce Brown had probably done us no favours by calling his classic '60s surf film *Endless Summer*, because it created this illusion that surfing was a summer sport. *Endless Autumn* would have been closer to the mark.

Then the rumours started up about a rebel tour. Surfer unrest was at an all-time high and some were impatient for the promised changes. Surf writer, filmmaker, promoter and former top pro surfer Derek Hynd warned me about it one night at the Surfer Poll Awards in California. We'd had a few drinks and he said, 'Rabbit, you have got the greatest challenge of all time on your hands.' As he does, he was speaking in riddles, but it wasn't long before I started getting whispers of the rebel tour, organised by Derek. And the surfers were interested in it, because of their dissatisfaction: they hadn't had a pay rise for 10 years. The judging criteria was ancient. Derek was promising better money and a new, innovative format. I was hearing that people had signed up. But one of the beauties of all of this was that it helped us usher through change quickly because of the threat of the rebel tour. There were people predicting the downfall of the ASP, the destruction of professional surfing. But the rebel tours were just about skimming off the cream and stuff the rest of them: offering big money to the top handful of surfers, with no thought for the career paths of those who'd be left out, careers we'd all been fighting so hard to create.

I had to win the war quickly. I felt a real immediacy in getting our tour right. I needed some divine intervention. I needed some things to start happening for us. There needed to be some real belief in destiny, that what I was doing was for the greater good, and the forces of providence would rally to our support. And some good things started happening. I was able to use those perceived threats to get through measures and get through reforms quickly.

Before the mid-year meeting in 2000, the surfers had a meeting of their own and formed the World Professional Surfers, to represent their collective interests. It was all quite fateful, because the mid-year meeting was going to be at Jeffreys Bay in South Africa in June, but some of the main players couldn't make that meeting, so it was postponed until July, in California. This gave the surfers time to rally and they came to that July meeting and took everyone by surprise, because nobody had ever seen the surfers come in with their act together. They came into that meeting as a block and they wanted a pay rise, they wanted a shorter season, and they wanted prime locations. They were ready to boycott events. A lot of event directors used to have pre-meetings and they'd come in with their act together. The surfers had never done that before — they'd always been ridden over roughshod. But they came to that meeting and took everybody by surprise. They wanted to restructure the whole tour, they wanted a jump in prize money from $120,000 to $250,000. We had been talking about incremental increases, but the surfers were adamant. It got very fiery for a while there. I remember for the first time the event directors went, 'Hang on', and they wanted to have a huddle. And so the two groups went into their huddles. But at the end of the day, the surfers were sticking hard and I supported them. There were five surfer reps, five event reps and me, and I held the casting vote. I was already trying to eliminate this us-and-them thing, but it was perceived at that meeting that I was the sixth surfer, which I wasn't. I just believed it was necessary. The majority of the guys in the field were going home losing money at each event. You could trace it nearly all the way back to my era when you had to get to the quarters or semi-finals to break even.

Then the surfers wanted a shorter tour. They wanted an off season, like other sports. They had sponsors' obligations for boat trips and photo shoots. Then there was family — their families were never seeing them and they were bringing home nothing. The burnout factor was a real problem. A lot of them had to hedge their bets and do the WQS as well, from January to December, and then start in January again. It was affecting their enthusiasm for the whole thing. The stoke wasn't there. They were jaded. I could see it. It was a sickness in the sport. So I supported the restructuring of the tour, and it was perceived later that the surfers had taken over, that Rabbit had thrown in his hat with the surfers. But in actual fact it was a 9–2 vote to restructure the tour.

THE BLOODBATH

One thing that Pete and I recognised was that we had to build security. The ASP tour had always just lumbered from year to year, and events were cancelled at the last minute or promoters were still frantically searching for sponsors at the 11th hour. One way to build security was to implement long-term event licences. Once we did that we'd all be on the same page. The event licensees would work for the common interest of the whole tour. They'd realise they were stakeholders in the success of the tour.

We introduced three-year event licences and we had to set a cut-off point, which was September 17, 2000. That fateful day, event licensees had to come in and put it on the table and say that they

Bustin' down the door

were locked in for three years on the tour. At the same time, we had increased sanction fees, and we still didn't have the long-awaited TV deals in place to take their events to the world. I knew it was a big ask. It was costing them about US$1 million to stage an event, and I was saying they had to come in on September 17 and put their money down. A lot of the licensees came together and formed a bit of a block. This was a real test for the ASP, because on September 17 I might not have any events and I might not have a tour. It was gnarly. It was really throwing the dice. But there were companies out there that did share the vision, that said, yes, this was a fair thing, the pay rise was justified, and fortunately some major heavy hitters came over the line.

The December meeting in Hawaii that year has become known as 'The Bloodbath'. That was when we had to ratify the September 17 confirmations. All we were getting then were pieces of paper with ticks in the boxes. But at the December meeting the licensees had to make their commitment, put their money down, and they had a licence for that event for three years — they were along for the ride. If they didn't, they were out. Again, it was the major surf labels who supported us, but they were competing against each other for positioning and that got really gnarly. There were some unbelievable stand-offs. There were times when it looked like the foundations of the ASP were going to break apart. It was absolute shuttle diplomacy, going between groups and trying to keep it all together.

There was a point when I was walking outside with Greville and I suffered a moment of doubt. I said, 'I think we've lost it.' He replied, 'No, Bugs, it's going to work out.' And he walked me around for a while. I was really shot. I'd just had a standup war with several very powerful figures. We were all shaken. And when I walked back in that room with Greville, it was like a peace dove had flown in the room. It was unbelievable. Rip Curl had made this fantastic compromise, and there was just a flow-on effect. I walked back in and all the tension had eased. There was a solution. I still don't know how it happened. I wasn't in the room. But people had gone, 'No, we've got to make this work'. And suddenly there was light, and we all took our places again and worked through it.

At the next meeting in March 2001, the event licences had come to fruition and everyone had had their wins and people ended up with their big events in the places where they wanted them. And suddenly there was this new vibe. It was like night and day.

Now it was up to us to come through with the oft-promised mega-TV deal to take this new-look pro tour to the world. When we were still working in Pete's apartment, before we even had an office, these two Poms turned up one day, from an English company called SSM Freesports. It was a sports media group, interested in getting involved with pro surfing. But we had a lot of work to do to come up with a mutually agreeable deal. The ASP board was understandably wary, after some unhappy media deals in the past, but we kept in touch with SSM Freesports, who had by then merged with Sportsworld Media Group, a huge, London-based sports marketing company. We had meetings, back and forth, and the lawyers were having a picnic. Eventually we signed off on a US$12.75 million deal. That money was to go into producing quality television, securing worldwide distribution, daily satellite feeds, highlights packages and the development of our website.

The night we signed that deal, in March 2001, a mini-hurricane hit Coolangatta right after we signed, the like of which I'd never seen. There was lightning and shrieking winds. It was a really powerful thing.

SMG had bought our media rights for five years, not in perpetuity, and their job was to go out there and get worldwide TV distribution. As I write, the ASP show is on in 36 countries.

Now, our job was to run a great world tour.

PETER WHITTAKER: 'Obviously, the whole negotiations with SMG were really critical. And Stuart Sawyer and the crew at SMG still scratch their heads about our methods of negotiation in the early stages. They basically couldn't figure us out. They kind of wanted us to write the terms of the agreement. We just told them the idiosyncrasies of the ASP, and they structured a deal that fitted around most people's needs. The night that we signed the deal, it was during the March meetings, and it was

Bustin' down the door

here in the office. It was about nine o'clock at night and we got it across the line and, of course, Stuart Sawyer and Bugs and I were pretty excited. We cracked a couple of ales during the signing, and Bugs and I went back to my flat to have a couple more ales. And this mini-cyclone started up outside. It was just totally tumultuous out there. It was like there was all this energy focused on the signing of the deal. It was an incredible moment. Rab was standing out in the middle of it with his arms in the air, facing the wind. And Stuart Sawyer, who's from England, went for a surf out there that day, and took off on a wave and, for the first time in his life, a dolphin jumped out of the water and surfed the wave with him. He was pretty well peaking. So it was a good day for deals.

'When that prize money increase went through, we were negotiating with SMG and it looked like the events would have to give up their media rights. And they were advanced enough in their own techniques of how to portray their events to the media; they'd become quite sophisticated at handling it themselves. So they were quite nervous about handing it all over. Fortunately, SMG have come through with the goods on the television side pretty much with flying colours. Essentially, the shows are evolving and the first reports from the industry are that everyone is happy, and the surfers are pretty happy, and now everyone realises that this is consolidating everyone's position. We're working on a five-year plan with SMG, to produce really good quality shows that are acceptable to the core market and the wider market and distribute them, get them out there into the world. As the distribution improves, our primary goal is to bring in a major global sponsor. I'd like to see the surfers get paid what the tennis players and golfers get paid for taking off at places like Teahupoo.'

If you look at the 2002 tour, the blocks are in place. We go to the best breaks in the world at the best time of year. The dream is getting closer. I've seen a lot of surfers finish their careers on a bitter note, and it really bums me out. They give it their all and there's nothing for them at the end of it. I couldn't do anything about those that had come through in the past, and I very nearly couldn't do anything about those that are here now. But I certainly can make things better for the future. We had a vision in the '70s of surfing for big money in perfect waves with mainstream media coverage, but we didn't know how to get there, and we didn't have the tools to get there, and the industry wasn't there. If I could contribute to putting those final bricks in place and the sport could really fulfil its destiny on my watch, that would be the most fulfilling thing for me in my professional life.

Those dreams I had when I was a schoolkid walking to and from school — thinking about a pro tour, about grand prix events, world titles, a career in pro surfing — they were just dreams. But they've been unwavering dreams. I've never departed from them. I'm very aware of the responsibility I have of first creating the impetus to move forward and then actually capturing the opportunities and seeing them. And I think maybe I can see them because no one's dreamed about them as much as I have. It would be a wonderful legacy that I'd like to leave, and it's certainly not mine alone. It will be a culmination of all the individual contributions, and all the people who left the tour bitter and twisted; it's their contribution too, it's the same dream and I'm just trying to harness that whole energy.

Now, I think the foundation stones are actually in place. The challenge is to see whether my mix works. And I still think we're going to need some incredible luck and a bit of divine intervention, and in that regard I know I've got a true heart. I trust the fact that I want things to turn out great for everybody.

PETER WHITTAKER: 'In the last two years it's been a total restructure from the bottom up ... All the events have been licensed for three years. There's been over $100 million worth of deals done in the last three years. It's all moving ahead pretty well. The surfers got their pay rise. It's been a rollercoaster in here. The industry hasn't been totally happy with the direction we took. For one reason or another, there were a lot of key players who were pretty pissed off with what

Bustin' down the door

we were doing. So we've had some pretty high and low times. There were events looking at whether they would stick with the tour. There was a real chance of the whole thing breaking down and fragmenting. And we weren't cash-flush. We were scraping through on a dime, so we had a lot of clawing back to do, which we managed to scrape through.'

A BIG YEAR

The personal highs and lows have been just as dramatic for me over the past few years as the professional ones. Without exception, 1999 was the biggest year of my life. The milestones were significant. I became CEO/President of ASP International, won a second world title, and met the woman who would deliver my greatest achievement of all: a baby boy.

The World Masters Championship had evolved from a simple idea to bring back the legends of the sport in a contest staged in prime surf. The first gathering was in Tavarua, Fiji. It was an all-in affair, bringing together 24 of the original pioneers of pro surfing. I went to Tavarua in 1997 with mixed feelings. I was not sure if it was a reunion, a big piss-up or a serious event. The vibe at Tavarua was magnificent. I hadn't seen Dane Kealoha for many years, and when we embraced on seeing each other, I knew this was a very important reunion.

While I hadn't competed at an international level for 10 years, I had kept in touch with my competitive spirit through Snapper club contests. In fact, in '96 I had managed, with the assistance of some D-bah barrels, to win the club open championship at the age of 42.

But at that first Masters, I could not summon the competitive juices. There was another, more important distraction preventing me from tuning into this inaugural Masters: my father, Bart, was barely hanging onto life in a hospital ward back in Brisbane. What had started as a summer ear infection had developed into this hideous, life-threatening brain infection. The prognosis he received when I was leaving Australia was not good.

This aggressive bug had eaten into his skull and appeared to be unstoppable. I could not get into the swing of things knowing that my father was in all probability on his deathbed.

I flew back to Brisbane and went straight to the Mater Hospital, where I met my sister Wendy. The doctor said there was no hope and that we should say our goodbyes. It was a rare and aggressive bug that had burrowed and spread into half his skull, creating incomprehensible pain and suffering for him. Yet Bart fought this insidious thing and won. Months later, he went on *60 Minutes* as the only known survivor of this kind of infection, and became a celebrated pin-up boy in the ear, nose and throat ward.

THE CRUELLEST BLOW

In '98, I arrived home from Mexico to the most devastating news. Two local surfers, Sean Fanning and Joel Green, had been killed in a car accident. Everyone in Coolangatta was totally shattered. Sean and Joel were two of the town's hotties, and along with Joel Parkinson, Mick Fanning, Dean Morrison and Damon Harvey, called themselves the CK6 — Coolangatta Kids Six. They represented the future. Sean and Joel were great young kids, both 19, a little older than the rest, and they had been driving home from a party at Kirra.

The accident happened within sight of the Fannings' home, right across from where the old Queensland Hotel used to stand. It was a tragedy that cast a pall of desolation and sadness over the whole town. I drove straight to the site of the accident. It was Monday morning. The tragedy had occurred on Friday night. A huge shrine of flowers was heaped around the Norfolk pines that the car had impacted. Young kids had gathered round it, their eyes red from crying. It was the saddest scene I had ever come across.

There is truly nothing more heart-wrenching than to see two young people cut down before their prime. Sean Fanning was a great young surfer, the older brother of Mick, and his death changed the lives of the CK6. Joel Green was just the nicest kid you could ever imagine, a young man who would make any parent proud. Joel was a hot surfer too, but there was more to Joel's act than just ripping waves. He was a leader, somebody that would have guided the CK6 toward their collective dreams.

In a surf town proud of its heritage, the death of Sean and Joel marked the saddest chapter of its history. The grieving process was long but necessary. A shrine to Sean and Joel has been erected on their beloved Kirra headland, and on special occasions, such as Mick winning Bells in 2001, the surfing fraternity gathers on Kirra Hill.

The Sean Fanning/Joel Green Memorial Event is held on that August weekend every year, and for the Coolangatta Kids, for Darrell Green, Liz Fanning and their families, it is a coming together to celebrate the lives of two beautiful young men who left us way before their time.

MY POLYNESIAN PRINCESS

While my time since March 1999 has been taken up mostly by ASP duties, I still had some charity and environmental involvement through Surfers Against Nuclear Destruction (SAND). One SAND fundraiser was held in conjunction with my Snapper buddy Greg Faulk's birthday at Currumbin Tavern on the ninth of the ninth, ninety-nine (9/9/99). The night was dedicated to raising money for the Coolangatta Special School, to buy surfing equipment for the school surfing program, of which I am a patron.

During the course of the night I was introduced to a beautiful Polynesian girl named Shelley. Later that evening I approached her for a dance, she knocked me back, and I went on my merry way. It was to be a fateful meeting on that special date.

Weeks later I headed for France and the third running of the Masters. I went with a mission this time. I was aware that I had won the third world title in history in 1978 and I felt this was my time. There were now two distinct divisions (35–40 and over 40). After four rounds, Michael Ho and I had a perfect 30 seed points, thus ensuring once again that we wouldn't meet until the final. The surf at Lafitenia stopped and for three days we played golf with Mickey Dora and just relaxed.

With time running out, the venue was changed to Anglet, situated on the northern side of Biarritz, and my old buddy Michael Ho and I both advanced into our long-awaited final together.

The grommet final between Tommy Carroll and Cheyne Horan was a classic.

Tommy had been outstanding all week, going through undefeated. However, Cheyne was tuned into the barrels, finally winning his world title in classic fashion.

The swell kicked as Michael and I paddled out, and traded barrels in beautiful conditions. Things were tight and I was out the back alone as a solid set approached. I let the first two go, and I then saw it, a double-up. I paddled hard, picked it up just before it doubled, dropped in, came off a square bottom, and pulled into a Kirra-like barrel.

I was so secure inside that wave, and came out with the spit. I knew I had a perfect 10 before they read it out. I was World Champion again, exactly 21 years after winning in '78! And just like that day at Pipeline, I had scored a perfect 10 to clinch the title. The victory created a very warm inner glow. Incredibly, two other Coolangatta residents, Mark Occhilupo and Joel Parkinson, won the ASP men's and junior world titles respectively in '99.

Arriving back in Australia a week later, I headed over to Straddie with the young guns of Snapper for the annual Straddie Assault. The wonderful thing about this weekend was that I was back in the grassroots. As there was no conflict of interest with ASP, I could still coach the Snapper squad.

We were going for a historic 13th consecutive victory in the teams title, and after a close tussle with our old rivals North End and Sunshine Coast club Coolum, Jay Phillips once again clinched victory for Snapper. Thirteen Straddie Assault victories in a row called for a huge celebration.

At the party that night, I again saw the beautiful Polynesian girl who had so captivated me at the SAND function, and this time when I asked for a dance, she didn't knock me back.

SHELLEY EMIA: 'I was working for *Groundswell* magazine, and my friends there said come to this SAND thing. And my

Bustin' down the door

boss said, "Go and get your photo with Rabbit, he's the CEO of ASP." I said, "What's ASP?" I went over there and he goes, "Hi, my name's Rabbit," and I said, "Rabbit — what kind of a name's that?" And he said, "You can call me Bugs." Then he asked me to dance and I said, "Ah, maybe later." . . . Then I saw him at Straddy and I thought I should go and say hello. He'd noticed me and I said, "How about that dance I owe you?" And he can dance. There's not many men you meet who actually can dance. And we danced our way into the mosh pit, and the rest is history . . . He was going, "Come to Hawaii with me." I was going, "Sure, I'll come to Hawaii with you," and I didn't think he was for real. But we just connected and we got so into each other so fast. He was pretty smooth . . . He was pretty straightforward. He knew what he wanted and he wasn't afraid to ask for it. He's definitely charming, He's just got this aura about him. He calls me his Polynesian Princess. The next night I took him back to my place and it was pretty magical. There was this big thunderstorm and there was lightning, and the lightning lit up the whole lounge room like fireworks. It was like a sign or something.'

THE GREATEST GIFT

1999 had been a year of unbelievable achievement. To round it out, I was inducted into the Sports Australia Hall of Fame, and at the last induction ceremony of the 20th century, I was asked to deliver an acceptance speech at a glittering function at Melbourne's Crown Casino. I was very inspired. With the Sydney Olympics just around the corner, they could have asked any one of hundreds of sporting legends to make a speech.

Accompanied by Shelley, I gave perhaps my best-ever speech that night. As a surfer it was a proud moment to address an audience that included Ian Thorpe, Cathy Freeman, Pat Rafter and countless past champions. I spoke about the spirit of Australia and what Australia meant to the world.

In August 2000, Jaggar Dean Hukatai Bartholomew was conceived. It was a Monday morning and I pulled the curtains open and was met by the brightest rainbow I'd ever seen right outside the window. We raced over to Rainbow Bay and the waves were a perfect three feet. I clearly remember coaching Shelley onto a beauty, then watching her surf into a rainbow at Rainbow Bay. I sensed something special had happened. Six weeks later, while in France for the WCT leg, I rang home to hear the news of Shelley's pregnancy.

Shelley came with me to the Masters, where I came third behind Michael Ho and Mark Richards, and she came to Hawaii at year's end. So, in effect, Jaggar has surfed waves at Guethary and Hossegor and the North Shore of Oahu, all from inside the womb.

On April 30, 2001, one of the best days of the year, the waves were pumping at Kirra. I paddled out and the signal was that if a pair of red boardshorts was hanging in the corner of the balcony, the contractions had started. Ninety minutes later I came out of a barrel, looked in and saw the red boardies flying in the offshore. It was time. I was so excited. Off to Murwillumbah we went. It had been 46 years since I had been in Murwillumbah Hospital — not since the day of my birth.

We went in on April 30 and, after a long ordeal and a tricky birth, an 8 lb 3 oz baby boy was delivered at 3.12 pm on May 1, 2001. Although I had heard it before many times, there is truly no greater experience than witnessing the birth of your child.

Shelley and I had tossed up names for months. Jaggar came from Shelley. We wanted a strong, unique name. Nobody, of course, believes me. They all think I named him after Mick. Heidi came to the hospital as support. She came up with Dean, which was appropriate as it honoured Dean Morrison.

Shelley wanted to honour her great grandfather, Hukatai. So Jaggar Dean Hukatai Bartholomew it was. It wasn't until a month later that we found out that Hukatai is Maori for 'master of the ocean'.

Jaggar has been a blessing to our lives. At 46 I'm a late starter, but I really don't think I would have been a devoted father in my 20s or even 30s. Then again, maybe I would have. All I know is that to create a beautiful little boy is the most special gift of all.

Just the other day I got up and I looked out the window and the whales were heading south, and I said to Shelley, 'Well, there's whales, honey.' I held Jaggar and pointed out the whales to him. Sure, he didn't see them, but he was chirping and giggling and somehow I knew he knew it was special.

On August 25 we held a dedication ceremony on the beach at Kirra. My old friend Guy Ormerod, who is now Pastor Guy, conducted the ceremony. In attendance was Joe Larkin, Joan Peterson, Barry Townend and both my parents. It was very special to have both of Jaggar's grandparents in attendance. It took the birth of Jaggar to bring Bart and Betty together for a special family occasion.

And now, somehow, it feels like the wheel has turned full circle. There are another three hot surfers in town — Joel Parkinson, Mick Fanning and Dean Morrison — who have captured the imagination of the surfing world. Twenty-five years after PT, MP and I jousted for supremacy in Coolangatta's perfect peeling tubes, Joel, Mick and Dean are just embarking on their international careers. In March 2002, Mick and Dean will join Joel on the World Championship Tour and make their debut at the Quiksilver Pro on the Gold Coast, in front of a hometown crowd. It'll be a proud day for the old town.

And as the only son among four daughters, I've finally ensured the survival of the Bartholomew name with the birth of my son. Jaggar's arrival has already helped heal old family hurts.

It's been a wild ride; there have been some deep and intense sections, some close scrapes with almost bare reef, but I'm glad I've made it through. And I know it has been my dreams — focusing on that light at the end of the tunnel, no matter how bumpy the passage — that's got me to where I am today.

cover photograph credits

COVER: Rabbit in action, '94. *Jason Childs/Sport the Library.*

BACK COVER LEFT TO RIGHT:

Bugs in his natural habitat — the Kirra barrel, '93. *Peter Morrison.*

The soul surfer. Mouth agape, hands behind his back, digging the view. Bugs, profoundly at home in a Duranbah barrel, '81. *Peter Crawford.*

The tail side is generally considered a move of the '90s. Rab was doing 'em back in '88. Slicing the top off a clean wall at Burleigh. *Peter Crawford.*

Rabbit's revolutionary line at Pipeline — turning square and hard off the bottom, '74. *Jack McCoy.*

The big-wave warrior — Bugs at his peak in Hawaii in the mid–'80s, freefalling out of the lip at huge Sunset. *Bob Barbour.*

index of names

Bells 128–30; 1976 Coke Surfabout
145; misses 1976 Pipe Masters 158; first
Stubbies contest 164–6; leads world
rankings 173, 174–5; 1977 Florida Pro
174; French debut 175–8; 1978 season
184–6; South Africa 188–90, 221–5;
wins World Title 198; 1979 Bells 204–6;
Japanese tour 208–10; regains number
one 212; 1979–80 Hawaii 218–19; La
Grande Plage exhibition 227; Lacanau
228–9; 1981–82 Hawaii 232–6; wins
$30,000 240–1; not advised of event
270; accepts defeat 271; Israel 277–9;
out of World Title competition 280;
1985 Hawaii 283–5; Op Pro riot 298–9;
wins 1999 World Masters
Championship 371, 373–4
early aquatic activities: Snapper Rocks
13–14; nearly drowns 14; begins surfing
25–7; watches Queensland Titles 27
early life: birth 11; family splits 16; the
nippers 19–20; called 'Rabbit' 20; early
income 21–2; finds fairy penguin 40
equipment: first board ride 14–16; rides
the swing 24; first surfboard 28; second
board 36; skateboards 37–8; cutback
boards 41–2; MP's boards 67–8; twin
fins 231–2
health: double pneumonia 35; collapses
279; malignant melanoma 307–8; severe
bronchitis 356
heroes: 38–9, 90, 114
homes: Rainbow Bay 17–18; Kirra 31–3,
350–1; Sydney 54–5; Surfers Paradise
55; Currumbin 139; Bilinga 163
media activities: filmed surfing 71;
magazine poster 94; Jarratt interview
120–1; magazine coverage 130;
'Challenge of the Sexes' (TV show)
146–7; nude surfing photos 145–6;
Band on the Run (movie) 172, 179;
surf movies 246–8; *The Performers*
(movie) 265
memories: Apprentice Awards speech
137–9; last great ride 288; proudest
336–7
relationships: falls out with MP 83;
reunites with father 92; rivalry with
Tomson 112–13; MP hostilities 124–6,
167; Hawaiian hospitality 133–5; and
hostilities 149–56; end of Kanga
partnership 156; Toni 195, 197–8, 217,
252; rediscovers youth 249; foster
parent to Dean Morrison 350–1; falls

in love with Shelley Emia 373, 374–5;
birth of son Jaggar 371, 376–7
school: wags school 33–4; schoolwork
suffers 53; backs WB's ambition 56–8;
weekly routine 60–1; repeats HSC
86–7, 91–2
social activities: Coolangatta 49–50,
139–41; first girlfriend 53; first time
drunk 69; eating contest 142–3; Surfers
arrest 194–5; gold top mushrooms
215–17; serious drinking 250–1; Tokyo
escapade 258–61; environmental issues
294; Christianity 300; Reg Riley's 21st
303–4; 'The Firewalkers' 304–5
writings: essay extract 83–4; letter to
father 113; article extract 147–9;
postcard to Wendy and Wayne 229–30;
and to Betty 279; letter to Heidi and
Cristel 281–2
Bartholomew, Wendy (WB's sister):
childhood 11; memories 19, 23, 55, 91;
dates surfer 29; Coolangatta 49, 60;
Victory Flats 68–9; lives with WB 186;
WB's career crisis 275; 372
Bedgood, Greg 361–2
Bendall, Ma and Pa 45–6
Bernado, Meg 355
Bertleman, Larry 77, 123, 233
Beschen, Shane 325
Bessas, Yves 177–8
Bevan, Dean 302
Bevan, Shane 302
Black, Graeme 28, 46–7
Blair, Larry 188
Bligh-Ware, Captain Ron 341
Boyum, Mike 213–15, 216
Bradshaw, Ken 150, 151, 219
Brooks, Rod 319
Brown, Bobby 65
Brown, Bruce 364
Brown, Ken 186–7, 193
Bryant, Peter (Mont): early role models 24;
memories 25, 35; wags school 34; paddle
race 97; drugs 141; nurses Perriot 163;
urges WB on 188; WB's surfing academy
293
Bryant, Timmy 25
Buchan, Adrian 352
Budroe, Noah 254
Buran, Joey 189, 225, 281, 298
Burness, Peter 173
Burns, Ronnie 254, 283
Burridge, Pam 262
Buttenshaw, Jason 305

Bustin' down the door

Bustin' down the door